The Center for South and Southeast Asia Studies of the University of California is the unifying organization for faculty members and students interested in South and Southeast Asia Studies, bringing together scholars from numerous disciplines. The Center's major aims are the development and support of research and language study. As part of this program the Center sponsors a publication series of books concerned with South and Southeast Asia. Manuscripts are considered from all campuses of the University of California as well as from any other individuals and institutions doing research in these areas.

RECENT PUBLICATIONS OF THE CENTER FOR SOUTH AND SOUTHEAST ASIA STUDIES :

Jyotirindra Das Gupta
Language Conflict and National Development : Group Politics and National Language Policy in India (1970)

Gerald D. Berreman
Hindus of the Himalayas (Second Revised Edition, 1971)

Richard G. Fox
Kin, Clan, Raja, and Rule : State-Hinterland Relations in Preindustrial India (1971)

Robert N. Kearney
Trade Unions and Politics in Ceylon (1971)

David G. Marr
Vietnamese Anticolonialism, 1885-1925 (1971)

Leo E. Rose
Nepal—Strategy for Survival (1971)

Richard Sisson
The Congress Party in Rajasthan : Political Integration and Institution-Building in an Indian State (1971)

Prakash Tandon
Beyond Punjab : A Sequel to Punjabi Century (1971)

David N. Lorenzen
The Kāpālikas and Kālāmukhas : Two Lost Śaivite Sects (1972)

Elizabeth Whitcombe
Agrarian Conditions in Northern India. Volume One : The United Provinces under British Rule, 1860-1900 (1972)

THE CLASSICAL LAW OF INDIA

THE CLASSICAL LAW OF INDIA

This volume is sponsored by the
Center for South and Southeast Asia Studies,
University of California, Berkeley

Robert Lingat, 1892-1972

THE CLASSICAL LAW OF INDIA

ROBERT LINGAT

TRANSLATED FROM THE FRENCH
with additions
BY J. DUNCAN M. DERRETT

UNIVERSITY OF CALIFORNIA PRESS
BERKELEY, LOS ANGELES, LONDON

University of California Press
Berkeley and Los Angeles, California

University of California Press, Ltd.
London, England

Library of Congress Catalog Card Number : 76-81798

ISBN 0-520-01898-2

Printed in the United States of America

The original edition of this work, *Les sources du droit dans le système traditionnel de l'Inde*, was published in 1967 by Mouton & Co., Paris and the Hague, as a volume in both the series *Le Monde d'Outre-mer Passé et Présent* (École Pratique des Hautes Études, Sorbonne) and the series *Les Systèmes de Droit Contemporain* (Institut de droit comparé, University of Paris).

TRANSLATOR'S PREFACE

AT THE end of the Second World War the Indian subcontinent found itself equipped (or perhaps, better, encumbered) with three main types of Hindu law. In matters of family law and some other topics of which the most prominent was the law governing religious endowments and charities, almost all Hindus amounting to a population of about four hundred millions were governed by a system professedly derived from the *dharma-śāstra*, the "science of righteousness", the ancient indigenous holy law of India. (There were a few exceptions among the Hindus—chiefly those who, in British India, had married under the Special Marriage Act, and those who, in French India, had "renounced" their religious law in favour of the civil law of France.) In the forms in which it was administered it was called "Hindu law". In the area known as British India, which was ruled by Britain through the Viceroy, this "Hindu law" had developed under the aegis of Common Law and Equity, modified occasionally by statutes, not all of which were clearly understood or put into practice by the public at large, into a system known since the 1920's by the pejorative but accurate name of "Anglo-Hindu law". The courts constantly referred themselves to the *dharma-śāstra* texts, but subject to a method which had been gradually devised during British rule. They also referred to previous decisions of the High Courts and the Privy Council. The result often coincided with what indigenous Hindu jurists of a century before might have recommended, and often did not.

In the French possessions another system was in force, which can be called "Franco-Hindu law". Characteristically, the French took considerable interest in the system, intellectually as well as practically, and there is a respectable bibliography, in which the name of L. Sorg figures prominently and honourably. In the Portuguese territories the legislation of Portugal made a substantial but uneven impact upon the indigenous laws. The tangled web of law (not unmarked by Goans who had adjusted themselves to the resulting chaos) awaited the skilled and authoritative treatment of the celebrated Portuguese jurist, Luís da Cunha Goncalves, himself born in Goa. To this day Franco-Hindu law and Luso-Hindu law, as we must call the personal law in force in the former Portuguese possessions, must be taken into account by any scholar and by any would-be reformer.

In the parts of India not subject to direct foreign rule, the so-called

Native or Princely States governed by Indian rulers under British paramountcy, other versions of Hindu law were in vogue. In some States little codes of their own devising obtained and to some limited extent still obtain as law.

Throughout India scholars and informed members of the public deplored features of the traditional system, particularly the absence of a divorce law and the right of Hindu males to have more than one wife concurrently, and sought for a method whereby these defects might be cured. They were met at every turn by the comment that the *dharma-śāstra* did not contemplate massive reforms, and that if an attempt were made to reform the system comprehensively, religion, as well as popular custom, would be outraged. The coming of Independence in 1947 gave Hindus the opportunity to effect dramatic reforms by legislation, and in 1955 and 1956 the four statutes forming the so-called Hindu Code were enacted by the Parliament at New Delhi.

These new laws have not satisfied all sections of opinion. There remain, moreover, large areas of the Hindu law which are only marginally affected by the reforms. Whether intellectually or practically, it is desirable to understand the scene in which these dramatic happenings took place; and it is high time that a concise and faithful picture be made available, wherefrom anyone may obtain a grasp of the nature of the legal system with which the foreign rulers worked and which the native population inherited.

During the long period of foreign rule Indian jurists and public men, some of them trained wholly or in part in Europe, gave voice to ideas about the *dharma-śāstra* which were gratifying to their fellow-countrymen. In a country which had become used to western jurisprudence and which fully accepted the rule of law as imported into India from England, it seemed natural to treat the re-discovered wealth of *dharma-śāstra* material as if it were a corpus of law similar in purpose and effect to the law to be found in Anglo-Indian legal publications. Many scholars, amongst whom K.P. Jayaswāl comes readily to mind, conceived the idea that the excellencies of the *dharma-śāstra* proved that Indians were fully capable of administering law to themselves long before foreign rule became inevitable.

This gratifying notion tended to lead imperceptibly to an assumption that the *dharma-śāstra* was not only law, in the modern sense, but also (at least for practical purposes) *all* the law which India had before the intrusion of the Muslims. The great difficulties of mastering the corpus of *dharma-śāstra* material, and the enormous heap of discordant and unreconciled decisions which emerged during British rule and which formed the pabulum of the writers of textbooks for legal practitioners, tended to dissuade people from undertaking an objective study of the subject in its true cultural setting. Practitioners did not want to know what the "true" Hindu law was, when the Privy Council had said authoritatively what the law for India (or for a part of India) must thenceforward be. Historians were, as is usually the case, impatient of the task of sorting through legal decisions, which are couched in a peculiar language and set in contexts of unexampled complexity and obliquity. The only man who set himself to explain what the *dharma-śāstra* taught and, at the same time, to sketch in the developments during the British period was P.V. Kāṇe, whose gigantic and solid encyclopaedia still daunts even the best-intentioned enquirer. Kāṇe's objectivity and accuracy were phenomenal; but he too had a motive, namely to show that India's *own* jurisprudence should be seen in its historical setting, and that when judged by the appropriate criteria it could stand comparison with any system likely to be compared with it. I do not think that anyone will blame Kāṇe or castigate his results for the motive which he had. Some will blame Parliament for not taking seriously the suggestions which, from time to time, he made for the guidance of the reformers.

After 1956, Hindu law suffered from a double disadvantage, in that the difficulty of the materials did not yield at once to a determined researcher, because there was no short and attractive guide to the subject; and in that the reforms gave a superficial impression of having rendered the learning of the past quite superfluous and obsolete. Many realised that the Hindu law was the oldest continuous system of law, and that its materials were, in their richness and diversity, superior to Roman law, while the longevity of its institutions altogether exceeded anything which any other system could proffer. Many were prepared to enquire—until they discovered that a knowledge of Sanskrit was required, if only to test the reliability of the many translations done by English and German scholars. True, this difficulty did not absolutely restrain those whose education had been of a classical type and whose minds had been broadened by contact with many and ancient cultures prior to their involvement with the dry and practical business of the law. But an uncertainty as to the value of what they read confined them to narrow and limited paths, in which an ultimate practical object was seldom out of view. Such was the work of J. Kohler. The speculative, if deep, studies of the *dharma-śāstra* and its companion sciences by J.J. Meyer only served to weaken the confidence with which students of a Bühler and a Jolly had been going to work. The only man who knew how to evaluate the material comprehensively was G. Mazzarella, whose enormous, but not prolix, publications defy all those who are not fluent in Italian and those who, possessing that language, are sceptical about the scientific content of the "social sciences". The recent work of W. Ruben illuminates the very early stages of the development of the *śāstra,* but avoids the jurisprudential questions raised in this present book. It stops at A.D. 500, when our commentaries begin.

Meanwhile the world has awakened to the intellectual value of non-western thought. Non-Christian is no longer anti-Christian. The world of ideas, as well as the world of space, has become perceptibly smaller. Asians, whether in Asia or in Europe and Africa and America, make their contributions to life and to intellectual endeavour. They need to understand their own culture; and we need to understand them. Previously we had the advantage of possessing fluent (I may also say, glib) accounts of Indian culture from Indians; but they were couched in language which borrowed far too much from our own environment. In order to communicate with us, they borrowed more than our language. Now we have Europeans who know the East well, not as exploiters, nor as sentimental wanderers, nor as lost souls trying to find their spiritual home, but as learners, sufferers, men and women who have not learnt about Asia from books alone, but have lived and perspired, imbibed the spirit of the lands in which they served, and struggled along with their inhabitants in a spirit of common enterprise and equality. Books by such authors come into quite a different category from the apologetic work of Asians or the fusty academic meanderings of the old-fashioned "philologist".

Robert Lingat worked for long in South East Asia, mastering languages and culture. He discovered that the core of society retained an historical tradition which was still alive and explained much that was otherwise inexplicable. That tradition went back directly to India. Much research into the history of the social institutions and even the political institutions of, for example, Cambodia has shown that culturally these regions were colonies of India. The traces of the *dharma-śāstra* which we can find there prove that India exported her concept of society and law, and probably she exported practitioners in it also. Lingat proceeded to trace back to India the concepts which were living realities in the regions where he served for so many years. Further study of India herself, and not merely from the classical literature, produced a view of that subject which had not been open to Indians or Europeans involved with India's own political, emotional, and intellectual problems.

This is why Lingat's book, translated here, is the best work ever written on this tantalising and difficult subject. No one who masters it can fail to tread securely in the maze of Indian legal history (if for the moment we neglect Muslim law, so ably served by others); and students of the comparative history of law will realise that they are handling here not merely a system of great age, but also one which is an important component of the modern world.

The original edition of this book appeared in 1967 and was intended for readers in those parts of the world in which French culture and the heritage of the Roman law are treasured. To make it fit for readers subject to the Anglo-American consortium of legal systems, in which of course India herself is included, numerous small adjustments were called for. These have no effect on the author's meaning. Because *"loi", "droit", "droit positif",* and similar expressions have no exact equivalent in English the author's beautiful, concise style has occasionally had to be abandoned for more cumbersome expressions which, I trust, will prevent unnecessary confusion.

Since 1967 several new publications have thrown light on matters falling within the scope of the book. The footnotes have been enriched with some additional, recent references, but the author's meaning has not been affected. There were a few places where, with the author's consent, I have thought fit to insert a "perhaps" or some similar *caveat* where an expression which was forcefully put can no longer be regarded as literally sound. But I believe it would take a minute comparison of the original and this translation to detect them, their contribution being minimal. The bibliography has been slightly amended in places, and the opportunity has been taken to remove misprints and incorrect references which so complex and detailed a work would be likely to incur even when undertaken by a meticulous publisher.

Since a work of outstanding merit, deserving that often abused epithet "seminal", depends fundamentally on the intention, and thus on the outlook, education, and qualifications of the author, I thought it proper to include Robert Lingat's *Curriculum Vitae* and his illuminating list of publications. These, together with an excellent portrait, he gladly provided at my earnest request; and thus what the reader has before him is Lingat's *chef-d'oeuvre* in English. His death in May 1972 deprived international scholarship of a combination of experience, intuition, insight, and sympathy which can hardly be looked for again. The question whether his work will be taken up and furthered, and by whom, now lies open for the English-speaking as well as the French-speaking world to answer.

AUTHOR'S PREFACE

IN THE following pages I propose to clarify the Hindus' understanding of Law before they encountered western notions on that subject. I am concerned essentially with aspects of private law, in other words those which obtain between individuals. Institutions of *public* law are the subject of a quite distinct science devoted to the art of government. It is true enough, as I shall demonstrate in due course, that one comes across not merely coexistence but even interpenetration between the two systems, political and juridical—the traces are evident in works appertaining to either discipline. But their points of view are nonetheless different; and the dichotomy between them is such that writers in each profess to be unaware of their counterparts in the other.

A feature of the originality of Hindu law, and at the same time of the difficulty which we experience in understanding the legal system of India, is that the law does not derive from written sources properly so-called. Its development owes nothing either to positive law in the sense of a legislative act, or to judicial decisions. Significantly, the rich vocabulary of Sanskrit does not contain a term corresponding to our word law, as we understand the term "law" (in English) or "droit" (in French) when we wish to refer to "English law" or "French law", signifying a group of rules which govern men actually and imperatively in a given locality and period of time. In building up their law the Hindus have not taken as their starting-point that element which has served in the West as a foundation for a specific discipline, namely the coercive element, which characterises a legal rule and distinguishes it from other rules which also control human activity. They have derived it from a more general notion which exceeds the domain of law in many respects without actually comprehending it entirely: duty. They did not attempt specially to define rules which people may be constrained by an external or physical sanction to observe[1] and which amount to specifically juridical duties. They relied on religious concepts peculiar to the Hindu world, and they taught people the rules of conduct which they ought to observe by reason of their condition in society—and amongst these rules the rules of law are to be found. The word *dharma* which is translated here

[1]Cf. the definition of Aubry and Rau: 'Law is the totality of precepts or rules of conduct to the observance of which it is permitted to constrain a person by exterior or physical coercion'.

"duty" in effect expresses conformity with what Hindus regard as the natural order of things, and this explains its association with law. But the rule of *dharma* can only become a rule of law by a process beyond the expression of it, a process which enables it to enter society armed with a power of constraint which is not inherent in it. Moreover, the jurist's task is not simply to discern amongst the enormous literature devoted to *dharma* whatever is particularly amenable to law. He must, indeed, concern himself with a great many of the duties which could not be the object of an external constraint (or, more simply, a legal action).[2] But, the jurist must go further and ask to what extent and under what form they could have been taken as rules of law by society. I say "could have been" and not "were" so taken, because we are in a position to grasp the machinery, but not its end-product. The latter, viz. the law in action, escapes us, precisely because we have no legal instruments such as legislative documents and reports of judicial decisions at our disposal.[3]

In short, we must study the role played in the evolution of law by the notion of *dharma* and by the precepts in and through which it is expressed : that is my task. I have chosen the period of the commentaries and the original treatises deliberately. In that period alone can we watch *dharma* and law face to face. In that period for the first time we can disentangle the broad features of a genuine juridical system. One might object that this amounts to a somewhat tardy attack on the subject : India had a long, rich story before the first commentators came upon the scene. But it struck me as a good method not to try to elucidate the sense and bearing of texts relating to *dharma* at any stage prior to their first being used for the construction of law. The theories and the means which the interpreters utilised to adapt them to social realities go to make up what I call the "traditional system of India", the classical system, by contrast with the system applied under British rule, in which western concepts predominate. It is "traditional", or classical, in two senses : not only does it rest upon concepts which are exclusively Indian; it possesses, also, the character of being an undisputed tradition.

[2]One must not forget, however, that this distinction is essential only for the western jurist. The commentators and authors of digests treat quite indifferently precepts which (it seems to us) derive from religion, ritual, morals, or even good manners, and those which have a juridical significance. They employ the same arguments relative to one and all of these and apply the same method of interpretation to them. It would be gravely misleading for us to attribute less value to the former group than to the latter, especially as they differ only in respect of the nature of the problems posed.

[3]This need is very scantily supplied by epigraphy and by the rare documents drawn by practitioners which have survived and been published. But we must make special mention of the *Lekhapaddhati* (Gaekwad's Oriental Series, Baroda, 1925), a manual of forms from Gujarat, bearing dates in the fifteenth century (and occasionally even earlier), which does provide numerous examples of forms of contract.

The interpreters are not mere theoreticians. They are exegetes. They absorbed from the very texts which they were interpreting the principles which allowed them to recognise a rule of *dharma* and to determine its import. These principles became apparent and indeed imperative, not as scholastic opinions but as fundamental data, the product of the ancient Sages' speculation. Consequently they were never questioned, except by certain heterodox circles which had no effect on the Hindu world, and it is only in our own days that they have been vigorously attacked at the heart of the Hindu world itself. Throughout the millennium in which their writings range, the interpreters or commentators started from the same premisses and employed the same methods of argument. Their intelligence was employed simply to apply the means at their disposal, with the result that the difference between the authors has no other significance for us than to inform us how varied were the solutions which practical problems could command. For our purpose it is not so tragic as it might otherwise be that a part of this literature is still buried in manuscript form, and that a part has disappeared altogether: even though there would have been found amongst the latter some works which would have been authorities at a given period and in a given region, the loss is serious only for the history of institutions. The lack of such works will not impede knowledge of the system which we are undertaking to investigate.

One may well ask if this system really proceeded from the texts upon which the interpreters believed it to be based, or if it became established only progressively, enveloped in a doctrine which emerged at the dawn of the interpretation itself. The question must remain open. No *independent* source has transmitted to us the texts under consideration. The state in which they have reached us, and the chronological difficulties which they raise, confine us to the paths which the commentators themselves have trodden. We are bound to limit our research and, at least provisionally, its result, to the period I have chosen.

These observations indicate the outline of my work. An early portion is devoted to *dharma,* to its sources, and to a rapid analysis of the literature which has risen from it. This is a purely descriptive section, intended above all to underline the size of the literature and the importance of the place it occupies in Indian thought. The *dharma-sūtras* which are the earliest expression of it have afforded me a starting-off point for a demonstration of the great sociological themes which provide the material of *dharma* with its framework and schematic arrangement, and for an *aperçu* of the vast domain open to the writers concerned and of the way in which they approached their task. It was, I felt, no duty of mine to linger long over questions of chronology which (as we shall see) held no interest whatever for the commentators and, as a consequence, had no bearing on the construction of the law. In any case, a few observations placed in an appendix serve to throw doubt on the very possibility of setting up a chronological classification of the texts which might be sufficiently advanced and sufficiently certain to satisfy the demands of critical scholarship.

In the second part, which is more systematic than the first, I endeavoured to discover how law-in-action *(le droit positif)* was born, i.e. by what means and in what measure the rule of *dharma,* which possesses *authority* for society, could receive from it that constraining force which turned it into a rule of law. This brought me to contrast the rule of *dharma* first with rules of customary origin and then with injunctions emanating from the king, viz. the two powers which are coercive in a society which has no legislation in the modern sense. Problems of this kind are not new: often propounded, they have been variously solved. I did not even have to alter the terms of them. I simply applied myself to the task of keeping to the orthodox position, which is that of the commentators, and to understanding it.

The classical Indian system was altered somewhat under Muslim rule, and more directly affected under British administration. As is generally known, it has given place to a system inspired from the West. But before it vanished as a whole from India it was propagated, not without undergoing changes which left its essential principles untouched, in the company of Buddhism in the Hinduised lands of Indo-China. It has finished, curiously, by uniting with our western system. I thought it would be interesting to present in conclusion a rapid survey of the outlines of that evolution, seeking out its seeds in the Hindu system.

It is hardly necessary to say that this work could not have been undertaken if I had not had at my disposal the five volumes of P.V. Kāṇe's *History of Dharmaśāstra,* that remarkable synthesis of the texts. The greater part of my references were obtained from that quarter, and my research grew out of reflections suggested to me as I read them. I must also express here my gratitude to the late M. Louis Renou, whose encouragement meant so much to me; and my thanks to M. Louis Dumont who was kind enough to read a part of my manuscript and to draw my attention to vistas which one who was too strictly educated in the law might well have overlooked.[1]

July 1965

[1]M. Lingat would have wished to draw attention to M. Dumont's *Homo hierarchicus* (Paris, 1967; Eng. trans., London, 1969) and D.G. Mandelbaum, *Society in India* (Berkeley, 1970) which in a sense complements it. [trs.]

ABBREVIATIONS

Āp.	*Āpastamba-dharmasūtra.*
Baudh.	*Baudhāyana-dharmasūtra.*
Bṛh.	*Bṛhaspati-smṛti,* ed. J. Jolly.
Bṛh. Aiy.	*Bṛhaspati-smṛti,* ed. K.V. Raṅgaswāmī Aiyaṅgār.
Dāy.	*Dāyabhāga* of Jīmūtavāhana, trans. Colebrooke (cited from W. Stokes's collection).
Dh.k.	*Dharmakośa,* the *Vyavahārakāṇḍa.*
B.E.F.E.O.	*Bulletin de l'École Française d'Extrême-Orient.*
B.S.O.A.S.	*Bulletin of the School of Oriental and African Studies.*
Gaut.	*Gautama-dharmasūtra.*
I.H.Q.	*Indian Historical Quarterly.*
J.A.	*Journal Asiatique.*
J.A.O.S.	*Journal of the American Oriental Society.*
J.A.S.B.	*Journal of the Asiatic Society of Bengal.*
J.B.R.S.	*Journal of the Bihar Research Society.*
J.O.R.	*Journal of Oriental Research,* Madras.
J.R.A.S.	*Journal of the Royal Asiatic Society of Great Britain.*
P.V. Kāṇe	*History of Dharmaśāstra,* by P.V. Kāṇe.
Kāt.	*Kātyāyana-smṛti,* ed. P.V. Kāṇe.
Kauṭ.	*Arthaśāstra* of Kauṭilya, ed. and trans. R.P. Kāngle.
M.	*Manu-smṛti,* ed. V.N. Mandlik, and Jhā.
Mit.	*Mitākṣarā* of Vijñāneśvara, ed. J.R. Ghārpure.
Nār.	*Nārada-smṛti,* ed. J. Jolly.
Nār.Sāmb.	*Nārada-smṛti,* ed. K. Sāmbaśiva Sāstrī.
Par.	*Parāśara-smṛti,* ed. V.S. Islāmpurkar.
Rāj. rat.	*Rājanīti-ratnākara.*
S.B.E.	*Sacred Books of the East.*
Sm.cand.	*Smṛti-candrikā,* ed. J.R. Ghārpure.
[trs.]	The sentence or note is owed in part or wholly to the translator.
Vas.	*Vasiṣṭha-dharmasūtra.*
Vīr.par.	*Vīramitrodaya, paribhāṣā-prakāśa.*
Vīr.vyav.	*Vīramitrodaya, vyavahāra-prakāsa.*
Viṣ.	*Viṣṇu-dharmasūtra.*
Vyav.cint.	*Vyavahāra-cintāmaṇi,* ed. L. Rocher.
Vyav.may.	*Vyavahāra-mayūkha,* ed. V.N. Maṇḍlik.
Yāj.	*Yājñavalkya-smṛti,* ed. J.R. Ghārpure.

CONTENTS

Part Two
FROM DHARMA TO LAW

PART ONE

DHARMA

CHAPTER I
THE SOURCES OF DHARMA

1. *The Concept of Dharma*

DHARMA IS a concept difficult to define because it disowns—or transcends—distinctions that seem essential to us, and because it is based upon beliefs that are as strange to us as they are familiar to the Hindus. The word itself is used in several widely different senses, even in a work with one consistent style like the code of Manu. The most general sense is provided by its root, *dhṛ,* which signifies the action of maintaining, sustaining, or supporting and which has produced *fre* in Latin (*fretus,* depending upon, daring to) and *fir* (*firmus,* strong in the physical and moral senses, whence solid, hard, durable).[1] *Dharma* is what is firm and durable, what sustains and maintains, what hinders fainting and falling.

Applied to the universe, *dharma* signifies the eternal laws which maintain the world.[2] This sense is related to a very ancient conception which the Hindus shared with the Iranians, according to which the world is not the product of a fortuitous concourse of elements, but is ruled by certain norms and sustained by an order necessary to its preservation. This order is an objective one, inherent in the very nature of things; and the gods are only its guardians.[3]

During the Vedic period the fundamental laws of the universe were identified with the laws of the sacrifice. Consequently *dharma* was *par excellence* the sacrificial act which maintains and even conditions the cosmic order. As we shall see below, it is in this sense that the Mīmāṃsā school use the word. Later on, that more or less magical act of sacrifice remains constantly present before the minds of the authors,[4] but the concept of *dharma* is widened : it envelops the moral world as much as the physical; and the norm of ritual becomes a norm of conduct. In

[1]A. Ernout and A. Meillet, *Dictionnaire étymologique de la langue latine* (Paris, 1932), s.v. *firmus* and *fretus*.

[2]'Dharma is so called because it protects *(dhāraṇāt)* everything; Dharma maintains everything that has been created. Dharma is thus that very principle which can maintain the universe' (*Mahābh.*, Śāntip., 109, 59).

[3]P. Masson-Oursel, *Esquisse d'une histoire de la philosophie indienne* (Paris. 1923), 35–6. Cf L. Renou, *L'Inde classique*, ss. 1152–3.

[4]Cf *M.*, III.75–6 : '. . . he who is diligent in making sacrifices upholds all this [world], animate and inanimate. The offering correctly thrown into the fire goes to the Sun; from the Sun comes rain; from the rain food; and from this all creatures [subsist]'. Cf XII.99.

external terms, *dharma* is the action which, provided it is conformable to the order of things, permits man to realise his destiny to the full, sustains him in this life, and assures his well-being after death. By its own virtue that act produces a spiritual benefit for him who has performed it, which will necessarily bear fruit in the other world.[5] Conversely, an act contrary to *dharma,* called *adharma,* necessarily involves a sanction, a "fall" for the one who does it, which will strike him in his future existence if not actually in his present life. "Destroyed, Dharma destroys; protected, he protects": so says Manu (VIII.15). In internal terms, *dharma* signifies the obligation, binding upon every man who desires that his actions should bear fruit, to submit himself to the laws which govern the universe and to direct his life in consequence. That obligation constitutes his duty: and that is a further sense of the word.

From there it is an easy step to the sense which *dharma* most frequently bears in our texts. This is the totality of duties which bears upon the individual according to his status *(varṇa)* and the stage of life *(āśrama)* at which he stands, the totality of rules to which he must confirm if he does not want to "fall", if he is anxious about the hereafter (cf *M.*, I.2; *Yāj.*, I.1). This is the sense which the word has in the epics, notably in the celebrated passage in the *Bhagavadgītā* where Kṛṣṇa, speaking to Arjuna who is hesitating to give the order to commence battle, tells him what is his duty *(sva-dharma)* as a Kṣatriya.[6]

This morality is addressed to man in society. It is based on a belief in retribution for one's acts and on the operation of transmigration.[7] Its foundation and its sanction are religious, but it is essentially social in the sense that, in a social order visualised as one with the natural order, the individual who obeys its precepts performs a duty which is as much social as religious. So far as this life is concerned, it provides him with reasons for acting and for fulfilling as his function, his role in society. It sees man's welfare in his works. And, in effect, this is the morality of action postulated by the literature which we must survey and the conception of law which emerges from it.

However, we must note that this is not the only morality which India has. Mystics extol disciplines of salvation whose object, by contrast,

[5] Cf the definition of *dharma* which Haradatta gives in his commentary on the *Āpastamba-sūtra*: *karma-janyo 'bhyudaya-niḥśreyasa-hetur apūrvākhya ātma-guṇo dharmaḥ*: 'Produced by the act, cause of [final] beatitude, a property of the soul having the name *apūrva* [devoid of cause], [that is] *dharma*' (*Ujjvalā,* on *Āp.*, I.1.1–2).

[6] But we are bound to note that even our sources illustrate the use of the word *dharma* simply in the sense of imperative rule or customary usage, without any religious connotation. Manu (IX.66) describes *niyoga* (see below) as 'a *dharma* of animals' *(paśu-dharma)*, i.e. a bestial usage.

[7] On its doctrines see L. Renou, *L'Inde classique,* ss. 1142–9, and P.V. Kāṇe, *Hist. Dharm.* V, ch.xxxv, pp. 1530–1612.

is to enable man to escape from the chain of rebirth by abstaining from and renouncing works of any kind. That is the life of the *saṃnyāsin,* practised in India at very early times and, some would say, not yet extinct. The writers on *dharma-śāstra* are perfectly aware of it, and they even go so far as to quarter it within the last stage of life. But this salvation-morality goes beyond their domain. The *saṃnyāsin* has renounced the world, he has freed himself from the relationships which are the web of mundane life; society's morality offers him no object or goal.[8] As is said in the *Mitākṣarā* (on *Yāj.,* I.8), "ascetics have no need of rules".

It follows as a matter of course that, for authors committed to the religious significance of actions, society's essential end is the realisation of *dharma,* when each individual can put his duties into effect. So their structure of law has *dharma* as its axis. But even in India religious aspirations do not monopolise all human activity. Manu himself remarks (II.2–4) that men seldom act without being prompted by interest, and that even the rule prescribed by *dharma* is sought out not for itself but for the spiritual advantages which it proffers. The pious intention is seldom pure. It is mixed with other motives of a less elevated complexion. Hindus contrast with *dharma* (which is the good) both *artha* (the useful) and *kāma* (the pleasurable), which also motivate human behaviour. Under the heading of *artha* the rule is assessed by the measure of profit, the advantage one draws from it; under that of *kāma* the measure is that of the pleasure which is experienced. Human activity may be summed up in that triad: *dharma, artha,* and *kāma.* A rule founded on *dharma* has an authority superior to that founded on *artha,* just as the latter has an authority superior to one motivated by *kāma.* But all three points of view are equally legitimate, and man is made in such a way that he is bound to consider all three of them as he functions in life. Side by side with the science of *dharma (dharma-śāstra)* there is, therefore, a science of *artha (artha-śāstra),* set out in treatises on politics as the practice of princes, just as there is a science of pleasure codified in the *Kāmasūtra.* For Manu (II.224), wisdom is to be found in a harmonious combination of the three prime motives of human nature. "There are those who declare", says he, "that the highest good, here below, consists in virtue *(dharma)* and in wealth *(artha)*; [others say it consists in] pleasure *(kāma)* and wealth, or in virtue alone, or in wealth alone; but the true opinion [is that it consists in] the conjunction of all three".[9]

However, the man who is anxious about his future destiny must search for the rules of behaviour in the science of *dharma.* It is true that

[8]Cf L. Dumont, 'Le renoncement dans les religions de l'Inde', *Archives de sociologie des religions,* 1959, pp. 45–69.

[9]On the *trivarga* see P.V. Kāṇe, II, 8–9 and L. Renou, *op. cit.*, s. 1150.

the criteria of interest and even (albeit rarely) of pleasure may play some part in the working out of law-in-action, but the rule of *dharma* will remain fixed at the very foundation of the concept of law.

To understand this concept we must first apply ourselves to *dharma* and examine the various sources from which it proceeds and in which it is expressed. After that, our task will be to understand how the passage was made from *dharma* to law, and at that point we shall find *artha* personified in the king.

The *dharma-sūtras* (*Gaut.,* I.1–2; *Vas.,* I.4–6) enumerate three sources *(mūla)* of *dharma*: the Veda, Tradition, and "Good Custom". The codes of Manu (II.12) and of Yājñavalkya (I.7) add one more: inner contentment *(svasya priyam ātmanaḥ, ātma-tuṣṭi)*. "The Veda, Tradition, and "Good Custom", and inner contentment, these are said manifestly to be the fourfold foundation of *dharma*" (*M.,* II.12). But if "inner contentment"—we should prefer to say the approval of one's conscience—really is a source of *dharma,* it does not strike us as quite properly placed here, following upon sources which possess an authority exterior to man. To understand why our authors set some store by it, it is sufficient to note that the list given by Manu and Yājñavalkya, like most lists of this type, amounts to a climax of esteem: the first of the sources of *dharma* is superior to the second, the second to the third, and so on. Consequently one should not have recourse to Tradition unless the Vedic texts are silent; only when the texts furnished by Tradition fail us may we refer to "Good Custom"; and lastly it is only when all the other sources are silent that the rule of *dharma* may be sought out in the approval of one's conscience. The commentators on Manu add the hypothesis that where one has a choice between two ways of acting conscience will show which is to be preferred. They believe, moreover, that the approval of conscience, as a rule of life, is not to be admitted except in the cases of individuals of great virtue. At that rate this source is in danger of being confused with "Good Custom".

It is evident, on the other hand, that in speaking of what is agreeable to the conscience, our authors do not intend that whatever suits someone can be considered as a rule of behaviour. Before referring to conscience it is fitting to look into the question whether it is not possible by analogy or by way of a natural consequence to deduce the required rule from those which have in fact been expressly formulated, or whether it is not possible to resolve the conflict between two rules which are only apparently contradictory. In other words recourse to reason and to logic should not be overlooked. In fact Gautama (II.2.23-24) recognises the usefulness of reasoning. Manu (II.11) is less hostile to reasoning than to sophistry which is aimed simply at undermining the authority of the written rule. Later authors, Yājñavalkya, Nārada, and Bṛhaspati, allow substantial scope for logic and exegesis as means of deciding upon the rule to be followed. When the Mīmāṃsā method came to be applied to the texts of *smṛti* it left very little room for *ātma-tuṣṭi.*

Only the Veda, Tradition, and "Good Custom" are sources in the sense in which we understand that word in juridical discussion. These we shall define one after the other. The two first are written sources, the last is an unwritten source.

2. *The Veda*

For every author *dharma* rests primarily and essentially upon the Veda or rather upon Revelation *(śruti)*. The Vedic texts are really revealed texts, divine words gathered directly by the inspired bards, the ṛṣis.

They consist of three collections of liturgical texts particularly named "Vedas": the *Ṛg-veda,* the *Sāma-veda,* and the *Yajur-veda*, to which a fourth collection, the *Atharva-veda,* was added at some later date.

For each Veda there existed several recensions, each belonging to a particular school of interpreters. Each school *(śākhā* or *caraṇa)* possessed its own collection of liturgical and sacramental texts called by the name *saṃhitā.* In addition, each Vedic school possessed, alongside its *saṃhitā,* treatises on ceremonial practices called *brāhmaṇa,* "guides", intended to explain to the Brahmins authorised to officiate what the relation was between the hymns or the formulae which they recited and the ritual actions which they were bound to carry out. *A propos* of these prescriptions, the *brāhmaṇas* have preserved for us numerous legends and some traditions of great age. The *saṃhitās* and the *brāhmaṇas* together make up *śruti*; but one must also bring within that expression the *āraṇyakas* and the *upaniṣads*, which were philosophical speculations.

It is very difficult to establish the age of the Vedas. The *Ṛgveda* is generally regarded as the most ancient. Max Müller places the majority of the hymns which comprise that collection in the eleventh century before our era. As for the *brāhmaṇas,* the same authority would place them at intervals between 800 and 600 B.C. Actually, there are some of them which could well be contemporary with the redaction of the Vedas, whereas others seem no older than the fifth century.[10]

For the Hindu all knowledge proceeds from the Veda, which is Knowledge.[11] All belief takes its source and its justification there. Consequently every rule of *dharma* must find its foundation in the Veda.

In actual fact the Vedic texts contain little enough in the way of rules

[10]For further detail on the Vedas and Vedic literature see L. Renou, *op. cit.*, ss. 513–618.

[11]*Veda* has the same root as *video*, which implies vision as a means of cognition. The perfect, which expresses a result gained, has the sense of knowledge (A. Ernout and A. Meillet, *op. cit.*, s.v. *uiso*).

of *dharma*. Strictly speaking, the Vedas *(saṃhitās)* do not even include a single positive precept which could be used directly as a rule of conduct. One can find there only references to usage which falls within the scope of *dharma*. By contrast the *brāhmaṇas*, the *āraṇyakas*, and the *upaniṣads* contain, apart from descriptions of certain practices fit to be invoked as precedents to support some rule, numerous precepts which propound rules governing behaviour.

But in reality, it seems that when a Hindu affirms that *dharma* rests entirely upon the Veda, the word Veda does not mean in that connection the Vedic texts, but rather the totality of Knowledge, the sum of all understanding, of all religious and moral truths, whether revealed or not. These truths are not human entities; they are imposed upon man who must simply submit to them; they exist by themselves and have always existed. They form a kind of code with infinite prescriptions of which only the Supreme Being can have perfect knowledge. This eternal code was revealed by Him to certain chosen ones, and that is what is called *śruti*. But only a part of that Revelation could be communicated to mankind; a good deal of it has been lost, moreover, due to the weakness of human memory. Therefore the Vedic texts are far from representing all the Veda. When a rule of *dharma* has no source, we must conclude that it rests upon a part of the Veda which is lost or somehow hidden from view.

We recognise in this theory the ancient belief in a cosmic and moral order which is at the foundations of the concept of *dharma*. To affirm that all *dharma* is to be found in Revelation amounts to an affirmation that the rule of *dharma* has a transcendent character. Primitive peoples often experience the need to materialise their concepts, and in this case the cosmic and moral order is represented in the form of a code capable of being consigned to writing.

It is this hypothetical or symbolic code, rather than the surviving Vedic texts, which the most ancient authors, the writers of the *dharmasūtras*, have in mind when they proclaim that the Veda is the primary source of *dharma*. They hardly do more thereby than express their adherence to common belief, without attaching any particular practical value to that source.

But in Brahminical circles the interpretation of Vedic formulae soon aroused some interest, and it was not long before also our writers had developed a tendency to define more accurately the authority which should be accorded to the Veda. In effect the *dharma* which is expressed in that part of Revelation which has reached us has, by reason of its origin, an absolute and unquestionable authority. But it was necessary that any passage in the Vedic texts which was actually invoked should really amount to a rule of conduct, that is to say, it should be an injunction *(vidhi)*. If it merely reported a fact, no rule of an imperative character could be derived from it; it was a simple *arthavāda*. For example, it is said in the *Yajurveda* (*Taittirīya-saṃhitā* III.1.9.4) that Manu divided his goods amongst his ten children. Is this only a story, suggesting no obligation upon fathers of families to follow Manu's example? Or is it a practice inspired in Manu by a consideration of the spiritual benefits which it might procure and which ought, thereafter, to be converted into a rule by any person concerned for his salvation? Upon the answer to this question depends the value of any Vedic text which is invoked as a source of *dharma*. In the same way the story of Ṛjrāśva in the *Ṛgveda*, the story of Śunaḥśepa (who was sold by his father) in the *Aitareya-brāhmaṇa*, and that of Naciketas (who was offered by his father to Yama) in the *Kaṭha-upaniṣad*, raise the problem of the limits of paternal authority.

A special school was formed to ensure the correct interpretation of the sacred texts, viz. the Mīmāṃsā school, the foundation of which is attributed to a sage of the Vedic period, Jaimini. Although the domain of Mīmāṃsā extends well beyond the search for *dharma*, its influence upon the development of the literature on *dharma* was considerable. The method of interpretation which it extols was adopted by the authors who belong to the epoch of the *sūtras*, and was thereafter constantly followed by the commentators. One could say that it became the Indian mode of juridical reasoning *par excellence*. Since its character is purely exegetical, its effect has been to reduce the scope of interpretation to a mere study of the texts, to distract writers and commentators at an early period from other sources of *dharma* than written sources, and, in that way, to bestow upon Indian jurisprudence a scholastic character which could not but be aggravated with the process of time.

In spite of the intervention of Mīmāṃsā, even though it has become a true and not simply a theoretical source of *dharma*, the Veda remains poor enough, as we have seen, in injunctions capable of being utilised to construct a science of *dharma*. It is from another written source, Tradition *(smṛti)*, to which however the same method of interpretation comes to be applied, that the authors and commentators must borrow in order to disentangle the rules of *dharma* and to make a specific discipline out of them.

3. *Tradition*

Tradition *(smṛti)* differs from Revelation *(śruti)* inasmuch as it is not a direct "heard" perception of the divine precepts, but an indirect perception founded on memory (*smṛti*: to remember, Lat. *memor*). A Sage remembers and transmits to men the traditions which he has gathered and which are the authorised means of acquiring wisdom.

In its largest sense *smṛti* signifies a complete portion of the sacred literature: the six *Vedāṅgas*, the epics (the *Mahābhārata* and the *Rāmāyaṇa*) and the *Purāṇas*.

All these works contain the rules of *dharma*. But those whose special object it is to expound them belong to the class of the *Vedāṅgas*. These (literally the "members" of the Veda) are considered as auxiliary sciences required for the interpretation of the Veda (envisaged as the "body"). They are subdivided into six kinds of treatises bearing (1) on phonetics and more especially on the euphonic rules peculiar to the Vedas; (2) on metres; (3) on linguistic analysis and grammar; (4) on astronomy, especially for the Vedic calendar which fixes days propitious for sacrifices; (5) on the explanation of the difficult terms of the Veda, i.e. etymology; and lastly (6) on the ritual to observe in the sacrifices: *kalpa* (rite, literally "form", "fashion").

All these works are written in the form of the *sūtra* ("thread", leading thread, whence rule), that is to say in aphorisms or highly condensed and abstract sentences, intended, no doubt, to be learnt by heart and unintelligible until they are explained and commented upon by the master.

The *sūtras* appertaining to ritual, or *kalpa-sūtras,* are the most important, which is easily understood when one realises the essentially ritualistic character of the Vedic religion.

The *kalpa-sūtras* are subdivided in turn into three categories of work. One deals with the great sacrifices: these are the *śrauta-sūtras*; the next with domestic cults: these are the *gṛhya-sūtras,* the last are particularly devoted to the duties and the privileges which are attached to the status of membership in the Āryan community: these are the *dharma-sūtras*.

The *śrauta-sūtras* set out in detail the rituals of the sacrifices which belong directly to the *śruti* or great sacrifices, the only ones dealt with in the *brāhmaṇas*. The *gṛhya-sūtras* are concerned with domestic rites which those scriptures mention only incidentally, and which are known to us only by tradition (whence the name *smārta-sūtra* also is given to them).[12]

It would be incorrect to see in those last rites a domestic cult opposed to a public cult. Brahminism does not know a public cult. As a general rule, all the acts known to it are individual, and are done for the advantage of an individual who pays the expenses involved (he is the *yajamāna*, the one for whom sacrifice is performed). There is no question of two cults, but only of different rituals. A certain number of acts are common to both rituals, for example the laying and maintaining of a sacred fire, and the daily offering made in this fire. But in their domestic form they are more simple, and they can be done with less preparation and with a smaller band of priests. Notably they can be performed by means

[12]On the ritual, cf L. Renou, *op. cit.*, ss. 697–744; Kāṇe, *op. cit.*, II, pt. 2.

of a single fire, whereas rituals celebrated according to the evolved ceremonial require at least three.

The ceremonies of the *śrauta* ritual are obligatory in theory but are not widely observed in practice. They are performed daily, or return at fixed intervals, or take place at the occurrence of exceptional events. They consist above all of offerings, of which the offering of *soma* (the *agniṣṭoma* ceremony) is the most important. All such ceremonies are costly. Some last for a day, but usually they last for many. There are some that last for several months, for more than a year, or even for several years. Some are reserved for kings, like the royal consecration *(rājasūya)* or the horse-sacrifice *(aśvamedha)*.

The domestic rituals constitute the least of the duties incumbent on the respectable and pious head of a family, particularly if he is a Brahmin. They are also the only rituals still observed to some extent up to our own time by Brahmins who pride themselves on their fidelity to the ancient ways.

In the first rank come the *saṃskāras* (literally, "preparation", "arrangement", whence consecration, sacrament), which mark the characteristic phases of life. Generally twelve of them are counted, from the *garbhādhāna,* a ritual intended to ensure conception, to *upanayana,* or initiation, and to *vivāha,* namely marriage.

At the time of initiation *(upanayana)* the adolescent boy, dressed in an antelope-skin, receives from his master or *guru,* the words of the celebrated verse of the *Sāvitrī,* along with the sacred thread and the staff. From that moment, which is considered as if it were his spiritual birth, he is "twice-born" *(dvija)* and responsible for his acts. Initiation is obligatory for all males of the free castes. He who abstains from it falls, he and his descendants, into the status of the "fallen", the excommunicate. In principle initiation should be followed by a more or less long noviciate, devoted to the acquisition of the Veda by the initiate. That is the status of the *brahmacārin.* At the end of the noviciate a special ceremony takes place which gives the Hindu the right and the duty to found a hearth and to become the head of a household.

Marriage has a great importance in the context of domestic ritual because as a general rule the cult of the sacrificial domestic fire commences with marriage. The fire employed for the marriage ceremony follows the young couple to their home and there forms the centre of their domestic cult. For women who (except perhaps in ancient times) do not undergo the sacrament of initiation, the marriage ceremony takes its place (*M.,* V.150; *Yāj.,* I.83; *Vis.,* XXV.5–6).

The domestic ritual includes also a whole series of minor sacrifices to be performed by the head of the household, or by his wife or a Brahmin. Essentially they consist of oblations of clarified butter or of offerings of flowers or fruits: for example, the five "great sacrifices" *(mahāyajña)* are offered every day to the gods, to "beings" (the offering of *bali*), to the spirits of the dead, to the Veda itself (a recitation of sacred texts), and to guests. Some ceremonies recur at a fixed date or at a particular season, such as the new-year rituals or the spring festival. From their very nature some cannot have their date fixed in advance, such as rituals for the choice of a house-site, rituals required by agriculture and cattle-breeding, rituals appropriate to the reception of guests of particular status. Finally there are funeral ceremonies, purificatory rites and other ceremonies connected with death, and there is the worship offered to the dead, i.e. the different kinds of *śrāddha*, a prominent feature of which is the offering of *piṇḍas* or "balls" compounded of rice boiled with milk.

The *gṛhya-sūtras* consist essentially of rituals. They confine themselves to a description of the rites incumbent on the *dvija*. Only exceptionally do they touch upon *dharma,* upon rules of conduct, moral duties, or rights and obligations. It could not be long before that sort of speculation occurred to authors of *sūtras*, independently. The post-Vedic epoch saw an affirmation of the supremacy of the Brahmin caste. The role of preceptor had devolved upon the Brahmins, and they were bound to compose manuals in which the teachings which they must inculcate in their pupils were condensed, in the form of formulae. Quite apart from this, appeals were commonly made to Brahmins to arbitrate between parties to a dispute or to give advice as to which rule should be followed in a particular difficulty (and this role is played by Brahmins, here and there, to this day). At royal courts Brahmins played the role of confessor or keeper of the royal conscience *(purohita)*, of councillor, or of judge. As a result there developed, alongside the *sūtras* devoted to domestic ritual, yet in close relationship with them, a literature which was equally *sūtra* in form but specially devoted to *dharma*: these are the *dharma-sūtras*.

Each school of the Veda should have, in addition to its *saṃhitā* and its *brāhmaṇa*, its threefold series (at least in theory) of the *kalpa-sūtra*: *śraūta*, *gṛhya*, and *dharma*.

Later, but still, it seems, at a relatively ancient period, *dharma* was subjected to specialised study. It began to be studied in special schools no longer attached to any one *caraṇa*, to any particular Vedic school. A science of *dharma* grew up *(dharma-sāstra)*, a discipline belonging exclusively to *dharma,* in which the rule of conduct was taught more systematically than in the *dharma-sūtras*. The new treatises were called *dharma-śāstras*. It is to this class of work that the celebrated Code of Manu belongs.

It is in the *dharma-sāstras* and the *dharma-sūtras* that Tradition, *smṛti*, came principally to be located, if one thinks of it in its capacity as a source of *dharma*. In fact the word can be used in a very wide sense to embrace both those classes of works. The Code of Manu is the *Manu-smṛti*. Such rules as were capable of being furnished by the Vedas were incorporated therein. The usages of the Sages played (as we shall see) an ever fainter role, and consequently it is the *dharma-sūtras* and the *dharma-śāstras* which, along with the enormous mass of commentaries and digests derived directly from them, constitute the actual corpus of the Hindu law, in so far as that finds its source in *dharma*.

Smṛti therefore has two senses: in the original, etymological sense it signifies remembered tradition or the knowledge one may derive from memory of the rules of *dharma*, in opposition to the *śruti* which is knowledge directly acquired through Revelation. In a second sense it signifies the whole of the literature constituted by the *dharma-sūtras* and *dharma-śāstras*, a literature regarded as having been inspired by the *smṛti*. The first sense is more prevalent amongst the old authors. Gautama (I.2) speaks of the *smṛti* "of those who know the Veda". Plainly he has in mind a source which was still alive. Similarly when Āpastamba speaks of "the consensus *(samaya)* of those who know *dharma*", he seems really to be referring to the same source. Manu still uses the word *smṛti* in the same sense (II.6,12), but he employs it equally in the second (II.9,10), and for later authors *smṛti* almost always means the inspired literature, *dharma-śāstra* (and *-sūtra*). Thus what had been a living source is fixed, congealed in the writings to which Tradition had been committed.

If one takes *smṛti* in its etymological sense of human tradition founded upon memory, its authority cannot but be inferior to that of *śruti*, which is direct revelation of the rule. But in course of time its authority grew to the point of equalling that of *śruti*. At a time when *smṛti* was considered to be conveyed entirely in a special literature—namely during the age of the commentators—two opinions on the subject were in vogue. For some (the followers of Śabara, the chief exegete of the *sūtras* of Jaimini) the works included in *smṛti* lay down rules of conduct which have been respected from time immemorial by Sages fully versed in knowledge of the Vedic texts. There is room, therefore, for presuming that the rules rest upon Vedic precept. Consequently, if *śruti* is silent, their authority is equal to that of the Veda. If, on the other hand a rule exists in *śruti* which contradicts what is conveyed by the *smṛti*, the former must, naturally, prevail. *Smṛti* thus has a secondary authority, dependent upon the non-existence of a corresponding rule in the *śruti*. On the other hand, for other commentators such as those who follow Kumārila (a later commentator upon Jaimini), the precepts of *smṛti* are invariably founded upon the Veda. If we cannot find the Vedic text which confirms them it is either because that text has disappeared, or is lost, or that—a preferable hypothesis—the weakness of our understanding or even our negligence impedes our having that profound knowledge of the Veda which the authors of the *smṛtis* must have had. Consequently those precepts have an authority equal to those of *śruti,* and, should a conflict occur between the two categories, it is permissible to infer a choice between them.[13] Common opinion favours the second theory. But, as we shall see, writers have, thanks to various arguments, managed often to remove completely any rule of *śruti* which embarrasses them, and to cause that of *smṛti* to prevail.

Another difficulty, hardly as serious as the other, arises from the development of the *smṛti*-literature itself. How is one to choose between different rules laid down in the texts when they disagree with each other? In such cases it is permitted to have recourse to an objective criterion, namely "Good Custom", and to a subjective criterion namely the approval of one's conscience guided by reason. Both of these tend to be blended in the act of interpretation, the role of which is precisely to resolve conflicts between different *smṛtis*. All writers agree in saying that one must apply to the *smṛti* texts the same rules of interpretation as are used for the text of the *śruti*, that is to say they must be interpreted according to the techniques of Mīmāṃsā. Later we shall investigate in some detail the way in which the authors of commentaries and digests have applied this method of exegesis.

4. *"Good Custom"*

The last source of *dharma* mentioned by all the authors is "Good Custom", the way good people live: *sad-ācāra*, the custom of the good, or *śiṣṭa-ācāra,* the custom of those who have undergone instruction.

We find also the term *śīla,* conduct, which some commentators make into a special source (Kullūka on *M.*, II.6). But the ancient writers make no such distinction and refer to *ācāra* as frequently as *śīla*. In effect, the practice of those who know the Veda blends with "Good Custom", for there is room to suppose that he who knows the law is guided by it in his conduct.

One must take care to avoid confusing this ideal "custom" with what *we* call custom, that is to say practices confirmed by immemorial usage, custom followed by everyone, habitual practices of a group, perhaps arising from convention. Custom pure and simple is indeed a source of law, but it is not a source of *dharma*.

Sadācāra is a religious life, exclusively orientated towards the acquisition of spiritual merit. It amounts to the practices observed from generation to generation by *śiṣṭas*, or those who are at once *instructed* and virtuous. They have not only plumbed the depths of the Veda and its related texts, but they can deduce from them all the consequences which are

[13] P.V. Kāṇe, III, 828–835.

implied, and, what is more, they conform to these teachings in their conduct (cf. *Baudh.* I.1.5–6; *Vas.*, VI.43).

For Manu (II.18) this custom is pure Āryan custom, that which the Āryans brought to India and which continues to be observed (in his view) by the pious inhabitants of *Brahmāvarta,* the sacred territory. In a conception which is the reverse of our notion of progress,[14] Hindus place the golden age at the dawn of creation. Consequently their custom is pure, in perfect conformity with *dharma*.

In course of time the sense of the expression *sadācāra* was modified until it signified every usage practised from time immemorial by virtuous and instructed people, without any special localisation, subject to the condition that no such usage should be motivated by any visible mundane purpose. This condition, to which we shall return later, is already formulated by the authors of the *dharma-sūtras* (notably *Vas.*, I.6–7).

The task of telling whether a particular practice conforms to *sadācāra* falls particularly on an assembly *(pariṣad)* to which the Upaniṣads often allude, sometimes under the name *samiti* or "gathering" (*Chānd.,* V.3.1; *Bṛhad.,* VI.2.1). The make-up of this assembly varies according to different authors. In the *dharma-sūtras* it comprises, in principle, ten persons (*Gaut.,* XXVIII.49–51; *Vas.,* III.20; *Baudh.,* I.1.7–9). The same number appears in Manu (XII.111), according to whom the assembly contains three men versed each in one of the three Vedas, one logician, one *mīmāṃsaka* (exegete following the techniques of Mīmāṃsā), one scholar in etymology *(nirukta),* one who knows the treatises on *dharma (dharma-śāstrin)* and finally three individuals, each of them representing the first three stages of life, namely one *brahmacārin,* one householder, and one hermit or ascetic. But Manu also provides (XII.112) that the assembly may be composed of three members only, each versed in one of the three Vedas: *Ṛg, Yajur,* and *Sāma.* Yājñavalkya (I.9) reduces the number of men competent to form a *pariṣad* to four, or to three.

But it matters little, basically, what the numerical composition of the assembly is. What really matters is the quality of the members. "They can be five, they can be three", says Baudhāyana (I.1.9), "one man [provided he is] without sin is sufficient to decide on the rule. But a thousand fools would be incompetent to do it". And he adds, "As an elephant made of wood, as an antelope made of leather, so is an ignorant Brahmin. Like them, he has nothing more than the name of his species" (I.1.10). Similarly Manu states (XII.113–114), "That which even a single Brahmin, instructed in the Veda, declares to be *dharma* must be considered as the highest rule, and not whatever may be proclaimed by myriads of ignorant men. Even thousands of Brahmins, if they have not fulfilled

[14]L. Dumont, *La civilisation indienne et nous,* Cahiers des Annales 23 (Paris, 1964), 33. Kāṇe, III, 885ff; V, 686ff.

their religious duties *(vrata)*, if they are not versed in the Veda, and if they subsist merely upon the name of the caste, are incompetent to constitute a *pariṣad* by assembling together".

The Brahmins do indeed form a class, and a powerful one at that, but they have never been organised as a college. They are entirely independent of each other, their class possesses no hierarchy, they have no sovereign pontiff. Provided they accept the letter of the Vedas and the sacred texts, and provided they perform the prescribed rituals, they retain a complete freedom of opinion. The Brahminical religion is a tolerant religion whose dogmas are very wide and capable of encompassing the most diverse metaphysics. It follows that no interpretation could derive authority from the number of those who assent to it. Its authority derives solely from the logical as well as moral value of the teaching involved. It was the same at Rome. The authority of the *prudentes*, who also were exegetes of a "good custom" laïcised into *boni mores* (good practices) or *jus naturae* (the law of nature), was founded in the esteem which they earned as well as in their inborn aptitude to grasp the rule of law and to deduce its logical consequences from it.

During the post-Vedic epoch *sadācāra*, expressed in *pariṣads*, was obliged to play an important role in the elaboration of the rules of *dharma*. To arrive at these Āpastamba (I.1.1.2) refers principally to "the agreement of those who know *dharma*" *(dharma-jña-samaya)*, and he mentions the Vedas only in the second place. But the development of a literature founded on the *smṛti* must, little by little, have deprived that source of all practical relevance. It is likely that the *dharma-sūtras* and the older *śāstras* did little more than collect the traditional rules propounded by *pariṣads*. Haradatta, a commentator on Āpastamba, explains *pariṣad* in terms similar to what Manu and the other *smṛtis* imply. The *smṛtis* were in fact called *pārṣada* works (works emanating in some way from *pariṣads*). On the other hand the authority attached to "Good Custom" is founded upon a presumption that it relies ultimately on the Veda. It follows that authority vanishes before a contrary Vedic text, for "the revealed texts have a greater force than any custom from which one might deduce *(ānumānika)* [the existence of a *śruti* passage prescribing the action]" (*Āp.*, I.1.4.8).[15] But its authority vanishes also before a rule of *smṛti*, that is to say, of the *dharma-śāstras*; for the authors of the latter are unquestionably *śiṣṭas*, and if *they* condemn a custom that naturally destroys the presumption that it is founded on the Veda. Finally the adoption of Mīmāṃsā techniques, which are exclusively exegetical in object, must have contributed towards the evaporation of this source, since it tended to confine commentators to a mere interpretation of the written rules.

[15] On *ānumānika*, see Bühler's note to his translation of that *sūtra* (*S.B.E.*, II, 15).

Pariṣad "colleges" disappeared in relatively early times, probably prior to the development of the literature comprised in the *śāstras*. Manu preserves the institution, but the fact that he allows a single qualified Brahmin the function of proclaiming *ācāra* ("custom") is significant. As his commentators Medhātithi and Kullūka see it, that source is involved only where the rules are of secondary interest. All essential rules from then onwards appear in the *smṛtis* themselves. The proper functions of *pariṣads*, which are above all to give decisions in particular cases and notably in questions of penance, have been fulfilled at later periods by Brahmins attached to the courts of Indian princes, such as the *paṇḍita* who bears the title *vinaya-sthiti-sthāpaka* ("he who established the lines of good discipline") in Gupta inscriptions.[16] In our own days they are fulfilled by caste meetings or by the heads of religious orders *(maṭha)*.[17] Interpretation in the proper sense of that word, namely that which enables principles or general rules to be singled out, finally passed to commentators and to the authors of independent treatises.

[16]A.S. Altekar, *State and Government in Ancient India* (Benares, 1955), 164.

[17]According to Kāṇe, II, 966–75, it was only after the British conquest that heads of *maṭhas* took over from Brahmins in general the privilege of deciding doubtful questions of a religious nature. For an instance of this jurisdiction actually being used, to the embarrassment of the regular courts, see *Madhavrao Raghavendra* v. *Raghavendrarao* Indian Law Reports 1946 Bombay, 375. And the svāmījī's *de facto* power to settle complaints is well illustrated at H.M. Sadasivaiah, *A Comparative Study of Two Vīraśaiva Monasteries* (Mysore, 1967), 158ff. [trs.]

CHAPTER II

THE DHARMA-SŪTRAS

THE DHARMA-SŪTRAS are works on *dharma* written in the *sūtra* form, that is to say in the form of aphorisms which condense the teaching imparted by a master, and were probably intended to be learned by heart by his disciples.

A score of such works have reached us, some of them in a fragmentary state. Half a dozen have been published, but the remainder exist only in manuscript.

Only the most important have been translated : Āpastamba, Gautama, Vasiṣṭha and Baudhāyana by Georg Bühler (*S.B.E.*, II and XIV), Viṣṇu by Julius Jolly (*S.B.E.*, VIII).

Originally, it seems, most of these *dharma-sūtras*, if not all of them, belonged to a collection of *kalpa-sūtras* and were attached to a particular Vedic school. But of all those which have come down to us there are only three (Āpastamba, Hiraṇyakeśin and Baudhāyana) for which we possess the *śrauta-* and *gṛhya-sūtras* which complete the triple series of the *kalpa-sūtra*.

In all respects the *dharma-sūtras* bear a close relation to the *gṛhya-sūtras* : the connection is not only linguistic but also in point of subject matter. There are *sūtras* which are common to both works, and these latter often refer to each other. Like the *gṛhya-sūtras*, the *dharma-sūtras* contain rules about the *saṃskāras*, including marriage; on the *āśramas*, including the duties of the *brahmacārin* and the householder; on funeral oblations, etc. But they seldom describe the ritual of domestic life; they touch upon it only in passing. Their domain is vaster and more ambitious. They intend above all to propound the rules to govern men's conduct, an intention which leads to the appearance of precepts of a character that can only be called juridical. Their principal interest for us lies precisely in their demonstration of how the study of ritual has led the writers to a study of religious obligation, which has itself led them to propound rules of law.

The period in which the *dharma-sūtras* were compiled, like that of the *sūtra* literature in general, follows that of the *brāhmaṇas*. A start was made about the sixth century B.C., one or two centuries before the rise of Buddhism, and theoretically the period ends with the birth of the *śāstra* literature, didactic treatises written in epic Sanskrit, several centuries before the Christian era. But composition in the archaic style of the *sūtra* went on long after the *śāstras* began to appear. Moreover, to arrive at a date for the principal *dharma-sūtras* involves considerable difficulty. Indologists are agreed in placing the *dharma-sūtras* of Gautama, Baudhyāyana and Āpastamba amongst the most ancient, also Hiraṇya-keśin and Vasiṣṭha. A special place must be made for the *dharma-sūtra* of Viṣṇu.

This chapter will be devoted above all to the problem of our texts' origins, and the next chapter will deal with their contents.

1. *The Dharma-sūtra of Gautama*

It is generally acknowledged that the *dharma-sūtra* attributed to Gautama is the most ancient of those which have come down to us.

Gautama is the name of a very ancient Brahmin family, many of whose members founded various Vedic schools which were all attached to the *Sāma-veda*. Though the text which has reached us is unattached we may well suppose that it once formed part of the *kalpa-sūtra* of one of those schools. Apart from that some internal evidence indicates that it had relations with a school of the *Sāma-veda*, of the Rānāyanīya branch localised in the Maratha country in Western India. The twenty-sixth chapter reproduces practically word for word a passage from a *brāhmaṇa* belonging to that Veda, the Sāmavidhāna. Further, the author betrays a preference for the *mantras* of the *Sāma-veda* in his choice of formulae to be used for purification.

The priority he gives to the *dharma-sūtras* of Baudhāyana and of Vasiṣṭha is supported by the fact that both these works refer to him, and they have actually borrowed a chapter from him. The *dharma-sūtra* of Gautama, on the other hand, names no other master but Manu (who may well *not* be the author of our *Manu-smṛti*). However, he often cites the opinion of the *ācāryas* (teachers), implying no doubt that the opinion on the point in question was accredited amongst those who had taught *dharma* before him. He alludes in many places to opinions professed by various writers. That shows that Gautama's *dharma-sūtra* is far from being the first treatise on *dharma*.

It is a fact hostile to the relative antiquity of this *dharma-sūtra* that the language in which it is written is less archaic and more conformable to the grammatical rules of Pāṇini than the *dharma-sūtras* of Āpastamba and Baudhāyana. But Bühler resolves this difficulty by noticing that Gautama's *sūtra* was detached from the *kalpa-sūtra* collection which it belonged to; it became a work of general authority instead of being a work of special application in a particular school. Its original language could easily have been revised and corrected by commentators. Bühler goes so far as to believe that the text itself may well have been altered, and he marks two or three passages which could have been interpolated.

But he adds that the general character of the work has not been affected greatly. The topics were arranged with too much method and with too much care to allow substantial modifications.

The use of the word *bhikṣu* to indicate ascetics instead of the more usual term *saṃnyāsin* (or *yati*), and also the rule according to which the *bhikṣu* should not change his abode during the rainy season (III.13) leads Bühler to think that the compilation of this *dharma-sūtra* must have been long anterior to the development of Buddhism, which appropriated the term. It is true also that one finds there the word *yavana*, which signifies the Greeks, and that many authors suppose that the Yavanas became known to Hindus only after the expedition of Alexander the Great, with the result that no work that contains the word *yavana* could have been written earlier than the fourth century B.C. A possible reply is that Hindus could very well have known of the Greeks long before Alexander's invasion, through Achaemenid Persia as an intermediary. Yet the *sūtra* which causes the difficulty cites these Yavanas as one of the mixed castes, which suggests that the Greco-Bactrian kingdoms were already in existence. However, the mention of an isolated name in a work subject to interpolation can hardly be a powerful argument in the face of characteristics consistent with a much greater antiquity. Thus the composition of the *dharma-sūtra* of Gautama could be placed, at the latest, four centuries before our era. Kāṇe places it between 600 and 400 B.C.

It is written entirely in prose. This distinguishes it from other *dharma-sūtras* all of which contain some verses, whether composed by their own authors or borrowed from elsewhere. It is divided into twenty-eight *adhyāyas* (literally "readings") of unequal length.

2. *The Dharma-sūtras of Baudhāyana, Āpastamba and Hiraṇyakeśin*

These three *dharma-sūtras* have a characteristic in common. They belong to branches of the same Vedic school, the school of the Taittirīya, specialising in the study of the Black *Yajurveda*,[1] of which we have the complete series of sacred texts, *saṃhitā, brāhmaṇa, upaniṣad* and *āraṇyaka*. We have, furthermore, the *śrauta-* and *gṛhya-sūtras* appertaining to each of these three texts.

According to the Brahminical tradition Baudhāyana was the first to compose a *kalpa-sūtra* collection in the Taittirīya school. His successor, so it is said, was Āpastamba, who founded a school of his own. Hiraṇyakeśin, disciple of Āpastamba, set up in his turn yet a third school. This is how three *kalpa-sūtras* came into existence, all attached to the Black *Yajurveda*.

[1]This recension is so called because prose portions are intermixed with the formulas and prayers, while the so-called White Yajurveda is free from such admixture.

It is generally agreed that the *dharma-sūtra* of Baudhāyana is earlier than the other two. The tradition we have just mentioned provides one reason. Another derives from a comparison of the rules expressed there with the corresponding rules of Āpastamba, who propounds generally stricter, more puritanical rules than does Baudhāyana. Further, the style of Baudhāyana is more archaic, ruder than that of Āpastamba. His plan is also much less systematic, which would be understandable if Baudhāyana were indeed the first *sūtra-kāra* of the school.

However, we have already seen that Baudhāyana's *dharma-sūtra* cannot be anterior to that of Gautama, for he expressly cites Gautama's opinion in two places and copies him virtually word for word.

Though the *sūtras* of Āpastamba and Hiraṇyakeśin have reached us in collections which have been systematically arranged, with a place assigned to every portion of the *kalpa*, the *sūtras* of Baudhāyana's school have come down to us in an incomplete fashion and as a distinct work. It is probable that the *dharma-sūtra* of this school was treated as an independent work, standing as an authority in questions of *dharma*. In consequence its text was bound to undergo certain changes. In Bühler's view only the first two portions (*praśnas*, "questions") out of the four which make up the surviving version actually belonged to the original composition, and he is not able to declare even those free from revision and interpolation.

The *Āpastamba-dharma-sūtra*, by contrast, has reached us in a much more satisfactory condition. It is contained in a *kalpa-sūtra* of thirty portions *(praśnas)* which have survived intact, of which it forms the twenty-eighth and twenty-ninth portions. The first twenty-four portions are devoted to *śrauta* rituals, the twenty-fifth to various ancillary matters, the twenty-sixth and twenty-seventh to *gṛhya* rituals, while, after we have done with *dharma*, the thirtieth section contains rules regarding the construction of altars. This huge work is certainly a whole and seems to have been composed by a single author. The subjects are systematically arranged. Further, the *gṛhya-sūtra* gives only the outlines of the domestic rituals, since the duties which are linked to the performance of them are explained in the sections set aside for the *dharma-sūtra*. Moreover, there are frequent cross-references from one part of the *kalpa-sūtra* to another. A few *sūtras* in identical terms are found in parts devoted to domestic ritual and parts devoted to *dharma*. Consequently the different parts of the work are really a unity.

Āpastamba, like Gautama, Baudhāyana and Hiraṇyakeśin, is actually a patronymic name. It belongs to a family of Brahmins dedicated to the study of the Black *Yajurveda*, one of whose members founded a school after Baudhāyana which was ritually specialised, a branch of the Taittirīya school. According to Brahminical tradition the Āpastambīyas originated in the South East of India, and their founder came from the Āndhra country (between the Godāvarī and the Kṛṣṇā rivers). This tradition is to some extent corroborated by a passage in the *dharma-sūtra* where the author refers disapprovingly to a custom of inhabitants of the North. Further, he cites the *āraṇyaka* of the Taittirīya according to a version current amongst Āndhra Brahmins. Right up to our own times Āpastambīya Brahmins have settled primarily in the territories belonging to the former Bombay Presidency, the Nizam's State, and the former Presidency of Madras (that is to say a large part of the present Andhra Pradesh and parts of Madras, with Maharashtra), whereas Brahmins of this school are rare in Northern India and those who are to be found in Central India have plainly immigrated into those regions. Pallava inscriptions, likewise in the Āndhra area, confirm that Āpastambīya Brahmins were settled in South India at an ancient period.

If the founder of the school came from the South we are led to suspect that it must have been relatively late in appearing. The South of India doubtless received the Brahminical civilization long after Hindusthan. The regions of the South are not mentioned in the Vedic texts and the Āndhras are actually indicated as barbarians in a *brāhmaṇa* of the *Ṛgveda*. The name of Āpastamba does not figure in the Vedic texts. The author of the *dharma-sūtra* represents himself as belonging to a late period (*avara*), that is to say at some distance of time from the Vedic period.

On the other hand the *dharma-sūtra* of Āpastamba suggests that a rich literature on *dharma* already existed. He cites ten authors by name. He certainly knows Gautama, with whom he shows some striking resemblances, and Baudhāyana, several of whose opinions he discusses. He refers to many authors without naming them. He cites one or perhaps more than one *purāṇa*.

Yet his style and grammar (which is far from the standards of Pāṇini) evince a great antiquity. There is no distinct reference to Buddhism, nor to any schism. Bühler himself was not able to place the date of composition later than the third century B.C. and he admits that that date could be too late by a century or a century and a half. Kāṇe places the work between 600 and 300 B.C.

But we are bound to notice that Hopkins places the composition of this work in the second century B.C. at the earliest. In his view the archaic character of the style is to be explained by the likelihood that the Āndhras will have retained such linguistic peculiarities long after the *sūtras* of Pāṇini had fixed the usage of the regions of the North.[2] His opinion remains an isolated one. Other scholars, on the contrary, regard the work as much more ancient and even consider it anterior to Gautama.[3]

[2] *Cambridge History of India*, I, 269.

[3] J.J. Meyer, *Über das Wesen der altindischen Rechtsschriften* (Leipzig, 1927) and B.K.

The *dharma-sūtra* of Hiraṇyakeśin, like that of Āpastamba, has come down to us with the complete series of *sūtras* of the school to which it belongs, the school of Hiraṇyakeśin Brahmins, which became detached at some undeterminable period from that of Āpastamba so as to form an independent school, though it maintained a certain relationship with it. It originated in the Koṅkan (on the West coast). Hiraṇyakeśin's *dharma-sūtra* has thirty-six sections *(praśnas)*, and it is the twenty-sixth and twenty-seventh which contain the *dharma-sūtra*. This work can hardly be regarded as an independent work, for many of the *sūtras* are borrowed word for word from Āpastamba. Its principal interest, therefore, is that it serves as the most ancient evidence of the authenticity of Āpastamba's text, and its value is considerable as a means of establishing it.

Bühler was content, when he drew up his edition of Āpastamba's *dharma-sūtra* to indicate the variants which appeared in that of Hiraṇyakeśin. The latter has some additions and some omissions. The style is revised; and the arrangement of the *sūtras* is different in places.

3. *The Dharma-sūtra of Vasiṣṭha and other ancient Dharma-sūtras*

Govindasvāmin, a commentator on the *dharma-sūtra* of Baudhāyana, cites a tradition that before the *dharma-sūtra* of Vasiṣṭha enjoyed a general authority it was studied and received as authoritative in a particular school of the *Ṛgveda*. Vasiṣṭha is the name of one of the most famous of the *Ṛṣis* of the *Ṛgveda*, a redoutable champion of Brahminism, a demigod born of the gods Mitra and Varuṇa and the *apsara* Urvaśī. The *dharma-sūtra* calls him "Vasiṣṭha the *Ṛṣi*" and thrice appeals to his authority. No doubt because of the tradition which relates it to the famous *Ṛṣi*, this *dharma-sūtra* has been held in great veneration and has been preserved up to our own time. Perhaps there was a family of Ṛgvedin Brahmins who claimed the *Ṛṣi* Vasiṣṭha as its mythical ancestor, and a member of that family was the author of a *kalpa-sūtra* of which only the *dharma-sūtra* has survived. Another possibility is that here we have an independent work adopted by a school of the *Ṛgveda* which happened to possess only *śrauta-* and *gṛhya-sūtras*.

In any case, the established relationship between this work and a school of the *Ṛgveda* presumes a considerable antiquity. In fact the *dharma-sūtra* of Vasiṣṭha greatly resembles the *sūtras* we have already examined, especially Gautama and Baudhāyana, to which it appears to be junior. Unfortunately, as in the case of Baudhāyana, the text has reached us in a retouched and interpolated condition. Nevertheless,

Ghose, 'Āpastamba and Gautama', *I.H.Q.*, 3 (1927), 607–11. For a critique of the arguments in favour of the priority of Āpastamba see S.C. Banerji, *Dharma Sūtras, A Study of their Origin and Development* (Calcutta, 1962), 44–49.

our existing version is that known to the ancient commentators, especially Viśvarūpa.

One of the interesting features of this *dharma-sūtra* is that in many places it cites the opinions of Manu, from which it follows that there existed at that time a work attributed to Manu. Primarily from this factor Bühler and other Indologists conclude that there must have been a *dharma-sūtra* of Manu behind the *dharma-śāstra* which has reached us : a hypothesis which we must consider later on.

Several of Vasiṣṭha's opinions are archaic. In many respects they differ from those of ancient authors like Gautama and Baudhāyana. Vasiṣṭha propounds rules on adoption which are not to be found in Āpastamba or Baudhāyana. He speaks of written documents as one of the three modes of proof, but the other authors are silent on the point.

Jolly admits that the composition of Vasiṣṭha's *dharma-sūtra* must go back several centuries before our era. Kāṇe places it between 300 and 100 B.C.

Most of the *dharma-sūtras* we have just reviewed imply that an earlier literature on *dharma* was already abundant. Of these ancient *dharma-sūtras* a few survive in manuscript form, but others are known to us only from citations either in the *smṛti* works or in the commentaries and digests.[4]

For example, Baudhāyana, Āpastamba and Vasiṣṭha refer to a *dharma-sūtra* of Hārīta which is often cited by the commentators, from the oldest to the most recent. Only one manuscript was known, and that was useless for purposes of publication. Jolly, who gives a résumé of its contents, considers it the most ancient of all *dharma-sūtras*. Like Āpastamba, the author belonged to a school of the Black *Yajurveda*.

By the same way, the oldest commentators, like Viśvarūpa, prove the existence of a *dharma-sūtra* of Śaṅkha-Likhita in prose. The fragments which they quote have been gathered by Kāṇe. The text is close to Gautama and Baudhāyana, and its date must be relatively old.

We may also mention the *sūtras* of Uśanas, of Kāśyapa, and of Atri. These three works bear the names of sages or famous *Ṛṣis* who were themselves reputed to be masters of *dharma*. They have reached us in two forms : in one we have incomplete versions in *sūtra* style, and in the other the versions are mostly versified. The same is the case with the *dharma-sūtra* of Śaṅkha-Likhita. A verse version has reached us which, however, is called a *smṛti*. It contains none of the numerous prose citations which appear in the commentaries. On the other hand a comparison between the two texts does reveal a tendency towards a more strict, rigorous approach to the subject. The very form of those

[4]S.C. Banerji (*op. cit.*, 244–344) has gathered citations from twenty-three of these *dharma-sūtras*.

last works foreshadows the literature of the *dharma-śāstras,* even if it does not already presuppose its existence.

We must mention, lastly, the *Vaikhānasa-dharma-praśna*, which includes a detailed account of the status of hermit (*vaikhānasa*, which is synonymous with *vānaprastha*) and that of the *saṃnyāsin*. The work appears to be comparatively recent, because it provides evidence of the cult of Nārāyaṇa (Viṣṇu), but it may well be founded upon an ancient manual. Kāṇe (I, 2d. ed., 260) dates the *sūtra* 300–400 A.D.

4. *The Viṣṇu-smṛti*

This work, known under the names *Viṣṇu-smṛti, Viṣṇu-sūtra* and *Vaiṣṇava-dharma-śāstra,* is very different from the *dharma-sūtras* which we have just studied. To start with, the *dharma-sūtras* represent themselves as human products, while the rules to be found in this work are attributed to the god Viṣṇu. He addresses them to the goddess Earth when, under the *avatāra* of the Boar, he raises the earth above the waters.

Further, the work is more extensive than the old *dharma-sūtras* (by about double). It is divided into a hundred chapters *(adhyāyas)*, as many as there are epithets for the name of Viṣṇu. However, some of these chapters are quite short.

Finally, while the old *dharma-sūtras* are written almost entirely in prose (mixed with verse in the ancient *triṣṭubh* metre), all the chapters possess a portion in prose, generally at the beginning, and a portion in verse, sometimes in *triṣṭubh* but often in the *śloka* metre, with the exception of the first chapter and the two last which are entirely in verse.[5]

As it stands at present, the work shows evidence of fairly recent redaction. Notably it mentions the seven days of the week, a Greek usage which does not appear in Indian epigraphy until the end of the fifth century A.D. and is not attested in literature until the next century. It enumerates the places of pilgrimage, many of which are situated in the Deccan (the south central portion of the peninsula). It describes numerous ceremonies and practices unknown to other *smṛtis,* omens of good and bad augury at the moment of leaving on a journey (amongst which appears the act of meeting an ascetic in a yellow robe—probably a Buddhist monk). Certain of its practices have a distinctly marked Vaiṣṇavite character. Many passages have no parallel in the old *dharma-sūtras*. Jolly therefore finds himself unable to date this edition before the third or even the fourth century A.D., and Kāṇe is of the same opinion.

Nevertheless certain portions unquestionably go back to an older period. If the style in general is classical and conforms to the rules laid down by Pāṇini, the prose passages are written in the laconic form of

[5]See L. Renou, 'Sur la forme de quelques textes sanskrits, I. La Viṣṇusmṛti', *J.A.*, 1961, 163–72.

the oldest *sūtras* and could not have been understood without the aid of a commentary. Even in the versified passages certain chapters, notably those which contain rules of a juridical character, contain a nucleus of great age, at least as old as the *dharma-sūtras* of Gautama and Āpastamba.

Jolly, following Bühler, conjectures that we have there the traces or the remains of a very old *dharma-sūtra* which has been retouched at some recent period by a member of a Vaiṣṇavite sect. Hindu commentators have already pointed out the close connections which exist between this work and the *kaṭha* school of the Veda, one of the oldest schools of the Black *Yajurveda,* of which a *gṛhya-sūtra* has survived. Many of the passages in Viṣṇu which relate to domestic rituals are in perfect agreement with the *kaṭha gṛhya-sūtra,* just as many of the *mantras* quoted throughout the work derive from collections belonging to the same school. Bühler and Jolly conclude from this that the *Viṣṇu-smṛti* was, in its original form, nothing but the *dharma-sūtra* of the *kaṭha* school of the Black *Yajurveda.* That school, which was born in the Punjab and Kashmir, is one of the oldest schools of the Veda. This means that the *sūtras,* composed so near to the first home of Āryan civilization in India, testify to an antiquity greater than those which have proceeded from other schools of the Black *Yajurveda*, such as that of Āpastamba, founded in South India. Bühler and Jolly believe in consequence that Viṣṇu is, in substance, much more ancient than Āpastamba, even earlier than the fourth or fifth century B.C. Yet because of the considerable retouching which the original work has undergone we must employ a good deal of caution in utilising the text which has come down to us.

The *Viṣṇu-smṛti* has another interesting feature, to which Jolly devotes some space. This is its relationship with later literature, especially the *smṛtis* of Manu and Yājñavalkya. Viṣṇu has 160 *ślokas* which are found in Manu, and several hundreds of *sūtras* only reproduce in prose rules expressed by Manu in verse. Jolly believes that the author of the *Viṣṇu-smṛti* could draw upon the same source as the author of the *Manu-smṛti,* and in these similarities he sees an argument in favour of the existence of a *dharma-sūtra* of the Mānava school (that is to say, the school of Manu or his followers), which was another school attached to the study of the Black *Yajurveda.*

Kāṇe disputes this conclusion and, it seems, rightly. Far too many verses are common to the two works. One must have borrowed from the other. Granted, indeed, that the surviving edition must be late, the most likely borrower is the author of our *Viṣṇu-smṛti.* Quite apart from Manu we find in that work very frequent agreements with the *smṛti* of Yājñavalkya and even with the *Bhagavadgītā.* We may join Kāṇe in the comment that it is highly unlikely that works of this order of celebrity could have borrowed from a work of relative unimportance such as the *Viṣṇu-smṛti*. If Viṣṇu does not actually cite Manu by name, and if that name is missing in certain verses which, in the *Manu-smṛti* itself, contain the name of Manu, this is not because both authors have drawn upon a common source, but simply because, since the *Viṣṇu-smṛti* represents itself as a direct revelation from the god, no human author could have been named! The retoucher who made a Vaiṣṇavite work out of the original composition has intentionally suppressed the name of Manu from the verses where he found it.

It is interesting to note that the *Mitākṣarā,* a commentary on the *smṛti* of Yājñavalkya of the early twelfth century, quotes Viṣṇu about thirty times but does not quote any *verse* from the *Viṣṇu-smṛti*. The authenticity of these versified portions can be open to doubt. They may not have formed a part of the work at the period when the *Mitākṣarā* was written: at any rate it is beyond doubt that they form the latest stratum of it.

CHAPTER III

INDIAN SOCIETY AND THE RULES OF LAW IN THE DHARMA-SŪTRAS

THE IMPORTANCE of the *dharma-sūtras* appears not least from the fact that they show us what part was allotted, in the Vedic schools, to the teaching of *dharma*. They taught *dharma* after they had taught ritual; it was taken for granted that ritual had been studied completely, and *dharma* made its appearance as a complement to that. If we are to judge from the number of *sūtras* devoted to *dharma* in a complete *kalpa-sūtra,* such as that of Āpastamba, the student's attention seems to have been directed, above all, towards a very thorough knowledge of the ritual performances. Unquestionably what was undertaken was to put him in a position correctly to fulfil the task of priest in the various cult activities in which he would be expected to officiate. This same spirit, ritualistic and even formalistic, prevails equally in the *dharma-sūtras,* which, to a certain extent, stop at rituals. Nevertheless there is a new element, an appreciation of *dharma,* of "duty" underlying all that formality. The teaching of *dharma* still occupied a very meagre place in the *brahmacārin's* education. Perhaps this was in response to a movement which manifested itself during the post-Vedic period which put the authority of the Veda itself and even that of Tradition in question. The movement denied the utility and efficacy of the religious practices and the rules of conduct which the Sages had prescribed. Possibly it was such criticisms which led the *ācāryas* of the Brahminical schools to complete their teaching of the rituals by speculations which brought out the moral and religious aspects of the rite, and explained its significance and the obligations which flowed from it. But there is another element in the *dharma-sūtras* which is entirely novel. Side by side with precepts which are still in strict relation to the rituals one comes across numerous rules tending to define social relationships and to regulate men's activities within their group—and from this time onwards there is the appearance of something resembling legislation. The study of the *dharma-sūtras* is essential if we are to do justice to the atmosphere which surrounded the birth of law in India and which impregnated it for ever afterwards. Above all it permits us to grasp how rules of this kind managed to find a place in their author's concerns, and how law came to be tightly bound up with *dharma*.[1] Moreover it helps us to understand these authors'

[1] *"Comment le droit s'est trouvé incorporé au dharma".*

point of view, for their particular vision gave them a rule of law which they saw not with the eye of a jurist but with that of a religious preceptor.

The interest of such a study is every bit as great when one considers that the *dharma-sūtras* represent the first phase of the written expression of *smṛti*. No doubt we are unable to attach much importance to dates, even the very approximate dates which are attributed to their composition. In course of time they underwent so many alterations that no one can predicate the definite authenticity of any of their rules. But that does not prevent our drawing at least from the form, to a considerable degree from the substance also, a reliable notion of what the first treatises on *dharma* were really like. Their material was already substantial by that stage. They contain in embryo all the later development of the *smṛti* literature. Topics are arranged there according to a plan which reappears in the Code of Manu. His and later *dharma-śāstras'* original contributions stand out the more clearly for that.[2]

In my present chapter the first two sections will be devoted to expounding two theories which appear to have been established at least in outline by the epoch of our *sūtras*. They are the theory of the four *varṇas*, and that of the four *āśramas* or stages of life. We are bound to tackle them first, for they are the very framework of the *dharma-sūtras*. The former of the two introduces the caste system, which is one of the most characteristic aspects of traditional Indian society. It raises most interesting problems, especially of its historical value and its practical importance. The latter theory, namely that of the stages of life, must not be neglected for all its frankly religious character, because it completes the picture of Indian society as our authors have drawn it. While the theory of the four *varṇas* seeks to define the positions of individuals in space (their relations with different social groups parallel to their own), the theory of the four *āśramas* follows them throughout their existence and leads them progressively to their final goal. Thus the two theories in combination provide a two-dimensional view of society, the former along the horizontal or static plane, the latter vertically or diachronically. Life itself is organised, in its individual and its social aspects, through the coordination of the two.[3]

1. *The Theory of the Four Varṇas*

The theory of the *varṇas* provides the authors of the *dharma-sūtras* with a framework within which they may lay down the duties of individuals according to their caste. The word used for caste is *varṇa* (literally,

[2]With rare exceptions I have not taken account of developments later than the rules found in the *Viṣṇu-smṛti*. For a more detailed and more comprehensive statement of the content of the *sūtras* see the work of S.C. Banerji, cited above at p. 22, n.3.

[3]P.N. Prabhu, *Hindu Social Organization* (Bombay, 1954), 74–5.

"colour"). We shall see that it does *not* signify any real castes, but rather the concept of caste to which our authors subscribed.

We cannot possibly set out here the scheme of castes as it has been described and studied by innumerable writers, nor even summarise the various methods proposed to explain its origin. We must presuppose that that scheme is already known to the reader in general terms. It remains for us to find out what may have been the relation between the theory of the *varṇas* and the reality. That theory belongs to *smṛti* and is found throughout Indian literature. It is fully formulated in the *dharma-sūtras*, to which alone we need resort for our information.

There are four *varṇas*, of the Brahmins, Kṣatriyas, Vaiśyas, and Śūdras respectively. "Amongst these *varṇas*, each preceding one is superior by birth to that which follows it" (*Āp.*, I.1.1.4-5).

This hierarchy is founded on a celebrated myth to be found in a hymn of the tenth book of the *Ṛgveda*, to which Gautama (IV.2) expressly refers. The four *varṇas* issued from Puruṣa, the first male: the Brahmins from his mouth, the Kṣatriyas from his arms, the Vaiśyas from his thighs, and the Śūdras from his feet. A hierarchy of functions and duties corresponds to this hierarchy of social groups.

"Brahmā", says Baudhāyana (I.18.2–5), "has placed *brahman* (sacred learning, mystic power) in the Brahmins, with the duty and the right to devote themselves to study and teaching, to perform sacrifices for themselves and for others, to make and to receive donations, in order to secure the protection of the Vedas.

"In the Kṣatriyas he has placed *kṣatra* (force, *imperium*), with the duty and the right to devote themselves to study, to make sacrifices and donations, to exercise force of arms, and to protect the wealth and lives of created beings, in order to secure the good government of the country.

"In the Vaiśyas he has placed *viś*, the power of work, with the duty and the right to devote themselves to study, to make sacrifices, to make donations, to cultivate the soil, to do business, to take care of cattle, in order to secure the development of productive labour.

"Upon the Śūdras he imposed the duty of serving the three higher *varṇas*."

Certain duties are common to the three higher *varṇas*: studying the sacred learning, sacrificing (that is to say, performing religious rites), making donations (that is to say, charity and pious offerings). These duties are not laid upon the Śūdras. In short the latter, though an integral part of Āryan society, do not participate in the cult. They can perform only the lesser sacrifices (*pāka-yajña*), very simple domestic rituals such as funeral oblations, which do not require the recitation of *mantras* (*Gaut.*, X.53; XI.65). Only the first three *varṇas* can and should receive the initiation which makes a *dvija*, a "twice-born", out of a young neophyte.

On the other hand certain duties are peculiar to each *varṇa*. The most noble occupations are reserved for the members of the superior *varṇas*.

To the Brahmins belong the sacerdotal function and a monopoly of religious teaching. Their name differs only in point of accent from the word *brahman* (neut.) which means the sacred word, the liturgical and cosmological power. Naturally, such functions secure for them a pre-eminent position. No one is above them. "Know that as between a Brahmin of ten years of age and a Kṣatriya of a hundred the relationship is that of father and son, but of those two it is the Brahmin who is the father", says Āpastamba (I.1.14,25), and Manu repeats this (II.135). The Brahmin is superior even to the king, who has only temporal authority. If a Brahmin meets the king on the road it is the latter who must give way (*Āp.* II.5.11.5-6; *Gaut.,* VI.25; *Vas.,* XIII.59; *M.,* II.139), for the Vedas affirm that Brahmins have no king but Soma, the god of the sacrifice (*Vas.,* I.45). The Brahmins are the depositaries and guardians of the sacred learning. Their families (*gotras*) have eponymous ancestors who were *ṛṣis* that actually received the revelation personally. Consequently, the duty to preserve the sacred word falls upon them, as does the duty to teach the Veda and its ancillary sciences, to teach other *varṇas* their *dharmas*; and, as a result, the functions of spiritual preceptor belong to none but them.[4]

The Kṣatriyas come after the Brahmins. In them resides *Kṣatra,* that is to say virtue, force, and right such as appertain to military men. Their special mission is to protect the people and to secure the safety of the country, in particular from external enemies, by means of their arms. Since even mere contact with a weapon defiles the Brahmin,[5] the Kṣatriya is the warrior *par excellence*. He alone has the duty and the right to carry weapons. In peace time, it is upon him that the task falls of maintaining order within the realm and concord amongst its inhabitants (*Āp.,* II.5.10.6). Moreover kings must be chosen from this *varṇa,* for the right to punish properly belongs to them (*Gaut.,* X.8).

It is up to the Vaiśya to secure the economic life of the country. He must devote himself to agriculture, commerce, and cattle-breeding (*Āp.* II.5.10.7). Lucrative business, like money-lending, is also permitted to him (*Gaut.,* X.49; *Baudh.,* I.10.2; *Vas.,* II.19).

The duty of the Śūdras is to serve the superior *varṇas*. Their merits increase as they devote themselves to the service of a higher *varṇa* (*Āp.,* I.I.1.6–7). The Ārya under whose protection a Śūdra is placed must secure his maintenance, even when he is no longer capable of work.

[4] 'The three other *varṇas* should live according to the teaching of the Brahmin. The Brahmin shall say what are their duties' (*Vas.,* I.39–40).

[5] 'A Brahmin shall not take a weapon in his hands, even if he intends only to examine it' (*Āp.,* I.10.29, 6).

And if his master falls into distress, the Śūdra must help him (*Gaut.*, X.61–62). If he cannot find employment with the superior castes the Śūdra has no course open but to maintain himself by occupations whose servile and, especially, manual tasks are despised by the Āryas (*Gaut.*, X.60).

We should note here that the occupations specifically assigned to the four *varṇas* are not simple professions, but rather social functions. The Brahmin's privilege is to study and to teach, but this is also his duty, as it is the duty of the Kṣatriya to defend the other classes or the duty of the Vaiśya to cultivate the soil or do business. The hierarchy between the functions does not prevent their being strictly complementary to each other. Each *varṇa* is equally necessary to social order. Each relies, or even leans, on the three others. Thus a Vaiśya or a Śūdra is fully quit of his social duty if he accomplishes his allotted task, however humble it may be. Our texts promise him then, as a recompense, the prospect of being reborn in a higher caste. At the same time they threaten the members of high castes who neglect their duties with rebirth in an inferior caste (*Āp.*, II.5.1.10–11; *Gaut.*, XI.29–30).[6]

Each man's lot is fixed for this present life by his birth, determined by his *karma*. *Varṇa* is therefore hereditary. One is born a Brahmin, one does not become one, even after prolonged studies, no more than a Vaiśya can become a Kṣatriya by the exercise of arms. But grave misconduct can lead to an immediate fall, exclusion from the community of Āryas, relegation to the rank of Śūdra.

In point of hierarchy, permitted and forbidden occupations, and heredity, the *varṇas* display traits in common with the castes, the *jātis*. But they are not, properly speaking, castes. No doubt the *varṇa* encompasses the *jātis*, and the two words can even be used indiscriminately the one for the other. But the *dharma-sūtras* invariably use the word *jāti* when they want to indicate the real castes.[7] There are only four *varṇas*, although the number of castes is unlimited (*M.*, X.4). In modern India, where castes proliferate, it is impossible to reduce them to so simple a framework as the Brahminical theory. The *varṇa* of the Brahmins holds its ground, no doubt; yet it does not constitute a caste, but rather castes distinct from each other. The *varṇa* of the Vaiśyas embraces so many professions that one can hardly make it out amongst the multiplicity and variety of castes. As for the Śūdras it is in vain that we search for a caste to which they could correspond. In its census operations

[6]This solidarity between the *varṇas* is placed in relief by a passage in the *Bṛhadāraṇyaka-upaniṣad* (I.4, 11–15) which shows the divine Brahman incapable of manifesting itself until it has produced the four *varṇas* and *dharma* which rules them all.

[7]Except perhaps in a passage in Āpastamba (II.3, 61) where *jāti* does seem to have been used for *varṇa*.

the Government of India long ago gave up all hope of usefully employing the Brahminical tradition.

It is true that the fragmentation which we see before us could be explained by the centuries, if not millennia, which separate the voicing of that theory from our own day. The *varṇas* could have divided in course of time. New conditions could have given rise to new castes. Such an explanation is not without a serious basis. Megasthenes was able to distinguish castes (*genea* or *merē*) in that part of India which he visited.[8] However, we cannot accept that explanation, at least so far as the age of the *dharma-sūtras* is concerned. From that very period, in fact, castes properly so called, actual *jātis,* have existed, and our authors were so aware of them that they constructed a theory to assign them to the four *varṇas* and to account for their existence. In their view the *jātis* were born of a mixture of the four *varṇas,* the issue of unions contracted between members of different *varṇas,* in short a cross-breeding of the *varṇas,* as well as arising from the relegation undergone by superior castes for not having kept to the rules and performing the duties of their respective castes. From the union of a male of higher caste and a female of a lower caste are born children belonging to special castes, the names of which are furnished by the *dharma-sūtras*. Thus the child of a Brahmin father and a Vaiśya mother is an Ambaṣṭha; of a Brahmin and a Śūdra woman a Niṣāda or Pāraśava; of a Kṣatriya and a Śūdra woman an Ugra, and so on (*Baudh.,* I.17.3-5; *Vas.,* XVIII.8-9; *Gaut.,* IV.16). Each of these names denotes a special caste with its own particular occupation. We find other names where the union is in the "inverse order", i.e. where the woman is of the superior caste. Then the relegation of the offspring is much more degrading. From a Kṣatriya male and a Brahmin woman is born a Sūta, from a Vaiśya and a Kṣatriya female is born a Māgadha, from a Śūdra and a Brahmin woman a Caṇḍāla and so on (*Gaut.,* IV.17; *Baudh.*, I.16.8.17.7-8). Unequal unions between these *jātis* produce new castes again. This system, called that of the "mixed castes" (*varṇa-saṃkara*), was already complicated in the *dharma-sūtras* and later achieves a high degree of complexity in the Code of Manu. It is obviously theoretical, invented to furnish an explanation for what was already a complex reality and at the same time to justify the existing hierarchy between the castes. Its artificial character will deceive no one. It is in keeping that Gautama (IV.21) derives the Yavanas, i.e. the Indo-Greeks, from an irregular union between Śūdra males and Kṣatriya females. Manu in his turn (X.43-44), depicts "as Kṣatriyas whom various misdeeds. . . . have reduced to the status of Śūdras, the tribes of Pauṇḍrakas, Codas, Drāviḍas, Kāmbojas, Yavanas, Śakas, Pāradas, Pahlavas, Cīnas, Kirātas, Daradas, that is to say all the non-Hindu warrior peoples of India or

[8] Arrian, *Ind.* xi–xii.

abroad, Dravidians and Chinese, Persians and Greeks, Scythians and aboriginals"[9] This evidently amounts to a system thought up rather late in the day to attach these nations to the Brahminical organisation.

In Senart's view the *varṇas* were never the origin of castes, but only of social classes. As far as the Vedic texts are concerned, the famous hymn to Puruṣa in the *Ṛgveda* is the only one to mention the four *varṇas* by name. This hymn is generally believed to have been written later and inserted into the collection only during the next period. It cannot prove anything for the Vedic period itself. In all other contexts the Veda uses the word *varṇa* in a sense analogous to race: *ārya-varṇa,* the "Āryan race" is opposed to *dāsa-varṇa,* the enemy race, those who are also called the Dasyu, the men with black skins. "This antithesis is the prototype of what is later expressed by *ārya* and *śūdra,* and a perfect equivalent to it."[10] Moreover, Āpastamba (I.9.27.11) and Vasiṣṭha (XVIII.18) employ the expression *kṛṣṇa-varṇa* for *śūdra.* The Śūdras were aboriginals whom the Āryas encountered when they immigrated from the North-west of India. However much cross-breeding took place between conquerors and conquered, between invaders and autochthonous peoples, the antinomy persisted. It is only reaffirmed in the later texts. The Śūdra is the population which was conquered or reduced to applying itself to such manual labour as the conquerors disdained to do.[11]

As far as the Āryan element of the population is concerned *(ārya-varṇa),* the Vedic hymns distinguish three broad categories which are surely at the origins of the three superior *varṇas*: the priests *(brahman),* the chiefs *(rājan),* and the clans *(viś),* that is to say the commonalty. A *Ṛgvedic* hymn (VIII.35.16-18) even shows them ranked in the well-known hierarchy: "The clans (*viś*) bow spontaneously before the chief *(rājan)* who is preceded by a Brahmin". *Rājan* signifies the chief and the aristocratic class of governors, of those who command. It is the origin of the *varṇa* of the *rājanya,* later Kṣatriyas. As for the *viś,* they are the mass of the people, the clans which surround the chiefs in war. The derivative *vaiśya* properly means head of a house (*vis*, Gk. *oikos*,

[9]E. Senart, *Les Castes dans l'Inde* (Paris, new ed., 1927), 123. In Sir Denison Ross's translation (*Caste in India,* London, 1930) the passage is at p. 102. An unexpected practical use for Manu X.43–44 and associated texts (e.g. *Mahābhārata,*Anuśāsana-parva, XXXIII. 18–19, XXXV.18) has arisen in India, now that Hindus may marry Christian European women. See Derrett at *Madras Law Journal,* 1970, vol. 2. Journal section, 1–8. [trs.]

[10]*Ibid.,* 145 (in Ross's trans., p. 123).

[11]This theory of the origin of the *śūdras* is nowadays disputed. According to R.S. Sharmā, *Śūdras in Ancient India* (Patna, 1958), the *varṇa* of the *śūdras* will have comprised besides non-Āryan tribes some groups which were of the same race as the conquerors, reduced to *śūdra* status after intestine wars or as a result of economic and other causes. See also W. Ruben, *Über die frühesten Stufen der Entwicklung der altindischen Śūdras* (Berlin, 1965), who criticises Sharmā's views.

Lat. *vicus*), head of a family, a sense still attested in particular in Buddhist literature along with the special sense which it has acquired in the theory of the four *varṇas*. The three groups distinguished in this way seem like three classes, analogous to those which one finds in all societies at a certain stage of development. We have no reason to suppose that there existed during the Vedic period any other barriers between these groups than those to which class pride might give rise. A number of Indologists have searched patiently to find there the essential elements of caste; but they have failed. All that we may conclude from research is that the sacerdotal class was already learned and ambitious, and was alone in a position to perform the complicated sacrificial rites. It must have tried in very early times to safeguard its interests and its prestige by isolating itself and by setting a greater value upon purity of blood than did the other groups. What could be more natural than that the class of chiefs, too, should try, there as elsewhere, to form a nobility with its own traditions, anxious to avoid marriages beneath them? However it still remains to be shown that the functions of Brahmin or of *rājan* were really hereditary at that early epoch. No one could dream of seeing a caste in the *viś*. In reality they amounted to the whole of the free population, all of the Third Estate.

The opposition between the two Vedic *varṇas, ārya* and *dasyu,* the latter soon to become Sūdra, as well as the division of the *āryas* themselves into three categories, gave birth in the next period to the theory of the four *varṇas*. That period saw the supremacy of the Brahmin class finally affirmed. There are legends which perhaps conceal some historical data and make out that the supremacy was not established until after violent conflicts between Brahmins and Kṣatriyas. However that may be, during that period Brahmins really became "earthly gods", as a hymn proclaims. They had no other king but Soma. Their class was closed to newcomers and isolated. It resembled castes which were already multiplying. At that point the hereditary principle was triumphant with the rule of endogamy, which did not permit a Brahmin's daughter to marry anyone but a Brahmin. Later on, when the Brahmins undertook to provide rules for Indian society nothing was more natural than that they should try to attach the *jātis,* which existed in reality, to *varṇas,* a division into classes which was more or less theoretical. Consequently they consolidated their privileges, giving as the basis for the rules of their caste the authority of the Vedas and the sacred tradition. The other castes managed equally to enter within the *varṇa* framework. Their multiplicity and diversity was explained through cross-breeding between the four "primordial" castes. The classical theory thus amalgamated the factual situation with the tenacious theories of the past. "Memories of the past and the realities of the present melted into a hybrid system. The living scheme of castes fell into a framework provided by the ancient distinction between the races and between the classes which were demarcated to that effect. . . The castes were superimposed on a régime to which they were originally strangers, less by any organic development than by an intellectual construction."[12]

Senart insists emphatically on the artificial character of this "construction", the fruit of "a scholastic speculation more disdainful than any other of facts and of history."[13] "The Hindu", he says, "never hesitates to generalise without bothering about limitations which we should regard as most essential. . . . A taste for classifications and a disdain for facts, a disregard for our sense of logic and a superstitious regard for formulas, everything conspires in their minds, along with the tyranny of the scholastic approach and the unquestioned domination of a priestly class, to hasten the incubation of systems, to lend to the most artificial constructs a wholly unmerited prestige."[14]

It is not our present task to assess the value of such generalisations about the spirit of India. But what Senart objects to, above all, in the Brahminical theory of castes is that they masked under a specious and incorrect simplicity a multiplicity and diversity of facts. There never was a Brahminical *caste,* but rather "innumerable castes, unequal in law, in rank also, separated in this respect by huge distances. . . . As for the Kṣatriyas and the Vaiśyas, their very name has only survived in a few traces, as suspect as they are rare. . . As separate, authentic castes one never comes across them. We shall never see more in them than generic names, a huge *cadre,* intended to embrace and also to conceal an infinite genuine fragmentation."[15]

I feel that this judgment is a little severe, and it probably rests on a misunderstandng. It is not free from a tendency which Senart himself rightly condemned in other Indologists, namely to see everywhere the priest's hand, and to attribute a very exaggerated importance to the priest's influence upon the organisation of society.

Further, the opinion of Senart on the origin of the *varṇas* cannot be sustained today without taking into account the results of Dumézil's research into the same subject. Senart sees no more in the *varṇas* than some classes such as one might find in any country. To him the Brahminical theory seems an artificial construction, really intended to secure to the class of Brahmins that supremacy which they had won in post-Vedic society. Dumézil shows, on the contrary, that the first three *varṇas* correspond to a very ancient tradition in fact to a tripartite conception

[12]E. Senart, *op. cit.*, 152–3 (Ross, p. 129).

[13]*Ibid.*, 152 (Ross, p. 129).

[14]*Ibid.*, 124–5 (Ross, p. 104).

[15]*Ibid.*, 124 (Ross, pp. 103–4).

of the world and of society which turns up at the very foundations of the ideology of the majority of European nations.[16] Indo-Europeans visualised the world and society as formed of three organs, ranked within a hierarchy and securing three functions, namely magical and juridical administration, military force, and fertility. Such a conception is found in a fossilized condition at Rome in the archaic triad of gods, Jupiter, Mars, and Quirinus, and the hierarchy of the three major *flamines* (priests). It is found also in many legends which form the beginnings of the traditional history of Rome. One finds it in the legends or legendary annals of Scandinavia and Ireland. In Greece the old traditions of the Dorians and Ionians kept the memory of a functional division of society into three parts, priests, warriors, and the Third Estate (or commons). Plato's ideal society seems like an Indo-European reminiscence, for it is constituted by the harmonious arrangement of three functions: the philosophers who rule, the warriors who fight, and the commons, made up of laborers and artisans alike, whose function it is to create wealth. In Iran, as Senart had already noticed, society is likewise divided into three or four Estates superimposed on one another, priests, warriors and herdsmen-agriculturalists. This is the conception which India had expressed in her turn by representing the whole Āryan community as divided into Brahmins, Kṣatriyas, and Vaiśyas. The Vedas only mention *classes,* but with a functional division of society into three parts which is common to Indo-Europeans, and which contains the principle of a hierarchy as well as a necessary solidarity amongst the three Estates. Our Brahmins did not have to invent it. It suggested itself, even if it did not impose itself upon them as a tradition enjoying a considerable prestige.

Now it is probable, as Senart thinks, that the segregation of these Estates and their hardening into castes was due in some measure to a racial reaction on the part of the Indo-Europeans to contact with non-Āryan peoples. We might even suggest that those non-Āryan peoples themselves furnished the invaders with certain elements of a caste-system. Whatever might be the origin of the castes properly so called—an origin which was certainly very complex—no one could nowadays sustain the theory that the doctrine of the *varṇas* was thought up to justify the caste system and to attribute a religious value to it, for the doctrine is far older than the system. But if, on the other hand, it is true that the castes were not born, as the Brahminical theory would have it, from a mixture of *varṇas*—or perhaps it would be more exact to say, if the castes were not born *solely* from a mixture of *varṇas*—one could still not contend that there is no link between *varṇa* and *jāti*. So it seems unjust to reproach our authors for having treated the *varṇas* as the prototypes of the castes,

[16]See, above all, the series: *Jupiter, Mars, Quirinus* (Paris, 1941); *Naissance de Rome* (Paris, 1944); *Naissance d'archanges* (Paris, 1945); *Jupiter, Mars, Quirinus* IV (Paris, 1948).

or rather for having tried to integrate the castes within the *varṇas*. Moreover they found in the *varṇas* a handy framework apt for the purpose of expounding the duties which are incumbent on each one according to his caste. And, if we reflect a little, they could hardly have proceeded otherwise. They found themselves confronted by a society already divided into very numerous castes, practising the most diverse customs. Even supposing that they were practically capable of going into the details of the rules which applied individually to everyone, that was not their mission. Their object was not to codify custom, which would be the task of jurists, but to teach each individual that rule of life which would secure his destiny. All the *dharma-sūtras* confine themselves to sanctioning within an authoritative formula the imperative force (so far as temporal power is concerned) of the rules which distinguish the different *jātis,* the real castes, from each other. In the process they take care to observe that these rules must not be repugnant to *dharma*. "The customs of countries," says Gautama (XI.20), "of castes *(jāti)*, and of families, are equally authoritative, provided they are not contrary to the [sacred] texts." And Vasiṣṭha (XIX.7), for his part, recommends the king, "while taking into account the customs of countries, castes *(jāti)* and families", to constrain the four *varṇas* to fulfil their respective duties.

While they reduced the innumerable castes of their days to the four main groups known to tradition, and while they invented the theory of the mixed castes in its totality, the Brahmins were by no means giving way to their "taste for classification". Thanks to their system they ended by keeping only those duties which, in their view, had a religious significance, i.e. the rules which they thought essential for the conduct of life, and by painting a simplified and perhaps idealised picture of the facts, which arranged them without distorting them. This way of describing caste within the framework of the *varṇas* had the great merit of not fixing the contemporary scheme in its then existing state, of not fixing custom which remained exterior to *dharma,* and thus of permitting substantial variations *within* the theoretical outlines provided by that tradition. Such a conception had obvious advantages over any codification of the actual usages of the different castes, had that been remotely possible. Indian society became able to adapt, to assimilate, and to renew itself. The names of the mixed castes given by Gautama and Manu prove that these possibilities did not remain in the realm of theory, but passed into actuality.[16a]

Above all, to identify the castes with the Vedic *varṇas* was to mark out a hierarchy without which the caste system would only have been a ferment of social disintegration, a fragmentation of autonomous groups, mutually isolated and doomed to proliferation. Senart himself

[16a] See below, Appendix by the Translator.

admits that it was the Brahminical theory which brought hierarchy to that anarchy of castes. It is probable that that hierarchy already existed as a fact. If it did the "Brahminical theory" not only made it precise but also legitimised it to some extent by deducing it from the Veda, presenting it as if it conformed to the natural order of things. Further, hierarchy is not simply a matter of a gradation in point of value. It has been emphasised that it implies that the elements are mutually complementary: the *varṇas,* and therefore the castes, are mutually dependent, and the whole social structure is maintained only through their harmony. From that moment the chief task to be performed by teachers of *dharma* was to take care to identify the obligations incumbent upon each individual by reason of his membership of a caste.

Now that we know the point of view our authors had, it is plainly useless to try to find out what was the true caste system of the days when our *dharma-sūtras* were composed by making a literal research into their propositions. The multiplicy of individual constitutions[17] disappears behind the simplified picture which the *varṇas* project. Nevertheless it is possible, since the *varṇas* are dealt with like castes, to make out the most general features of the system and, by comparison with our contemporary facts, to draw some useful inferences about the development of the institution of caste. It is obvious, too, that our authors were not so disdainful of facts as they had been made out to be, and that their theory was supple enough to cope with the already complex reality which lay before them.

It is in this way that the rule that caste functions are specialised undergoes considerable modifications. Members of one *varṇa* are absolutely forbidden to apply themselves to occupations reserved for higher *varṇas.* For example, the priestly function can be exercised only by a Brahmin. A Vaiśya cannot bear arms, except in self-defence or to prevent a mixture of castes (*Vas.,* III.24). Yet Āpastamba (II.2.4.25) admits that in times of distress a Brahmin can receive religious instruction from a Kṣatriya or even a Vaiśya. This is an isolated and exceptional provision, it is true, but none the less noteworthy in an author taken as severe in his views. On the other hand all our *dharma-sūtras* admit that in times of distress the members of one *varṇa* may have recourse for their subsistence to occupations proper to inferior *varṇas* (*Gaut.,* VII.6-7.26; *Vas.,* II. 22-23). A Brahmin may enter into business and even do the humblest work without being degraded. But certain traffic is always forbidden to him, and certain professions are accounted too impure (*Gaut.,* VII. 8-15; *Āp.,* 1.7.20.12-13; *Baudh.,* II.1.76-78; *Vas.,* II.24-29). And by "times of distress" *(āpad)* is meant not merely periods of famine or calamities, but difficult periods which frequently arise in this Age of

[17]In the sense of legal statuses, *statuts particuliers.*

Iron. Further, Gautama permits a Brahmin to apply himself to agriculture or commerce at all times, just as if he were a Vaiśya—provided that he does not do the work personally. He authorises him even to lend money at interest (X.5-6). Baudhāyana (I.2.2-5) reports certain customs peculiar to Brahmins of the North and to those of the South, customs which are elsewhere forbidden. This indicates that even within a *varṇa*—and a *varṇa*, too, as precise as that of Brahmins—there were already different groups entirely separated by the customs peculiar to them. Briefly, the *dharma-sūtras'* doctrine was as elastic as modern custom is. What degrades a man is not so much the exercise of a profession or a craft as the impurity of the contacts which it involves, or rather the gravity of the breach of the caste rules for the time being. No one can accuse our authors of being over-severe at this point. Once again, they were satisfied to point out what the duties were. The Brahmin who lives only to study and to teach is certainly superior to the one who takes refuge in the occupations of the Vaiśyas: nevertheless the latter does not necessarily lose his caste.

There is a point at which the theory parts company with the facts of modern life, namely at the relations between the *varṇas*. The first three are not separated from each other by the multiple taboos which even the higher castes erect between each other out of that care to avoid contact which manifests itself by so many curious scruples. All that one can notice is a tendency on the part of the Brahmin caste to isolate itself by more rigorous precepts in matters relating to the notion of purity. These precepts could still be explained by the Brahmins' sacerdotal functions.

There is a real aversion only between the three higher *varṇas* taken together, i.e. the twice-born, and the Śūdras. The latter do indeed constitute the impure caste, contact with which and even, in some cases, mere sight of whom taints. Āpastamba (I.3.9.9) and Vasiṣṭha (XVIII.11-13) account the Śūdra like a burial place, and that is why the Veda may not be recited in a Śūdra's presence or must be interrupted when a Śūdra comes on the scene. It is a capital sin, involving exclusion from caste, for a Brahmin to teach the Veda to a Śūdra. The Śūdra cannot even hear the sacred word. "If he intentionally hears the recitation of the Veda, let his ears be filled with melted zinc or lac. If he recites Vedic texts, let his tongue be cut off", enjoins Gautama (XII.4-6). "The Śūdra who assumes an equal place (with that of a member of a superior *varṇa*) in speech, on the road, a bed or a chair, shall be flogged" (*Āp.*, II.10. 27.15; *Gaut.*, XII.7.cf.*M.*, VIII.28).

Senart's view is that there must survive in this aversion of the twice-born for the Śūdras the contempt of the conquering Āryas for the aboriginals, the Dasyu, the black-skinned ones. However, at the time when the *dharma-sūtras* were written the Śūdras were no longer enemies. but an inferior class of various races. probably mixed but speaking the language of the Āryas and participating in Indian social life. integrated within the framework and forming a *varṇa*. We have seen that they might perform very simple domestic rituals. without recitation of *mantras*. The original place of the Dasyu is occupied by the barbarians. the *mlecchas* (those who "jabber"), who are outside the *varṇas* and outside Hindu society as well. A Brahmin should never speak as much as a word to such people (*Gaut.*, IX.16), and he is forbidden to learn their speech (*Vas.*, VI.41). So by this time, the Śūdra has someone below him. Moreover the aversion seems to be blunted or to have been blunted from time to time. Āpastamba (II.3.4-9) authorises the master of the house to use Śūdras to prepare food destined for the Viśvedevas. provided that they do so under the direction of members of the superior castes, and he lays down that such food is fit for the gods and will be eaten by the master and mistress of the house. But the same author elsewhere (I.6. 18.13-14) reports that there are those who do not allow a Brahmin to accept food offered to him by a Śūdra unless he has no other means of livelihood. This is the rule to be found in Gautama (XVII.5) and Vasiṣṭha (XIV.4). and Manu hallows it (IV.223). Mere contact with a Śūdra taints a Brahmin, and he must purify himself from it. If a Śūdra touches him during his meal he must stop eating (*Āp.*, I.5.17.1). He must not even touch food brought to him by a Śūdra. even when the latter has not actually put his hand on it (*Āp.*, I.5.16.22). In times of distress these rules are almost entirely waived. Thus a Brahmin is permitted. subject to a light purification (by gold or the fire). to accept food "even from a Śūdra who lives under his protection [and who makes this offering of food to him] for the sake of obtaining spiritual merit" (*Āp.*, I.6.18.14).

On a par with the rules of commensality. and by a natural connexion between the ideas. the rules of marriage are much less severe in the Brahminical theory than they are in the modern caste system. The law of endogamy is one of the essential elements of that system.[18] One cannot contract a legitimate marriage except with a woman of the same caste. The rule is hardly relaxed in favour of sub-castes within the same caste. Yet all our *dharma-sūtras* accept marriage between different *varṇas*. Baudhāyana (I.16.2-5) allows members of each *varṇa* to marry, apart from a wife of their own *varṇa*, another wife in each of the inferior *varṇas*, so that a Brahmin may have four wives (including a Śūdrā), a Kṣatriya three. a Vaiśya two. and a Śūdra one. But Gautama (XV.18), as well as Āpastamba (I.6.18.33) and Vasiṣṭha (XIV.11), forbids one to invite

[18]The relaxation introduced in India in 1949 (Act 21 of 1949). and confirmed in the Hindu Marriage Act (s. 5 of Act 25 of 1955). is a fundamental reform. confined at present to India. and very rarely utilised by any but the most sophisticated Hindus. [trs.]

to a meal in honour of the dead (a *śrāddha*) "him whose only wife is a Śūdrā", and he allows a child born of a Brahmin father and a Śūdra mother "if he is obedient like a pupil", nothing more than maintenance out of the estate of his deceased father if the latter left no other issue (XXVIII.39). The marriage of a *dvija* with a Śūdrā cannot in general have the rank of a marriage between two *dvijas*, because a Śūdra woman cannot participate in the domestic cult. Vasiṣṭha says (XVIII.18), "a Śūdrā, who belongs to the *kṛṣṇa-varṇa* ("dark *varṇa*"), [is married] for pleasure, not in order to perform a duty". Finally marriage with a Śūdra woman ends up by being regarded as an irregular and blameworthy union. Āpastamba (I.9.27.11) holds it a sin, expiable by a penance for three years, for a Brahmin to have "served" a woman of the *kṛṣṇa-varṇa* one day and one night, that is to say, according to certain commentators, to have cohabited with a Śūdra woman. Vasiṣṭha (I.24) allows no more than three wives to a Brahmin, two to a Kṣatriya, and one to a Vaiśya as to a Śūdra. He expressly forbids marriage between a *dvija* and a Śūdrā, "for such a union involves unquestionably the degradation of the family and, after his death, the loss of heaven" (I.25–27). Baudhāyana (II.2.7) in effect relegates to the rank of Śūdra any Brahmin who begets a son on a Śūdra woman. The rule is hallowed by Manu (III.15–19). The *dharma-sūtras* thus establish an unpassable barrier between *dvija* and Śūdra.

But one finds nothing of the kind in regard to unions between members of the three higher castes. Only *pratiloma* unions ("against the hair") or forbidden. These are in the inverse order of castes, i.e. with a woman of a superior *varṇa*. Such unions cast the unfortunate offspring into very low castes. It follows that a Brahmin girl cannot be married except in her own caste, whereas a Kṣatriya girl can be married to a Brahmin or to a man of her own caste. But, by contrast, we have seen that all the *dharma-sūtras* recognise marriages in the order of *varṇas*, i.e. contracted with a woman of the next inferior or more inferior *varṇa*. This system of hypergamy (more properly "hypergyny") is still in vogue in our own day for marriages between sub-castes. In principle a male of a superior sub-caste can take a woman from a lower sub-caste, whilst refusing to give his own daughters to that sub-caste. It is true that the *dharma-sūtras* regard such unions with disfavour. The desirable marriage, which secures to sons born of it all the qualities necessary to perform the domestic cult, is the union contracted according to the prescribed rituals with a woman of equal *varna*. Children born of unequal marriages belong to special groups of inferior rank, a subdivision of the *varṇas* which is the source, according to the Brahminical theory, of the true castes. But this system is far from being absolute or rigid. According to Gautama (IV.16) and Baudhāyana (I.16.6), the son born of a marriage with a woman of the next inferior *varṇas* is a *savarṇa*, i.e. he belongs to the "same *varṇa*" as his father. Gautama (XXVIII.35ff.) allows him, if he is the eldest son, the same share in his father's estate as the younger son born of a woman of the same *varṇa* as her husband, provided only that he is virtuous. The same rule is found in Baudhāyana (II.3.12). It would seem to follow that the children born of a woman of the immediately lower *varṇa* are of the same rank as those born of a woman of equal birth.[19] One must of course except the case of a Vaiśya who marries a Śūdra woman: the child born of such a union is a *rathakāra* (*Baudh.*, I.17.6).

When the degree of inferiority is greater between the *varṇas* of the father and the mother the child is not a *savarṇa*, and a smaller share is allotted to him in the paternal estate. But the taint resulting from the inferior status of his mother is not indelible. It is removed at the end of a certain number of generations (seven according to Gautama IV.22 or five according to an even older author cited by Gautama at IV.23), if the daughter born of the mixture of castes and her descendants have contracted marriage with males belonging to the father's *varṇa*. For example, if an Ambaṣṭha girl, born of a Brahmin male and a Vaiśya woman, marries a Brahmin, and her daughter and *her* descendants do the same, the son will be a Brahmin in the seventh generation, or even the fifth according to some authors. Baudhāyana (I.16.13-14) admits that even the posterity of a Niṣāda, born of a Brahmin and a Śūdra woman, can arrive at Brahmin rank in the sixth generation. Conversely, the descendants of children born of the mixture of castes fall finally to the *varṇa* of the mother when successive marriages are contracted with men belonging to that *varṇa*. This dual theory called *jātyukarṣa* ("elevation of caste") and *jātyapakarṣa* ("collapse of caste") is taken up again by Manu (X.64-65) and by Yājñavalkya (I.96). Therefore not only is the principle of endogamy not strictly followed, according to which only a child born of parents belonging to the same group should be integrated within that group, but even the principle of the heredity of the caste is frankly breached, since at the end of a period, assuredly a long one, the descendants of one *varṇa* can rise to a higher *varṇa* or descend to an inferior *varṇa*. Perhaps this is the point at which the Brahminical theory differs most from the facts of modern life.[20]

Finally, although the *varṇas'* only function for our authors is to provide

[19]Baudhāyana, I.17, 3–5, says expressly that the son of a Brahmin male by a Kṣatriyā is a Brahmin, and the son of a Kṣatriya male by a Vaiśyā is a Kṣatriya.

[20]However one should note that according to H.A. Rose, *Glossary of Tribes and Castes*, cited by H. Hutton, *Caste in India* (4th edn. Bombay, 1963), 64, there exist near the northern frontiers of India regions where the progeny of a male of high caste by a woman of low caste can, after several generations, be accepted as belonging to the higher of the two castes. C. v. Fürer-Haimendorf, 'The inter-relations of castes and ethnic groups in Nepal', *B.S.O.A.S.* 20 (1957), 243–54. [trs.]

them with a framework within which they might settle the *jāti-dharma,* this is by no means an artificial scheme. The rules of conduct incumbent on everyone according to his caste, the precepts which they contain touching the permitted and forbidden occupations, the relations between the castes, and the rules about marriage form a picture whose resemblences with and also differences from the modern facts present an image, perhaps simplified but probably correct on the whole, of the reality which they had in front of them. There are moments when we feel that that reality hindered them in formulating a gradation of values which, as spiritual preceptors, they would have preferred to be more systematic. Generally speaking, caste as it appears through the provisions of the *dharma-sūtras,* is not so closed nor so firmly subject to strict rules as in modern India. The hereditary principle is far from triumphant there. Several generations, consequent upon successive marriages, can raise or lower themselves in the social scale. If we put aside certain functions reserved for Brahmins and Kṣatriyas, the first three *varṇas* share all the non-servile occupations. Endogamy applies rigorously only in regard to Śūdras who can marry only women of their own caste. Over-severity is thus a product of a later development of manners. To that the teaching of the Brahmins may well have contributed something, not to speak of other factors. We have already noticed that some of our authors are more rigorous, even more puritanical. Vasiṣṭha (I.25) says that there are those who permit marriage between a *dvija* and a Śūdra woman, privided no Vedic texts are recited at the ceremony. He himself, and all the others, condemn such a union in formal terms. All agree in extolling and placing in the first rank a marriage between spouses of the same caste. Āpastamba goes further. He censures those who approach a woman of another caste (II.6.13.4) and he pronounces clearly in favour of monogamy. He does not allow a *dvija* to take a second wife unless the first has remained barren or cannot participate in the cult; moreover it must be before he has celebrated any sacrifice conjointly with her (II.5.11. 12-13).

Thus we can grasp certain indications by which our authors attempt to act upon a mass of diverse customs, to orientate them towards a morality which they hold to be higher, and to organise them into a coherent whole. They praise certain usages, while proscribing others in the name of the moral law whose interpreters they are. They lay down the general duties which it will be society's task to sanction in order to develop in a sound direction. That is where their mission ends. For the remainder, that is to say for all the special rules of the various castes, we have castes, we have seen that the *dharma-sūtras* refer us to custom, to established usage. Respect for such is a condition necessary to social peace, and that is why the *dharma-sūtras* make it a duty of the king to see to it that this usage should be observed. But respect for custom has not any bearing on the spiritual future of the individual, and consequently our authors do not esteem it. Nevertheless, a large field is left in which custom may evolve and conform to the image of the great ideal castes which the *varṇas* are. By the same token we see that it would be useless to expect a faithful description of caste from our writers. If they are not theorists pure and simple, neither are they jurists or legislators.

2. *The Theory of the Four Stages of Life*

To the division of society into four *varṇas* there was added, so far as the Āryas were concerned, a division of life itself into four steps or stages called *āśramas* (from the root *śram,* to labour, and particularly to devote oneself to austerity). Men became successively student, householder, hermit or anchorite, and ascetic.

The first stage commences with the ceremony of initiation (*upanayana*), a very important ceremony, since it confers a second birth on the neophyte and makes a *dvija* of him. The preceptor (*guru* or *ācārya*) who places the sacred triple thread upon the youth, hands him the antelope skin to cover himself and the *brahmacārin's* staff, and teaches him the formula of the *gāyatrī* is considered as his spiritual father. This spiritual parentage is held to be superior to natural parentage (*Āp.,* I.1.1.16-18). Prior to his second birth the young man cannot participate in religious life; he is on the level of the Śūdra (*Baudh.,* I.3.6; *Vas.,* II.6; *Gaut.,* II.1). In principle, initiation takes place at the age of eight for a Brahmin and three and four years later for a Kṣatriya and a Vaiśya. Thereupon the young *dvija* goes to live with his preceptor in order to study the Vedas and the ancillary sciences under his direction. For each of the Vedas twelve years' study is considered requisite, so that the period devoted to study can be prolonged up to 48 years, though it can be reduced to a minimum of twelve years (*Āp.,* I.1.2.12-16; *Gaut.,* II.45-47, etc.). In any case it is not necessary to prolong study of the Vedas beyond the point at which the student has them by heart, and Baudhāyana (I.3.5) quotes a passage from the revealed texts according to which "one must kindle the sacred fire [i.e. after finishing one's studies] when one's hair is still black". In exceptional cases one may stay all his life attached to a *guru* in the status of *brahmacārin.* In that case, when the *guru* dies, he should serve his son, or an older fellow-student, in the same way as he served the *guru* himself (*Gaut.,* III.4-9).

The word *brahmacārin* is not well rendered by our word "student", for it implies a life devoted not only to study but also to the practices of austerity which are intended to purify the pupil's soul. He must learn to master his senses, to keep himself from all impure contact, to be satisfied with a frugal way of life, to practise the virtues appropriate to his status, such as humility and obedience. Instruction is inseparable from moral education.[21]

The end of the first phase of life is marked by ceremonies including a purificatory bath (*snāna*), whence the name *snātaka* which is given to the *dvija* who has finished his studies and has returned to his paternal home. The *snātaka* is subjected to special obligations, to a kind of life which is not yet that of the householder but which prepares him for it.

Soon after his return to the paternal hearth he must contract marriage and enter the second *āśrama*, that of the householder (*gṛhastha*). Marriage is a social and religious duty for every Ārya, bound as he is to continue the family and to secure the perpetuation of the domestic cult. Thus the *dharma-sūtras* consider the householder phase as the most important for it is the one upon which the three others depend (*Gaut.*, III.3; *Vas.*, VIII.14; *Baudh.*, II.11.27; *Viṣ.*, VIII.14–15).

The third step commences when the householder "sees he has wrinkles and white hairs" and he has seen "the son of his son" born (*Viṣ.*, XCIV. 1-2. Cf *M.*, VI.2). Then he should go and live in the forest like an anchorite (*vānaprastha*).[22] His wife can accompany him or even stay at home with the children. He has a fixed abode, a hermitage, and so he is still bound to sacrifice morning and evening, to make the daily five great sacrifices, as before, and to keep the ritual fire. But he should give himself over to meditation and to study. He should submit to various kinds of mortification, clothing himself in bark or the skins of animals, live chastely, expose himself in summer to the heat of the sun in the middle of four fires, lie on the ground during the rainy season, wear damp clothes in the winter, abstain from speech for long periods, practice prolonged fasting, sustain life generally only with fruits, flowers, roots and vegetation growing in the forest, finally only with fruits which drop spontaneously from the tree.[23] If he wishes to drive his austerities further he may even more substantially reduce his diet and leave for the "great journey" (*mahāprasthāna*): turning to face the North East, living only on air and water until he falls exhausted (*Āp.*, II.9.23.2; *Baudh.*, III.3.13–14. Cf *M.*, VI.31). But normally the austerities which he undergoes during his life as a hermit are intended to prepare him for the fourth and last stage.

"He who has passed from one *āśrama* to another", says Baudhāyana (II.17.16), "who has offered oblations in fire and overcome his senses, becomes at length, worn out by alms-giving and offerings, an ascetic."[24]

[21]On the importance of the education given during the *brahmacārin* stage see K.V. Raṅgaswāmī Aiyaṅgār, *Some Aspects of the Hindu View of Life according to Dharmaśāstra* (Baroda, 1952), 142–4.

[22]Gautama, III.2, uses the word *vaikhānasa*, which seems older.

[23]Baudhāyana, III.3, classifies the different sorts of *vānaprasthas* according to their diet or their manner of eating it.

[24]This stage is referred to by various names: *parivrājaka* (the wanderer), *saṃnyāsin* (the renunciate), *muni* (the silent?), *yati* (he who masters his senses), *bhikṣu* (mendicant).

His entry into this new phase of existence is marked by an imposing ceremony which Baudhāyana describes (II.17.18-42), wherein he performs a last sacrifice (*iṣṭi*) of particular solemnity, after which he throws into the fires of the altars the sacred utensils and announces in a loud voice his resolution to become an ascetic. He is thereupon dead to the world, and when he actually dies, no funeral ceremonies will need to take place. He himself will not need to observe mourning for any of his relatives, save only for a ritual bath if he receives news of the death of father or mother (*Vas.*, X.27). Thereafter, "he will live without fire, without home, without joy, without protection. Maintaining silence and not opening his mouth except to recite the Veda, begging no food but what will suffice to keep him alive, he will wander without care for this world or for heaven" (*Āp.,* II.9.21.10). He should always live alone, without a companion. He is not allowed to settle in one spot except during the rainy season (the *vassa* of the Buddhist monks) (*Gaut.*, III.13). He should live only on alms, should eat only once a day and then only certain natural products, and should cover himself with rags or even go naked (*Āp.,* II.9.21.11–12). Thus liberated from all ties with the world, indifferent to joy as to pain, to truth as to lies, he will search only for the Ātman (the Spirit) (*Āp.,* II.9.21.13).

The theory of the four stages of existence is fully established by the epoch of the *dharma-sūtras,* but it appears after Vedic times. The word itself is not found in the *saṃhitās* or the *brāhmaṇas*. The first two stages, however, are known from the Vedas onwards. The *Ṛgveda* (X.136.2) speaks of the *munis* clothed in air and rags. The *Chāndogya-upaniṣad* (II.23.1) distinguishes three orders (*skandhā*) of life following the rule of *dharma* as practised, which could correspond to the first three *āśramas* (the ascetic does not figure there), but each of these orders enables one to attain heaven after death. The *āraṇyakas,* on the other hand, presuppose that the life of the hermit was already organised. What they have in mind is clearly an autonomous mode of life. It is only in the *dharma-sūtras* that the four *āśramas* appear as successive stages of life.[25]

Some Indologists, like Deussen, are full of admiration for this theory. "The whole history of the world has little to equal the grandeur of this conception", he writes.[26]

Others, by contrast, see nothing there but a completely theoretical ideal and accuse the Brahmins, once again, of a large appetite for generalisation and for scholastic classification.

This does not mean to say that they deny that hermits and mendicant monks actually existed in India, side by side with *brahmacārins* and

[25]Or in other post-Vedic texts, such as the *Jābāla-upaniṣad.* Kāṇe, II, 418–22.

[26]P. Deussen, *The Philosophy of the Upanishads*, tr. A.S. Geden (Edinburgh, 1908), 367. Also in Hastings' *Encyclopedia of Religion and Ethics*, II, s.v. *āśrama*.

householders. If the stage of the student has been reduced in our own day, more often than not to the initiation ceremony itself, we know that it was not always so. Megasthenes tells us of the thirty-seven years of austere life which the Hindu "sophists" must pass with a teacher before founding a family. What Al Bīrūnī tells us about the student and the householder agrees entirely with the Brahminical rules. If the stage of the anchorite seems to have fallen into desuetude very early, the fact that it was practised in the past is attested by inscriptions and by Buddhist sculptures, as well as by the evidence of the Greeks, who called the anchorite ὑλόβιος (*hylobios*), a literal translation of *vānaprastha*. Finally the mendicant monks of the Brahmins live on into our own day in the *saṃnyāsins* of the Śaivite sects and the so-called *fakirs*. Their doings astonished Alexander's Macedonian comrades as they astonish travellers now. From their habit of going naked the Greeks called them gymnosophists.[27] If the *yogins* and *fakirs* of today are often professionals living on the credulity of the public, sincere examples are not wanting, and the custom of ending one's life in asceticism is not lost. In 1886 the Prime Minister of the State of Bhavnagar crowned a distinguished career by becoming a *saṃnyāsin* seven years after his retirement.[28]

It is clear that our Brahmins did not invent these four stages from top to bottom. Everyone agrees that the Ārya who is faithful to the duties of his caste must pass a part of his youth with a master, prior to taking a wife and obtaining a son who will continue the tradition of family ceremonies. But it is denied that the two other stages were ever obligatory. "We are a long way out", writes Senart," if we follow the texts and imagine all the Brahmins exclusively devoted to study and penance, dividing their careers into four periods and devoting the last two to the life of the hermit and to the profession of a wandering *fakir*! The Compilers of these books have simply welded into a system some isolated facts, more or less exceptional in themselves, and conferred an imperative quality upon what was only a perfectionist's ideal, realised only in the rarest cases."[29]

I feel these criticisms, too, unwarranted. One could reply first that, as with the theory of the four *varṇas,* our authors had not the least intention of codifying custom, but rather of teaching everyone what his duties were according to his age and status. Moving from this position they found in practice four modes of existence, which sought to coordinate and present in an order that could satisfy their intent. Since they were bound to fix the rules of life of the hermit and the ascetic, it is natural enough that they tried to integrate these rules in the picture as a whole,

[27] *Der kleine Pauly* II, 891 (Gymnosophisten).

[28] L.S.S. O'Malley, *Popular Hinduism* (Cambridge, 1935), 210.

[29] E. Senart, *op. cit.*, 125–6 (Ross, p. 105).

and to present the four modes of existence as a progressive elevation, an upward movement towards salvation.

But such a reply would make too great a concession to the critics. We must not attribute to the writers' exposition a rigorous quality which it never had, at least so far as the *dharma-sūtras* are concerned. Here too they did not "theorise" as much as is often said, and they did not give their "system" so "imperative" an aspect as is often assumed.

Although we find expressed the idea of a plan of four stages of life successively to be undergone by all the Āryas, it is never formulated as a mandatory rule or a *dharma* in that sense! Just as it is exceptionally allowed that one should prolong the *brahmacārin* phase throughout one's life, so it is admitted (not unreservedly, it is true) that one may pass immediately from the *brahmacārin* stage to that of the religious mendicant or ascetic, as soon as the period of study is over (*Baudh.,* II.17.2-5; *Vas.,* VII.3. Cf *Yāj.,* III.56). On the other hand, the order of succession between the third and the fourth *āśrama* is inverted in Gautama (III.2) and Āpastamba (II.9.21.1), which indicates the preference these authors have for the ascetic stage which, naturally, renders the hermit stage superflous; the choice is however, left to the individual. Gautama (III.36) goes further. The Vedas, he says, expressly prescribe no stage but that of the householder. In their eyes this alone is obligatory. In his commentary on that passage, Haradatta adds that the two last stages were founded for those who were unfit to set up a hearth. For Vasiṣṭha (VIII.17) equally the two last stages are facultative.[30] He declares that the Brahmin who fulfils his duties as master of the house cannot fail to reach the heaven of Brahmā after his death (X.31 and Bühler's note). Thus it is not necessary to pass the last portion of his life in mortification and austerity. Basically all our authors are hostile to mere asceticism. Baudhāyana (II.17.3-5) recommends it only for those who are childless or widowed, and generally after one has attained one's seventieth year and after the children are fully established in performance of their own duties.

We have already noticed that the *dharma-sūtras* regard the stage of householder as the most important, because without him there could be no *brahmacārin,* no anchorite, no mendicant monk. "Just as all rivers and all streams find in the ocean their place of rest, so men of the various stages (*āśramas*) go and take refuge under the protection of the householder" (*Vas.,* VIII.15. Cf *M.,* VI.90. Manu returns more than once to the superiority of the *gṛhastha.*) Āpastamba (II.9.23.3-12 and 24.1-8) discusses at length the opinion, based on a passage in a *purāṇa,* that attributes excellence to a chaste life, which he refutes by citing the Veda: "Thou art reborn in thy issue; this, O mortal, is thy immortality....

[30]'Facultative' in the sense that they are optional, one may enter them if one wishes.

They live with us, says Prajāpati, they who fulfil the following duties: study of the three Vedas, studentship, the procreation of children, faith, religious austerities, sacrifices and gifts. He who praises other duties becomes dust and perishes" (the same *sūtra* is in *Baudh.,* II.6.11.34). It really seems that we have here an allusion and a reply to a movement of ideas which was directed against *dharma* and against the doctrine of the efficacy of acts. In the opinion of our authors one must, above all, be quit of the sacred triple debt: towards the Sages by studying the Vedas, towards the gods by performing sacrifices or religious rites, and towards one's ancestors by founding a family and having children to continue the cult of the *pitṛs* (forefathers) (*Baudh.,* 16.4-7; *Vas.,* XI.48).

If our authors envisage a situation where the father of the family becomes old, abandons his property to his children and then retires to the forest, it is probably because they were bound to take account of a widespread custom amongst primitive peoples, obliging the aged to yield control to younger people. Some savage tribes actually go so far as to drive old men and women to suicide when they are no longer of any use. Europeans long ago were content to place a senile parent under the guardianship of his children. Perhaps it was partly to avoid this humiliating wardship that the custom was introduced whereby parents voluntarily gave up their assets—the origin of the distribution of an ascendant's goods as we find it in modern law. The causes which explain our voluntary surrender of assets can account for the third *āśrama* of the Brahminical theory. The speculative and religious nature of the Hindu and the peculiar point of view with which the authors with whom we are dealing approached social rules have simply given to this phase of life a unique character. This is therefore no theoretical construction, but rather perhaps a religious transposition or sublimation of an ancient, barbarous custom.

As for the fourth *āśrama,* it is doubtless the result of a defensive policy on the part of our Brahmins *vis-à-vis* the ascetics who competed with them in the field of religion. Baudhāyana (II.6.11.28) goes so far as to say that the last two *āśramas* were invented by an *asura* (demon) (Kapila, son of Prahlāda) to annoy the gods, since the latter could not receive offerings from *vānaprasthas* or *parivrājakas.* There has never been a time in India when there were not mystics disdaining knowledge and seeing the surest road to union with God in penance and austerity. The *Ṛgveda* already knows the *muni,* "the ecstatic visionary who lets his hair grow and who goes all naked or barely covered with a few rags

[31] *Partages d'ascendant.* This is unknown to the common law, but is held in common by the Hindu law and the laws of most continental countries. In India fathers frequently distribute their estates during their lifetimes, even prematurely: see *Athilinga* v. *Ramaswami* Indian Law Reports 1945 Madras, 297. [trs.]

of an orange hue. People thought he was in intimate commerce with the gods, and in one hymn the sun is praised under the simile of a *muni*".[32] With the infusion of Dravidian elements, or simply under the influence of the hot-house which is the Hindu environment, it is probable that such mysticism developed dangerously. Beside recluses in the forest who were still attached to Brahminism, there were all kinds of ascetics, practising ecstatic methods, mortifying themselves and living on alms. They enjoyed great prestige amongst a credulous population, gaining reputations as sorcerers, healers, soothsayers, and so on. In fact these people came from every corner of the Hindu world, from all castes.[33] Their way of life placed them outside Brahminical precepts. Hence the Brahmins thought of canalising and damming up this current of mysticism by making it into a fourth *āśrama*. No one who becomes a *saṃnyāsin* is under any further obligation to keep up a domestic cult. He no longer has a hearth. He has destroyed his sacrificial instruments. According to Vasiṣṭha (X.18), he should not carry any visible sign of his status. He could, or should, have shaved his head, removing the top-knot which every Hindu keeps on his crown (*Gaut.*, III.22; *Vas.*, X.6). He should even have removed the sacred thread which distinguished him from the non-Āryas. Thanks to the creation of the fourth *āśrama* the door is now open for a broad assimilation which might permit some check to be offered to a competition which was dangerous for the orthodox ascetics. At the same time our authors lay down rules to safeguard Brahminical tradition. They forbid the Ārya to become an ascetic or a hermit before he has passed through at least the *brahmacārin* stage (*Āp.*, II.9.21.3-4,8; *Gaut.*, III.1), or even before he has been a householder (*Āp.*, II.9.22.7-8). Āpastamba (II.9.24.8) and Baudhāyana (II.6.11.34) threaten with hell anyone who seeks final emancipation without having first paid the triple debt (cf *M.*, VI.35.37). All require the *saṃnyāsin* as well as the hermit to recite the Vedas, a step which effectively debars from that way of life all who are not *dvijas*.

Despite our Brahmins' efforts, the life of the *saṃnyāsins* escaped their control and went on more or less outside the orthodox framework. Eventually it was acknowledged that no rule of *dharma* survived for the *saṃnyāsin*. People of low caste, Śūdras, became ascetics. However, the authority of our authors continued in the juridical field. According to the case-law of the Anglo-Indian courts no juridical effect was allowed (except where a properly proved custom established the contrary) to a Śūdra's taking to asceticism. The law treated the ascetic's links with his family as still unbroken.[34]

[32] *Works* of Barth, *Quarante ans d'Indianisme. Oeuvres de Auguste Barth*, 4 vols. (Paris, 1914–8), I, 42.

[33] Arrian, xii.9 : 'One may become a "sophist" no matter which class one comes from'.

[34] Kāṇe, II, 952. On the impropriety of an ascetic's attempting to leave the stage of *saṃn-*

3. *The Rules of Law in the Dharma-sūtras*

The *dharma-sūtras'* object is to teach men their *dharma,* the rules of conduct which produce spiritual merit according to their caste and appropriate to the stage of their lives. The general plan, though often somewhat irregularly observed, consists of taking the Brahmin as a basis, following him through the four *āśramas*, and then of formulating rules peculiar to the three other *varṇas*.

Consequently the *dharma-sūtras* contain a great many precepts on the duties of the student, regulating minutely his daily life and his deportment towards his master, his master's wife and children, explaining how one should meet them, greet them, and behave in their vicinity. Similarly they prescribe the periods of the year and the localities where teaching should take place, showing in which circumstances teaching should be interrupted, and the like. Once the study stage is over the Brahmin who has now returned to the paternal home but is not yet married—the *snātaka*—is bound to observe numerous duties special to his status, and these are set out in equally minute detail. Similarly, the life of the householder is enveloped in a network of precepts which govern even the most humble of his activities. Details are given of the foods he may eat, and those he may not; and of the people from whom he may accept it. The gifts and charitable acts which he must perform are laid down—and the merits which arise if he performs them (*Gaut.,* V.18ff.; *Baudh.,* II.5.19–20). A considerable number of rules are devoted to the manner of treating guests, according to their caste and the time of their arrival, since hospitality is a truly religious duty and "the guest furthers one's attaining heaven, whether he is welcome or one is indifferent to him", say Āpastamba, who compares attentions paid to a guest to sacrificial rites (II.3.7.1–10). A Brahmin ought not to refuse hospitality even to a Śūdra (*Āp.,* II.2.4.19; *Baudh.,* II.5.14). He should feed him after having given him work, or, without treating him like a guest, he should get his servants to feed him (*Gaut.,* V.43–45). "Lacking other things, a place to rest in, water for washing, grass, and a kind word are never found wanting in the house of a good man", says Āpastamba (II.2.4.14) with Vasiṣṭha (XIII.61) and Gautama (V.35–36), and Manu repeats this (III. 101).

Our authors are keenly preoccupied by notions of purity and impurity. They enumerate multiple sources of impurity and show what are the purificatory practices by which one may purify oneself and the things one uses. Naturally obligations relating to domestic sacrifices occupy a large place in our collections, though the rules of the sacrifices themselves

yāsa, and the Hindu law's insistence upon a final breach with the family, with the special exception of Śūdras, see the interesting comparative study by Y. Kṛishan at *Annals of the Bhandarkar Or. Res. Institute* 50 (1969), 75–89. [trs.]

come from the *gṛhya-sūtras*. The precepts about *śrāddhas* are particularly detailed. These are sacrifices for the dead which consist essentially of a feast to which an uneven number of Brahmins are invited (*Gaut.*, XV.7). Our authors lay down what qualifications are required of possible candidates for an invitation, indicating who must be rigorously excluded, and they lay down the time and place where such feasts should take place, and the deceased relatives to whom the offerings of *piṇḍas* (rice balls) should be made. The duties of the anchorite and the mendicant monk are laid out generally in much less detail, except in Baudhāyana, who distinguishes between various kinds of hermits according to their mode of life (III.3.1–15). Some *sūtras*, like the *Vaikhānasa-dharma-sūtra*, are undoubtedly more particularly orientated towards the duties of the two last *asramas*.

The whole of these duties is called *ācāra*. This amounts to the practices of the *śiṣṭas*, though consigned to writing.

Every breach of these duties or ritual obligations is a fault, a sin which will infallibly (unless the sinner performs the due penance) involve punishment, if not in this life then in the next world or in after-lives.[34a] He will go to hell, will be reborn in a lower caste, or even in the form of an animal. These sins are classified according to the gravity of the sanction which is attached to them. Our authors distinguish between sins "which cause fall" (*pātaka* or *pātanīya*), i.e. those that involve exclusion from caste, and those which involve only a temporary defilement (*aśucikara*). In the first category, a distinction is introduced again between cases where the exclusion is final and those where the culprit can be readmitted, and between those cases where readmission into the caste is easy and those where it is not. This leads to a classification of faults which is already advanced, although not fully developed until Viṣṇu and Manu. It betrays the great importance which the caste system had for society.

The ceremony of excommunication from the caste is described by Gautama (XX.2–7) and Vasiṣṭha (XV.11–14), and recurs in Manu (XI.183–188). It consists first in performing the funeral of the culprit. Then a slave brings an old broken vessel picked up from a rubbish-heap, fills it with water taken from a pot belonging to a slave-woman and, facing the South,[35] turns it over with his left foot, saying "I deprive so-and-so of water". With untied hair and wearing the sacred thread over their right shoulders and under the left, the culprit's relations touch the slave. After taking a purificatory bath, they return home. No Ārya may speak to the excommunicated person, nor sit near him, nor have any relationship with him. Anyone who speaks to him must perform a penance, and one who continues to remain in contact with

[34a] See U.C. Sarkār at *Viśveśvarānand Indological Journal* I (1963), 91–101. [trs.]

[35] The South is the most inauspicious quarter, the direction of the abode of the Dead. [trs.] For the ceremony see P. Rolland, *K.A.N. Sastri Vol.* (Madras, 1971), 487–91.

him for a year exposes himself to the danger of being excommunicated (*Vas.*, I.22; *Baudh.*, II.1.2.35). The excommunicated individual is naturally excluded from all the functions and ceremonials of the caste. He loses his rights of succession, and if he was the eldest son he loses his right of primogeniture and the privileges attached to it. On his death he goes to hell (*Gaut.*, XXI.5–6). However, his children must maintain the excommunicated parent, although without being allowed to appropriate his goods (which, according to Haradatta, are confiscated to the king). Gautama (XXI.15–16) and Vasiṣṭha (XIII.47) declare that the mother is never an outcaste to her son. Āpastamba (I.10.28; 9–10) says that he must continue to serve her, provided he does not perform sacrificial acts in her company. Baudhāyana (II.2.3.42) says that he must secure her maintenance, but without speaking to her. Excommunicated people can live together outside inhabited places, may sacrifice for each other, teach each other, and intermarry. If they have sons, these could be admitted into the society of Āryas, provided that their parents are separated from them (at an early stage?). But this is not allowed by Āpastamba (I.10.29.8–14) nor by Baudhāyana (II.1.2.18–25), who admits however that they may be reintegrated after they have done penance. Vasiṣṭha for his part (XIII.51–53) wants the sons of the excommunicate to share their parent's condition, but not the daughters, for these will enter the families of their husbands upon their marriages.

The ceremony for readmission to caste is the antithesis of that of excommunication. A new or golden vessel is brought; it is filled with spring water or water from a sacred stream; then the relatives of the excommunicate pour the contents over him and bathe along with him in a sacred pool. They offer the vessel to him. The excommunicate recites *mantras*, makes a sacrifice, and gives presents to a Brahmin or to his preceptor (*Gaut.*, XX.10–14). The ceremonies which follow are the same as the sacrament for the new-born (*Vas.*, XV.21). After society has readmitted him he is submitted to a last test, according to Manu (XI.197). He must offer grass to cows; only when they accept this fodder from him can he be considered definitely to be worthy of readmission. Āpastamba alludes to this test (I.9.24.20), if his commentator Haradatta is to be believed.

A sinner must purify himself in this life if he wishes to avoid the punishment which threatens him in the next world. Consequently, he will not be reintegrated into his caste until he has expiated his guilt by means of penance (*prāyaścitta*, "prime thought", or "thought about finding").[36] In very early times the question was raised whether the theory of *karma* was not contradicted by this notion of penance. It gave rise to a short discussion in Gautama (XIX.2–11), Baudhāyana (III.10.2–9) and

[36] On the various proposed etymologies for this word see Kāṇe, IV, 57–61.

Vasiṣṭha (XXII.1–8), where the efficacy of penance is affirmed on the authority of Vedic texts. The accepted explanation is that penance balances the effects of an act of an *adharma* (non-*dharma*, or anti-*dharma*) character. Penances are prescribed for the culprit by his *guru*, whether the latter was approached by the former of his own free will, or some relative of the culprit or leader of the caste has put the matter before the *guru*. Even if the misdeed in question is not one which involves automatic fall from caste, the sinner risks being excommunicated if he fails to perform the prescribed penance. Threat of exclusion plays a role at all times as an indirect sanction obliging the culprit to rectify his fault. These notions of sin and expiation, which are very ancient, led our authors to classify penances according to their relative severity in a table corresponding to their classification of sins. All our *dharma-sūtras* devote at least one chapter to this subject, a section resembling the Penitentials of the Middle Ages. Their theory of penance is already a learned one. We find their source in the *brāhmaṇas* of the *Sāma-veda*, especially the *Sāmavidhāna* (ed. Burnell, 1873), from which Gautama and Baudhāyana have borrowed. The doctrine is identical, and the list of sins hardly differs. Account is taken of the degree of reflection and the age of the culprit, and how far the act was intentional (*Āp.*, I.29.2–4). Self-defense is admitted as a ground for absolution (*Āp.*, I.29.7; *Vas.*, III.15),[37] but repetition of a sin aggravates the penance. The latter applies to accessories and accomplices as well as to the wrongdoer himself (*Āp.*, II.29.1).

There is a great variety of penances. Those which match the gravest crimes amount to a death-sentence, for they force the culprit to commit suicide. Thus he who murders a Brahmin must, in order to gain absolution, seek death in battle or cast himself into fire (*Vas.*, XX.27; *Āp.*, I.9.25.11–12; *Gaut.*, XXII.2–3). One who drinks fermented liquor from which he must abstain dies purified if he swallows such liquors heated to boiling point (*Āp.*, I.29.25.3; *Gaut.*, XXIII.1). He who has defiled the bed of his *guru* must lie on a red-hot bed of iron, or embrace an iron figure of a woman which has been made red hot, or even cut off his genitals and, holding them in his joined palms, walk towards the South[38] without stopping till he drops dead (*Āp.*, I.9.25.1–2; *Gaut.*, XXIII.8–9; *Vas.*, XX.14; *Baudh.*, II.1.1.13–14). For minor sins there is a whole range of penances: fasts more or less prolonged during which the fasting becomes more severe (*kṛcchra, tapta-k., ati-k., cāndrāyana*); recitation of *mantras* (especially of the *sāman*) accompanied by other observances such as fasting or mortifications; fines in the form of gifts to be made

[37]Even the killing of a Brahmin is not sinful if done in legitimate self-defense (*Vas.*, III.17–18; *Baudh.*, I.10.18, 12–13). The contrary view is found, but at much later periods.

[38]See above, p. 53, n.35.

to Brahmins; ascetic practices; various weakening practices, continence, control of the breathing, and postures which involve more or less strain. There are some odd ones, such as the penance of *pañca-gavya*, to which Vasiṣṭha (XXVII.14) and Baudhāyana (IV.5.14) allude and which consists of swallowing the five "products of the cow", namely milk, curds, butter, urine and dung. One who has killed a cow must look after a herd, watch over the animals with the greatest care, and feed exclusively on *pañca-gavya*. Vasiṣṭha (XXII.12) and Gautama (XIX.14) also mention going to certain holy places on pilgrimage as having expiatory virtue.[39]

There are some discrepancies in the fixing of penances, and at times the same sin can be the object of different prescriptions even in the same author. So for the intentional killing of a Brahmin Gautama provides (XXII.4–8), in place of the suicide of the culprit, a period of austerities lasting twelve years, which could however be shortened if he saves the life of a Brahmin or if he thrice recovers from the hands of brigands the stolen property of Brahmins. For the same crime Āpastamba (I.9.24.11–15) also concedes that the culprit may be purified by twelve years of austerity, unless he has killed his *guru* or a learned Brahmin, in which case he must live in the same austerity all his days. On the other hand there are certain general penances which enable even the gravest sins to be expiated. A sinner can be purified by performing certain sacrifices. Thus he who offers the horse-sacrifice[40] overcomes all sins; this sacrifice destroys the sin arising even from Brahmin-slaying (*Vas.*, XXII.6). And in many cases, the recitation of prayers suffices to purify the sinner from numerous sins he may have committed. According to Baudhāyana (IV.5.31) "he who, at sunrise, murmurs the *gāyatrī* 1,008 times is freed from all sin, provided he has not killed a learned Brahmin".

What impression can we form of Indian society, what indications do we have of the rules effectively governing social relations, when we look at the sum total of these precepts?

We must enter a preliminary caveat here. The teaching of *dharma* proceeds from Brahmins who were extremely preoccupied with questions of purity and impurity, of guilt and expiation, and with ritual observances and the regular practice of the same. For them the different phases of life were really the *āśramas*, which were a series of attempts to regulate the conduct of life according to rules laid down in advance. Only a narrow circle was involved, perhaps hardly representative of the total population but enjoying, for all that, a considerable authority within it. Our authors figured as "confessors",[41] but with a wider field of activity because of the breadth of the concept of *dharma*.

[39]For a detailed account of penances see Kāṇe, IV, chh. iv and v.

[40]A sacrifice confined to conquering kings who have proved they possess imperial qualities.

[41]*Directeurs de conscience*. Referees on matters of morals and religion, or duty generally, as is not seldom experienced to this day.

The precepts which set out what *ācāra* is belong essentially to religious law. But, to our eyes, some of them possess a juridical character. They deal, besides, with institutions which used to belong to religious law in Europe but which, in India, existed until a very recent date in secular law. So it is, for example, with the rules relating to marriage which find their place, naturally, at the commencement of the duties incumbent on a man entering the second *āśrama*. The *dharma-sūtras* lay down the conditions for a valid marriage. They show, somewhat rapidly, the rules of endogamy and exogamy. For a marriage fully efficacious from the religious point of view one must marry a girl of the same *varṇa*, but belonging to a different *gotra*. She should not be related to her future husband through an ancestor nearer than six degrees on the father's side or four degrees (counting exclusively of the intended spouse) on the mother's side (*Gaut.*, IV.2; *Vas.*, VIII.2), or six degrees in both lines according to Āpastamba (II.5.11.16). Gautama (IV.1–2) and Vasiṣṭha (VIII.1) add that she should not have the same *pravara*, or mythical pedigree.[42] The girl must not have been married already. A father is advised to marry off his daughter *before* she reaches marriageable age, even while she still goes about naked (*Gaut.*, XVIII.21–23; *Baudh.*, IV.1.11; *Vas.*, XVII.70).[43] Indeed the father commits a sin if he keeps a marriageable girl at home, a sin equal to that of killing an embryo (*Vas.*, XVII.71; *Baudh.*, IV.1.12). Thus a marriageable girl who has not yet been given in marriage may choose a bridegroom for herself after three years of waiting (*Vas.*, XVII.67; *Baudh.*, IV.1.14), or even after three menstrual periods, as Gautama says (XVIII.20). The forms of celebration of marriage are described in the *gṛhya-sūtras*. The *dharma-sūtras* enumerate the different rituals, six in Āpastamba and Vasiṣṭha, but eight the Gautama and Hārīta, a number which becomes classical in the later literature.

An even smaller number of precepts assigned to the same *āśrama* deal with relations between husband and wife and with the rights of the married woman, both personally and in respect of her property. A woman always requires protection; she is always within someone's power. "As a child she is under the protection of her parents; when she is married under that of her husband; in old age under that of her son", declare Vasiṣṭha (V.3) and Baudhāyana (II.3.45), and Manu repeats this (IX.3). Gautama (XXVIII.24) however makes allusion to the personal property of a woman which, at her death, will pass to her unmarried daughters or, in default of them, to poor married daughters. This alludes to the special devolution of women's absolute property, called *strīdhana*.

The rules relating to partition of family assets are set out by Āpastamba

[42] On the words *pravara* and *gotra* see Kāṇe II. 482–99.

[43] *Nagnikā*. Kāṇe. II. 440.

immediately following the duties of the householder. It is before the stage of hermit or ascetic, i.e. in the lifetime of the father, that family property should be divided among sons, according to the theory of the four *āśramas*. The rules of this "partition of goods" are also applicable to problems of actual succession which may arise at the father's death. In all the *dharma-sūtras* the rules of succession have a large place in the collection of duties which makes up *ācāra*. Everything that concerns sonship and parentage will be found in general either there, or in passages dealing with *śrāddha* ceremonies. The heir is he who performs the funeral rites, who offers the rice-balls called *piṇḍas* to the ancestors. The succession to property is a corollary of succession to *sacra*, or the religious obligations of the family.[44] Thence comes the scheme of different orders of heirs: the sons, the *sapiṇḍas*, the teacher or fellow student *(sa-brahmacārin)*, the king (except for Brahmin decedents, whose estates can pass only to Brahmins) (*Āp.*, II.6.14.1–5; *Vas.*, XVII.81–87). After the *sapiṇḍas*, Baudhāyana (I.5.11.12) introduces the *sakulyas*, i.e. ascendants (and their issue) who are entitled only to the *lepa* (residue of the offerings of *piṇḍas*) and Gautama (XXVIII.21) the *sagotras* and *samānārṣas*. The meaning of these words is later taken differently by different commentators, and different kinds of sons, amounting to twelve, are enumerated (*Baudh.*, II.2.3.15–30; *Vas.*, XVII.12ff.). Vasiṣṭha (XV.1–4) admits that parents have the right to give, sell, or abandon their children; but this precept appears in connection with adoption, and the same writer forbids giving or receiving an only son in adoption. He devotes several *sūtras* to adoption (XV.5–10).

In connection with the occupations allowed to Vaiśyas and, in times of distress, to members of the first two *varṇas*, Vasiṣṭha (II.41–51) and Baudhāyana (I.5.10.21–22) fix the maximum interest rates (15% in principle, but variable according to the caste of the borrower, the nature of the commodity borrowed, and also according as the loan is, or is not, backed by a surety or other security) (cf *Gaut.*, XII.29). In passing Vasiṣṭha (II.44) lays down the rule that in principle the lender of a sum of money cannot demand a total of interest higher than the amount of principal lent: "For gold, double; for cereals, triple (the amount of the loan)"—a rule which has lasted to our own day under the name of *dāmdupat*.[45]

The majority of these rules are taken up again, explained, developed and completed in the later literature of the *śāstras* and the commentaries. They doubtless reflect practices in vogue at our authors' periods. But, integrated within *ācāra*, they have become something different from mere customary rules. They have received a religious value, the notion

[44]The principle is neatly formulated at Viṣṇu XV.40: *yaś cārtha-haraḥ sa piṇḍa-dāyī*.
[45]Derrett, *Introduction to Modern Hindu Law* (Bombay, 1963), ss. 824–9. [trs.]

that it was a sin not to conform to them! By the same token our authors were led to make a choice, to recommend certain rules which perhaps were followed only by an élite, to leave in the shade or even to condemn expressly others which were perhaps in general use, in short to apply to the mass of customs a process which may, or may not, have been uniformly effectual. Their hesitations and contradictions indicate the difficulties they had to surmount or circumvent in order to try to make the rule they wished to see adopted triumph over its competitors.

We may take as an example the forms of marriage. The *dharma-sūtras* describe the eight forms which we meet later in Manu. The first four (only three in Āpastamba and Vasiṣṭha) consist essentially of the gift of the girl by her father to the bridegroom. The fifth is marriage by purchase of the bride (the rite of the Āsuras, or *mānuṣya*). The sixth is marriage by mutual consent (the rite of the Gandharvas). The seventh is marriage by rape (the rite of the Rākṣasas, or *kṣātra*). Finally the eighth, ignored by Āpastamba and Vasiṣṭha, is a violation of the woman who is asleep or unconscious (the rite of the Piśācas [devils]). It will be conceded that our authors must have met these different kinds of union, and that each of them was regarded as regular by at least one section of the population.

They commence by classifying them hierarchically. The first is superior to the second, the second to the third, and so on. "The quality of the child to be born depends on the quality of the marriage rite" (*Āp.,* II.5.12.4; *Baudh.,* I.11.21.1). For Āpastamba (II.5.12.3) and Baudhāyana (I.11.10–11) only the first three or four forms, i.e. those where the marriage is a gift of the woman, are regular *(dharmya)*; the others are all degrading. Gautama (IV.14–15) is of the same opinion, but adds that certain authors allow the two following.

Marriage by purchase is forbidden to members of the higher castes. Āpastamba (II.6.13.11) does not recognise the parents' right to sell their children. He tries to prove that the word "sell" which figures in certain Vedic texts or in the *gṛhya-sūtras* in connection with gifts made at the time of the marriage is used metaphorically, for these are the rites which give effect to the marriage (II.6.13.12). The same opinion is found in Vasiṣṭha (I.36–38). Baudhāyana (I.11.21.2–3) declares that "the woman who has been bought is not a wife; she cannot participate in sacrifices offered to the gods and to the *manes* (shades). Kaśyapa says that she is a slave". And he condemns energetically the father who gives his daughter for money, saying that he commits a great sin and destroys his family to the seventh generation. However, the same author allows marriage by purchase for Vaiśyas and Śūdras "who are not particular in what concerns the choice of their brides" (I.11.20.13–15) (or "who lack scruples or rules").

Marriage by mutual consent is not allowed by Baudhāyana (I.11.20.12) except in the case of Kṣatriyas, but he adds that some authorities recommend the rite for all the castes "because it rests on mutual affection" (I.11.20.16). Apart from that he authorises, as does Vasiṣṭha, a mature girl's choosing a bridegroom for herself if she had remained unmarried for three years.

Marriage by rape, simply mentioned by Āpastamba, Gautama, and Vasiṣṭha, is allowed by Baudhāyana (I.11.20.12) for the Kṣatriyas only, "for force is their attribute".

The last form, ignored by Āpastamba and by Vasiṣṭha, is allowed by Baudhāyana (I.11.20.14) for Vaiśyas and Śūdras for the same reason that induced him to allow marriage by purchase.

From the whole of these rules one can only conclude that our authors have tried to induce those who wished to raise themselves or to maintain themselves in superior castes to accept an obligation to contract a marriage consisting in a simple gift of the girl by her father. They tried to proscribe marriage by purchase and reserve marriage by mutual consent for Kṣatriyas alone. Then they formally condemned the lowest types of union, tolerating marriage by rape only in the case of Kṣatriyas. Further, whatever the *form,* no marriage was regular unless it was accomplished with the aid of the rituals laid down in the *gṛhya-sūtras*. "The girl who, after being carried away by force, is not married with the sacred formulas can be given in marriage to another man: she is equal to a virgin", says Vasiṣṭha (XVII.73). We notice that our authors endeavoured to circumscribe and even banish practices of which they disapproved. But it would be going too far to suppose that their precepts were actually accepted as a whole in the society of their times.

A similar conclusion is to be drawn from a glimpse of the precepts relating to the different kinds of sons. In order to secure the perpetuity of the domestic cult ancient Āryan custom seems to have made comparable to an *aurasa,* or real son born of a regular marriage between his parents, all kinds of people who had no blood relationship with the head of the family, whenever the latter shows signs of remaining childless: the son born of a daughter designated by her father to provide him with a son *(putrikā-putra)*; the son born of *niyoga*. i.e. procreated by one other than the husband himself after his death or even during his lifetime *(kṣetraja)*; the adopted son (*dattaka, kṛtima,* i.e. "fictitious"); the son born in the house but to an unknown father *(gūḍhaja* or *gūḍhotpanna)*; the abandoned and subsequently found child *(apavidha)*; and so forth. The *dharma-sūtras* classify and arrange the different categories of sons hierarchically. They retain some as heirs, but admit others to sucession only in default of the first (*Vas.*/ XVII.25.39; *Baudh.*, II.2.3.31-32; *Gaut.*, XXVIII.32-33). They are not always in agreement on the order which should be given to these different categories. Gautama gives the tenth rank to the son born of an appointed daughter (*putrikā-putra*), while Baudhāyana places him in the second rank. The adopted son (*dattaka*) is placed by Gautama (XXVIII.32) in the third rank as heir, Whereas Vasiṣṭha (XVII.28) places him in the eighth position and denies him the status of an heir. They insist on the primacy of the *aurasa*. born of a regular marriage of two spouses of the same caste (*Vas.*, XVII.13; *Baudh.*, II.2.3.14). He alone is identified with his father.[46] Again, they surround the "formalities" of *niyoga* with severe restrictions (*Gaut.*, XVIII.4-7; *Vas.*, XVII.56-66; *Baudh.*, II.2.4.7-10). If these rules are not observed the son belongs to his begetter (*Vas.*, XVII.63; *Gaut.*, XVIII.11-14). Baudhāyana (II.2.3.18-19) even declares that the *kṣetraja* should be considered as having two fathers and as belonging to two families. In principle, the child belongs to his begetter (*Gaut.*, XVIII.9; *Āp.* II.6.13.6). Similarly, our authors recommend the head of the family to keep a watch over the women: "Through his negligence a husband loses all value from the birth of a son" (*Baudh.*, II.2.3.34-35, citing a *gāthā* of Aupajaṅghani, a *ṛṣi* of the Black Yajurveda). "He who gave the seed takes the son, after his death, into the world of Yama" (*Āp.*, II.6.13.7, citing the same *gāthā*). All this tends to lead to a condemnation of practices like *niyoga*, which Āpastamba (II.10.27.4) forbids "because of the weakness of the senses of men (of our epoch)". And he adds, "If the vow (of the spouses) is transgressed (husband and wife) will go together to hell; the reward (in the after-life) arising from obedience to the restrictions of the law is to be preferred to a progeny obtained in that fashion (i.e. by *niyoga*)" (II.10.27.6-7).

Another example could be taken from the rules relating to partition of family property. All the *dharma-sūtras* recommended partition. either after the father's death, or—as Āpastamba considers preferable (II.6.14.1)—even in the father's lifetime prior to his entering the third or the fourth phase of life. It actually follows from a passage in Gautama (XV.19) that the son *may* force a partition on his father. But he condemns this practice by excluding such sons from participation in *śrāddha* feasts, thereby depriving them of their rights of succession. Partition during the father's lifetime should not take place without his permission: such is the rule laid down by Baudhāyana (II.2.3.8), implicit in Āpastamba (II.6.14.1). But Gautama (XXVIII.3) tells us that the whole estate could be passed to the eldest son. who would then be bound to secure the maintenance of the family and to behave towards his brothers as a father would do. He also gives several rules about the organisation of this joint

[46]Baudhāyana. II.2.3. 14 cites a verse (found in the *Mahābhārata* and elsewhere): 'Thou art produced from my various limbs. thou art born from my heart. thou art myself under the name of "son" . . .'

family. In particular he shows that a learned member can withdraw, at his option, whatever he may have acquired by his own means (XXVIII.30). At all events he holds partition to be spiritually preferable (*dharma-vṛddhi* takes place) (XXVIII.4). Āpastamba (II.6.14.10-14) and Baudhāyana (II.2.3.2–3) are more forthright : they rely on the Vedic text to which we have already referred (Manu's partition of his goods between his issue), and lay down that partition should take place.

These rules evidence contradictory practices in which one is already able to see the seeds of the two great systems of succession still (with some minor modifications) in force in India today, that of the *Dāyabhāga* and that of the *Mitākṣarā*.[47] Our authors pronounce in favour of the principle which results in multiplication of domestic cults. But we should not attribute a legal value, an imperative quality, to their precepts. As Gautama actually says, the father increases his *dharma* (or increases *dharma*) by proceeding to partition; but that does not mean that partition was the rule in Gautama's time (cf *M.*, IX.111).

The authors vary in their interpretation of the rules affecting partition. They debate the shares to be allotted to different sorts of sons, and the special share *(uddhāra)* to be given to the eldest. Reconciling different views, Baudhāyana (II.2.3.3–4) admits that the father may partition his assets equally amongst all the children (save the daughters), but he could just as well make differences between them according to their seniority and the castes of their mothers (*ibid.,* 9.12). Unequal partition is the only one indicated by Vasiṣṭha (XVIII.42-51) and, with some variations, by Gautama (XXVIII.5-17). Āpastamba (II.6.14.1.11-14) declares on the contrary that equal partition between sons conforms to the Veda. Our authors are far from agreed as to what rights should be allowed to daughters in the succession. Vasiṣṭha (XVII.46), Baudhāyana (II.2.3.43) and Gautama (XXVIII.24) permit them to inherit only certain of the mother's goods and exclude them from all rights in succession to their father. On the other hand Āpastamba (II.6.14.4) calls the daughter to succeed to her father, but only in the absence of all relations and even pupils, and immediately before the king would take by escheat. There is no greater agreement on the rights of the widow, whom only Gautama calls to succeed the husband in default of sons, in competition with (or after?) *sapiṇḍas* or *sagotras*. Āpastamba (II.6.14.9) confines himself to allowing her as part of the estate her own jewellery and the assets she received from her own family, unless indeed she is included amongst the *sapiṇḍas* called to the succession in default of sons (*ibid.,* 2). To sum up, here we do not really come across formal rules. One may simply note a tendency, still a shy one, towards equality of sharing at a partition, and to the total exclusion of females.

[47]Derrett, *Religion, Law and the State in India* (London, 1968), ch. xii.

If a great part of what we call personal legal status is found amongst the precepts of *ācāra,* the criminal law appears in its turn, in large measure, in the theory of sins and penance.

A number of penances have all the rigour of penal sanctions. I have already mentioned some that amount to a death sentence. Fines appear in the guise of gifts to be made to Brahmins. This form of penance is common. Penance can include mortifications or prolonged austerities which inflict punishment no less severe than imprisonment would have been. Frequently penance, like punishment, acquires an exemplary quality. Thus the killer of a Brahmin or the culprit who has committed a crime of equal gravity must beg in seven households of the village during his years of penance, crying out, "Who will show charity towards an *abhiśasta* (accursed one)?" (*Āp.,* I.9.24.15; *Gaut.,* XXII.4). The adultress's penance in Vasiṣṭha (XXI.1–5) includes an ignominious parade, seated on an ass naked and smeared with butter.

Penance varies, as does punishment, with the gravity of the offence. For the killing of a Brahmin the period of austerity is twelve years, of a Kṣatriya six years, of a Vaiśya three years, of a Śūdra one year. The fine which accompanies this decreases likewise with the caste: 1,000 cows for a Kṣatriya, 100 for a Vaiśya, 10 for a Śūdra, plus a bull in each case (*Gaut.,* XXII. 2-16; *Āp.,* I.9.24.1-25; *Baudh.,* I.10.19.1-2). We find the same gradation, with different figures, in Baudhāyana (II.1.6-10) and Vasiṣṭha (XX.31-33) who increases to three years the length of the penance required for the murder of a Śūdra.

Again, we have seen that before determining the appropriate penance account was taken of the element of intention, as well of the age of the culprit and whether or not he had relapsed into guilt; that, again, self-defense would eliminate guilt (*Āp.,* I.10.29.7; *Vas.,* IX.15); and that accomplices follow the principal offender in point of guilt (*Gaut.,* XXI.2; *Āp.,* II.11.29.1). Gautama (XXI.19) even adds that he who, being able to prevent the commission of an act of violence against a defenseless person, abstains from intervening to save him, incurs the same guilt as if he had himself committed the act.

It is true that penance, as distinguished from punishment, is voluntary. But we must not forget that the threat of exclusion from caste is an indirect means of constraint, often quite sufficiently efficacious to make the culprit perform the prescribed penance.

Penance is thus not simply expiatory. It is also deterrent. There has been some debate whether punishment was derived from penance, or the other way about. We are tempted to see the concurrence of the two as Barth did:[48] "Expiation and punishment are correlative conceptions, and it does not seem that the second developed after the first and at its

[48] *Works* (see above, p. 51, n. 32), III, 71–2.

cost. . .Short of presupposing an absolute theocracy I cannot visualise any form of society, and certainly not a society at the nomadic stage, where a single religious penance, undergone voluntarily, could, with everyone's consent, have sheltered the culprit from all claims on the part of the community or its chief, and the legitimate vengeance of the party wronged." In effect, confusion between penance and penalty frequently occurs, the penance being equivalent to the penalty and taking the form of a punishment.

However, the system is imperfect and incomplete. It is imperfect because, in spite of everything, the real object of penance is to cleanse the sinner of his guilt. The fact that it has the quality of chastisement as well is a secondary consideration. Even if it takes that form at times, it does not have chastisement as its nature or its object. Further, the multiplicity of penances and the enormous importance attached to practices which are purely expiatory, such as pious donations and the recitation of prayers, often attenuate or even reduce to vanishing point whatever penal content they have. Finally, as regards the Śūdra, penance as such is somewhat illusory, since he cannot be outcasted if he fails to perform it.[49] It must be imposed upon him, and thus it becomes a veritable penalty. But it is not the role of Brahmins to punish! That is the king's prerogative. It is his task to keep the various members of the community to their proper duties by means of appropriate punishments, of which he is the sole judge. Penal law, properly so called, derives exclusively from secular power.

The system is also incomplete in that, so far as it acts as a deterrent, it secures no compensation to the victim or person wronged. The fines in the form of donations go to the Brahmins, not to the victim. Here too we must be on our guard against too absolute a view of the matter. Penance inflicted on the wrongdoer often provides a kind of public reparation for the victim, sufficient to assuage his desire for vengeance. Occasionally, too, the penance devised takes into account reparation due to the victim. Thus Baudhāyana (I.10.19.1) provides that the cows to be offered in a case of homicide are given by the culprit *vaira-niryātanārtham,* "in order to escape vengeance", while the supplementary bull is given *prāyaścittārtham,* "to expiate his sin".[50] The cows given by the sinner originally represented the blood-price, the *wergeld,* paid once—and perhaps still paid in Āpastamba's day—to the relatives of the victim. This would tend to prove that at least in this instance it is the penal law which was the source of the penance or had served as a model for it. But in reality, as is the case with penalites, there is much confusion

[49]Manu, X.126, declares that the Śūdra cannot commit a sin which causes fall from caste *(pātaka)*.

[50]See Bühler's note on *Baudh.*, I.10.19. 1 and *Āp.*, I.9.24. 1.

between the two conceptions, and it is doubtless quite natural that compensation should be transformed into a simple penance by a process analogous to that which, in Europe, changed compensation into a penal fine.[51]

If the penal or expiatory aspect, in the form of penance, holds so important a place in the *dharma-sūtras* this does not mean that their authors were unacquainted with the concept of compensation. Their self-imposed task was to teach *dharma,* to clarify the saving or expiatory virtue of the actions in question. They were concerned above all to tell the transgressor of the law how he could purify himself from his sin, to reestablish the (occult) order broken by his guilt and the balance of his own *karma* which he had upset. This only qualified Brahmins had authority to do. As for compensation for the wrong inflicted by his crime, this was a matter exclusively for the temporal order, which derived from the king's power. It was, in general, the same with all private disputes which could arise between individuals. The solution did not interest Brahmins in their capacity as *gurus,* since it was to be found, not in the *ācāra* or religious usage, but in practice, in custom as we understand it. Nevertheless, though it was foreign to their concerns, our Brahmins were led to penetrate into that domain and to make some room in their *sūtras* for questions of a purely juridical character.

Their intervention seems to have been a consequence, a natural prolongation of the teaching of *dharma*; it was imperceptibly and almost by force of circumstances that spiritual preceptors had to emerge as jurisconsults. Having to teach the duties of the four *varṇas,* they could not fail to specify those which were peculiar to the Kṣatriyas. The duty of the Kṣatriya is above all to protect the other *varṇas* againt their enemies. He alone has the right and the duty to bear arms. He commits no sin in killing enemies (*Gaut.,* X.17). And here our authors remind the Kṣatriyas of the laws of war: "The Āryas do not kill those who have put down their weapons, nor those who beg for mercy, their hair loosened and their palms joined, nor fugitives", declares Āpastamba (II.5.10.11). They spare also "those who have lost their horses, their chariots or their weapons" (*Gaut.,* X.18). They do not use barbed or poisoned weapons (*Baudh.,* I.18.10). But this little war code, where one also finds rules relating to the distribution of booty (*Gaut.,* X.20–23) and precepts upon how to engage in combat (*Vas.,* III.17–19), touches only one part of the attributes of the warrior caste. To the Kṣatriyas, and especially to him amongst them who is chosen to be king, belong equally the cares of government and the mission to ensure peace amongst the subjects by a good administration of justice. All the *dharma-sūtras* have a more

[51]According to *Baudh.,* I.10.19. 1 the cows go to the king. In his view, therefore, it is a penalty.

or less extended chapter on the official duties of the king *(rāja-dharma)*, in which the uncontested supremacy of the Brahmin caste is affirmed. The chapter is very short in Baudhāyana. He contents himself with reminding the king that the taxes he levies on his subjects are due to him only by way of payment for his doing his duty of protecting the people (I.18.1) and with bidding him to chose a Brahmin as his chaplain *(purohita)*, whose advice he should follow (I.18.7-8). The growing authority of this chaplain or confessor, and of Brahmins in general at the courts of princes, explains why the other authors are bound to detail these pieces of advice, of which there was a wide variety. They are concerned with brief recommendations as to the locating of the capital and the palace, which should include a hall of audience *(āmantraṇa)* and a hall open to all *dvijas* (*Āp.*, II.10.25.2-13); the appointment of functionaries charged with the administration of towns and villages and the revenue, and those responsible for thefts committed within their jurisdictions (*Āp.*, II.10.25.4-9); the rates of duties, varying with the subject's profession (*Gaut.*, X.24-28,31) or the nature of the commodity taxed (*Baudh.*, I.10.14); individuals who ought to be exempt from taxation (*Āp.*, II.10.26.10-17; *Vas.*, XIX.23-24); and the king's duty to come to the aid of women whose husbands had been killed in war (*Vas.*, XII.20). These rules, as a whole, form an embryo administrative code.

Finally our authors do not omit the two special functions of the king, his special *dharma*: to protect—and to punish (*Gaut.*, X.7-8; *Vas.*, XIX. 1.8). The king must protect his subjects against external enemies, taking command of the army and securing its victory. Further he must protect them against disturbers of the public tranquillity, those who hinder others from accomplishing their own duties, people who are like thorns *(kaṇṭha-ka)* in society, following the metaphor which Manu later made classical.

The king must be watchful lest the subjects transgress their duties (*Vas.*, XIX.7). In this respect he is only the servant of *dharma* and the Brahmins' auxiliary. They prescribe the penance: he must see that it is carried out and punish the recalcitrant (*Āp.*, II.5.10.12-16; 10.1). Here the penalty seems like a complement to the penance. But it is really an independent notion. The king does not intervene in order that the culprit may be purified from his guilt, but in his capacity as judge, having as his mission the task of protecting the community and defending it against those who injure it. That is his *dharma*, and the king who neglects it can be liable to a penance himself (*Gaut.*, XII.48). "If the king does not punish an act deserving of punishment, the guilt recoils onto him" (*Āp.*, II.11.28.13). Vasiṣṭha (XIX.40-41) explains the penance which the king and his chaplain, should perform, if he leaves the culprit unpunished. The right to punish is considered the essential prerogative of the king. The only passage of the *dharma-sūtras* in which the king is compared to a god is that which deals with the right of punishment (*Vas.*, XIX.48. cf *M.*, V.93). He is free to fix the nature and extent of the punishment as he thinks fit, for his decision is inspired above all by temporal considerations. He acts in the interests of the community.

However we get the impression that the *dharma-sūtras* wish to guide him in this duty as in others. They do not fail to remind him of the Brahmins' immunity. According to Gautama (VIII.12-13), that immunity is practically total: a Brahmin, he says, ought not to be beaten, nor put in irons, nor condemned to a fine, nor banished (from the village or the realm), nor censured, nor abandoned. Other authors content themselves with exempting him from all corporal punishments. However grave his crime he cannot be punished with death. The heaviest punishment that may be imposed on him is banishment. Baudhāyana, however, permits the king, before banishing him, to brand him on the forehead with a sign which recalls the crime he has committed. Gautama himself (XII.47) provides for branding. Āpastamba (II.27.17) allows the Brahmin culprit (who has killed, stolen, etc.) to be blinded (but the commentator understands merely that he should be blindfolded...).

Next, the *dharma-sūtras* furnish principles for determining the punishment to be inflicted. Before giving sentence, says Vasiṣṭha (XIX.9) the king must take account "of the place and the time (when and where the crime was committed), the functions, the age, and the associations (of the culprit) and of the part of the body of the victim which has been struck", if it is a question of blows or injuries. For Gautama (XIII.51-52) the sentence must be framed with an eye to the status of the criminal, the force he used, the nature of the crime and the fact whether or not he had relapsed into crime. Pardon could be granted on the unanimous advice of an assembly of men learned in the Vedas. Āpastamba gives the spiritual preceptor, the officiating priest, a *snātaka*, or the king the right to intercede for an accused if he had not committed a capital offense, in order to obtain a commutation of the penalty. But our authors are capable of going further and, for certain crimes, they detail the nature and the amount of the penalty. Thus Gautama (XII.8-14) gives a schedule of fines for insulting people, the amounts varying with the *varṇa* of the offender and that of the person insulted. The same author (XII.15-16) likewise fixes the amounts of fines for theft. It is eight times the value of the object if the thief is a Śūdra, doubled if he is a Vaiśya, and doubled again (thus amounting to 32 times the value) if the theft was committed by a Kṣatriya. As a general rule the penalty increases with the status of the culprit (*Gaut.*/ XII.17). The same author gives another schedule of fines for damages caused to crops by straying animals. The rate varies according to the animal (XII.22-26). Thus parallel to the scale of sins and penances there arose a scale of purely penal sanctions, an embryo of criminal law, as we understand it, whereby the State deters individuals from committing crimes.

Nevertheless, we cannot establish a line of demarcation between religious sanction and penal sanction. At times they seem to have been cumulative. Thus Āpastamba provides banishment for the *dvija* who commits adultery with a Śūdra woman (II.10.27.8). Sometimes the two sanctions seem to have been mutually exclusive. On this subject we seek in vain for a generalisation. Yet Vasiṣṭha declares (XIX.45), "Criminals who have been punished by the king are purified and go to heaven, like virtuous people who have done good deeds" (cf. *M.*, VIII.318), thereby admitting that the chastisement administered by the king avails as a penance. Again, we find in all *dharma-sūtras* (*Vas.*, XX.41; *Baudh.*, II.1.16-17; *Āp.*, I.9.25.4-5; *Gaut.*, XII.43-45) a provision according to which the thief (of gold belonging to a Brahmin) who voluntarily comes before the king and confesses his crime, carrying a club or a stake on his shoulder, is purged from the sin of the theft as soon as the king has struck him a blow with the club, whether he dies on the spot or survives. This provision, like that of Vasiṣṭha cited above, passes into Manu (VIII.314-316,318). "Whether he is killed or pardoned, he is purified; and if the king does not strike him the sin recoils upon the king" (*Gaut.*, XII.44-45; *Baudh.*, II.1.17). The religious law and the secular law thus interpenetrate each other. The two domains are never clearly distinguished. However, the rules of penal law occupy little space in the *dharma-sūtras*. They are not arranged systematically, as are sins and penances. The topic was plainly secondary and accessory so far as our authors are concerned. We have every right to presume that Hindu princes exercised their right to punish without waiting for the *sūtra-kāras'* precepts on that subject! What we have in front of us are the Brahmins' earliest efforts to provide rules for the chief's justice, which up to that point must have been arbitrary or customary in character, and to integrate it within their already learned system for expiation of sins.

Another function of the king, an essential attribute which is also a corollary to his duty to give "protection", is to arbitrate differences between his subjects on matters which did not come within *ācāra*. Disputes in the realm of private law form what is generally called *vyavahāra* (business). Here again the topic does not interest our authors directly; it arises exclusively from duties bearing upon the king's conscience. Organisation of justice is his concern alone: it is *his* justice. Apart from that, the control of such disputes belong to custom properly so called, usages observed amongst the people in their transactions. The king's only course is to refer to the customary rule and to pass sentence against the party who has infringed it.

Now ordinary custom, the breach of which does not constitute a sin, is foreign to the teaching of *dharma*. But just as our authors were brought to concern themselves with the law which really belonged to the king, namely the punishment of criminals, they are led to advise the king in his exercise of the other important prerogative of his, namely the right to put an end to private differences. Hence we have certain rules, not however very numerous, on the composition of the tribunal, on the choice of judges, on the modes of proof, and on procedure in general.

Amongst approved means of proof the first place is naturally occupied by the evidence of witnesses. All our authors devote at least some *sūtras* to the subject. Gautama actually devotes a chapter to it (XIII). The witness must take an oath before deposing. He must be reminded of the torments that await him in the other world if he does not tell the truth. False evidence is in any case punished by a public admonition and an even graver sanction. As once with courts in Europe, the evidence of a single witness will not normally suffice. In principle as many as three are required (*Gaut.*, XIII.2). The witness, questioned by the judge, is bound to reply on pain of a penal sanction (*ibid.*, 6). Āpastamba (II. 5.11.3) is the only writer to mention, alongside witnesses, ordeals *(divya)* as a means of proof. But he does not describe them, and he does not explain what their probative worth is. The subject is regulated by custom. Vasiṣṭha (XVI.10.14-15) is the only one to speak of title deeds (*likhita*, written evidence) in connection with the proof of property. He seems not to admit the evidence of witnesses in the context unless written evidence is lacking or the deeds produced by the parties are in mutual contradiction. We would be wrong to rely on the silence of the other *dharma-sūtras* on this topic as evidence of their antiquity relative to Vasiṣṭha. They must have known of title deeds. If they keep silent about them it was because the topic comes within the province of the customary law.

The rules of procedure are naturally the same in civil suits as in criminal. However, certain differences are to be observed. In civil cases witnesses tendered by the parties should be beyond suspicion of partiality towards either side. They should be selected from among individuals who are irreproachable and worthy of being believed by the judge (*Gaut.*, XIII.2; *Āp.*, II.29.7). According to Vasiṣṭha (XVI.30) a witness should belong to the same caste as the party on whose behalf he appears: "Women should testify for women, *dvijas* of the same rank for *dvijas*, honest Śūdras for Śūdras; and men of lower castes for those belonging to the lower castes" (cf. *M.*, VIII.68).[52] In a criminal case, on the contrary, no objection can be raised to a witness (*Gaut.*, XIII.9). On the other hand Gautama (XIII.27) and Vasiṣṭha (XVI.3) seem to suggest that

[52]But the preceding *sūtra* would appear to contradict this rule.

the king cannot act *ex officio* except in a criminal matter. The rule is not formally expressed until the time of the *dharma-śāstras*. It is a rule which implies a juridical quality well worthy of note.

The *dharma-sūtras* allot very little space to these procedural rules. But, just as the Brahmins are called to assist the king in his judicial functions and even to replace him in those functions, it is inevitable that such topics, marginal to the essential preoccupations of our authors, should gradually take and keep the attention of professors of *dharma*. Viṣṇu has more detailed rules than Gautama on oral evidence. He devotes a special chapter to written evidence and four chapters to ordeals.

Our Brahmins were originally even less interested in the regulation or determination of disputes than they were in the methods to be followed in hearing and disposing of the cases. Such regulation belonged entirely to the temporal sphere and was governed by custom. Baudhāyana is practically silent on this sphere. In fact, as Gautama in particular says (XI.20-25), the rule must be found out from the practices of countries, of castes, of corporations, and of families. The king must thus enquire about the practices in vogue amongst authorised representatives of the groups of society, and deduce from them by analogy or inference the proper solution of the case submitted to him (*Gaut.*, XI.20-24). However, the same author adds that in difficult matters where the solution is doubtful, the king should take counsel with the Brahmins and make a decision conformable to their advice (*ibid.*, 25). And so we find Brahmins occupying themselves with *vyavahāra*, or disputes between individuals. We grasp that, in order to ease their own mission as well as the king's, the authors of the *dharma-sūtras* must set forth rules to be followed for the solution of the most common cases. The result is that the civil law carved itself a place alongside and, as it were, in the margin of *dharma*. It was still a little place, where the most diverse propositions succeeded each other with no order at all. Thus Gautama, the richest (or, should we say, the least poor?) in this class of rule, deals successively with compensation in cases of theft;[53] money-lending (maximum rates of interest, limits to the accumulation of interest, different species of interest, etc.) (X.29-36); then acquisition by possession alone (length of time, things susceptible of being acquired in this way, exceptions in favour of certain persons) (XII.37-39); debts which should be paid by heirs (XII.40-41); the liabilities of a depositary, or a borrower, or of a purchaser where the object has been lost (XII.42)—the whole intermixed with rules of a penal character.

Vasiṣṭha and Āpastamba are much more brief. The first devotes several

[53]The king must secure the restitution of the stolen object. Otherwise he is liable to pay its value out of his own coffers (X.46–7), a rule which survived at least in theory into the early British period.

sūtras to the servitude (or easement) known as right of passage, fixing the width of the path involved (XVI.11-12), to the means of proving title to land and to acquisition by possession (XVI.16-18), then to debts which can be recovered from heirs (XVI.31). Āpastamba is content to lay down certain rules relative to leases of farms, the responsibility of herdsmen, and compensation payable when uncontrolled cattle do damage. Our authors naturally take an interest in the most common causes of litigation. That is why rules concerning agriculture, cattle-breeding, and landed property are relatively numerous. Hence also the rules about loans and deposits, the two contracts typical of a society still subject to a closed economy. But certain of these provisions already witness the exercise of a juridical mind. They are set down in a form which can be recognised as scientific. We may take some *sūtras* from Gautama as examples. "One becomes owner by succession, purchase, partition, taking possession, and finding. One must add for the Brahmin acceptance of a donation, for the Kṣatriya conquest, and for the Vaiśya or the Śūdra labour" (X.39-42). Or again, "The property in an asset is acquired by him who has possessed it for ten years under the eyes of the true owner, provided the latter is not deprived of reason or become senile (*bāla*). Nevertheless the goods of *śrotriyas*,[54] ascetics, or officers of the king cannot be acquired by prescription" (XII.37-38. Cf. *Vas.*, XVI.16-18). One reads in Āpastamba (II.11.28.1): "If the tenant-farmer cannot produce any fruit from the soil, he must pay the owner the value of the harvest which the land could have produced". It is evident that our authors are well aware of other rules of the same kind and that they proffer nothing more than a selection, leaving to custom what really belongs to its sphere. Civil law, henceforward, is none the less grafted onto the study of *dharma* and is to be developed considerably in later literature. Viṣṇu contains a long chapter (196 "verses") on topics of civil and criminal law, followed by a special chapter (43 "verses") on the recovery of debts. But, as with the old *dharma-sūtras*, the rules follow without any order, and with no apparent connecting link between them. They do not aim to cover the whole field of private law.

This analysis of the *dharma-sūtras* shows that the substance of the little treatises is already quite complex. Their authors are above all keen to teach members of the higher *varṇas* their *ācāra*, or religious custom, along with practices of an expiatory and purificatory character. But they touch law properly speaking only in an indirect and accessory manner, whether in connection with institutions having a bearing on *ācāra*, or in connection with the duties of the king. However, they already contain the germ of what will later have all the apparent characteristics of law-giving. I say "apparent" because, if the rules which they extol

[54]Learned Brahmins, thoroughly versed in the Vedas (and observing their rituals).

appear to have been borrowed from custom, their method nonetheless implies a selection, always and exclusively consisting of *advice,* which they give in order to secure that superior order of things which it is their mission to proclaim, but which it can never be their business to impose.

CHAPTER IV

THE DHARMA-ŚĀSTRAS: THE MANU-SMṚTI

IT IS generally agreed that the great treatises on *dharma*, as closely attached to *smṛti* as to the *dharma-sūtras*, follow, historically speaking, immediately after the latter. The name *dharma-śāstras* is reserved for this new category of writing. These works, the most celebrated of which are the *dharma-śāstras* of Manu, Yājñavalkya and Nārada, differ from the *dharma-sūtras* in three main respects.

1. In point of form they differ because, while the *sūtras* are (as in the case of Gautama) entirely in prose, or in prose mixed with verse, the *dharma-śāstras* are written entirely in verse, the metre, *śloka* (*anuṣṭubh*), being that used in the two great epics, the *Rāmāyaṇa* and the *Mahābhārata*. The style is less archaic and very close to classical Sanskrit. It is no longer elliptical. It attempts to be clear, easy to comprehend.

2. As for subject-matter, the *dharma-śāstras* deal with the same subjects as the *dharma-sūtras,* but they are much more extensive works and they give a much larger place to rules of a juridical character. The *sūtras* are concerned, above all, to lay down the duties incumbent on members of the different castes, and confine themselves to giving several particular solutions, or to expressing certain general principles to regulate disputes which arose. The *dharma-śāstras* by no means neglect the observances and practices of religion or ritual, but they undertake to give in detail the rules which should guide the king in the exercise of his functions. The role assumed by these subjects in the new treatises is immediately apparent if one turns to the chapters where the duties of the king are set out, including his judicial functions, and where we find what might be called the "legislative" element. Though the *sūtras* devote but a small fraction of their texts to these topics, they occupy considerably more than a third of the texts of Manu and of Yājñavalkya. The *dharma-sūtras* include rules which are developed only in the contexts of family and succession law. As for the remainder they are quite inadequate and give only isolated rules, without coordination and without plan. In the *dharma-śāstras*, by contrast, the rules intended to assist in the administration of justice are methodically classified, studied under a fixed number of heads. There we find a branch of the science of *dharma* which is tending to disengage itself from the others, and to be envisaged as an autonomous discipline.

3. The *dharma-sūtras* form a part of the *kalpas* belonging to Vedic

schools. They have close connections with the *gṛhya-sūtras* and the rituals of the respective schools, prolonging and completing them. They are essentially manuals intended for Brahmins belonging to a *caraṇa,* having in mind the teaching which should be given to students. Their authority, at least originally, does not extend beyond fairly narrow circles. Moreover, they contain little or no philosophical speculation. They profess to be nothing more than treatises written by ordinary mortals and based on traditions of the Sages, including the practices of those who are versed in the Vedas and observe Good Custom. Āpastamba and Gautama recognise this expressly. Āpastamba laments occasionally the vices and "weakness" of men "of late times", and Gautama inveighs against those who would wish to imitate some of the irregular activities of the Ancients, whose subsequent disgrace was only prevented by their generally high level of virtue. The *dharma-śāstras,* on the other hand, arrive surrounded by legend attributing a mythical origin to them. They purport to be the Word of Brahmā, gathered by demigods or Sages, and transmitted in an abridged form to our days. At the same time they bear no relation to any school of the Veda in particular. They evince no preference for any particular ritual. They are fully detached from the *gṛhya-sūtras.* They appear to be works which are specially and uniquely devoted to the study of *dharma.* As a result the rules which they prescribe are authoritative for all the Āryas, and no longer limited to the circle of any *caraṇa.*

The *dharma-śāstras* evince then not only a widening of the teaching of *dharma,* both in its content and in its importance, but also a specialisation in what is now an independent discipline.

This specialisation is marked by the appearance of special schools of *dharma,* distinct from all *caraṇas.* According to Bühler, it is due to a development of the six so-called ancillary sciences, taught nominally as a complement to the study of any particular Veda, as if they were *aṅgas* (limbs) of the Veda.[1] In the Vedic schools the essential object of teaching was to provide a complete and profound knowledge of the sacred texts. The student had first to know the *saṃhitā,* the text of the *mantras* and *brāhmaṇas,* the method of breaking up words and phrases, the different kinds of recitation. This essential task must have occupied a large part of the time devoted to study. For the ancillary sciences, such as grammar, astronomy, ritual, and so forth, the time must have been limited. While the *aṅgas* amounted to brief treatises it was still possible for the student to learn them and understand their contents during the period of instruction. But this became practically impossible when, due to the progressive growth of materials and the improvement

[1] *The Laws of Manu* (Oxford, 1886), Introduction, xlvi–lvi. The idea is taken up again by A.B. Keith, *History of Sanskrit Literature* (Oxford, 1928), 403–5.

in techniques of dealing with them, these sciences gave rise to substantial works. This was the case with the science of grammar, which attained a high degree of complexity as well as perfection with Pāṇini and his commentators. It is also the case with ritual. The *sūtras* dealing with the latter amounted to treatises of an imposing bulk. Thereafter the members of Vedic schools must have faced a choice between two methods: either they could learn by heart all the Vedic texts of their school, with the *Vedāṅgas*, without trying to understand what they learnt, or they could resign themselves to learning and studying only a certain number of those treatises. Students who chose the first method became, as Bühler says, living libraries, but they were unable to use the learning which they carried within them.[2] Those who opted for the second method could become scholars in the science of ritual, of grammar, or of astronomy, but they could not rival the former class in verbal knowledge of the sacred texts. Consequently the Vedic schools had to lose their high authority as centres of intellectual life for the Āryas, and they were supplanted by special schools in which only one science was taught.

This specialisation is not a recent phenomenon. It goes back to the distant past. Very early, even before historical times, some sciences became detached from the course of studies of the Vedic schools, and were taught in special schools whose teaching was accepted as authoritative everywhere. One such school was devoted to grammar, a science particularly esteemed amongst the Hindus, who applied their philosophical talents to it at very early period and excelled in it. No surviving grammatical treatise belongs to any Vedic school. The *sūtras* of Pāṇini, which belong to the class of *aṅgas* and go back to the *sūtra* period (fifth or fourth century B.C.), are accepted by all schools. Similarly for astronomy: the oldest treatises which survive show no relationship to the Vedas or Vedic schools, apart from their being attributed to some *ṛṣis* or descendants of a *ṛṣi*.

In what concerns *dharma*, the fact that the Vedic schools as late as those of Āpastamba and Hiraṇyakeśin possessed *dharma-sūtras* proves that this subject continued longer than the others to be a part of the courses of the *caraṇas*. However, certain *dharma-sūtras* themselves show that there already existed special schools of *dharma* in their own times. Vasiṣṭha (III.20) and Baudhāyana (I.1.8) enumerate amongst individuals capable of forming a *pariṣad*, (i.e. a meeting qualified to propound a rule where the formal texts were silent), "he who recites

[2]Precisely the same dilemma was experienced in the Land of Israel by the first century, and developed there and in 'Babylonia' in the next four centuries amongst Jewish scholars. The expounder of the Law required the services of a 'Tanna', whose task it had been to memorise, but not to expound, maxims and propositions embodying the sacred learning. B. Gerhardsson, *Memory and Manuscript* (Copenhagen, 1964). [trs.]

dharma (*dharma-pāṭhaka*)", along with "him who knows the *aṅgas*". This shows that at the time of Vasiṣṭha and Baudhāyana, there existed people who were already devoted to the study of *dharma* in general and who knew more than one *dharma-sūtra*—otherwise it would have been sufficient to call to such a *pariṣad* "he who knows the *aṅgas*". Special schools of *dharma*, and perhaps even special manuals, must have existed in the time of the *sūtras*. As soon as *dharma* was studied independently and methodically as a *śāstra* (discipline), the imperfections and gaps in the *sūtras* could not have failed to make themselves evident. The very importance and abundance of the topics which they embraced must have led the study of *dharma* to become detached from the mass of Vedic studies and constitute an autonomous discipline in itself. However the role which Brahmins played as the king's councillors, a role which grew with time, especially in judicial administration, demanded that questions of juridical significance should be submitted to a much more complete and systematic development. Thus schools of *dharma* came into existence just as already there had arisen schools in which nothing but grammar or astronomy was studied. The name *dharma-śāstra* can conveniently be reserved for treatises composed in such schools, in contrast with the *dharma-sūtras* that appertained to Vedic schools.

But we must note in passing that the word *dharma-śāstra* is often applied to the *dharma-sūtras*, since they too had as their object the *disciplining* of students in *dharma*. On the other hand it is not utterly impossible that the oldest *dharma-śāstras* were composed in the form of *sūtras*. If we could not have attributed to particular Vedic schools the *dharma-sūtras* which have come down to us in isolation, such as those of Gautama or Viṣṇu, they would have had to be placed with the *dharma-śāstras*. Thus it is really only a question of a convenient nomenclature. As far as the commentators are concerned the two kinds of work have equal authority.

We are bound to add to Bühler's explanation for the appearance of *dharma-śāstras* certain factors of a social character without which the success and the development of this new kind of literature would be hard to understand. It is possible that, as N.C. Sen-Gupta thinks,[3] a need made itself felt in post-Vedic society for some law-statement in the largest sense of the word, to safeguard the cultural unity of all those elements in the population which claimed a part in Brahminical tradition. That tradition was a heritage from Vedic times, but was profoundly changed by contact with non-Āryan cultures. The authors of the *dharma-sūtras* struggled to define it and to preserve it, fighting against practices which they considered to be aberrations. But their influence was practically confined to the narrow circle of the Brahminical schools, and each

[3]*Evolution of Ancient Indian Law* (Calcutta, 1953), 15.

school codified for its own purposes what it held to be the law of the Āryas. The authors of the *dharma-śāstras* want to substitute for these fragmentary and limited pictures of Indian society, or even to superimpose upon them, a new picture gathering together all characteristics and offering, as it were, a synthesis of the *dharma-sūtras*. We might suppose that the Hindu élite which remained faithful to its Vedas reacted to historical circumstances, such as the formation of the great empires or even the expansion of doctrines subversive to its own, by becoming aware of the community of beliefs and rituals which, in spite of local variations, united them all. It is just this awareness of a community of culture which can account for the appearance of the *dharma-śāstras*. Those works could well offer some kind of code of Indianness.

The *dharma-śāstra* literature, which could have commenced after the era of the *sūtras*, is very rich, for it did not come to an end until the ninth century A.D., by which time the earliest surviving commentaries must have appeared. Those which enjoy the highest authority and are generally regarded as the oldest are those of Manu, Yājñavalkya and Nārada.

THE MANU-SMṚTI

The *Manu-smṛti* or *Mānava-dharma-śāstra*, which we call the Code of Manu, is much more celebrated than any other *smṛti*. As a source of *dharma* it is classed in India at the head of all *smṛtis*, immediately after the Veda. It has enjoyed the same prestige in further India, in Champa, Cambodia, Indonesia—and has followed the Indian civilization everywhere, even if not always in Brahminical forms.

It is also amongst the first Sanskrit works to be translated into a European language. Sir William Jones' translation *(Institutes of Hindu Law or the Ordinances of Manu...)* was published in Calcutta in 1794, after *Sacontalā or the Fatal Ring* (1789, 1792) by the same translator, and the *Bhagavad-Gītā* and the fables of the *Hitopadeśa* translated by Charles Wilkins (1785–1788). A second edition appeared in Calcutta and London two years later, in 1796. This translation, a most meritorious work, remains the basis for all later works on the *Manu-smṛti*, save the most recent. Another English translation was commenced by Arthur Coke Burnell and finished after his death by Edward W. Hopkins, the celebrated specialist in the epics, and was published in 1891 in the Trübner Oriental Series. The best and unquestionably the richest in references is that of Georg Bühler (called *The Laws of Manu*) published in 1886 in the *Sacred Books of the East* collection, where it appears as Vol. 25. He provided an important preface on the different problems raised by the work attributed to Manu. Finally a new English translation was provided by Gaṅgānātha Jhā, along with a translation of Medhātithi's commentary and followed by a collection of numerous extracts from other commentaries. The five volumes, in several parts each, with three volumes of copious notes, appeared from Calcutta between 1921 and 1929.

The *Manu-smṛti* was translated into German by Hüttner in 1797, and Julius Jolly provided a translation of Book VIII and the beginning of Book IX in the *Zeitschrift für vergleichende Rechtswissenschaft* (vols. 3-4).

A. Loiseleur-Deslongchamps, pupil of A.L. Chézy, the first holder of the chair of Sanskrit at the Collège de France, published in 1833 a French translation called *Lois de Manou* under the auspices of the Société Asiatique. This remained for long the only one in that language. It was reproduced in 1841 in the collection of sacred books of the Orient published by Pauthier, and was thereafter translated into Portuguese. It has often been republished and was for some time available in a popular edition. "It is generally exact and faithful, certain errors of detail apart, and it moves at an elegant pace", says Strehly, but, "for the ease of non-Indologist readers", he adds one could wish for "a more coherent commentary, with much more information". G. Strehly, in his turn, published a new translation in 1893 under the title *Les Lois de Manou* for the *Annales du Musée Guimet* (it is vol.2 of the *Bibliothèque d'études*). The French translator had previous versions at his disposal, and he notes, where appropriate, how they interpreted the passages in question. The commentary is less sober than that of Loiseleur-Deslongchamps. But there are no references to other *dharma-śāstras* or to the *dharma-sūtras*, and this leaves a considerable superiority with the work of Bühler referred to above.

1. *Analysis of the Manu-smṛti*

The work has a total of 2,694 *ślokas* or couplets, and is divided into twelve Books (*adhyāyas*, "readings").

In Book One the Great Sages (*maharṣi*) approach Manu and ask him to tell them the *dharmas* of all the castes "for you are the only one who knows the effects, the true nature, and the object of this universal order established by Him who is self-existent (Svāyambhū or Brahmā), unknowable and unfathomable" (I.3).[4]

Manu replies and describes the creation of the world by Brahmā and his own birth, as issue of Brahmā himself by way of Virāj. Manu in his turn created the ten Great Sages (amongst whom we notice Vasiṣṭha, Bhṛgu and Nārada) and from them came as issue seven other Manus, charged with the task of successively creating and recreating the world

[4][The French original here was taken from G. Strehly's version.]

during the alternate periods of creation and destruction of the cosmos called "periods of Manu" (*manvantaras*).

Manu received from Brahmā the content of the *dharmaśāstra*. He taught it in his turn to the ten Sages. He then ordered Bhṛgu to recite it from one end to the other, "for this Sage has learnt it entire from me" (I.60). Bhṛgu takes up the tale and continues it till the end, saving the rare interruptions due to questions put by the *ṛṣis*. He gives the names of the six Manus descending from Manu Svāyambhū. Each one during his period created and protected created beings. That gives him the opportunity to tell of the division of days and nights for the gods and for men, and the length of the four ages *(yuga)* of which one Manu-period is composed. In the course of these ages *dharma* declines. Likened to a bull, it has four feet in the first, but it is progressively deprived of one foot in each of the following ages. The life of men goes on diminishing also, and their duties change. For the protection of the world the Most Resplendent one has assigned distinct occupations to the members of the four *varṇas* born from his mouth, his arms, his thighs and his feet. There follows praise of the Brahmin (I.92-101), later praise of the *śāstra* of Manu. The Book ends with a table of contents of the whole work (I.111-119).

This first book, which is but an introduction—yet how imposing it is! —does not correspond to anything to be found in the *dharma-sūtras*. Only the first chapter of the *Viṣṇu-smṛti* offers a remarkable analogy to it. On the other hand, the five Books which follow deal with the same matters as the ancient treatises and in the same order—or disorder—in which the majority of them (notably Gautama) rejoice.

Book Two, after explaining the sources of *dharma*, lists the first *saṃskāras*, from birth to initiation, and fixes the point at which each *varṇa* should be initiated, etc., sets out in detail the conduct proper to a Brahminical student, namely his duties towards his preceptor (his spiritual father), and how he should receive his instruction and connected matters.

The three following Books are devoted to the second stage of the life of the *dvija* in which he takes a wife and become a householder. Book III commences with marriage: the qualities required of a spouse, the eight forms of marriage, which of them are authorised for each *varṇa* and what religious effects are attached to each of them. Next we find precepts on the duties of the spouses, next a series of verses on the respect due to women. Manu expresses in passing (III.51) his rejection of the sale of a daughter by her father. Next he enjoins upon the householder the performance of the five daily sacrifices, called the great sacrifices *(mahā-yajña)*, for "he who is diligent in performing sacrifices sustains all this (world), animate and inanimate" (III.75). Thence we pass to an eulogium of the status of householder, superior to the three other stages of life because they subsist by means of him (III.77-78). Next come the rules relating to hospitality. Like the *dharma-sūtras*, Manu regulates minutely the duties to be rendered to the guest according to his *varṇa*, the moment when he should arrive, and the quality of the offering to be made to him. The remainder of Book III (122–286), more than a half, is devoted to the monthly ceremony of *śrāddhas* in honour of deceased relatives, which consists essentially in the offering of rice-balls called *piṇḍas* and in a feast to which, in principle, the only proper guests are learned Brahmins who represent the *manes*. Manu relates who, in default of Brahmins, can be invited to *śrāddhas*, and who, on the other hand, should by no means be allowed to attend (III.150-167), and how the offerings themselves should be offered.

Book IV explains the way of life and the means of subsistence permitted to a Brahmin who has left his studentship, or to a householder, regulating his behaviour in minute detail, including how one should answer the calls of nature (IV.48–51, 56). There follow precepts about the Brahmin's first duty, the study of the Veda and the teaching of it, on the solemnity with which the period of study should be commenced *(upākarman)* and that with which it comes to an end *(utsarga)*, the places and the circumstances in which one should give up recitation of the Veda. After this Manu returns to rules of conduct, notably to presents which it is desirable to accept and those which should be refused. The remainder of the book contains rules relating to diet. There is a long list of foods which are impure by reason of the identity of the one who offers them or are soiled by impure contact (IV.205-220). In conclusion, a fine encomium of charity (IV.227-235) and of the practice of virtue appears, since man will not have any companion in the other world but the fruit of his actions (IV.238-243).

The first third of Book V is devoted again to precepts about food. There is a long list of foods forbidden to Brahmins and to *dvijas* by reason of their natural impurity (V.5-26). There are cases when one is permitted to eat meat (only in the course of a religious ceremony; one should not kill an animal except with a view to sacrificing it) (V.27-56). There follow numerous rules (90 *ślokas* out of 169) on the impurity caused by the death or the birth of a relation or by an impure contact, and also on the means of purification. The last verses speak of the duties of women. They are perpetually incompetent and "should never do anything on their own sole authority, even in their homes" (V.148). "The authority of the husband derives from the gift (of the girl by her father)" (V.152). She should remain faithful to her husband even after his death. "A virtuous woman who remains chaste after her husband's death goes to heaven, even if she has no child, just like Brahmins who remain chaste from their youth and die without posterity" (V.159-160).

Book VI, the shortest by far (97 *ślokas*), deals with the last two phases of life, the stage of the hermit and that of the mendicant monk. Manu comes back at the end to the announcement about the superiority of the stage of the householder (VI.89-90).

The five Books which we have rapidly analysed hardly contain anything new by comparison with the earlier literature. Bühler, who has made a minute comparison between the text of our *dharma-śāstra* and that of the *dharma-sūtras* which have come down to us,[4a] concludes that more than three-quarters of the verses contained in these five Books have precepts corresponding to them in the *dharma-sūtras*. However, Manu is no mere copyist. Most often he amplifies or develops the rules in the *sūtras*. He insists upon some more than others. The portions who have no point of correspondence with the *sūtras* are principally philosophical digressions, which disclose speculations quite foreign to the authors of those *sūtras*.

In the three following Books (VII to IX) our *dharma-śāstra* differs profoundly from the *dharma-sūtras* and suggests no more than a distant resemblance to them. Here his originality is to be found.

After setting out the duties of the anchorite and the mendicant monk, and finishing the study of the four stages of life, Manu conforms to the plan of the *dharma-sūtra* of Āpastamba and other *dharma-sūtras*. In Book VII, he attacks the topic of *rāja-dharma*, the study of the duties incumbent upon the king. First we have a eulogy of punishment, which alone keeps the ruler's subjects to their duties (VII.17-25). Then Manu sets out the qualities which the king must cultivate and the vices which he should avoid (VII.30-53). Precepts follow on the choice of ministers and ambassadors, and on the choice of site for the capital and fortresses (VII.54-76). Manu next tells of the laws of war. With the *dharma-sūtras* he recalls that an Ārya never strikes an enemy on foot (while he is himself in a chariot), nor a suppliant, nor him who surrenders at discretion, nor non-combatants, nor him who is already fighting with another adversary, and so forth (VII.91-93). For the protection of his realm the king should appoint a chief for each village *(grāma)*, a chief for ten towns, and a chief for twenty, a chief for a hundred, a chief for a thousand, each chief being subordinate to his superior in the hierarchy (VII.115-117). Manu fixes the reward to be provided for these functionaries, as well as the minimum salary to be given to palace servants. Several verses follow on the taxes which the king may levy (VII.127-137). One is reminded in passing that a learned Brahmin cannot be obliged to pay any taxes. Then Manu passes to advice on policies to be followed with regard to neighbouring states and on the conduct of war when that could not be

[4a]See also G.B. Beaman, *On the Sources of the Dharmaśāstras of Manu and Yājñavalkya* (Leipzig, 1895).

avoided "for when two adversaries are locked in combat there is no certain means of knowing on which side victory or defeat may emerge" (VII.199). "A well-instructed prince should try to triumph over his enemies by conciliation, corruption, or division, employed together or separately—never by warfare at the outset" (VII.198). But if these three expedients have not succeeded, then, assuming that his preparations are adequate, he should fight to vanquish his enemies. Manu lays down the policies to pursue with regard to conquered countries. He extols alliance rather than annexation: "While acquiring gold and territory the king does not prosper as much as he would if he had made a faithful ally, who could become powerful in the future" (VII.208). On the other hand the laws and customs of neighbouring countries must be respected by the conqueror, just as they are (VII.203). The book ends setting out the king's timetable, from when he should take his midday meal to his bedtime.

Only a quarter of the matter dealt with in Book VII can be traced in the *dharma-sūtras*. It is evident that here Manu encroaches upon the domain of politics rather often. This is not an absolutely novel feature, but it is much more frequent in Manu than in the *dharma-sūtras*. It is a manifest sign that the Brahmins have acquired an important place in the king's councils.

Books VIII and IX demonstrate an even greater originality than Book VII, as much by the arrangement of the topics as by the novelty of the matters taken up. The two Books are devoted to the regulation of disputes in private law so far as they appertain to the justice given by the king. While the *dharma-sūtras* propounded rules for the solution of only certain of the most common disputes that the king would have to know, Manu tries to embrace all the types of litigation that could possibly arise, and to enumerate the different types of dispute. At the beginning of Book VII (4-7) he declares that all disputes brought to the royal court are reducible to eighteen heads. These are the celebrated eighteen *mārgas* ("paths, roads") or *vyavahāra-padas* ("footings of 'business'") which constitute for India the first attempt at methodical classification of contentious business, the first systematic proposition of law. These eighteen "heads" are: (1) non-payment of debts; (2) deposit; (3) sale by one not the owner; (4) relations between partners; (5) recovery of things given; (6) non-payment of wages; (7) breach of regulations of certain associations and corporations; (8) resiling from sale; (9) disputes between the owner of a herd and his herdsmen; (10) disputes relating to the boundaries of villages and properties; (11) assault; (12) insults by word of mouth; (13) theft; (14) acts of outrage; (15) adultery and rape; (16) duties of husband and wife; (17) partition (of heritage); and (18) gambling and wagering.

As Jolly has shown, this classification is reasoned; the topics are not thrown together by chance but in a certain order, corresponding to the economic conditions of the period.[5] The first nine *mārgas* are really concerned with obligations. The non-payment of debts, or rather the non-repayment of money lent, naturally occupies the first place because of its great practical utility. Then comes the title "deposits", a contract of great importance as a result of the insecurity of property, etc. The tenth deals with disputes about boundaries, that is to say with actions about immovable assets and the right of property itself. The five following "heads"—assault, insult, theft, etc.—concern crimes against the person. All that concerns the law of the family is contained in the two penultimate *mārgas*.

In the course of Book VIII precepts relating to the first fifteen "heads" are propounded. As an introduction several rules are set out on the composition of the tribunal, which should be presided over by a Brahmin in the king's absence; on the duty of the king to protect handicapped people, children, women without families, and the sick; on the part which comes to the king from lost property which is found, and from treasure-trove. Along with the first *mārga* we are also given the rules relating to proof. If the debtor denies a debt, the burden of proof falls on the lender (VIII.52). Something is said about proof by witnesses; the persons who may be entertained as witnesses; which penalties strike those who perjure themselves, both in this world and the other. In default of witnesses to discover the truth, the judge can take recourse to the oath and to ordeals. Apart from the oath Manu mentions only the water and fire ordeals (VIII.114-115). It is also à propos of the recovery of debts that Manu enumerates the weights and measures used in such transactions and fixes the interest which should be paid; he deals with securities, viz. pledge and suretyship, with acquisition by prescription, and with what vitiates consent.

In some confusion at the end of the book are thrown a series of rules on points which have not found a place under the fifteen rubrics previously dealt with. Here are found rules concerning the king's duty to fix the prices of merchandise; here also are rules for the rates of tolls payable according to the nature of the vehicle, and about the seven kinds of slaves and the servile status in general.

Book IX begins by expounding the duties of husband and wife, which forms the sixteenth *mārga*. Manu insists on the need to watch women and to keep them in lifelong tutelage. He discusses at length the question which has already preoccupied the authors of *dharma-sūtras,* namely to whom belongs a son: to him who has begotten him or to the husband of the mother? He concludes that the son ought to belong to the last,

[5] J. Jolly, *Hindu Law and Custom* (Calcutta, 1928), 35.

just as, barring a special agreement to the contrary, the harvest belongs to the owner of a field and not to him who scattered the seed (VIII.31-56). In passing he prohibits the husband's sale of his wife (VIII.46). There follows another discussion on the practice of *niyoga,* which Manu prohibits after having seemed to admit it (VIII.57-58). He concedes, however, that the brother of a bridegroom-to-be is bound, if the latter dies, to marry his betrothed (VIII.69–70). He deals next with the cases where a wife could be repudiated or replaced, and he condemns the practice of paying a bride-price, even if the father is a Śūdra (VIII.98). The title of "duties of husband and wife" ends with the principle of indissolubility of marriage (VIII.101-102).

Only about a quarter of the *ślokas* contained under this head can be found in the *dharma-sūtras*. By contrast there are relatively few new rules in the portion devoted to partition of heritage, which forms the seventeenth *mārga*. Manu deals first with partition amongst children, with the preferential share for the eldest son, with the share to be given to the son of a *putrikā* (daughter appointed by her father to provide him with an heir in the absence of male issue of his own), with the adoptive son (*dattrima,* which is identical with the *dattaka*), and with the *kṣetraja* (born of a woman authorised to bear a child by someone other than her husband). Then he passes to partition amongst sons born of different women. He lists and defines the twelve sorts of sons, the legitimate son *(aurasa)* and those who are qualified to replace him in the funeral ceremonies. The rules about devolution of the inheritance in the absence of sons are outlined succinctly (IX.185-187). In default of natural heirs, the inheritance passes to the king, unless it is the estate of a Brahmin (IX.189). Rules follow relating to assets which are the property of the wife *(strī-dhana)* and to the devolution of them. Some verses on the grounds for disqualification from succession, and a few more on the possible prolonged indivision of an estate bring the title of partition to a close.

The eighteenth and last *mārga* gives rise to only ten *ślokas* (IX.221-231). Manu condemns and prohibits gaming and wagering which, he says, "are nothing less than manifest theft" (IX.222). One verse (IX.233) seems to express the rule of *res judicata,* and the following provides a right of appeal to the king from all unjust decisions passed by a minister or the judge.

The penalties and penances prescribed for four of the Great Sins (murder of a Brahmin, the drinking of spirituous liquor, theft, sexual intercourse with the *guru's* wife) and several precepts on the king's fulfilling his role as giver of justice bring to an end the exposition of the royal administration of justice.

The king is further bound to maintain internal order by seeking out the "thorns" of the kingdom, criminals and wrongdoers of all sorts. He must have public places watched, punish the officials or neighbours of any place where a crime is committed, and deter the commission of crimes by the imposition of appropriate penalties. A series of additional rules follows (IX.252-293), almost all of them foreign to the *dharma-sūtras,* the majority relating to criminal law properly so called.

The king's mission is then evoked in a series of *ślokas* where his activity is compared to that of the gods and the elements (IX.303-312). But immediately afterwards the status of Brahmin is extolled, for even if he is ignorant or employed in lowly avocations, he must always be honoured as the highest divinity (IX.313-322).

Book IX finishes (326-336) by summarily listing the duties of the Vaiśyas and the Śūdras. For these last "obedience towards Brahmins [who are] learned in the Vedas, householders and renowned [for their virtues] : that is their supreme duty, which will lead them to bliss" (IX.334), and it will enable them to be reborn in a higher caste (IX.335).

Book X deals with the mixture of *varṇas* and the means of subsistence allowed in times of distress, when the normal rules cannot be followed. The *dharma-sūtras* deal with these questions either à propos of marriage or à propos of succession. They list one or two groups of castes called "mixed" and confine themselves to describing rapidly their origins and sometimes their modes of subsistence. They add a few precepts about the alteration effected on the status of individuals born of a mixture of *varṇas* at the end of a certain number of generations, and also the signs whereby an individual of low birth may be recognised. Manu takes up all these questions, but he goes into much greater detail and introduces a large number of names of mixed castes unknown to the *sūtras*. The rules which follow on the occupations proper to the castes and their means of subsistence in times of distress bring, by contrast, little which is quite new.

The first forty-three verses of Book XI deal with rules about the gifts to be made to persons in need and especially to Brahmins, and on the performance of sacrifices, for which Brahmins lacking the necessary objects are permitted to take them from others. The remainder of the book is devoted to penance and to expiation. Those who have not expiated their misdeeds are reborn with deformities and diseases varying according to the nature of their acts (XI.48–53). Hence the necessity for purification. Sins *(pātakas)* are then classified according to their gravity into Great Sins *(mahā-pātakas),* Secondary Sins *(upa-pātakas),* sins involving loss of caste *(jāti-bhraṃśa-kara)* or likely to consign the sinner to a mixed caste *(saṅkarī-karaṇa),* sins rendering one unfit to receive donations *(apātra),* and sins merely involving taint *(malāvaha)*. Appropriate penances *(prāyaścittas)* are provided for all these kinds of sins, with much precise detail. Manu attaches a purificatory effect to confession and repentance. "In so far as a man guilty of a sin confesses it spontaneously he is absolved from it, as a snake (sheds) his skin; to the extent that his spirit regrets his evil deed, to that extent his body is freed from that wrongdoing" (XI.229–230). But above all, men are absolved from their misdeeds through austerities, and Manu understands by austerity *(tapas)* the performance of the task allotted to each one according to his caste (XI.235–245). The Book ends by noting the *mantras* which should be recited as a penance when the sin has remained a secret.

The whole of Book XI faithfully reflects the spirit of the *dharma-sūtras*. The portion relating to penance and the classification of sins finds a close analogy in the *Viṣṇu-smṛti*.

Book XII, the last, resembles the first in its philosophical and religious character, which gives it a feature in common with *purāṇa* literature. It commences by classifying the acts which result in different human conditions: it explains how the three essential qualities (the *guṇas*) of a soul, namely goodness *(sattva)*, passion *(rajas)* and ignorance *(tamas)* influence transmigration.[6] It sets out the penalties which await in the other world those who commit wicked acts; and also which await them in future lives. By contrast it enumerates the acts whose performance will procure supreme bliss. For Brahmins the best means of attaining final bliss are austerity and the sacred learning, i.e. knowledge of the Veda and of *dharma*. This is why Manu introduces several *ślokas* here to indicate those who are authorised to decide the rule to be followed in any case which is doubtful or not provided for (XII.108–115). This is the only passage in Book XII which has a corresponding passage in the *dharma-sūtras*. The last verses recall the divine origin of the treatise revealed by Bhṛgu, and exalt the Supreme Male (Puruṣa) whom "some call Agni, others Manu, Lord of Creatures, and others Indra, others the vital breath, others the eternal Brahman" (XII.123), into whom is absorbed only a man who "by means of his (individual) soul recognises the (universal) soul in *all* beings" (XII.125).

This analysis shows what a large scope is to be found in the *Manu-smṛti*, which condenses a vast literature. It is a veritable encyclopedia of religion, morality, politics, and law. Nearly half the work exceeds the framework of the *dharma-sūtras*. *Dharma* is entirely detached from the teaching of ritual, and its study is founded directly on that of the Veda in the largest sense of that word, namely the philosophical and social concepts of the Hindu world. The teaching of the *dharma-sūtras* is found therein in its entirety, but it is encased in an exordium and a peroration which curiously heighten its tone and significance, and it is intermixed or interpenetrated

[6]On the three *guṇas* see L. Renou, *L'Inde classique*, s. 1432. Kāṇe, V, 1357. S. Rādhākṛishṇan, *Indian Philosophy* (London, 1941), II, 262–6, 310–1.

by a philosophy far removed from the normal dry approach of the *sūtras*. This method of presentation by itself would be enough to place the Code of Manu in a class apart.

But for us its originality resides above all in the important place assumed by questions of a juridical character and in the attempt at classification represented by the eighteen *mārgas*. The scope of royal justice is also delimited, doubtless still with a certain amount of hesitation, and disengaged from questions properly appertaining to religion. Yet there is no point at which the latter loses its rights, since it is always with reference to *dharma* that Manu advises the king how to conduct litigation.

This is the moment to observe that if the work was intended to reach a much larger audience than the *dharma-sūtras* reached, it was none the less addressed essentially to Brahmins and to Kṣatriyas, the latter represented above all by the king—that is to say to the ruling and educated elements of the population.

2. *The Origin of the Manu-Smṛti*

The mythical character which the *Manu-Smṛti* attributes to itself makes research into its true origins rather difficult. The Manu who revealed the Law of Bhṛgu is descended from Brahmā, the Self-Existent, and he is himself the progenitor of humanity, which has taken his name (*manava* = man). His nature enables him to participate in the divine and the human condition. The *Ṛgveda* names him amongst the most ancient sages, and a celebrated passage presents him as the father of a family dividing his wealth amongst his sons. In the *smṛti* itself (VII.42) a verse refers to him as a king who obtained sovereignty by humility. As the father of humanity it is natural that he should have been regarded as the ancestor of kings, and as an offspring of Brahmā he is regarded as the mediator between the Supreme Being and the race of men. Likewise he appears as the discover of sacrifice, and especially of funeral rites. The revelation of rules on which the social and moral order is founded is understandably attributed to him. From Vedic times onwards he is seen as the first legislator. This function remains especially attached to him in the countries of further India, whose indigenous codes take shelter under the authority of his name even though their precepts have basically little common ground with those contained in our *Manu-smṛti*.

To attribute the work to Manu was to evidence the unparalleled authority which it enjoyed, but not to reveal its sources to us. No one believes now that the Laws of Manu are really primitive. Many passages show that the author, far from having been the first legislator, had numerous predecessors. He reports controversies on many subjects, even contradictory opinions, just as the *dharma-sūtras* had done before him. He expressly says that "some" authorise something, and "some" forbid it. Further some passages allude to the existence of a *"dharma-śāstra"*, a term which could equally designate the *dharma-sūtras*. He might even be referring to Gautama and Vasiṣṭha. Finally there is an allusion to heretical sects, atheists who reject the authority of the Veda, which could well have Buddhists in mind, which at any rate suggests a period well after Vedic times. It is unquestionable that the work presupposes a rich previous literature on *dharma*.

How is the birth of the *Manu-smṛti* to be accounted for? Max Müller suggested in 1859 *(A History of Ancient Sanskrit Literature)* a hypothesis which, taken up again by Bühler, is still of fairly general currency in Europe. The *Manu-smṛti* was (so it was said) a refashioning of an ancient *dharma-sūtra* originally attached to the *kalpa-sūtra* of a particular Vedic school, the Mānava school, a subdivision of the school of the Maitrāyaṇīyas devoted to the study of the Black Yajurveda. The existence of such a school is attested by tradition, which attributes to the *ācārya* Manu the composition of *śrauta* and *gṛhya* ritual-manuals. Only the names of these ritual works were known in the time of Max Müller, but the texts have since been recovered. Moving from the existence of a *Mānava-gṛhya-sūtra* and taking his stand on the traditional opinion according to which every Vedic school possessed its complete collection of *kalpa-sūtras*, Max Müller concluded the existence of a *Mānava-dharma-sūtra*, completing the *śrauta-* and *gṛhya-sūtras* of the same school. There was a confusion between Manu, the human author of the *sūtra*, and Manu, the mythical ancestor of the human race. After the formation of special schools of *dharma*, the *Mānava-dharma-sūtra* was chosen for preference over all others because of its attribution, and it served (so it was said) as a basis for the composition of the *śāstra* which has come down to us.

The ingenious hypothesis of Max Müller, who relied on little more than the similarity of the names, seemed at first to be confirmed by later research. It was possible to attach to particular schools the isolated *dharma-sūtras* which have survived. Gautama is an example. We have traced out the *gṛhya-sūtras* and *śrauta-sūtras* corresponding to certain *dharma-sūtras* and shown the links which permit us to see in them all the work of a single school. At the same time we have grasped the tendency of the *dharma-sūtras* to separate themselves from the manuals of ritual, and to be treated as independent works which are authorities for all *caraṇas*. Above all we have had the case of the *Viṣṇu-smṛti*, which (as we have seen) arose from a *dharma-sūtra* peculiar to the *kaṭha* school of the Black Yajurveda. In the hands of a Vaiṣṇavite, it became transformed into a work of divine inspiration. So it appeared quite plausible that our *Mānava-dharma-śāstra* had as its origin nothing but the *dharma-sūtra* of that Mānava school which produced those *śrauta-* and *gṛhya-sūtras*.

Most unfortunately, the later discovery of the ritual-manuals of that very Mānava school, as well as other works of the same school, tended to contradict rather than to confirm Max Müller's hypothesis, as Bühler was bound to admit. There are actually serious divergencies between some rules in the *Manu-smṛti* and the manuals of the Mānava school, the details of which are given by Bühler. The agreements which can also be shown prove nothing, because the rules were common to the manuals of all schools. Though Bühler persisted in believing in the existence of a *dharma-sūtra* of the Mānava school which must have served as the basis for our *smṛti*, it seems better to give up the hypothesis for want of evidence to support it. Between the *Mānava-gṛhya-sūtra* and the *Mānava-dharma-śāstra* there is nothing in common but the names.[7]

But Max Müller's hypothesis has not been altogether fruitless. In order to prove the existence of a *dharma-sūtra* of Manu earlier than our *smṛti* Bühler and other Indologists have tried to find whether there was not, in the *sūtra* literature, allusions to or borrowings from a treatise on *dharma* attributed to Manu. These researches led to a double conclusion. First they have established that there existed, from a very ancient period, a floating mass of adages or precepts in verse form which formulated a rule of law or a moral duty. These precepts, *dharma-ślokas*, analogous to the maxims *(brocards)* of Europe but in a popular and spontaneous style, are found in the *sūtras*. Sometimes they are anonymous, but sometimes they are attributed to Manu: *manur abravit* "so said Manu". Here, no doubt, Manu is the mythical progenitor of humanity, and the rule is attributed to him only because his authority is immemorial and beyond discussion. There was certainly no question of an individual author for them. It is however possible that the founders of special schools of *dharma*, the *dharma-pāṭhakas* whom the *sūtras* mention, had themselves launched these aphorisms which summed up in a happy formula solutions which they had reached. In this way a rich stock of current maxims grew, covering little by little the diverse fields of juridical activity. It expressed immemorial custom and the reflections of the Sages, in either case fathered on Manu, who was the first to have revealed the Law to men. If thereafter someone collected all these isolated precepts and classified them methodically following a *dharma-sūtra* framework, he would have put together a work bound to enjoy high authority. No subterfuge was necessary to attribute it to Manu, since the compiler had contented himself with collecting "the sayings of Manu", that is to say the rules about which everyone (i.e. nearly every Ārya) was agreed.

[7]This is a continuing debate. L. Renou, *Les écoles védiques* (Paris, 1947), 194–5 and the bibliography at the note. A recent commentator, S.C. Banerji, cited above at p. 22, n. 3, at pp. 39–44 recognises the force of the arguments supporting the existence of a *Mānava-dharmasūtra* but holds that they are not decisive. See Kāṇe, I[2], s.13, p.149.

That just such a work did exist from an early period is the other conclusion to which the researches undertaken by Bühler, Hopkins, and other Indologists have led. Beside that floating mass of maxims attributed to Manu one finds, in the *sūtra* literature as well as in the *purāṇas* and the *Mahābhārata*, passages which suggest that their authors were acquainted with a treatise owing its authority to Manu. The *Mahābhārata* possesses a good number of verses in common with the *Manu-smṛti*. Bühler thought that not less than a tenth (260) of Manu's verses could be found in the epic (especially in Books XII and XIII), where they were sometimes even given a better reading, but where they appeared without any significant order. It is natural to wonder whether the author of the *Mahābhārata* and that of our *smṛti* did not utilise a common source, which must have been the original *Mānava-dharma-sūtra*. But the most conclusive evidence for the former existence of a Manu treatise earlier than our *smṛti* is to be found in Vasiṣṭha's *dharma-sūtra*. Many passages in this text attribute opinions to Manu which are much too complex and elaborate to have been conveyed in the form of adages. Moreover Vasiṣṭha actually quotes the text of a "Mānavam", that is to say a treatise by Manu.

However, if these opinions agree more often than not with those of our *smṛti* they also differ occasionally from them. And then again the citation of the Mānavam is in prose, and not in *śloka* metre as is the *smṛti*. So it seems well established that there existed in Vasiṣṭha's time a *dharma-śāstra* attributed to Manu, but written partly in verse and partly in prose, close to but not identical with the *Manu-smṛti*. Following Max Müller's hypothesis, Bühler sees this as the *dharma-sūtra* of the Mānava school. But it is possible to see it merely as the product of a special school of *dharma*, independent of every Vedic school, for we know that such schools did exist at a very early period. The name of Manu was attached to this treatise because, as we have seen, it completed the traditional teaching of the *sūtras* with the aid of precepts attributed to the first lawgiver.

Thus the original of our *Manu-smṛti* does not have to be a *dharma-sūtra* of any Vedic school, and particularly of the Mānava school, chosen simply because of the similarity of the name of its founder with the Manu of mythology. One can see it rather as an attempt, perhaps the first, which a school of *dharma* made to formulate, apart from all *caraṇas*, the general rule of conduct for Āryas. Yet this first *Mānava-dharma-śāstra* was probably close in form and in substance to the *dharma-sūtras*, and it remains likely that one of them supplied him with his framework. As the citation in Vasiṣṭha shows, it was written, just like the *sūtras*, partly in prose and partly in verse. The *Manu-smṛti* itself has preserved in the details of its lay-out many traces which can hardly be explained by any reverence for the traditional ground-plan of those *sūtras*. The place occupied by certain topics within the total composition, however, is not intelligible except upon the footing that they already occupied the same position in the *sūtras*.

It is not possible to settle the contents of the early treatise which was the foundation of the *Manu-smṛti*. A minute comparison such as Bühler made between the text of that *smṛti* and those of the *dharma-sūtras* is helpful in that it shows what a considerable contribution the editor of our version of Manu must have made. But similarity or analogy with a *dharma-sūtra* could not be a sure criterion for distinguishing a prototype from that which followed it, once it became uncertain whether the *Manu-smṛti* really was a reworking of a *sūtra* belonging to a particular Vedic school. From the very beginning it ought to contain a great many rules foreign to the *sūtras*, particularly in the portions relating to the duties of the king and to the administration of justice, for these must have been developed extensively by that time. But the original work undoubtedly underwent numerous additions and profound alterations before it could reach its present form. For example, the celebrated division of the eighteen *mārgas* seems to have been introduced all at once, for it is unknown to the ancient authors who refer to the original treatise and also to the *Mahābhārata*, the composition of which seems virtually contemporary with that of our *Manu-smṛti*.

Could there have been *several* successive versions of the work attributed to Manu? We have noticed that the *Manu-smṛti* itself purports to be revelation not direct from Manu, but as propounded by the great *Ṛṣi* Bhṛgu, a revelation of the law of Brahmā as he, Bhṛgu, heard it from Manu's mouth. Then Manu says, at the beginning of the first Book, that after having received the law from Brahmā, he taught it in turn to ten Great Sages created by him (I.58). So the *Manu-smṛti* ought to be attributed not to Manu, but to Bhṛgu, or at least ought to be considered to be the Bhṛgu (i.e. Bhārgava) recension of the *Mānava-dharma-śāstra*. Some later texts in India do actually refer to it in those terms, and an inscription in Champā belonging to the end of the twelfth century does the same (an inscription to which we shall return). Are we to think that there were many recensions of the fundamental text? What then is the place occupied by our *smṛti* in this series of recensions? According to the prose introduction to the *Nārada-smṛti* (in the text edited by Jolly), Manu composed a *dharma-śāstra* in 100,000 *ślokas*, divided into 1,080 Books, which were successively reduced to 12,000 *ślokas* by Nārada, 8,000 by Mārkaṇḍeya (another of the ten Sages), then to 4,000 by Sumati, the son of Bhṛgu. So our text, which has only 2,685 *ślokas* would be only the last link of a long chain.

But the *Nārada-smṛti's* own composition proves that it belongs to an epoch well after that of the *Manu-smṛti*. The legend appearing in it seems to have drawn upon a very old tradition echoed in one *purāṇa*[1] (the *Bhaviṣya*) and in the *Mahābhārata*, according to which Brahmā composed an enormous work in 100,000 chapters (or *ślokas*) on *dharma*, *artha*, and *kāma*, a work which was reduced to more and more modest proportions by a succession of Sages. This legend in turn could have had its origin in the actual conversion into a *dharma-śāstra* of that considerable quantity of aphorisms of which we have already spoken. The author of the *Nārada-smṛti* took possession of the legend and deliberately adjusted it in order to increase the prestige of his production.

The digests of the Middle Ages also contain citations taken from a Bṛhan-Manu ("Great Manu") and a Vṛddha-Manu ("Old Manu"), which are not to be traced in the *Manu-smṛti*. But the opinions expressed therein betray a much more developed juridical technique than is to be found in our Manu. On the contrary, these works look as if they were amplified versions of the *Manu-smṛti*. The version of Bhṛgu seems to have been the earliest, and the surviving text looks like the first of the *dharma-śāstras*; that is, it was the first treatise entirely versified in form, in which the study of *dharma* is propounded as a science *(śāstra)* in its own right.

3. *The Date of the Manu-Smṛti*

The most serious argument in favour of the relative antiquity of the *Manu-smṛti* is furnished by the as yet imperfect character of its rules on procedure and private law. If one compares its rules with those of the *dharma-sūtras*, then with those of the other *dharma-śāstras*, one arrives at the impression that they are somewhat more explicit than the former, and yet not a little inferior to the latter. As far as procedure is concerned, the *Manu-smṛti* still gives more attention to the moral aspect of the judge's function than to a demonstration of the trial, which is described much more clearly and with more detail in the codes of Yājñavalkya and Nārada. In that respect it is to be classed immediately after the *dharma-sūtras*, with which it agrees particularly in not mentioning written plaints and written evidence, as well as in the brevity of its rules on ordeals. As in the case of certain *dharma-sūtras*, the silence about documents is not to be explained by any suggestion that Hindus were unaware of writing, but simply that the author of the *Manu-smṛti* was still, in spite of everything, imbued with the spirit of the *sūtras*. He attached more importance to morality than to technical aspects, and only interested himself to a moderate degree in questions relating more to custom than to *dharma*. Many passages of Manu do imply that documents were in general use, especially in commercial transactions, and the work points to the existence of a developed maritime commerce. If the *Manu-smṛti* is silent on the use of documents as a means of proof and differs in this respect from

[1]See F. Lászlo, *Die Parallelversion der Manusmṛti im Bhaviṣyapurāṇa* (Wiesb., 1971).

the other *dharma-śāstras*, that is best explained by the supposition that the author knew only the *dharma-sūtras*.

Not less significant is the brevity of the rules about ordeals. Among the *dharma-sūtras* only Āpastamba recommends as a general rule the employment of the "divine proof" *(divya)*, and he gives no details. On the other hand, the codes of Yājñavalkya and Nārada describe five kinds of ordeals and Nārada, in particular, enters into the details of the rules which must be observed. The *Viṣṇu-smṛti* itself expatiates sufficiently long on ordeals. Once again the silence of the *dharma-sūtras* does not imply that ordeals were unknown in ancient India, but simply that the authors considered that this topic should be left to custom. The authors of the *dharma-śāstras*, on the other hand, wanted to fill the gap left by their predecessors. Yet they were probably satisfied to bring various local customs into a system which was gradually completed. Thus, the fact that the rules in Manu are placed midway between those of the *sūtras* and those of the other codes which are in verse is one more reason for holding that the *Manu-smṛti* was the oldest of the surviving *dharma-śāstras*. Finally, in its treatment of litigation before the king, which is a new section, the *Manu-smṛti's* inferiority relative to works of the same class is evident in various ways. After the attempt at classification into 18 *mārgas*, the rules of law are often ill arranged. Twice, at the end of the eighth and the ninth Books one finds a series of precepts which are isolated and could have figured under one or other of the eighteen "titles" of litigation. Further, the rules of a juridical character are constantly intermixed with moral exhortations, a characteristic which disappears in the *smṛtis* of Yājñavalkya and Nārada. Certain "heads" of litigation are treated in a most summary fashion and give rise to the enunciation of only particular solutions, insufficient to enable us to deduce a general principle from them. Another gap to be observed in the *Manu-smṛti* is the almost complete absence of legal definitions. On all points the superiority of the codes of Yājñavalkya and Nārada is evident. The inferiority of the *Manu-smṛti* can only be explained on the basis that it was compiled at a period when interest in questions of a juridical character was indeed awakened, but when the study of them had not yet reached the degree of perfection demonstrated in the other *smṛtis*. This seems to be the strongest argument to bring to the aid of the opinion of practically all Indologists that the *Manu-smṛti* is older than the other *dharma-śāstras*.

So it is possible to accept as true the statement made in the work itself that the version of Bhṛgu was the first and by far the most ancient of the versified versions of a primordial work attributed to Manu. But if the relative antiquity of the *Manu-smṛti* can be established plausibly within juridical literature as a whole, the task becomes much more delicate when we attempt to fix an historical date for its composition.

Sir William Jones attributes to the *Manu-smṛti* a very high antiquity, between 1280 and 880 B.C. Chézy, followed by Loiseleur-Deslongchamps, makes the compilation go back to the thirteenth century B.C., principally because it makes no mention of the Buddha "who, according to common opinion, lived about a thousand years B.C." (!) (from the *Preface* to Loiseleur-Deslongchamps' translation) and because of "the antique simplicity" of its religious doctrines. Monier Williams (in his *Indian Wisdom*, 1875) more judiciously proposes the fifth century B.C.

In our days opinion has settled against so early a date. Burnell takes note of the age of the philosophical doctrines appearing in Manu and presumes that Book VII, concerning as it does politics and the proper conduct of kings, is an addition made for the advantage of some powerful king and patron of letters, attributing the inspiration of the work to the founder of the Cālukya dynasty, Pulakeśi, who reigned in the middle of the sixth century A.D.[8] As their inscriptions show, the kings of this dynasty did actually take the title Mānavya, which can be explained by the custom of princes to take the *gotra* of their *purohitas*. Though the reasons behind this hypothesis are ingenious they have not convinced all scholars.

Manu's mention of Yavanas and Śakas, that is to say the Greeks (or Indo-Greeks) and the Scythians, amongst the "mixed castes" leads Bühler to think that the work could not have been composed before the third century B.C. But the presence of these words in a single couplet (X.44) can hardly be conclusive of the date of the whole poem, especially when Bühler himself admits the possibility of an interpolation for the word Pahlava which he finds in the same list! The *dharma-sūtra* of Gautama also mentions Yavanas as one of the mixed castes, and Bühler does not hesitate to excise the passage as interpolated.

Our only relatively solid landmark for the dating of the *Manu-smṛti* is Medhātithi's commentary, the *Manu-bhāṣya*, the most ancient of the surviving commentaries if we exclude that of Bhāruci, which Medhātithi used but which is much less rich in incidental information than Medhātithi.[9] Medhātithi himself, about whom we know hardly more than his name, lived probably in the second half of the ninth or the beginning of the tenth century. He frequently cites readings and opinions of his predecessors (including Bhāruci), but he seldom names them, being content to refer to them *en masse* as "the ancient commentators" *(ciraṃtana)*. From such meagre data Bühler arrives at the conclusion that

[8]Introduction (p. xxvii) to his translation of the *Manu-smṛti*, *Ordinances of Manu*, completed and edited by E.W. Hopkins in 1891.

[9]Derrett, 'A newly-discovered contact between Arthaśāstra and Dharmaśāstra: the role of Bhāruci', *Z.D.M.G.*, 115 (1965), 134–152; 'A jurist and his sources: Medhātithi's use of Bhāruci', *Adyar Library Bulletin*, 1966, 1–22. [trs.]. Kāṇe, I[2], 568–71.

the *Manu-smṛti* could not have been composed later than the second century A.D. One can only admire the boldness of his reasoning. It is true that he appeals to other arguments which he regards as subsidiary, especially the dates of the compilation of the *Nārada-* and the *Bṛhaspati-smṛtis*, works held to be later than Manu. But the dates presumed for these two *smṛtis* do not rest on any sure criteria. It is true that inscriptions begin to make some reference to a work or treatise attributed to Manu by about the end of the second century, but the allusions are vague enough, and no one can say for sure whether they really refer to our *smṛti*. The oldest certain citations of our text do not appear until the works of the great religious teacher and *mīmāṃsaka* Śaṅkarācārya, whose age is not far antecedent to Medhātithi's.

Thus, failing all external evidence, we cannot assign the composition of the *Manu-smṛti* to any date more nearly approximate than between the era of the *sūtras* (itself vague enough) and that of the earliest commentary upon it. Indologists have been virtually forced into the position of adopting Bühler's opinion and agreeing to place the work between the second century B.C. and the second century A.D. The rediscovery of the commentary of Bhāruci has had little effect in principle, since however much older Bhāruci may be than Medhātithi there remains no sure method of assessing the gap that must exist between the earliest surviving commentary and the text of Manu himself.[10]

It is to the same period around the beginning of our era (perhaps broader still, three centuries on either side, according to Winternitz) that Indologists are more or less agreed today to place the composition of the *Mahābhārata*. Between the epic and our *dharma-śāstra* there is an undeniable relationship. The immense epic poem purports also to be a religious, moral, and political encyclopedia for the Hindu world. Indeed it also can be classified as *smṛti*. Like the *Manu-smṛti* it aims to broaden sacred learning, to free it from the monopoly of the Vedic schools, and to render it accessible to every educated Hindu. Further, the *Mahābhārata* has many verses in common with the *Manu-smṛti*, and it actually cites the *śāstra* of Manu. It is true that Indologists are not in agreement as to the relative date of the epic and the *Manu-smṛti*. Bühler, following Hopkins, believes in the relative antiquity of the epic, and he sees in the passages common or virtually common to both the borrowings by both authors from a common source, namely the *Mānava-dharma-sūtra* of which he supposed the *smṛti* to be a reworking. On the other hand, Kāṇe pronounces in favour of the seniority of Manu, arguing that while the *Mahābhārata* several times names Manu as the author of a *śāstra*, it is not named by Manu once. Whatever might be the outcome of this discussion the two works certainly belong to the same epoch in

[10] [trs.]

point of style, vocabulary and character, to such a degree that research designed to determine the age of the epic will serve indirectly to throw light on that of Manu. It follows that the rather adventurous hypothesis of Bühler gains a certain amount of support. Whichever of the two works preceded the other, it is clearly within those two extreme dates, two or three centuries B.C. and A.D., that most probably both the epic and the *Manu-smṛti* must have been composed. That is a vague approximation indeed, but we must be content with it in default of any precise reckoning.

It is worth adding that it was precisely in the course of the first centuries of our era that Indian culture took a firm root in the countries of further India, and the Hinduised kingdoms of Fou-Nan, Champā, and the Malay Peninsula appeared.[11] This "Hinduisation", due solely to the prestige which Indian civilisation exercised on the populations of Southeast Asia, and by which they have remained characterised ever since, implies that culture in India itself had at last ceased to be the monopoly of restricted circles of cultivated Brahmins, and had found an expression in works which had effectively popularised it. Likewise it is just round about the commencement of our era that one is tempted to place that awareness of a community of culture of which we have spoken above, and which is betrayed by the appearance of the *dharma-śāstras*. The Code of Manu carried with it, through the majesty of its tone and the breadth of topics treated in it, the radiation of a triumphant civilization which could not fail for long to exercise a seductive influence outside India itself.

[11]G. Coedès, *Les Etats hindouisés d'Indochine et d'Indonésie* (Paris, 1948), 36–40.

CHAPTER V
THE OTHER DHARMA-ŚĀSTRAS

AMONGST THE *dharma-śāstras* whose texts have come down to us in full only two, namely those of Yājñavalkya and Nārada, deserve to be placed close to Manu in point of the importance of their contents and form. But numerous other *dharma-śāstras* have enjoyed an authority equal to these works of front rank and have contributed equally to the formation of the traditional system. Some, by no means the least important, are known to us only from quotations given by commentators and compilers of digests.

1. *The Yājñavalkya-Smṛti*

The *Yājñavalkya-smṛti* was published and translated into German by A.F. Stenzler in 1849. Editions have multiplied since that date, as have translations.[1] The text arrived at with the aid of the surviving commentaries does not suffer from too many variants having an appreciable difference in meaning.

Like Manu, Yājñavalkya is a mythical personage. He figures amongst the most illustrious Sages of the Vedic age. In the *Mahābhārata* and in other sources, he purports to have received the White Yajurveda as a revelation from the Sun, and likewise the *Śatapatha-brāhmaṇa* and certain other sacred texts. The *Bṛhadāraṇyaka-upaniṣad* shows him in the aspect of a celebrated theologian. He is also credited with a well-known treatise on *yoga*.

Though the author of the *dharma-śāstra* affirms his identity with one of the Vedic Sages (III.110), no relationship can be made out, whether in substance or in form, between our text and the works attributed to that Sage. On the contrary, we can see in the *dharma-śāstra* some connections with the White Yajurveda, which leads Jolly to think that the *smṛti* arose from a *dharma-sūtra* belonging to a school attached to that Veda. Stenzler previously drew attention to the correspondence which exists between certain passages in the *smṛti* and the domestic ritual-manual of one of these schools. Jolly notes that "evident" connections also exists between the *Yājñavalkya-smṛti* and the *gṛhya-sūtra* of the Mānava school which itself belongs to the Black Yajurveda. He further concedes that the author, whilst taking a *dharma-sūtra* of the White

[1] As a general rule the relevant bibliographical data are to be found at the end of this volume.

Yajurveda as his basis, must have utilised other *dharma-sūtras* and also our Manu as well. In the end there seems to be no reason whatever for holding that Yājñavalkya had any particular *dharma-sūtra* as his point of departure, or for relating it to any particular Vedic school. All that we, with Kāṇe, can guess is that the author of the *smṛti* could well have belonged to a school of the White Yajurveda and that in consequence the *mantras* of that Veda and the ritual-manuals relating to it were more familiar to him than other Vedas and *sūtras*.[2]

Whoever might have been its author, the *dharma-śāstra* of Yājñavalkya early acquired a great notoriety, attested by the numerous commentaries written round it. One of those commentaries, the *Mitākṣarā,* acquired during the British period and as a result of the system of legal administration in the Anglo-Indian courts the status of a quasi-legislative instrument in certain contexts. The result was as J.C. Ghose puts it, that "If it is true that all Hindus bow before the authority of Manu, we must not forget that in reality they are ruled by the Code of Yājñavalkya".[3]

This fame is explained by the intrinsic qualities of the work. Of all the *smṛtis* which have come down to us that of Yājñavalkya is assuredly the best composed and appears to be the most homogeneous, even though it may have been made up of elements borrowed from various sources. We are struck, especially if we have just read Manu, by the sober tone, the concise style, and the strictness with which the topics are arranged. We find none of those lyrical flights which are, after all, the literary beauty of Manu. The cosmogony which occupies practically the whole of the first Book of Manu is entirely omitted. But there are some digressions, of which the most curious is a description of the life of the embryo and of the human body which is given a propos of the duties of the ascetic, and which extends to not fewer than forty couplets (III.69–109).[4] Yet we come across no repetitions, no contradictions, none of those "second thoughts" which make the meaning of Manu at times somewhat less than definite. The author has obviously sought to make his formulas as brief as is consistent with clarity: he succeeds more often than not. There are cases where he appears to compress two *ślokas* of Manu into one. The result is that he reduces to one thousand or so the 2,694 couplets of Manu, even though several topics, especially in private law, are dealt with far more completely and in greater detail.

The work is divided into three Books *(adhyāyas)* of about equal length, the first devoted generally to religious custom *(ācāra),* the second to administration of justice *(vyavahāra),* and the third to penance

[2]The question is still open to debate. L. Renou, *Les écoles védiques* (Paris, 1947), 196.

[3]*Principles of Hindu Law* (Calcutta, 1906), xi.

[4]There is a French translation in Renou's *Anthologie sanscrite* (Paris, 1947), 202–4. For English versions see Bibliography below.

(prāyaścitta). This tripartite division, which bears witness to the author's readiness to systematise, provides a logical classification within the vast domain of *dharma*, and it has proved fundamental for the development of commentators' expositions.

As for the material substance in it, the *Yājñavalkya-smṛti* is in general very close to Manu, but it occasionally manifests a remarkable independence. Thus it refuses absolutely to accept the validity of marriage between a Brahmin and a Śūdra woman (I.56). The author does *not* formally condemn *niyoga* (I.69). He recognises the rights of succession of the widow and the daughter in the absence of male issue (II.135). Some of Manu's favourite ideas are etiolated: there is a damper on the glorification of the king, and an almost complete silence about the privileges and immunities of Brahmins!

On the other hand, the second Book, which corresponds to Books VII and IX of Manu, gives more numerous and more detailed rules, which could conceivably have been intended to complete Manu's Code. While in the domain of judicial proof Manu makes proof rest essentially on oral evidence, with the two ordeals of fire and water merely mentioned, Yājñavalkya gives preference to documentary evidence above other modes of proof and gives very detailed rules about the drawing up of legal documents (II.84–94). He gives the whole law of ordeals, describing five kinds in practically the same terms as Viṣṇu (II.95–113). Likewise he gives the principles regulating possession and acquisition by possession alone (II.24–29), to which Manu makes a bare allusion. In the same Book, Yājñavalkya takes up in a slightly different order the eighteen titles of litigation propounded by Manu, but the prescriptions required turn out to be more developed, so that these topics, which have a fully juridical character, hold a much more important place in the work as a whole than they do in the *Manu-smṛti*. Good examples of this are the importance assumed by rules relating to suretyship (II.53–54) and the regulation of commerce (II.244–258).

The evident technical progress which the work demonstrates, as well as the form of the whole, hardly permits a doubt that as a complete composition it must be later than that of the Code of Manu. Yet debate rages on the question when that composition must have been made. Jolly proposes the fourth century A.D. at the earliest. His reason is that the *Yājñavalkya-smṛti* must be placed after Manu by several centuries, and naturally before his earliest known commentator, Viśvarūpa. He takes account also, as does Stenzler, of the knowledge which the author seems to have had of Greek astronomy, and the use he makes in two contexts of the word *nāṇaka*, which means a coin of a type which cannot have begun to circulate in India until a somewhat late date. In turn, R.G. Bhandarkar takes up an argument of Stenzler which appeared to have been abandoned, proposing to come down as late as the sixth century. He relies on a passage in the first Book dealing with the worship to be paid to Ganeśa.[5] None of these arguments has convinced Kāṇe, who believes that at the latest the composition of the work must be placed in the first two centuries of the Christian era, and that it could even have occurred as early as the first century B.C.

2. *The Nārada-Smṛti*

There are two versions of the *smṛti* attributed to Nārada, a short version (called the Vulgate) and a longer version. The short version, which was the first one to be known outside India, was translated into English by Jolly in 1876. The longer version, believed to represent the original work, was furnished by a manuscript where the text is accompanied by the commentary of Asahāya, an author who is thought to have lived in the seventh century. This was published by Jolly in 1885, but since the manuscript stopped at verse 22 of section V, the text had to be completed with the aid of the short version. Further, Jolly added under the title of appendix *(pariśiṣṭam)* a chapter on theft taken from an old Nepalese manuscript. In 1929, K. Sāmbaśiva Śāstrī made a new edition of the long version, accompanied this time by a complete commentary by Bhavasvāmin, of uncertain age but generally agreed to belong to the beginning of the seventh century.[6] These two texts are very close to each other, though there are numerous variations in wording. The order of topics is the same.[7] But we must take note that when Jolly published a new translation in 1889 he added, by way of complement, more than a hundred other verses which are attributed to Nārada by commentators or authors of digests and which cannot be found in the text which he edited. It seems then that there were other versions of the *Nārada-smṛti* than those which have survived.

As we have seen already in connection with the origins of the *Manusmṛti*, the *Nārada-smṛti* purports to be a recension of the law of Manu which is *older* than that of Bhṛgu. According to the preface to the version commented upon by Asahāya, which is in prose while the rest of the work is in verse, Manu, the mythical ancestor of humanity and child of the Self-Existent, had composed a book in 100,000 *ślokas* and 1,080 chapters to serve as a basis and rule for human activity. Manu communicated this to Nārada, one of the ten Great *Ṛṣis* created by him, who, realising that

[5] *Vaiṣṇavism, Śaivism and Minor Religious Systems* (Strasburg, 1913), 148.

[6] This is the date adopted in the *Dh. k.*, p. xxx. According to Burnell, a Bhavasvāmin, author of a commentary on the *Baudhāyana-śrauta-sūtra*, lived in the eighth century (Kāṇe, I, 32).

[7] It is worth noting that the prose introduction to Asahāya's version is not present in that of Bhavasvāmin, nor II.1–44, III.1–18. On the other hand we do find there the chapter on theft, and that upon ordeals, which the editor thought were only résumés.

so vast a work could not be retained by mortal minds, made an abridgement in 12,000 *ślokas* and transmitted it to Mārkaṇḍeya, another *ṛṣi*. He, in turn, reflecting on the shortness of human life, reduced Nārada's abridgement to 8,000 *ślokas* and communicated them, so reduced in bulk, to Sumati, son of Bhṛgu. At last Sumati made a new abridgement in 4,000 *ślokas*. It was this highly condensed version by the son of Bhṛgu of the colossal work of Manu, which was brought to the knowledge of men, the gods alone being able to read the text of Manu in its original state. But one chapter of the first abridgement, which was devoted to the administration of justice, namely that of Nārada (the ninth), *had* been preserved and was transmitted to us in the *dharma-śāstra* that bears his name.

We have already seen that this legend of successive recensions of an original Code of Manu relied upon an ancient tradition, which was known to the author of the *Manu-smṛti* himself. However, very late sources, notably an inscription of Champā of the end of the twelfth century,[8] describe the *Nārada-smṛti* as the recension by Nārada *(Nāradīya-saṃhitā)*[9] of the Code of Manu, just as they represent the *Manu-smṛti* as the recension by Bhṛgu *(Bhārgavīya-saṃhitā)* of the same work. Nevertheless the fable which the legend contains itself betrays the seniority of the *Manu-smṛti* over the *Nārada-smṛti,* since it admits that prior to the "revelation" of the *Nārada-smṛti* the recension of Bhṛgu was the only one known to men.

A comparison of the contents of these two *smṛtis* fully confirms that Manu was the senior in age.

After the prose preface which we have just analysed, the *Nārada-smṛti* contains by way of introduction three chapters on the subjects of general procedure and judicial organisation. Then come the rules relating to control of litigation. Nārada[10] places them like Manu under 18 titles or heads which correspond, apart from slight modifications, to the 18 *mārgas* of Manu. Like Manu, Nārada deals with proof in connection with the first title, that which deals with recovery of debts, and, like him, gives in a kind of appendix a series of rules intended to complete the duties of the king in judicial contexts. So there is a remarkable correspondence between Nārada and the eighth and ninth Books of Manu in regard to the order of treatment. Apart from that, about fifty couplets are common to the two works, and in the numerous cases where the two authors express themselves in a different form their opinions are very close to each other in substance.

[8]L. Finot, *Notes d'épigraphie indochinoise* (Hanoi, 1916), 183.

[9]This is the name which the *Nārada-smṛti* bears in Bhavasvāmin's version (which has no prose introduction): *nāradiya-manu-saṃhitā*.

[10]When I speak of 'Manu', 'Yājñavalkya', 'Nārada', and so on, I mean, naturally, the author or compiler of the Codes attributed to Manu, Yājñavalkya, Nārada, etc.

But in the *Nārada-smṛti* the topics handled by Manu are classified or distinguished into more numerous, and sometimes even entirely new, categories. Thus the 18 titles of litigation are subdivided into 132 ramifications (*Int.*, I.20). Manu mentions only the two ordeals of fire and water (VIII.114–116); but Nārada enumerates five, describes them at length, and even adds two more (I.247–348). Manu distinguishes only seven kinds of slaves (VIII.415), but Nārada mentions fifteen, of which only the first four cannot be manumitted (V.26–29). Nārada classifies assets into three types, according to the manner in which they were acquired, and each of these types is subdivided into seven varieties (I.44–47). Similarly the problems to which gifts can give rise are set out under four heads which are themselves subdivided into thirty-two sections (IV.2–3). These new classifications and sub-classifications, unknown even to Yājñavalkya, show the importance accorded to the study of problems of a juridical character in the schools of *dharma*. This importance stands out from one fact alone, namely that Nārada has about a thousand verses, while the second Book of the *Yājñavalkya-smṛti,* which corresponds to him, has no more than 307.

On the other hand the rules of procedure, which often agree with those of Yājñavalkya, demonstrate an appreciable progress in the analysis of court-work. Those which concern framing of the plaint, methods of entering a defence, disqualified witnesses and such matters are set out with much more detail and contain a number of additional provisions.

Nārada is especially to be distinguished from the other *smṛtis* by his great concern for precision. Thus he gives a group of rules on juridical capacity and on the effect of documents executed by persons under an incapacity (I.26–42). The purchaser's exercise of his right "to resile" *(kraya-vikrayānuśaya),* that is, the freedom which is allowed him to rescind a sale, is limited and regulated (IX.1–7). Similarly hiring of labour and engaging of services are dealt with at length and give occasion for several new rules (VI).

Speaking of the *Nārada-smṛti* and emphasising its clarity, brevity and precision, A. Barth wrote in 1876, "If we except the monuments of Roman legislation, antiquity has not perhaps left us anything which is so strictly juridical. I imagine that a jurisconsult would immediately feel at home in running over these briefly formulated definitions and precepts, disposed, as they are, according to a simple and well-conceived plan".[11] Rodolphe Dareste, the legal historian, gave his own appreciation of our *smṛti* and actually asked in all seriousness whether Nārada "could not have had some acquaintance with Roman law . . . Why could he not have had before him some texts of Ulpian or of Paulus? His method of proceeding by definition and division recalls that of Gaius".[12] His

[11] *Works* (see above, p. 51, n. 32), III, 232.

[12] R. Dareste, *Etudes d'histoire du droit,* I (Paris, 1889), 99.

suggestion has little probability, but that it could have been proposed by a scholar of such standing testifies loudly to the scientific quality of the *Nārada-smṛti*. The frequent philosophical or moral speculations of Manu have entirely disappeared. It is very significant that Nārada deals exclusively with the juridical portion of the *dharmaśāstra*, the *vyavahāra*, and leaves to one side the religious portion, sacred custom and penance. It is true that several authors of the Middle Ages (Hemādri, Mādhava, and Devaṇṇa-bhaṭṭa) quote verses of Nārada which deal with *ācāra*, *śrāddhas* and *prāyaścittas*, which shows that at their times there used to exist works attributed to Nārada which dealt with the other aspects of *dharma*. But they had before them works quite distinct from our *smṛti*, for the text on which Bhavasvāmin and Asahāya commented—the only two commentators whose productions we have upon this *smṛti*—is devoted exclusively to *vyavahāra*.

So far as his content is concerned Nārada, like Manu, exalts the function of the king, created by the gods to maintain peace and social order. He places the accent on the personal power of the king whose will should encounter no obstacle. If, in general, he seldom strays from decisions laid down solemnly by Manu or Yājñavalkya, a number of his opinions stand out by reason of their innovative quality. This can be very striking, as when he permits five cases when a wife may remarry (XII.97), or when he limits or even abrogates the privilege of the eldest son as he declares that even a younger son can take over control of the family property if he is particularly fit to do this (XIII.5), or even when he allows unmarried daughters a share in succession to their fathers (XIII.50).

Such rules, and the general character of the work, led Jolly and Kāṇe to place its composition after the Codes of Manu and Yājñavalkya, perhaps about the sixth century of our era (as Jolly suggested) or between the second and the fourth as is the opinion of Kāṇe.

3. *Other Smṛtis*

The list of *dharma-śāstras* is far from coming to an end with the name of Nārada. Kāṇe (I^2, p. 304) estimates the number of these works known to writers of the Middle Ages at about a hundred. Some survive only in the form of abridgements, and the majority are known to us only from quotations which the authors of commentaries and digests preserve for us.

But we should make an exception of the *Parāśara-smṛti*, which bears the name of a celebrated *ṛṣi*, the author of several Vedic hymns and the father of Vyāsa, the traditional author of the *Mahābhārata*. The work is relatively short (592 verses); according to Kāṇe (I, p. 195) it must have been composed between the first and the fifth centuries and so could have been earlier than the *Nārada-smṛti*. It deals only with religious custom *(ācāra)* and penance *(prāyaścitta)*, but in the fourteenth century its commentator, Mādhava, completed it with a long digression on the subject of judicial administration, the basic text not providing any rules on that subject. A particularly notable verse of the text (I.24) says that in the four Ages of the world the four *dharmas* successively proclaimed by Manu, Gautama, Śaṅkha-Likhita and Parāśara were (or are) authoritative. Parāśara does indeed declare that he expounds rules of conduct valid in the Kali Age. But, as Kāṇe notices (III, p. 885), a considerable number of important institutions are sanctioned in the *smṛti* which are elsewhere prohibited as incompatible with the conditions of the Kali Age.

A number of *dharma-śāstras* have been quoted so abundantly by authors of commentaries and digests that it has been possible if not actually to reconstruct their text, at least to determine their characters and tendencies. Such is particularly the case with the two *smṛtis* attributed respectively to Bṛhaspati and Kātyāyana.

Bṛhaspati is, in the *Ṛgveda*, the name of a deity. He is the *purohita* of the other gods, with whom he intercedes in men's favour. He was thus perfectly qualified to be counted amongst the makers of codes of *dharma*. The *dharma-śāstra* which bears his name seems to have enjoyed a considerable authority amongst commentators, from the oldest to the most recent. Jolly gathered and classified 717 verses dealing with the administration of justice. Hẹ provided a translation of this collection immediately after his translation of the longer version of the *Nārada-smṛti*. K.V. Raṅgaswāmī Aiyaṅgār, took up this work later and gathered a total of 2,400 verses of Bṛhaspati cited by jurists. The most numerous relate to the administration of justice, but a not inconsiderable proportion (more than a third) deal with the sacraments *(saṃskāras)*, rites for the dead *(śrāddhas)* and penances *(prāyaścittas)*.[13] The original work thus embraces the three branches of *dharma* and seems in bulk at least to equal, if not surpass the Code of Manu.

Bṛhaspati follows the *Manu-smṛti* very closely. He considers it as the highest authority (*Bṛh., Aiy.*, saṃskāra, 13). He refers to it and quotes it often, and in many contexts he seems to be merely a commentator on Manu, whose terms he explains and whose precepts he develops. He throws new light on certain topics such as documentary evidence, which he deals with minutely, and the regulations or by-laws passed by members of certain local or professional bodies, the function of which he explains (XVII.5–24, taking the place of Manu's three verses, viz. VIII.219–221). At times he swerves from the decisions recommended

[13] *Bṛhaspati (Reconstructed)*, Gaekwad's Or. Ser., 85 (Baroda, 1941). The text should not be read without reference to the remarks of Renou in his 'Notes sur la Bṛhaspatismṛti', *Indo-Iranian Journal*, 6 (1962), 82–102 and *Etudes Védiques et Pāṇinéennes*, XI (Paris, 1963). And see Kāṇe, I², 491–5.

by Manu, especially in his favourable treatment of the rights of women in their father's or husband's property.

If it is hardly doubtful that Bṛhaspati is later than Manu, his position relative to Yājñavalkya and above all to Nārada is the subject of some discussion. Jolly and Kāṇe place him clearly after Yājñavalkya, but they see him as approximately contemporary with Nārada. Raṅgaswāmī Aiyaṅgār does not share their opinion but puts Bṛhaspati earlier than both Nārada and Yājñavalkya.

Kātyāyana, like Bṛhaspati, is frequently cited by both ancient and modern commentators. Fragments of his work, 973 verses concerning the administration of justice, were gathered and published with an English translation by Kāṇe in 1933. Later 121 more verses on the same subject were recovered by Raṅgaswāmī Aiyaṅgār in his edition of the *Vyavahāra-nirṇaya* of Varadarāja.[14]

Kātyāyana, like Bṛhaspati, is named at the beginning of the *Yājñavalkya-smṛti* amongst the Sages who had codified *dharma*. But the *smṛti* which we know from the jurists' citations is generally held to be well posterior to the Code of Yājñavalkya. According to Kāṇe, the author took Nārada and Bṛhaspati as his model. He completed their work and clarified some of their rules. He often refers to the opinion of Bhṛgu, by whom he means apparently Manu. The rules which he attributes to Bhṛgu are however not always to be traced in our *Manu-smṛti*, which discovery served as an argument for the theory of successive recensions of Manu. Kātyāyana deals in considerable detail with the personal property of women *(strī-dhana)*. In him we see the first *smṛti* author to have defined the various categories of such property carefully, to have fixed the woman's powers in respect of it, and to prescribe rules of devolution to be applied to those assets when their owner died.

We have a work attributed to Kātyāyana, the *Karma-pradīpa* ("The Lamp of *Karma*"), devoted to religious custom. One may well ask whether it is not by the author of the *Kātyāyana-smṛti*. If that really was the case there must have existed a vast work passing under the name of Kātyāyana and covering the whole domain of *dharma*. Jolly and Kāṇe are in agreement that the composition of his *smṛti* must be placed somewhat later than Bṛhaspati.

After Bṛhaspati and Kātyāyana the names most often cited are those of Vyāsa, whose *dharma-śāstra*, according to Kāṇe, was contemporary with those of Yājñavalkya and Bṛhaspati, and which, to judge by the citations, gave special attention to procedure and proof; Pitāmaha, who seems to have been an authority on ordeals; Yama; Śaṅkha (or Śaṅkha-Likhita) to whom is also attributed a *dharma-sūtra*; Saṃvarta;

[14]Varadarāja, *Vyavahāranirṇaya*, Adyar Library Ser. 29 (Adyar, 1942).

Hārīta; and Aṅgiras—to mention only those names which will recur in the later part of this book.

It sometimes happens that several *dharma-śāstras* are attributed to the same mythical personage. To distinguish amongst them their authors (or perhaps commentators) have qualified their names with the prefix *vṛddha* (old), *laghu* (small), *madhyama* (middle), *bṛhat* (long), and so on. Thus besides an unqualified "Manu", which means our *Manu-smṛti*, reference is made to a Vṛddha-Manu, or a Bṛhan-Manu, and likewise to a Vṛddha-Yājñavalkya, Bṛhat-Parāśara, Vṛddha-Kātyāyana, and so on. These names may refer to collections of verses omitted from the current versions, or perhaps abridgements, or even entirely independent compositions. These compilations could go back to a relatively ancient period, for Viśvarūpa, a commentator of the beginning of the ninth century, already knew the *Vṛddha-Manu* and the *Vṛddha-Yājñavalkya*. On the whole these texts, which are sometimes rather tendentiously called "spurious", tend to expand, qualify or correct the law laid down in the "genuine" *smṛtis* of which we have spoken at length above.[15]

The *dharma-śāstra* literature continued to be produced, according to Kāṇe, up to the ninth or even the tenth century, that is to say well up to the period in which the first commentaries appeared.[16] Medhātithi, the great commentator on Manu who is attributed to the ninth century, actually says (on *M.*, II.6) that in his day an author could compose a work having as much authority as the *Manu-smṛti*. But it seems that what he had in mind was a doctrinal work rather than a real *smṛti*, for he adds that such a work would have authority only for subsequent generations, after it had received the approbation of the sages and those who were fully trained in *dharma*. That seems to have happened with the *Smṛti-saṅgraha* and the *Caturviṃśati-mata*, which are unknown to commentators prior to the twelfth century. The first purports to be a compendium *(saṅgraha)* faithful to the views of the great writers; the second purports to embrace the substance of the teaching of no less than twenty-four Sages (Manu, Yājñavalkya, Atri, Viṣṇu, and so on) on religious usages and penances.

[15][trs.]

[16]This is also the view of A.S. Altekar, *Sources of Hindu Dharma* (Sholapur, 1952), 20.

CHAPTER VI

THE COMMENTARIES AND THE DIGESTS

IT IS generally agreed that the literature of the commentaries and independent treatises followed immediately after that of the *dharma-śāstras*. There was no loss of continuity, and the last *smṛtis* could well have appeared long after the first commentaries had become available. This concomitance of the two types of literature, and *a fortiori* their overlapping, has a certain improbable element about it. One has only to look at the status attributed to the *dharma-śāstras* by the time of the commentators. In that period the human origin of those works had indeed been completely obliterated. It was an article of faith that the precepts which they contained derived from Sages of the remotest antiquity, and their authority was accordingly beyond dispute. They appeared as if they were scripture, timeless, eternal; the whole of them, along with the epics and the *purāṇas*, brought to men the voice of a tradition which was both holy and in conformity with the order of nature. The commentators and authors of juridical treatises could not imagine their role as anything other than that of *interpreters*, concerned only to explain the meaning of texts whose authenticity and religious importance they did not doubt for one moment. So it seems more probable that a long interval elapsed between the publication of the last works appertaining to the *smṛti* category and the appearance of the first commentaries. Yet at the same time the date of composition of the *dharma-śāstras* which are regarded as "late" and that of the most ancient commentaries which survive are equally impossible to determine with any exactitude. I am on the whole inclined to think that after a period of silence, perhaps between the sixth and the ninth centuries, a veritable renaissance of *dharma*-literature occurred. Its products began to build up from then onwards without interruption until well into the nineteenth century.

This new class of literature includes two main kinds of works: the commentaries and the treatises. The commentaries (*bhāṣya, vṛtti, vyākhyā, vivaraṇa*, etc.) were devoted to one particular *smṛti* and were intended to explain its text. As is natural enough, these came first. By contrast the treatises *(nibandhas)*, a form preferred by jurists from the twelfth century onwards, attempt to embrace the whole of the *smṛti* literature or one of its branches; to this end they group under certain rubrics extracts from different *smṛtis* relating to the same topic, but linking them together with more or less evolved commentaries such as this arrangement of texts evokes. Because of the analogy presented with Justinian's *Digest*, the British—perhaps Colebrooke was the first to do this—gave the treatises the name of "digests".[1] There is not really a clear line of demarcation between the two different types of work. The commentators are usually not content to explain simply the text of one *smṛti*. They quote corresponding passages from other *smṛtis*. They indicate how far the texts agree, and they try to reconcile them if necessary. The result is that some commentaries seem almost like real digests. This is notably the case with the *Mitākṣarā*, or the *Parāśara-mādhavīya*. These, though they purport to be commentaries, the one on the *Yājñavalkya-smṛti* and the other on the *Parāśara-smṛti*, are in reality sizeable compilations, making substantial use of a range of works outside the text upon which a commentary is being made.

The first interest to be derived from a study of the commentaries and the digests is that they enable us to be better acquainted with *smṛti* literature. A number of *dharma-śāstras* which were accessible in the Middle Ages have disappeared by now and are known only by the quotations to be found in these writings. Sometimes the quotations are so abundant that there has been little difficulty in gathering them and either reconstituting the orignal work or, at the very least, forming a general impression of its contents. That has been the case with the *smṛtis* of Bṛhaspati and Kātyāyana. Even when these quotations were originally taken from an author whose work we do possess, they are still useful since they can offer significant variant readings. These variants must have come from different versions which were once every bit as authentic as those which have survived, but which have since been lost. Not the least valuable profit to be obtained from the study of commentaries and digests is that one is put on one's guard against assuming (as would otherwise be natural) that any particular versions of the *smṛtis* are "original" or "primitive". In reality the text only ceased to be subject to variants and interpolations when literature intended to interpret it began to circulate. In this very sense one could say that the "composition" of the *smṛtis* was prolonged until the age of the commentaries.

But if these works really continued or took up anew the work of the *dharma-śāstras*, their character is profoundly different. During the period when they were made the literature deriving from *smṛti* was at an end. The different sources of *dharma* had dried up, with the exception of *sadācāra* which, at a late date, appeared once again in certain writers but with a new meaning. Thus the task was to use existing written sources and to draw from them conclusions about the rule to be followed.

[1]In the preface to his translation of Jagannātha Tarkapañcānana's digest (1797). The word is already to be found in a letter of Sir William Jones to the Supreme Council of Bengal in 1788, a portion of which is cited in that preface.

This was indeed a considerable task in view of the mass of texts which might be consulted and the inevitable divergencies, let alone contradictions, which their comparison would bring to light and which would then have to be resolved.

The need for unification and simplification which drove the jurisconsults of the Late Roman Empire and Byzantium to compile codes and to proffer selected extracts from the classical jurists made itself felt in India once the *śāstras* had been consecrated as an inspired literature. As long as India lived subject to its own traditions that need did not cease to be felt. But there was a big difference from the situation in the Roman Empire. What we have in India is a new flowering of writing, as considerable, perhaps even more considerable in bulk than the anterior literature upon which it was founded. True, our writers brew the same old texts over, again and again. They repeat them, and themselves, and they copy from each other. Yet they were none the less achieving a work of simplification and synthesis. First of all the great number of their sources and the variety of topics with which they dealt caused them to multiply the divisions within the realm of *dharma,* each of these divisions or subdivisions giving rise to a treatise or a chapter. Instead of the simple tripartite division of the *Yājñavalkya-smṛti* into *ācāra, vyavahāra,* and *prāyaścitta,* we find in the *Kalpataru,* one of the most ancient digests which we possess (twelfth cent.), the rules of the sacred books spread under *fourteen kāṇḍas* or sections, wherein texts are collected successively concerning the duties of the *brahmacārin,* those of the householder, daily observances, offerings to the *manes,* donations, the ritual for the consecration of idols, the rituals of worship, pilgrimages, etc. Sometimes *vyavahāra* is subdivided into *vyavahāra* properly so called, treating of the composition of courts of justice and procedure, and *vivāda,* dealing with the 18 titles of litigation. Certain works or portions of works collect the rules relating to adoption, or partition of inheritances, to the duties peculiar to the Śūdras, etc. As a result, precepts scattered in innumerable sources are found methodically classified. This classification, which presupposes a considerable spoliation or stripping down of the texts, is proof enough by itself of a powerful effort at synthesis. At the same time it reveals all the amplitude and diversity of the domain of *dharma* itself.

But the authors generally do not stop there. They also comment upon their texts, explaining terms where passages are obscure and clarifying them with examples. They are not content to bring them together. They try to harmonise them, to disengage from them a coherent system of rules. When their precepts disagree they must try to justify one way out of the conflict. Either they must show that the discord is only apparent, or they must prove that one solution is superior to another. By this work of interpretation, the commentaries and the digests appear to have been the sequel and goal of the *smṛtis* of which they provide the gist. However, this new contribution to the teaching of *dharma* no longer has the character and value of the rules which the *śāstras* themselves contain. In the place of books held to be inspired we are handling human compositions whose origins are not wrapped in any mystery. The names of the commentators and authors of treatises are known to us, and, what is more, in the majority of cases, the period and the milieu in which they lived are also known, if not some details of their lives as well. Many of them were ministers or councillors of kings or princes well known to history. Further, their way of approaching problems, and even the solutions which they recommend, could not have had the authority of the precepts laid down in the *smṛti*. They are no more than personal opinions, whose value is no higher than their power to convince other people. Moreover, commentators and digest-writers had no hesitation in criticising the views of their predecessors or contemporaries, and such discussions and criticisms take up at times a considerable amount of room in their writings. Thus although the whole of the precepts on which their interpretation rests is immutably fixed, it is by its very nature diverse and variable. It reflects the evolution of ideas and manners. It is a living and a direct source of law.

Some commentaries or treatises have acquired in matters of juridical importance so great an authority that they have ended up by casting the *dharma-śāstras* quite into the shade. It is a fact that when the British took in hand the administration of justice in India it was not the Code of Manu which was cited before their judges, nor even the *smṛti* of Yājñavalkya or that of Nārada, but this or that work which had been accepted by the parties subject to the jurisdiction as the correct expression of the law applicable to them. Thus it is hardly surprising that the commentaries and treatises were known to Europe before the great works which were actually their basis, with the sole exception of the Code of Manu which the enthusiasm of Sir William Jones introduced to Europe from 1794 onwards. Three years later Colebrooke produced his translation of a premier digest, which had been written, however, on the instructions of Jones himself. Later a whole series of translations of juridical works was to appear, and naturally these were the commentaries or treatises chosen first on account of their practical value. British judges had an urgent need of these translations in order to be less dependent upon their native assistants. It was only after these translations had answered the calls, above all, of simple utility, that the first translations of the *dharma-sūtras* and *dharma-śāstras* appeared, whose interest was entirely intellectual. The commentaries and treatises or at least some examples of those classes have thus assumed in British India a legal character, and the Anglo-Indian courts, and their successors in independent India, have referred to them constantly.

The intervention of British methods of administration undoubtedly resulted in increasing the authority which these sorts of work could enjoy, beyond, indeed, what could have been done by the patronage of princes or Hindus of high prestige. But, leaving aside for the present the role of interpretation in the adaptation of the rules of the *śāstras* to social reality, i.e. to law, it is equally beyond doubt that the appearance of this kind of literature soon began to impede access to the original texts themselves. They were concise, and they were archaic: by the Middle Ages many passages of *smṛti* were unintelligible without commentary. We can be sure that the bare text seldom circulated. On the other hand the digests offered the advantages of methodical classification of the *smṛtis*. Infinitely more commodious to handle, for they amounted to a complete library; easier to understand; and more useful since they tried to reduce divergencies between the source materials, it seems natural enough that they should have ended up by being substituted for those sources. In Further India where the name of Manu honours the first juridical compilations, we can be sure that it was not the real text of the *Manu-smṛti* which was used for the purpose, but some treatise in vogue amongst the Indian colonists, or some version strictly associated with one or more commentaries.[2] In modern India compendia of quite localised usage often take the places, in certain ritual contexts appertaining to *ācāra*, of the great treatises themselves, which remain unknown to the public. This shows us the importance of the role which the commentaries and treatises have had to play at all times during the passage of the rule of *dharma* into law-in-action.

The abundance as well as the frequent high quality of this literature demonstrates the interest which the Hindus have evinced in the science of *dharma* throughout their long history. It has been of dimensions of which one could not have dreamed unless one had passed all the surviving specimens in review. We are virtually forced to limit ourselves here to pointing out some of the more celebrated works or those which are most helpful for our present purpose. The bulky first volume of Kāṇe's *History of Dharmaśāstra* presents a more complete picture.

1. *The Commentaries*

Of all the *dharma-śāstras* it seems that the *Mānava-dharma-śāstra* is the one upon which commentaries have been most frequently written. The oldest commentary on Manu to reach us is that of Bhāruci. Except

[2]F.H. Van Naerssen has showed that the author of a work in Old Javanese of the Majapahit period, the *Aṣṭadaśavyavahāra*, had before him and incorporated into his commentary certain Sanskrit commentaries on the *Manu-smṛti*, amongst which it seems possible to recognise the *Manvarthavivṛtti* of Nārāyaṇa. 'The Aṣṭadaśavyavahāra in Old Javanese', translated from Dutch in the *Journal of the Greater India Society* 15 (1956), 111ff.

in a few places it is not an extensive commentary. It was possibly a South Indian production and betrays a knowledge of an *arthaśāstra* text little if at all removed from the Kauṭilīya *Arthaśāstra*. It was amongst the sources used by Medhātithi.[2a]

Medhātithi is placed in the ninth century or at the latest at the beginning of the tenth.[3] One knows nothing about him save that he lived in Kashmir. The text of Manu which is commented upon in his very voluminous *Bhāṣya* is close to that with which other sources provide us, suggesting that the Code of Manu was already in a nearly fixed state. Medhātithi cites numerous *smṛtis,* and earlier commentators whose names he seldom specifies. Bühler pays homage to his erudition and to his skill in construing difficult passages. He praises the clarity of his eludication of the text, and he objects only to what appears to him to be an excessive veneration for the opinions of his predecessors. The *Bhāṣya* of Medhātithi was translated in its entirety, albeit somewhat hastily, by Gaṅgānātha Jhā.

There are no less than five other commentaries on Manu, amongst which the most extensive is the *Manvartha-muktāvali* of Kullūka, which provided the greatest assistance when the first English and French translations of Manu were made. The author wrote at Benares and lived probably in the fifteenth century according to Bühler (Kāṇe's opinion, which is much more probable, places him before the fourteenth century and assigns his *floruit* to c. 1250). His commentary is rather long, but it is never prolix, always clear and precise. Though he prides himself on the superiority of his knowledge to that of his predecessors, he lacks originality. He is often content to plagiarise without acknowledgement older works such as Medhātithi's *Bhāṣya* and the *ṭikā* of Govindarāja which, according to Kāṇe, was composed in the second half of the eleventh century. Three other commentaries upon Manu which deserve mention are those of Nārāyaṇa, whose work belongs to between 1100 and 1300, Rāghavānanda who belongs to the fifteenth century at the earliest, and Nandana, who appears to have been even later.[4] Rāghavānanda was a favourite author in Bengal, and Nandana seems to have been a southerner.[4a]

After Manu the *smṛti* most frequently commented upon is that of Yājñavalkya. The oldest of his commentators, Viśvarūpa, wrote the

[2a][trs.]

[3]Kāṇe (I², 583) places him between 825 and 900. Medhātithi (on *M.*, II.22) alludes to successive invasions of Mlecchas who failed to find an enduring footing in Āryan territory. It is not improbable that he refers to Muslim incursions. If he does we may well conclude that Medhātithi wrote his *bhāṣya* prior to the conquest of the Punjab by Mahmud of Ghazni (998–1030).

[4]In V.N. Mandlik's edition Manu's text appears with six commentaries.

[4a][trs.]

Bālakrīḍā (Child's Play), a work belonging to the beginning of the ninth century according to Kāṇe and thus a contemporary of Medhātithi if not even earlier.[5] The portion corresponding to the second Book of Yājñavalkya is really poor, but the developments which emerge in the course of the other two Books run to a considerable length.

The commentator *par excellence* on Yājñavalkya is a *yogin,* Vijñāneśvara, who lived at the end of the eleventh century in the reign of Vikramāditya VI of the Cālukya dynasty of Kalyāni (in the former Nizam's Dominions, now Mahārāshtra), one of the great emperors of the Deccan (1076–1127). Though his commentary, the *Ṛjumitākṣarā,* more commonly known as the *Mitākṣarā* ("measured in its syllables"), purports to be an abridgement of Viśvarūpa's commentary, it is a large work, using a crowd of texts coming from various *smṛtis* and taking into account the opinions of numerous earlier glosses. Though it has the form of a commentary it is a veritable treatise on *dharma* in which the author discusses and criticises the views of his predecessors and utilises with ease all the resources of a subtle dialectic. His merits early secured him a wide distribution and an eminent place in the literature of interpretation of *smṛti.* Under the influence of the Anglo-Indian courts it obtained in certain contexts, especially those related to the law of inheritance, the status of a legislative text throughout the Indian subcontinent, except for Bengal and Assam, where the *Dāyabhāga* prevailed. In 1810 the portion which deals with succession and the joint family was translated by Colebrooke[6] and that which deals with procedure was translated by W. Macnaghten in 1829. Today we have a complete translation from the pen of J.R. Ghārpure.

The *Mitākṣarā* was commented upon in its turn by Viśveśvara (the *Subodhinī*) in the second half of the fourteenth century, by Nanda-paṇḍita (in the *Pramitākṣarā*) who is also to be found as a commentator on the *Viṣṇu-smṛti* and an author of a treatise, and, at the end of the eighteenth century and beginning of the nineteenth century by Bālambhaṭṭa (in the *Bālambhaṭṭī*) who was one of the paṇḍits of Colebrooke.

Apart from the *Mitākṣarā* we have three other commentaries on the *Yājñavalkya-smṛti.* One is attributed to Aparārka, king of the Koṅkaṇ and a subject of the Cālukyas, who reigned at the beginning of the twelfth century (1110–1140). Like the *Mitākṣarā,* it is a veritable digest. It is more voluminous and richer in citations of every kind of source (there are very many extracts from *purāṇas* as well as *dharma-sūtras*), but the author's argumentation is more sober.

[5] Viśvarūpa is certainly later than Kumārila, but it is difficult to decide his *terminus ante quem.* Kāṇe, I, 261–3.

[6] This translation was translated, in its turn, into French by G. Orianne, puisne justice at the royal court of Pondicherry, in 1844.

The second commentary, the *Dīpakalikā*, which is a contrast by its brevity, was written by Śūlapāṇi, and the third, the *Vīramitrodaya*, by Mitra-miśra. These two authors will reappear later in our story.[7]

Nārada was commented upon very early, since his earliest known commentator, Asahāya ("the incomparable"), is cited by Viśvarūpa and Medhātithi. But his *bhāṣya* has come down to us only in a reworked and incomplete form.[8] He commented also upon Gautama and Manu. Kāṇe places him between the sixth and the seventh century, a period which is perhaps a little remote for him (Jolly proposes about the eighth century). We noted above the commentary of Bhavasvāmin which was published in 1929.

The *Viṣṇu-smṛti* was commented upon by Nanda-paṇḍita, the prolific author who commented also upon the *Mitākṣarā* and the *Parāśara-smṛti*, and wrote the *Dattaka-mimāṃsā*, and more works on law, philosophy and even poetry. His commentary on the *Viṣṇu-smṛti*, the *Vaijayantī*,[9] was composed in Benares in 1622 at the request of King Keśava-nāyaka of Mathurā. It is a work of great merit, abounding in citations and interesting digressions.[10]

The *Parāśara-smṛti* was made the object of a voluminous commentary called the *Parāśara-mādhavīya*, by Mādhava, called Vidyāraṇya ("Forest of Learning"), an allusion to his status as *saṃnyāsin* at the end of his life. The writer was celebrated above all for his philosophical works, being the *guru* and minister *(mantrin)* of King Bukka, who ruled at Vijayanagara in the middle of the fourteenth century. His commentary covers about 2,300 pages of the edition printed at Bombay. It is a veritable encyclopedia of *dharma*, according to Jolly. In fact Mādhava completed the *smṛti* of Parāśara by interpolating into his commentary a digression which deals with *vyavahāra* and which occupies more than quarter of the volume. This digression is called *Vyavahāra-mādhava*. The portion devoted to succession was translated into English by Burnell in 1868.

The *dharma-sūtras* too had their commentators. Haradatta, from South India, who (according to Kāṇe) lived between 1100 and 1300, wrote the *Ujjvalā-vṛtti*, a commentary on the *dharma-sūtra* of Āpastamba, and the *Mitākṣarā*, a commentary on the *dharma-sūtra* of Gautama. Bühler has a high opinion of his knowledge, and refers to him constantly. Maskarin, whose date is even more uncertain,[11] commented upon

[7]Extracts from these three commentaries are given by Ghārpure in his translation of the *Mitākṣarā*.

[8]Extracts are provided by Jolly, in his translation of the *Nārada-smṛti*.

[9]The name of Indra's banner.

[10]Extracts are given by Jolly in his translation of the *Viṣṇu-smṛti*, but the whole text is now available in a luxury edition from the Adyar Library (1964).

[11]Kāṇe places him after Haradatta, though some suppose him to have lived in the eighth century. See p. 273 below. [trs.]

Gautama, and Govindasvāmin, certainly a late author, wrote a commentary on the *dharma-sūtra* of Baudhāyana.

2. *The Digests*

Even though commentaries continued to be written until a very late period, indeed right up to our own times,[12] the general tendency from the twelfth century onwards is to compose treatises or digests.

One of the most ancient which we possess is the *Kṛtyakalpataru* (or *Kalpataru*),[13] composed by Lakṣmīdhara, chief minister *(mahā-sāndhi-vigrahika)* of Govindachandra, king of Kanauj (1104–1154), in the first part of the twelfth century, half a century prior to the Muslim invasion, about the same period as Aparārka. This is a large work (it is exceeded only by the *Vīramitrodaya* in point of size), including about 30,000 *ślokas*. It is roughly a third of the size of the *Mahābhārata,* though it is hard to compare exactly a verse work with one in mixed verse and prose as is Lakṣmīdhara's. No digest gathers so rich a collection nor arranges texts so logically. He has gathered texts from *śruti* as well as *smṛti,* and in the latter must be included the epics and *purāṇas*. He usually limits himself to arranging the citations, grouped methodically under fourteen *kāṇḍas,* adding only a very brief commentary. His influence was great up to the sixteenth century : many later writers borrowed extensively from him.

The *Smṛticandrikā*[14] of Devaṇṇa-bhaṭṭa, composed about 1200, is an equally important work which has enjoyed high esteem not only in the South of India, whence its author originated, but also in the North. It has three divisions *(kāṇḍas)* : *āhnika, vyavahāra,* and *śrāddha*. It has very numerous citations (especially abundantly from Kātyāyana and Bṛhaspati). But the author is not content with merely quoting them. He quotes and criticises the views of other interpreters and expresses his own point of view. A Tamil summary, the *Vyavahāra-saṅgraha,* composed about 1830, was translated into French by Sicé.[14a]

Hemādri, minister and chancellor *(śrīkaraṇādhipa)* of King Mahādeva, one of the last of the Yādava dynasty, who ruled at Devagiri (Daulatābād) from 1260 to 1273, wrote the *Caturvargacintāmaṇi* (The Philosophers' Stone for the Four Classes), a gigantic work dealing above all with rituals and religious observances, but occasionally also with matters connected with *vyavahāra*. The four volumes published in the Bibliotheca Indica amount to 6,000 pages.

[12]Kṛṣṇa-paṇḍita wrote, in the last quarter of the nineteenth century, a commentary on Vasiṣṭha's *dharma-sūtra* which was available to Bühler.

[13]*Kalpataru, kalpavṛkṣa,* or *kalpadruma* means 'wishing-tree', 'tree of abundance' (i.e. repertory, florilegium), the title of several works.

[14]*Candrikā*, 'moonlight' (i.e. illumination), figures in the title of numerous works.

[14a]*Abrégé substantiel du droit* (Pondicherry, 1857).

From the thirteenth to the fifteenth century juridical literature blossomed in Mithilā (modern Tirhut), in the East on the borders of India and Nepal, to such an extent that the authors came to form a special school. Thanks to its geographical position, Mithilā could escape the worst of the ravages of the Muslim invasions.[15]

In the first quarter of the fourteenth century, Caṇḍeśvara, prime minister of the king of Mithilā, Harasiṃha-deva, composed a digest in seven parts or "treasure-mines" *(ratnākaras)*. One of these parts, the *Vivāda-ratnākara,* contains a detailed exposition of the 18 titles of litigation, accompanied by a great number of citations. In 1324 Harasiṃha-deva, vanquished by the Muslim armies, retired to Nepal. At the request of his successor, King Bhaveśa (or Bhaveśvara), a feudatory of the Sultan of Delhi, Caṇḍeśvara wrote the *Rāja-nīti-ratnākara,* which deals with the functions of the king.[16] The most celebrated representative of this Mithilā school is Vācaspati-miśra, who was a minister or councillor of Kings Bhairavendra and Rāmabhadra of the Kāmeśvara dynasty, and who lived in the second half of the fifteenth century. A prolific author, he has left especially a series of works called *cintāmaṇis,* of which the *Vivāda-cintāmaṇi,* which deals with the 18 heads of litigation, and the *Vyavahāra-cintāmaṇi,* which deals with procedure, are well known. The same author wrote various treatises called *nirṇaya* (solution), such as his *Dvaita-nirṇaya* on controversial points of *dharma* (composed at the command of Queen Jayā, spouse of King Bhairavendra), *Mahādāna-nirṇaya* (on gifts), and *Suddhi-nirṇaya* (on purification).[17] This class of work, which was in fashion from the fifteenth century, presents rules which are apparently in conflict with each other and attempts to reconcile them. We need only mention the *Vyavahāra-nirṇaya* of Varadarāja, which is a minor digest, the succession chapter of which was translated in 1872 by Burnell.

A king of Orissa of the Gajapati dynasty, Pratāparudra-deva, who reigned at Kaṭaka-nagarī (Cuttack) (1497–1539) had the *Sarasvatī-vilāsa*[18] composed, probably in the first quarter of the sixteenth century, by a group of paṇḍits. This treatise was intended to embrace all *dharma.* He declares at the outset of the work that he wished by means of this composition to spare all future interpreters the pain of obtaining an agreement from the commentators, and to render superfluous the works

[15] M. Chakravarti, 'Contributions to the History of Smṛti in Bengal and Mithilā, Part II, Mithilā', *J.A.S.B.*, 1915, 377–406.

[16] On the author's bibliography see K.P. Jayaswal's Introduction to his edition of the *Rājanītiratnākara* (Patna, 1924).

[17] On the life and works of Vācaspati Miśra see the Introduction by L. Rocher to his edition of the *Vyavahāracintāmaṇi.*

[18] 'Possessing the charm (or grace) of Sarasvatī (goddess of eloquence and learning)', a not uncommon title.

of predecessors from that time onwards. The work is divided into several *kāṇḍas*, of which the *Vyavahāra-kāṇḍa* is the most important, and indeed the only one of which any knowledge is generally available.

Nanda-paṇḍita, who lived at Benares at the end of the sixteenth century or at the beginning of the seventeenth, was the author of numerous works on *dharma*, some composed at the request of reigning princes or important persons. We have already mentioned his commentary on the *Viṣṇu-smṛti*, written at the request of a prince of Karṇātaka. He also commented on the *Parāśara-smṛti* and the *Mitākṣarā*. He got together a digest called the *Smṛti-sindhu*, at the request of King Harivaṃsa-varman and the Māhendra dynasty. His most celebrated work is the *Dattaka-mīmāṃsā*, a treatise on adoption which was soon adopted by the British authorities as if it were a classical work on the subject, along with the *Dattaka-candrikā*,[19] a work of authority in practice and purporting to be by one Kubera-bhaṭṭa. Both treatises were translated by Sutherland in 1821.

Another Benares writer was Kamalākara-bhaṭṭa, a contemporary of Nanda-paṇḍita. He belonged to a family of jurists likewise hailing from the Deccan. His father Rāmakṛṣṇa wrote a digest. His uncle Śaṅkara-bhaṭṭa is the author of the *Dharma-dvaita-nirṇaya*. He himself composed numerous works. The most important are the following: (1) the *Nirṇaya-sindhu*, written in 1612, devoted mainly to ceremonies of a religious character; he mentions, according to Mandlik, thirteen works of *śruti*, 131 *smṛtis*, 68 *purāṇas* and 272 *nibandhas*, *ṭīkās* and commentaries; (2) the *Śūdra-kamalākara*, a treatise on the duties and religious obligations incumbent on the Śūdras; and lastly (3) the *Vivāda-tāṇḍava*, devoted to procedure and to rules of a juridical character, analogous to the *Vyavahāra-mayūkha* of his cousin Nīlakaṇṭha, though somewhat less extensive.

Born at Benares to the same illustrious family of jurists coming from the Deccan, the cousin and rival of Kamalākara, Nīlakaṇṭha wrote the *Bhagavanta-bhāskara* in the first half of the seventeenth century at the request of a Rajput prince, Bhagavanta-deva, who reigned at Bhareha (Baicho) at the confluence of the rivers Chambal and Jumna.[20] It is a real thesaurus of *dharma* (97 *smṛtis* are quoted), divided into twelve *mayūkhas* ("rays"). Its author, writes Kāṇe, remains unequalled amongst all commentators for his perfect knowledge of the vast *smṛti*-literature, for the brevity of his exposition, the conciseness and smoothness

[19]This work, which was at first attributed to Devaṇṇa-bhaṭṭa, was suspected of being a forgery made in Colebrooke's circle. Alternatively it has been attributed to a writer of the 16th century. Derrett, *Religion, Law and the State in India*, 255–6.

[20]For Nīlakaṇṭha see the Introduction to Kāṇe's edition of the *Vyavahāramayūkha* (Poona, 1926).

of his style, the clarity of his views and the sobriety of his judgments. The part of the work which is best known is the *Vyavahāra-mayūkha*, which was translated into English by Borradaile in 1827 and later by other scholars including Kāṇe himself. We can only mention among the other portions his *Nīti-mayūkha,* the *Prāyaścitta-mayūkha,* and the *Pratiṣṭhā-mayūkha,*

Even more voluminous than the *Bhagavanta-bhāskara* is a work of the same epoch (the first half of the seventeenth century), the *Vīramitrodaya,* itself a vast treatise covering the whole domain of *dharma.* Its author was Mitra-miśra, who belonged to a family originating from Gwalior. He wrote the work at the request of Vīrasiṃha (Vīr Singh), a king who reigned at Orccha (Bundelkhand) from 1605 to 1627 and who, at the instigation of the future emperor Jahangir, caused the assassination in 1602 of Abul-Fazl, the friend of the emperor Akbar and his historian.[21] The work is divided into *prakāśas.* The *Vyavahāra-prakāśa* is probably the most extended treatise on that subject. It has four chapters, the first relating to the composition of courts and the rules of procedure, the second to the different modes of proof, the third to the 18 titles of litigation and the last, which is very short, dealing with the matters which the king may take up *ex officio.* The author frequently discusses the opinions of his predecessors and flatters himself that his work will render a reference to other *nibandhas* superfluous. Mitra-miśra also wrote a commentary on the *Yājñavalkya-smṛti,* and that too bears the name of *Vīramitrodaya.*

Viśveśvara-bhaṭṭa, an author already mentioned as the writer of a commentary on the *Mitākṣarā,* was originally from the South of India. He migrated to the North and wrote several works under the patronage of King Madanapāla, a vassal of the Sultan of Delhi, who reigned at Kāṣṭhā (Kāṭha) on the Jumna, to the North of Delhi, in the second half of the fourteenth century. The most important of these works is the *Madana-pārijāta* which deals with all the matters comprised within *dharmaśāstra,* with the somewhat unfortunate exception of *vyavahāra,* which is represented only by its chapter on succession. The fact that this chapter was chosen for treatment, and thus given some sort of priority, throws light on the relative importance of succession as a topic at the period. We may also mention the same author's *Smṛti-kaumudī* which is devoted to the legal status of the Śūdras.

With Jīmūtavāhana, the author of the *Dharmaratna,* there appeared one of the most celebrated jurists of India. His period is not quite certain. Jolly and Rājkumār Sarvādhikārī place him in the fifteenth century,

[21]The work's title plays on the words Vīra and Mitra and can be translated either 'the brilliance (literally, dawn) of the gods Vīra and Mitra', or 'the brilliance of the friend of Vīra (*sc.* the king)'.

which appears to be too late. Kāṇe, for excellent reasons, chooses between 1090 and 1130.[22] All that we know for certain about him is that he belonged to a family of Brahmins of Bengal. The *Dharmaratna* survives in only three parts, one of which, known by the name of *Dāyabhāga,* relates to the management and partition of family property and its descent on the death of the ancestor; a second, called *Vyavahāra-mātṛkā,* deals with judicial organisation and procedure; and the third, *Kāla-viveka,* deals with the fixing of times suitable for performing ritual acts and religious duties. The *Dāyabhāga* is the most celebrated of the three. The rights of inheritance and the powers of the head of the family as described by him are based on doctrines fundamentally different from those presented in the *Mitākṣarā.* The differences are reflected in Anglo-Hindu law by the coexistence of two great "schools" that of the *Dāyabhāga* and that of the *Mitākṣarā,* the one an authority in Bengal and Assam, and the other in the remainder of India.[23] The *Dāyabhāga* has been commented upon by more than a dozen authors, amongst whom Raghunandana (below) is prominent. A more recent commentary, the *Dāya-krama-saṅgraha* of Śrī Kṛṣṇa Tarkālaṅkāra, was translated into English by P.M. Wynch in 1818 and into French later by G. Orianne.

After Jīmūtavāhana, the most famous member of the Bengal school is Raghunandana, called Smārta-bhaṭṭācārya (Preceptor of the Scholars in Smṛti), but a predecessor of his is still consulted, namely Śūlapāṇi, the author of a commentary on the *Yājñavalkya-smṛti* which we have already referred to. Kāṇe places him between 1375 and 1460.[24] His commentary is brief but throws light on Bengal opinions of the period. He wrote a series of little treatises intended to form, when collected, a large digest bearing the name *Smṛti-viveka.* Fourteen of these sections have reached us. The best known is the *Śrāddha-viveka,* which has been commented upon several times and is consulted for opinions outside the scope of its nominal subject-matter, *śrāddhas.*

Raghunandana is certainly the most famous disciple of Jīmūtavāhana. Perhaps he was the greatest of the jurists of Bengal. Apart from his commentary on the *Dāyabhāga* which we have already mentioned he wrote a treatise named *Smṛti-tattva* (The Fact, or Truth, about Smṛti), divided into twenty-eight sections all called *tattvas.* This is a work of great erudition on the different branches of *dharmaśāstra,* in which he cites not less than 89 authors. The *Dāya-tattva* which deals with inheritance and partition is the best known, having been translated by the

[22]For a discussion of dates proposed for him see M. Chakravarti, cited above, p. 116, n. 15, 'Part I. Bengal'. *J.A.S.B.* 321–7. This writer would place Jīmūtavāhana at the beginning of the twelfth century.

[23]See above, pp. 98, 110, 113, and below, p. 177.

[24]For Śulapāṇi see Chakravarti, cited above, p. 116, n. 15, at pp. 336–343.

celebrated Hindu practitioner and jurist, G.C. Sarkar Śāstrī. The *Śuddhi-tattva* contains, incidentally, one of the fullest Sanskrit authoritative sources on the practice of suttee *(satī)*. Raghunandana seems to have lived in the first half of the sixteenth century.[25]

From the beginning of the same century or the end of the previous one, we possess the *Nṛsiṃha-prasāda*, a vast work divided into twelve *sāras* (Wholes) which cover all the realm of *dharma*. Its author, Dalapati (which could conceivably be a title, "general"), was minister and archivist of a king called Nijāmasāha who ruled at Devagiri (Daulatābād) and whom he praises at the beginning of the *Saṃskāra-sāra*. This Nijāmasāha is no other than the founder of the Muslim dynasty of Ahmednagar, Ahmed Nizam Shah, who ruled from 1490 to 1508.

A work of a similar type is attributed to Ṭoḍar Mal (Rāja Ṭoḍara-malla), the famous general and finance minister of the Emperor Akbar. It is entitled *Ṭoḍarānanda* (The Joy of Ṭoḍar) and is divided into several *saukhyas* (Delights). The *Vyavahāra-saukhya* does *not* deal with the 18 titles of litigation, which are merely enumerated, but with the duties of the king as judge, with procedure and the organisation of the courts. The other *saukhyas* deal with times propitious for marriage, gifts, *śrāddhas*, astronomy, etc. Ṭoḍar Mal died in 1589.

In the seventeenth century Ananta-deva, the descendant of a Mahratta holy man, composed the *Smṛti-kaustubha* at the request of Bāz Bahādur Candra, king of Kumaon, a vassal of Delhi, who reigned over Almora and Nainital from 1638 to 1678, in the time of Aurangzeb. It is a lengthy work, divided into *kaustubhas*,[26] subdivided in turn into *dīdhitis* (rays). In this digest he used five *śruti* works, 104 *smṛtis*, 28 *purāṇas*, and 92 commentaries or *nibandhas*. The *Saṃskāra-kaustubha* is the most popular. The section relating to adoption, the *Dattaka-dīdhiti*, forms an important treatise on the subject. The *Rājadharma-kaustubha* is especially interesting for its rules on succession to the throne and for its description of coronation ceremonies.

Mention should be made too of the *Smṛti-muktāphala* of Vaidyanātha Dīkṣita, a work composed in South India. Though not devoted directly to *vyavahāra* it contains information occasionally availed of for the development of Anglo-Hindu law.[27] Jolly and Kāṇe date it about 1600. Ghārpure, who published the text, places its composition between 1686 and 1696.

[25]For Raghunandana see the last-mentioned article at pp. 351–7 and 363–375. See also Bhabatosh Bhaṭṭāchārya, *Raghunandana's Indebtedness to his Predecessors*, referred to at *Indian Stud. Past and Pres.*, 9/2 (1968), 113.

[26]*Kaustubha* was the mythical jewel produced from the churning of the ocean and worn by Viṣṇu and Kṛṣṇa.

[27][trs.]

In the eighteenth century one Ratnākara compiled at the request of king Jayasiṃha of Mathurā (Jai Singh of Jaipur) the *Jayasiṃha-kalpa-druma* (1713). We should also not overlook the *Dharma-sindhu* (Ocean of Dharma) by Kāśinātha, composed in 1790–1791, devoted primarily to religious observances. The work is very popular in the Deccan, and we have da Cunha Goncalves's authority for the assertion that it is the prime *śāstric* source to be consulted in the former Portuguese India,[28] for it deals incidentally with matters like the right to be adopted.

When the British took into their hands the administration of Bengal several digests were compiled at their request. The earliest is the *Vivādār-ṇava-setu* (Bridge over the Ocean of Litigation), compiled in 1775 for Warren Hastings by a group of eleven paṇḍits of Bengal and Northern India. Since it was translated into English by N.B. Halhed from a Persian version (called Tarjamah i Dharm-shāstra) made from the paṇḍits' Sanskrit original by Zain al-Dīn 'Alī Rasā'ī and was published under Halhed's name in London in 1776, the work is conveniently known as *Halhed's Gentoo Code*. It was translated from the English of Halhed into French and German in 1778. A critical edition of the Sanskrit text is awaited, for the demand for copies was such that interesting variations are said to have crept into it. Another work of the same type and purpose was compiled in 1789 by Trivedi Sarvoruśarman at the request of Sir William Jones. It is called the *Vivāda-sārārṇava* but has never been published.

The most remarkable of these digests is the *Vivāda-bhaṅgārṇava* (Ocean of Solutions of Cases) composed also at the instance of Sir William Jones by Jagannātha Tarkapañcānana. Apart from the section dealing with criminal law, this work was translated by Colebrooke and published in English in Calcutta in 1797 under the title *A Digest of Hindu Law*. A second edition in three volumes appeared in London four years later. This translation, along with Jones' *Manu*, formed a point of departure for the study of Hindu law in Europe. It was long a source of information and reference for the Anglo-Indian courts in Bengal and elsewhere, and its usefulness is by no means exhausted in such contexts. As a collection of texts it is "simply invaluable", according to J.D. Mayne, the writer on Anglo-Hindu law. The author has been accused of not knowing how to come to a decision between divergent opinions, and it has been characterised as "the best book for an advocate and the worst for a judge". But this may conceivably not do justice to the author's own intentions.[29]

To end we should pay a tribute to the *Dharma-kośa*, the brain-child

[28][trs.]

[29]The needs of the British administration provoked a veritable flowering of treatises until the middle of the nineteenth century. Derrett, *Religion* ...., ch. 8 ('The British as patrons of the *śāstra*.'). [trs.]

of an ascetic and an enthusiast for *dharmaśāstra* in Maharashtra some thirty or so years ago. It is a digest of a new type, intended not so much for the assistance of the courts as for the intellectual study of Hindu institutions. It gives texts relating to *dharma* (including *śruti, smṛti* and *arthaśāstra*), divided under various rubrics and classified as nearly as may be according to the commonly accepted chronology. The most significant commentaries are extracted, and the extracts follow immediately after the texts. Three volumes complete the *vyavahāra-kāṇḍa*: the first deals with rules of procedure and evidence, and the two others with fundamental rules of substantive law.

APPENDIX

SOME REFLECTIONS ON THE CHRONOLOGY OF THE DHARMA-ŚĀSTRAS

THE CHRONOLOGY of the *dharma-śāstras*, like everything relating to ancient India, is bedevilled by uncertainty. Following upon Bühler and Jolly but improving on both, Kāṇe has assembled in the first volume of his imposing *History of Dharmaśāstra* (1930, ²1968) all the data which we have in order to place the composition of the works in time or, at the very least, to classify them chronologically. He has examined and discussed the principal opinions on this subject published in Europe and in India, and he has attempted in his turn to disengage the elements which permit us to limit the problem of dating within some determined historical period. No one is surprised to learn that this labour occupied the entire leisure of the author for five years, and one cannot but pay homage to his conscientiousness, his erudition, the sharpness of some of his observations and the clarity of his reasoning in general. Since the time of publication this volume (of which a second edition is awaited) has become a classic, and his conclusions, which are often especially wise, are very generally accepted. Yet complete unanimity is lacking, and the recent work of the late K.V. Raṅgaswāmī Aiyaṅgār[1] tends to place Kāṇe's chronology in some doubt.

In my own view almost insurmountable obstacles stand in the way of any solution being given to the chronological problem. They force it to depend on deductions which are bound always to have a purely hypothetical character.

To begin with, there is the total lack of reference to historical events. This is so often insisted upon as a trait common to the *dharma-śāstras* that repetition is hardly necessary. Their attribution to mythical persons does not allow us to assign them to any age at all. But when we reflect on the truly historical movements which India has known during the very long period within which these writings must be placed—the development of Buddhism, the campaign of Alexander, the rise and the fall of the great native empires, the first invasions or incursions of Muslims—we cannot hide our astonishment at the perfection with which the authors of their works have managed to dissimulate the epoch at which they wrote and the circumstances which led them to write. Unless,

[1]Notably the important Introduction to his edition of the *Bṛhaspatismṛti*, Gaekwad's Or.Ser., 85 (Baroda, 1941).

of course, anything of their personality which was then apparent has been effaced little by little in the course of the transmission of their texts. Indologists such as Burnell, who searched for some clue in the ideas and political theories of the code of Manu have been led to conclusions which have not carried conviction. The link proposed between the author's thought and the data of history seemed much too vague or fragile. Thus it is that Jayaswāl supposed that the exaltation of the royal function in certain passages of the *Nārada-smṛti,* where royalty is propounded as of practically divine origin, revealed that it was composed in the period of the powerful Gupta empire, in the fourth century A.D.[2] The connection is possible enough, but one can hardly say that it impresses one as plausible. One is tempted to say the same of the hypothesis formulated about the date of compilation of the *Devala-smṛti,* a hypothesis taken in some quarters as axiomatic. The work provides purificatory rites to be undergone by Hindus forcibly converted to Islam, in order that they might be readmitted to Indian society. A.S. Altekar does not hesitate to connect these precepts with the conquest of Sindh by Muslims, and to attribute the book to a "social thinker of Sindh", which would place its composition in the ninth century at the earliest.[3] No doubt the connection is plausible. But we need something more than a simple mention of *mlecchas* before we can be convinced, since Muslims were by no means the first "barbarians" to come into contact with the Hindus.[4]

It seems even more hazardous to try to determine the epoch in which a book was compiled from the religious or philosophical colouring of a passage, as Burnell has done for Manu, and Stenzler and Bhāṇḍārkar have done for the Code of Yājñavalkya. The appearance and development of a philosophy or a sect involve too much imprecision to offer a footing upon which any sort of reliance can be placed. It is only where the work reveals a decidedly sectarian character that we can assign it to a late epoch. Even the case of the *Viṣṇu-smṛti* shows that in so doing we are bound to be very discreet.

Nor is any real help to be obtained from a general examination of the style, for all our *smṛtis* are written in classical Sanskrit and depart only by accident from grammatical tradition. All that we can say is that

[2]*Manu and Yājñavalkya* (Calcutta, 1930), 74–5. And an economic historian of ancient India, S.K. Maity, unhesitatingly bases his findings upon the *smṛtis* of Nārada, etc., as if they belonged to this epoch. [trs.]

[3]*Sources of Hindu Dharma* (Sholapur, 1952), 19. A footnote to Kāṇe's account of Devala is provided by Bhabatosh Bhaṭṭāchāryya at his *Studies in Dharmasastra* in *Indian Studies: Past and Present* (Calcutta, 1964), 8–10. [trs.]

[4]I might add that some of the verses of the *Devala-smṛti* are attributed to Āpastamba by the author of the *Mitākṣarā* and by Aparārka (Kāṇe, I. 121). No doubt this would, in the eyes of modern scholars, have been a work distinct from the *dharma-sūtra* of Āpastamba, but it enjoyed an equally high authority in the eyes of commentators.

the versified literature of the *smṛtis* is in contrast with the form and style of the literature of the *sūtras*, and succeeds to it. But the epoch of the *sūtras* is itself very uncertain. It would be naive to suppose that it came to an end the moment versified *smṛtis* made their appearance. As Barth wrote, "the (Vedic) schools are ancient, that may well be ... but we need other proofs beyond a few barbarisms and other sins against Pāṇini's grammar before we can admit that the voluminous collections of their *sūtras* go back to the same period and that the *dharma-sūtras* in particular form a part of those collections from that period."[5]

Finally epigraphy for its part provides nothing helpful for dating them. It seems that very few ancient inscriptions textually reproduce a passage identifiable in a particular *smṛti*. The allusion made in many of them to Manu or even to a work attributed to Manu is not sufficient to affirm that what was meant was the text we know by the name of Code of Manu. The references which explicitly or indirectly recall the *smṛtis* of Bṛhaspati or Vyāsa are quite worthless for, even as dates *ante quem*, they are far too late to be of any significance. The same must be said of the quotation of Vasiṣṭha XXVIII.16 in the Ragim copper-plates of Tīvara-deva, dated in the last quarter of the *eighth* century by Fleet (*Gupta Inscriptions*, No. 81).

There are those who take account of the use of certain isolated words, such as *yavana, nāṇaka, dīnāra, pustaka*, etc., to date a whole work, or at least to fix a date after which it must have existed. Apart from the fact that we are not agreed as to the time when these words passed into the language, nor in some cases what they actually meant thereafter, it seems bold indeed to attach the chronology which some think possible to the entire work or even to the verse in which the relevant word is found. Even if we admit that Yavanas means Greeks (which is not certain), and that accordingly wherever the word is used to designate a caste it could not have been used with this meaning until after the rise of the Indo-Greek kingdoms, it remains always open to wonder whether the word itself or the verse where it is found was really part of the original text. Although Hindus are represented as being endowed with prodigious memories, I beg leave to doubt, especially when we are dealing with a text which is *not* liturgical and which must as a matter of principle remain intelligible, that it has come down to us intact, free from supposed corrections, amendments, or additions, throughout a long oral tradition or after multiple successive scribal copies. No one is unaware of the risk involved when one evokes the possibility of interpolations. It is an argument used with irresponsible freedom in many fields.[5a] But when we see serious commentators of the standing of

[5] *Works*, V, 93.

[5a] [trs.]

Medhātithi or Vijñāneśvara[6] doubting the authenticity of certain verses transmitted with the *smṛti*, one may well question the reliability of the reasoning which would rely on one word or an isolated verse in order to date a whole work.

Another fact which may corroborate the possibility of interpolation is the diversity of attribution frequently encountered with regard to the same text in the commentators. In the introduction to his edition of the *Bṛhaspati-smṛti*, Aiyaṅgār cites a large number of examples where a verse is attributed by some to Bṛhaspati, by others either to Manu or Kātyāyana, or to Nārada, or to Vyāsa, and so on.[7] In the introduction to his edition of the *Kātyāyana-smṛti* Kāṇe cites numerous cases where a verse of Kātyāyana is attributed either to Bṛhaspati, or to Nārada, or to Manu, Vyāsa, Devala, or Pitāmaha.[8] Aiyaṅgār and Kāṇe do not absolutely reject the hypothesis of mere error of attribution on the part of the commentators. But they are led to contemplate the possibilities that the author of one *dharma-śāstra* borrowed from another, or both borrowed from a common anterior source—of course quite a hypothetical one—now lost; all of which comes down, in either case, to admitting the possibility (on a substantial scale) of interpolations.[9]

On the other hand, it is generally admitted that the great *smṛtis* which have come down to us entire, such as the Code of Manu and that of Yājñavalkya, are not homogeneous compositions. For example, without entering into details, the first Book of Manu and his last seem really to form just a framework added at one go to the collection of rules which form the main body of the code, themselves of various origins.[10] As for the *Yājñavalkya-smṛti*, it is not out of the question, even since the ingenious theorising of Kāṇe, to see as a relatively recent addition to the other two books the portion devoted to *vyavahāra*, which is repeated practically word for word in the *Agnipurāṇa*. Kāṇe himself goes so far as to admit (I, p. 174) that the original underwent a certain amount of rewriting between 800 and 1100, although he places the composition of the work in the first two centuries of the Christian era. As for the *Nārada-smṛti* everyone agrees in general that the prose prologue which describes its origin is a text which was originally quite independent of the original.[11] Despite the fragmentary nature of the work which he has reconstructed, Aiyaṅgār does not hesitate to recognise that the *Bṛhaspati-smṛti*, the composition of which he dates about the beginning of our era, has

[6]Medhātithi on *M.*, IX.93; *Mit.*, on *Yāj.*, I.256.

[7]K.V. Raṅgaswāmī Aiyaṅgār, *Bṛhaspati (Reconstructed)*, Introduction, 145–8.

[8]Kāṇe, *Kātyāyanasmṛti-sāroddhāra* (Bombay, 1933), pp. viii–ix.

[9]The matter is debated at length by Aiyaṅgār, *op. cit.*, 145–51.

[10]G. Bühler, *Laws of Manu* (Oxford, 1886), lxvi–lxxiii.

[11]In any case the prologue is wanting in the version upon which Bhavasvāmin commented.

undergone revision and addition, and even a new edition in the fifth or sixth century.[12] If the *dharma-śāstras* have reached us arranged in this way and made-up to this sort of appearance, it can hardly be good sense to try to date their composition by relying upon isolated passages, and it would hardly be good sense even if they contained a definite historical allusion.

It is the absence of or inconsistencies between internal criteria, which might otherwise have sufficed to determine the age of the composition of any work, which has developed amongst scholars another method, consisting in looking for indications adequate to mark it as anterior or posterior to some other work. In this way a beginning has been made at a *relative* chronological classification which permits us to place the *dharma-śāstras* in a scale of regular succession after the Code of Manu, which is considered the oldest of them all, up to the period of the first commentators. If these two limits are taken into account all that is left to do is to imagine what interval might have occurred between the composition of two successive *dharma-śāstras* in order to arrive at an approximate dating.

We must recognise that this method has given results which are intellectually much more satisfactory. Some discussion is necessary, however, because the criteria for chronological classification are sometimes slender enough.

We have, though there is no need to insist upon it, the lists of *smṛti-kāras* which certain *dharma-śāstras*, like Yājñavalkya (I.4–5), themselves give. Apart from the fact that there we have isolated verses particularly subject to alteration, falling under the objections which we have already noticed, we have no means of being certain that the often mythical persons figuring in those verses have any connection with the works attributed to them amongst surviving literature. The fact that Yājñavalkya cites Kātyāyana amongst his predecessors (or contemporaries) does not hinder Kāṇe from considering the latter "much later". The fact that Yājñavalkya himself is cited in Śaṅkha-Likhita does not hinder him from holding that the latter is much older than the *Yājñavalkya-smṛti*.[13] In any case Yājñavalkya does not fail to place Śaṅkha (and) Likhita on his own list! So we cannot place any reliance on the fact that one author is cited by another in order to establish an order of precedence, for even authors who are said to belong to distant epochs actually cite each other. Thus Pitāmaha cites a *śloka* which he attributes to Bṛhaspati, from which Kāṇe concludes that Bṛhaspati is much older than he (I², p. 516). But Aiyaṅgār (Introduction, p. 105) produces a *śloka* of Bṛhaspati who refers to Pitāmaha, and concludes that "the assertion of Mr. Kāṇe is

[12] Aiyaṅgār, *op. cit.*, 97, 158.
[13] Kāe, I², 429–30 (cf 142!); 496, 501.

open to question". Of course we can always suggest that the name in question refers to two different works, only one of which has come down to us, the other being an earlier version, now lost. But this kind of argument has hardly any more weight than the mere fact that it is offered.

Yet again, chronological classification of the *dharma-śāstras* is usually based upon a comparative examination of their contents. The method is a delicate one and presupposes a vast collection of references. Kāṇe, in the wake of Jolly, has recourse to such with great ingenuity and incomparable learning. The order of priority at which he arrives, if not his actual dates, will strike many as proved or at least plausible. From the fact that one work presents, in relation to another, new elements or developments, a more developed working out of the institutions of law, a greater care for precision or a more marked technical character, it is natural enough to hold it to be later than the other. It is possible to arrive by this means at a succession or progression : Manu, Yājñavalkya, Nārada, Bṛhaspati, Kātyāyana (to cite only the principal *smṛtis*). This is a highly probable order. However, the method is not beyond criticism, because we are free to suspect that the differences which have been detected are due primarily, or notably, to the nature of the works concerned. J.J. Meyer makes this very observation à propos of the date of Nārada, whom he places before Yājñavalkya and even before Manu. If the *Nārada-smṛti* clearly has a more juridical character than the other two, says he, it is not necessarily because it is more recent. It could be because its author was essentially a practitioner, with first-hand experience of the courts, while Manu and even Yājñavalkya remained essentially moralists.[14] After all is it not an analogous argument used in connection with Manu himself, to explain his silence on documentary proof and his brevity regarding ordeals? In much the same way the highly schematic stratification which is G. Mazzarella's contribution to the study of the *dharma-śāstras* is open to suspicion.[15] Although he is able to check legal development by reference to cultures other than the Indian, it is not clear that he has exhausted other possibilities to account for differences between the Indian sources, which he regularly attributes to "epochs".

If we were to neglect this line of criticism we should soon come across another kind of difficulty which risks rendering altogether illusory the work we have undertaken. It should be clear that while we seek to place

[14]J.J. Meyer, *Über das Wesen* ... (cited above, p. 22, n. 3), *passim*. Aiyaṅgār (*op. cit.*, 136) takes up the same point, 'Nārada is clearly a compendium for professional men, Manu's for scholars'. See also p. 121 regarding the rules relating to procedure which are set out in the *Bṛhaspati-smṛti*.

[15]Derrett, 'Juridical ethnology: the life and work of Giuseppe Mazzarella (1868–1958)', *Zeitschrift für vergleichende Rechtswissenschaft*, 71 (1969), 1–44. [trs.]

the *dharma-śāstras* in point of time this is not merely, as is the case usually with literary works, in order to assign to them a more or less approximate *date*. It is also, and even primarily, with the intention of grasping what was the evolution of ideas on social relationships, quite apart from the question of technical progress. Even if a classification on the basis of purely technical criteria reveals tendencies progressively realised, it often rebuffs us by the anomalies which it high-lights. For example, given the increasing importance of adoption amongst the legal means of securing continuity of legal personality, it seems rather paradoxical that there should be in a *dharma-sūtra,* i.e. in a work thought well prior to *dharma-śāstra* literature, namely the *dharma-sūtra* of Vasiṣṭha (Kāṇe places it between 300 and 100 B.C.), the greater part of the texts which were available to commentators when they wanted to regulate the institution. A whole chapter (the 15th) is devoted to the subject, whereas the *smṛtis* hardly do more than mention the name of the *dattaka*. Conversely it is curious to observe, as indeed Aiyaṅgār does (p. 115), that the provisions regarding ordeals become abundant as the works containing them become more recent. In the *dharma-sūtras,* Āpastamba (II.11.29) barely mentions this mode of proof; Manu (VIII.174) lists two kinds of ordeals; Yājñavalkya (II.95–99) five or six, Nārada and Kātyāyana (411–461) seven, Bṛhaspati and Pitāmaha (in 200 verses) nine. It seems as if with the development of judicial procedure the recourse to ordeals would, on the contrary, have inspired progressively less interest.

It can also happen that the same author proffers propositions which at times estrange him from and at other times connect him with authors placed before him, in such a way that it is impossible to trace a definite design. The line is a zigzag which passes from recent writers to old writers and from the latter again to the former. Thus the eulogy of the *satī* in the *Vyāsa-smṛti* seems to Jolly to indicate that the work is not old. But the *Parāśara-smṛti* (IV.32–33), which Kāṇe (I., p. 193) places between Yājñavalkya and Nārada, equally extols the *satī*. In reverse, Manu appears to dissuade from this practice (according to Medhātithi, on *M.,* V.157). But *Bṛhaspati,* who is ordinarily so faithful to Manu's teaching, actually recommends it (*Aiy.,* p. 133). Aparārka cites a text of Āpastamba which inflicts a severe penance (*prājāpatya* penance) on the widow who resiles from her resolve to mount the pyre of her husband. The *Mitākṣarā* (on *Yāj.,* I.86) cites many verses on suttee *(satī)* which it attributes to Śaṅkha and to Hārīta, authors of *dharma-sūtras*.[16] Yājña-valkya seems to state a newer rule than Manu when he calls the widow to succeed to her deceased husband in the first rank if he died without

[16]K.V. Raṅgaswāmī Aiyaṅgār, *Rājadharma* (Adyar, 1941), 186–9; Kāṇe, II, 629. Viṣṇu XXV.14 (older or younger?) for his part offers the widow the choice between leading a chaste life or mounting her husband's pyre.

sons. from which Kāṇe concludes that Yājñavalkya should be posterior to Manu who seems actually to refuse the widow all rights of succession to her husband. But Nārada, whom Kāṇe believes more recent than Yājñavalkya, does not recognise the rights of succession of a widow. Bṛhaspati returns to the position of Yājñavalkya and proclaims loudly what the widow's rights are. But Kātyāyana (928) who generally follows Bṛhaspati, drives the widow from the succession (cf. 922–927). Aiyaṅgār gave some attention to the wife's legal status as represented by the different *dharmaśāstra* writers (p. 135) and concluded that the vacillation of opinion is such that it is impossible to draw from the degree of interest they show in the question any indication whatever as to the relative age of the works themselves. Remarks of this kind could be cited again and again, which subtract all credit from a method often practised by scholars as a secondary device, which consists in guessing the epoch of a work's composition from the presumed evolution of manners. Quite apart from the fact that the historian has no knowledge of any such classification, one has only to fear that it will end by inserting into the texts a logical evolution which exists nowhere except in our own minds. Could there not have been in India any backward movements, or local variations? And could one never have encountered divergent opinions in the works of a single author?

The upshot of these observations is that it seems we must renounce all hope of arriving at certain dates. This does not mean to say that so far as the great *smṛtis* are concerned, whose texts have come down to us intact, we could not hold a chronological classification to be generally valid if it is based on a comparative examination of the contents envisaged from the point of view of its technical character. That is how it seemed probable that the version of Manu's Code with which the commentators have furnished us was, in general and upon the whole, earlier than all other *dharma-śāstras*. But we are bound to admit that all the parts of the work do not necessarily date from the same epoch, that certain rules could have been introduced at a later date than that of the composition of the original work, and that, conversely, certain rules appertaining to the original failed to find a place in the versions which Manu's commentators make known to us. Otherwise it is inexplicable how so many verses attributed to Manu either in *smṛtis* or in the digests of appreciable antiquity cannot be found in the complete version of the Code. It is hardly an adequate reply that what we have there are adages, maxims, precepts fathered on Manu as the human race's first legislator: for that very reason, they ought to have found a place in our Code.

In conclusion, we are led to think that, during the long period of time in which the different *dharma-śāstras* were composed, these texts remained open. They underwent alterations or reworkings which are not betrayed by any criterion. Mutual borrowing occurred, a sort of interpenetration which explains the difficulties which one experiences in classifying the texts in some order of priority, even if it appears that one is more recent than another in point of its more advanced technique. The commentaries whose authority was established by the end of the ninth century had the advantage of putting an end to these reworkings and fixing the texts. But (of course) they fixed them in general in the condition of the manuscripts as they found them, for it is unusual for a commentator to dispute the authenticity of a proposition or passage which he found in his source.

Yet after the appearance of the first commentaries, the same influences probably continued to operate on the *dharma-śāstras* which we know only from the extracts quoted by the writers of the Middle Ages. At any rate these, and they are really numerous, could not conceivably be subjected to any chronology. In their case the additional and delicate question arises whether they are authentic. The term "spurious" is sometimes heard in their connection. We know that, when making a citation, the commentators and digest-writers confine themselves to giving the name of the author, without offering any other indication and without (with the rarest exceptions) bothering to specify the title of the work from which the extract is taken. There are even texts which are cited as part of *smṛti* without attribution to any particular author. There are thus cases where we lack even the most elementary means of verifying a citation. Not only is the same extract frequently attributed (as we have seen) to different authors, but it is equally common for the same name to apply to different writers. Numerous passages may be attributed to the author of a well-known *smṛti* preceded with the qualifications "Laghu-", "Vṛddha-", "Bṛhat-", and so on, about which it would be impossible to say what, if any, their relation is with the *smṛti* of that name (they could have borrowed from older or different versions, and could as well have come from works which were always independent). And the mere name of an author does not always suffice to identify him, because an unavoidably limited number of persons had acquired the reputation as a promulgator of *dharma*. Thus when an extract attributed to Nārada cannot be found in recensions of the *smṛti* which have come down to us, we cannot be sure that it is the same Nārada.[17]

Every criterion of form proves useless. One begins to snatch at criteria of substance and to suppose, for example, that different works must be involved when the texts express inconsistent opinions. We know the usefulness of that criterion in the field of Roman law when attempts were successfully made to reveal the interpolations in the *Digest*. It is not clear that it could be used efficaciously in our present domain, where it is not exceptional to meet contradictory opinions in the same *smṛti*.

[17]Kāṇe, I, 238, à propos of Vyāsa. [Elaborated at I^2, 533.]

Moreover it is difficult to see what precise conclusion one could arrive at with reference to the thought of an author of whom we know only some isolated verses which we have no means of replacing in any context whatever.[18]

The authenticity of the attribution and, consequently, the very value of the extract in its capacity as a rule of *dharma* rests entirely and definitively upon the authority enjoyed by the commentators or digest-writers who selected and fixed it. From then onwards it becomes part of a mass of texts whose dates, relative to each other, were of no interest whatsoever to their interpreter.

[18]From the work which Renou devoted to the text of Bṛhaspati as published by Raṅgaswāmī Aiyaṅgār it appears with full force what difficulties one must encounter, if one attempts to establish the original form of the *smṛti*. Not only is the attribution of numerous verses to Bṛhaspati himself not certain, whether because some commentators have attributed them to other sources, or because the Bṛhaspati to whom they are attributed may not be the one to whom the verses on *vyavahāra* are assigned (Kāṇe, I, 126); but apart from that the commentators' citations demonstrate multiple variants, between which it seems seldom either easy or judicious to make a distinct choice, especially when, as often happens, these variants relate to legal doctrine, and some commentators rely upon one reading while others rely upon another. We may take as example *Bṛh. Aiy.*, I, 19, where the variant *vardhate* ('increases', 'prospers') is taken up by Devaṇṇa-bhaṭṭa (*Smṛ. cand.*, II, 11) instead of the reading *avahīyate* ('is supplanted') which is furnished by the *Vyav. cint.*, 715 and the *Kalpataru*, Vyavahāra-kāṇḍa, 261. It would be gratuitous to suspect the good faith of these writers. It is more to the point to recognise the character of these texts as having halted at an indecisive stage of development. This character is emphasised, moreover, by the sufficiently common fact that *ślokas* (couplets) make their appearance with two lines which, in other *smṛtis*, each form a part of two quite different *ślokas*!

PART TWO

FROM DHARMA TO LAW

THE PROBLEM

In the old Vedic schools the study of domestic ritual was completed very early on by the rules of a discipline primarily of religious inspiration, which were intended to define *dharma*, or the conduct of the individual according to his age and station in life. Though fairly scanty in the *dharma-sūtras,* precepts of a juridical character took a more and more important place in the *dharma-śāstras*. At the same time, they were expressed in a more and more certain and scientific form. The immense literature of the commentaries and digests finally presents a sum-total of all those works whose authority was confirmed by time. Study of the sacred tradition is prolonged by it right up to our own days, but at the same time it is limited, for only texts in which that tradition is embodied may be utilised.

Yet the rules of a juridical character which one finds in the *dharma-śāstras* continue, as in the times of Gautama or Āpastamba, to be incorporated with rules of a purely religious and ritual inspiration. It matters little that they are enunciated à propos of the duties of the householder or those of the king, that they appear in the *ācāra* section or the *vyavahāra* section. Their object is to certify the *virtue* of the act in question. When Yājñavalkya for example provides (II.24) that he who sees his land occupied by another for twenty years, without making any objection to this, is subject to a loss in respect of that land, etc., that rule, for all its completely juridical tone, is of virtually the same nature as that which enjoins upon a *dvija* the duty of not marrying a woman of a *varṇa* higher than his own (I.57). In either case the precepts put into the mouth of Yājñavalkya express or rather determine the requirements necessary to maintain the cosmic and moral order. It is the duty of men to profit from this if they want salvation. Thus the king, or his delegated judge, knows that he will commit a sin if, when a suit for repossession of land is before him, he does not apply the rule laid down, and likewise a Vaiśya knows that he will commit a sin if he marries a Kṣatriya woman. The two sins would not have the same degree of gravity, but of necessity both would involve a sanction in this world or in the next if they are not effaced by an appropriate penance. These are not simple recommendations which wisdom would tender, or rules of equity that ought to be obeyed. The rule of *dharma* retains its peculiar quality even when it involves juridical consequences. Its authority resides essentially in the faith of the Hindu in a divine regulation of the world, the law of which is expressed by that rule.

Hence we are led to wonder in what measure the rules of law which we meet in the *dharma-śāstras*—presuming that they do really belong to *dharma*—actually express juridical solutions. They are enunciated in order that spiritual merit may be gained or secured. It is unquestionably a religious duty to conform to them, and in this respect they are certainly amongst the origins of law. But what is their exact significance? Are they direct sources of law, i.e. have they the quality of legislation, the authority of which bears directly upon the judge? Or are they sources of law only in the sense that religion and morality are amongst the sources of law in Europe—that is, have they managed to exert an influence upon the development of social institutions as an historical or explanatory cause of law rather than a true *source*?

From the day that the British took into their hands the administration of justice in India, they were confronted by the problem of the value suitable to attach in practice to the *śāstras'* precepts. This problem has remained open to controversy ever since. In 1772, Warren Hastings laid the foundations of the jurisdiction of the courts which the East India Company should institute by virtue of the Diwani grant obtained a few years earlier from the Emperor at Delhi. He provided that in certain matters, such as those concerning succession, marriage, caste and religious institutions, the Hindus and Muslims would be ruled by their respective laws. Likewise, after the Indian Empire had been joined to the Crown of the United Kingdom, in her Proclamation of the 1st November 1858, Queen Victoria solemnly renewed the promise made to her subjects to respect their laws and customs.[1] But, so far as the Hindu element of the population was concerned, where were these laws and customs to be found? The Regulation of 1772 provided that in the cases in which the Hindu law must be applied the British judge must be assisted by a native Law Officer, whose opinion he must seek before making his decision. This system owed something to methods known to the Muslim courts, and it was not abolished until 1864. Its result was to give the judges the impression that the *smṛti*-literature had the status of legislation. The Law Officers were not professional jurists in the western sense (India had none, so far as we know), but men educated in the *śāstras,* one might say "doctors in *dharmaśāstra*". They always cited as authorities for their opinions texts taken from the *dharma-śāstras* or from works relying upon the latter. In truth the judges were not slow to perceive that the texts often had only a slight connection

[1] 'We disclaim alike the right and desire to impose our convictions on any of our subjects... We will that generally in framing and administering the law due regard be paid to the ancient rights, usages and customs of India.'

with the point of law in issue. There were times when they seemed to be cited only as a matter of form, or to illustrate the paṇḍit's own learning. There were times when they appeared to contradict the opinion proffered. Harmony between the opinions themselves was not always maintained, and the paṇḍits were not always consistent with themselves. Thanks to translations, the British judges gained well before 1864 some personal acquaintance with the alleged written law which their paṇḍits relied upon, and they ceased to follow their opinions blindly. This critical spirit, however, went only so far as to cast doubt on the interpretation of the texts. It never reached their juridical quality. The result was that the legal force attributed to precepts of the *śāstra* came to be confirmed. Once a text had been produced as the basis for a rule of law, the British judge had only to attempt to find its sense and implications and to apply it with all the consequences it seemed to involve.

Now it was not long before realisation began to dawn that the paṇḍit, in conformity with national usage, most frequently gave opinions which conformed to his compatriots' (or some of his compatriots') conception of what would be just; and that the vanity or the corruption with which he tended to be accused by no means always explained the useless ostentation of texts with which he amused himself or the text-torturing in which he indulged. It was early discovered also that precepts of the *smṛtis* were not always obeyed with rigour, that they were not all understood in the same sense, and that at times even custom contradicted them flatly and prevailed in practice without discernible objection. Further, a Regulation was passed in the Bombay Presidency in 1799 which required the courts to ascertain in each case whether there did not exist a customary rule which might furnish a solution to the dispute and, if there was, to apply it to the exclusion of all provisions emanating from the written texts (Bombay Regulation IV of 1799). But though it was recognised that custom took precedence over the law of the *śāstras*, the difficulty of its proof when the existence of a custom had to be established, and the infinite diversity of the customary rules forced the judges, more often than not, to fall back on the precepts of the *smṛtis* under the influence of their paṇḍits, or rather to the interpretation of those precepts which had been established locally. Resistance to improper application of the written law was accentuated in regions or circles where the judges were better informed about actual customs. Hindu law defied attempts to grasp it.

In the last quarter of the nineteenth century a lively reaction occurred against the use which the courts were making of the "Brahminical codes" and their substitutes. It tended even to deny their practical value. Some suggested that they be replaced by a new legislation made entirely by British authority. Others proposed that custom alone should be the guide, since in their view custom was the only real law which India had ever known.[2]

The most impetuous champion of these reforming ideas was James H. Nelson, a District Judge in the Madras Presidency. His three works, *A View of the Hindu Law. . .*, *A Prospectus of the Scientific Study of the Hindu Law*, and *Indian Usage and Judge-made Law in Madras*, published respectively in 1877, 1881, and 1887, resounded somewhat loudly. They are fighting works, almost pamphlets.[2a] Because of his practical responsibility Nelson had personal acquaintance with the difficulties of which he speaks, and he was perfectly *au fait* with the problem. In spite of his exaggeration his critique could not fail to arouse attention and was bound to lead to a better understanding of the Hindu law.

Nelson takes up the cudgels against the case-law handed down by the High Court at Madras, which he attacks as being biassed in favour of the Sanskrit texts and which he accuses of an excessive reluctance to apply the customary law although a recent statute (The Madras Civil Courts Act, 1873, sec. 16) had recognised its legal force. He cites several principles solemnly laid down under that system which led to decisions as unjust as they were contrary to established customs. But his criticism had a more general bearing. He was inspired by views advanced by Burnell,[3] and his critique amounted to a denial of the juridical value of the *smṛtis* and digests. In Nelson's view those works

[2]The same problem arose before the courts of the French possessions in India, the French government having undertaken to administer justice to Hindus 'according to the laws, usages, and customs of their castes'. But it seems that the court at Pondicherry, guided by earlier practice, was quick to recognise the fundamental importance of custom. See Léon Sorg, *Introduction à l'étude du droit hindou* (Pondicherry, 1895).

[2a]Derrett at C.H. Philips, ed., *Historians of India, Pakistan and Ceylon* (London, 1961), ch. 26.

[3]Burnell, to whom Nelson dedicated his first work, wrote in the preface to his translation of the *Dāyavibhāga* portion of the *Parāśara-Mādhavīya*, which he published in 1868, the following, which Nelson quotes at p. 133 of his *View*: 'The digests however were never intended to be actual codes of law; they were written in a language understood by a very few, and because of the Vedic quotations in them, they must have remained almost exclusively in the hands of the Brahmans. Again they refer for the most part to the Brahmans only, and utterly ignore the numerous un-Aryan peoples scattered about India, and which form the greater part of the population of the South, whose usages (whatever they may call themselves) can in no wise be referred to the Dharmaśāstra. There is not a particle of evidence to show that these works were ever even used by the Judges of ancient India as authoritative guides; they were, it is certain, considered as merely speculative treatises, and bore the same relation to the actual practice of the courts, as in Europe treatises on jurisprudence to the law which is actually administered.' Burnell's views here, and in his edition of a part of the *Varadarājīyam* (1872), were not free from exaggeration, and were expressed in an over-dramatic style. That the *śāstras* (interpreted in a very wide sense) were actually consulted in legal contexts is proved by the important inscription from South India published in *Ann. Rep. S.I. Epigraphy*, 1936–7, pp. 92–3 (A.D. 1584). See appendix below. [trs.]

never were taken to be sources of law! It was a great blunder to place them in the same category as the *Institutes* of Justinian or the Napoleonic Code. Their reputation was in any event a recent one, and was due in no small measure to the enthusiasms of European Sanskritists. Prior to the publication undertaken by Sir William Jones, he argued, a Madras paṇḍit would have been astonished to hear the Code of Manu referred to as a source of law. *Smṛtis* were purely literary and theoretical works. They had no contact with reality. They were the fruit of speculations altogether out of touch with practice and propounded ideal rules for which not a single Hindu cared in the business of life, if we except a few very restricted circles of Brahmins. They were of no weight at all so far as concerned the crowds of inferior castes and the peoples of Dravidian race. Their authority was practically nil even for the Āryans and those who pretended to be Āryans. If the experience of the author was of any value, a native of South India, whatever his class, would be highly embarrassed to say according to which of the *smṛtis* or which of the digests he claimed to be judged. In fact the *dharma-śāstras* had nothing to do with law at all. Hindu law was entirely customary. Far from simplifying the British judges' task, recourse to Sanskrit texts which were inaccessible except by way of translations had created greater difficulties. In order to extricate themselves, the judges had often been led to abandon this alleged written law in order to substitute for it their own sense of equity. This method has given rise only to arbitrary and incoherent decisions. An artificial law resulted from it, a veritable monster engendered by "Sanskritists without law and lawyers without Sanskrit". In his view this monster should be executed and buried without delay, and then a commission should be got together to gather and to arrange in a simple form the practices and primitive customs which were common to all the castes or the majority of them.

The works of Nelson have the merit of putting the problem clearly. The remedy he suggests seems rather naive, but his critique is in general well founded. It is marred only by his exaggerated tone and by his prejudices against what he calls the "Sanskrit Books", prejudices which were not justified.

Jurists naturally replied to him.[4] But the most pertinent reply, because it takes the problem as a whole, is that made by the celebrated Indologist. Auguste Barth (to whom Nelson dedicated his second book) in his reviews in the *Revue critique* for the years 1878, 1882, and 1888.[5]

[4]Mr. Justice Innes made a detailed reply in 1882. Sarvadhikari discussed some of Nelson's opinions in his Tagore Law Lectures for 1880, 'On the Hindu Law of Inheritance'. J.D. Mayne, in his turn, drew attention to the weaknesses of Nelson's argument in the preface to the third edition (1883) of his classic treatise *Hindu Law and Usage*.

[5]*Works* (see above, p. 51, n. 32), II, 39–40; III, 296–304 and 403–13; IV, 47–52.

Barth criticises Nelson with some severity for arguments which leave no stone unturned in an attempt to lower the authority of the Code of Manu, the *Yājñavalkya-smṛti* and the *Mitākṣarā*. But he is not far from him in thinking that the *smṛtis* are basically literature and nothing more. "The treatises", says he, "are almost all of them apocryphal. They have a character which is primarily didactic and often purely literary. They never had the force of positive ordinances, and the doctrine itself which they propound, half religious and half juridical, undoubtedly shares the fate of holy and ideal books. They agree only moderately with the way of the world and are more respected than obeyed."[6] So he does not accord them the status of legislation. Yet he adds, "If it would be an error to place the *śāstras* on the same level as the Law of the Twelve Tables or the *Code Civil*, it would be no less an error to attempt to judge them by the same standard. We must take them for what they are, a written tradition, and that at epochs and under influences sundered by many diversities, not compiled by legislators but by scholars unrelated, for the most part, to public authority.[7] Apart from certain doctrines relating to social pretensions rather than to civil law properly so called, or wherever that tradition is outside reality, those scholars did not work otherwise than in good faith and were never inspired simply by personal fantasies."[8]

Barth admits, then, that *dharmaśāstra* authors were not pure theoreticians or simple poets, but that they tried at least in some domains to make a practical work, taking their inspiration from custom in order to enable their conception of wisdom to prevail. Likewise, in opposition to Nelson, he recognises that the *smṛtis* have exercised an undeniable influence over Indian society and that their precepts in certain contexts have acquired a legal force. He may be going a little too far when he says, "We do not hesitate to concede that in civil questions, in what concerns the constitution of families, the management of property, contracts, partition, succession, all questions of which the codes treat in a practical fashion and conformably to conditions obtaining amongst the majority of the inhabitants, we can really speak of a 'Hindu law' as having been effectively recognised from the Himalayas to Cape Comorin". It is true that he adds, "Only, we must not claim more for this law than it claims for itself, and never lose sight of the qualification it constantly exhibits, that its validity stops where a contrary custom prevails".[9]

[6] *Ibid.*, III, 299–300.

[7] A gratuitous assumption. Except for indications, in certain cases, which are in any event hypothetical, about their countries of origin, we know nothing about the personalities of the authors of the *dharma-śāstras*.

[8] *Works*, III, 405.

[9] *Ibid.*, III, 302.

Without any other definition of its nature, Barth recognises that the *dharma-śāstras* have enjoyed a certain authority and that authority has not been without effect. "Mr. Nelson", he says, "rightly attaches great importance to the fact attested by judicious and well-informed observers that at a recent period as much as in the time of Megasthenes, the inhabitants of the various regions of India did not refer to any written law in order to regulate their differences.[10] But when he concludes from this that before William Jones's publication one would have astonished a paṇḍit of Madras by citing the Code of Manu to him as a book of authority in matters of law, his conclusion is certainly erroneous. The paṇḍit would not have spoken of the code as an Englishman would speak of an Act of Parliament, but he would certainly have recognised in it one of the numerous expressions of the eternal *dharma*."[11]

He concludes, "The history of the juridical literature of India, whether native or European, imperfect, uncertain, full of *lacunae* as it is, like everything applying to the past of that singular country, is not really the formless chaos nor the tissue of contradictions that it appears to be to the rather overheated imagination of Mr. Nelson. What is true is this: Britain, in undertaking to respect as far as possible this multiple tradition, and at the same time, to apply it with the aid of institutions and methods without which justice cannot be imagined in the West, has assumed a task which was difficult from the first, and its complications have become gradually more obvious as we have learnt better to guage the present as well as the past conditions obtaining in that land."[12]

The eminent Sanskritist here put his finger on the true cause of the discomfort experienced by the British judges. The principal lesson to be drawn from this long controversy amounts to this, that the Hindu concept of law marries ill with our methods of administering justice. Our judicial system demands an imperative rule, emanating from an organ having legislative power, or appertaining (in the case of the common law) to a source the authority of which is equal to that of legislation until it is validly repealed. Now there never was in India, prior to the British period, a power able to pass legislation, in our sense of that word, at least in matters of private law. However, law did not reside entirely in custom. Certainly the *dharma-śāstras* were not Codes in the European sense of that word. But their precepts did not thereby lack a certain authority in the eyes of all Hindus, specially because of their origin but also, and particularly in the judge's eyes, because they were the only ones which were the fruit of a profound study and, as a result, offered some framework of juridical reasoning. The written law

[10]Cf. Derrett, *J.A.O.S.* 88 (1968), 776ff.
[11]*Ibid.*, III, 405.
[12]*Ibid.*, III, 408.

of the *śāstras* and the customary laws of the different groups of humanity thus existed side by side, equally respected though often in notable disagreement with each other. The former acted upon the latter and restricted its mobility; but the latter also acted upon the former through the medium of interpretation. The result was an extremely variable and diverse law, the application of which required the judge to use a power of *assessment* quite incompatible with our conception of the judicial function. What was needed was a judge who had the power to apply as the case demanded the law of the holy *ṛṣis* or the custom of ancestors, a judge who could decide with sovereign independence and total liberty so far as the choice of law was concerned, in short an arbitrator rather than a judge. And Barth was wise enough to detect that that was how it was.[13]

To understand the notion which the Hindus had of law prior to the intervention of western concepts, it is important to try to define the authority which they attributed to the *dharma-śāstras*. The precepts to be found in those works could stumble against several sorts of obstacles: particularly that of custom, and that of the governmental policies. We must, then, look into the relations that obtained between custom and the written law of the *śāstras,* on the one hand, and, on the other, the role incumbent on the king in the application of that written law according to traditional notions. In either case the preliminary labour done by interpretation pioneered the road and prepared the passage from *dharma* to law.

[13] This law . . . is addressed rather to arbitrators than to judges and contains at least as many recommendations as it does precepts.' *Ibid.*, IV, 50.

CHAPTER I
INTERPRETATION

1. *The Scope of Interpretation*

THE APPEARANCE of the commentaries and the digests marks an important phase—perhaps we ought to say a turning-point—in the evolution of juridical thought in India. A technique of interpretation,[1] already provided with all its principles and all its methods from the oldest works which have come down to us, is there put to work and is applied without alteration until the British period began and even thereafter. The law which was effectively in force during this long period was born of that technique, and it is no exaggeration to say that it was only with that interpretation that a true juridical science began in India.

If it were really permissible to believe, as many scholars do, that the succession of *dharma-śāstras* represents a series of stages passed through, one after another, in the elaboration of law, this presumption would certainly have to be abandoned from the moment when the era of the commentators commenced. According to the Hindu interpreter, all the *dharma-śāstras* were the expression of the same eternal law, that is to say it is from the whole of written tradition, and not from this or that *smṛti* in particular that one must deduce the rule to be followed. Thus Bhāruci and Medhātithi, the oldest commentators on the *Manu-smṛti* who have survived, do not rest content with commenting upon the text of Manu; they compare the verses of Manu with material taken from other *smṛti* works to which they attach the same authority, and, where it is appropriate, they reconcile the propositions. All other commentators do the same. This doctrine of consensus to which we shall return is one of the essential and characteristic traits of Hindu interpretation. It is in the *smṛti,* founded on the Veda, or Truth, that rules of conduct must be found, and precepts responding to the very nature of things. Here, in its own ideal image, Indian society has ceaselessly

[1]I take the word interpretation in the sense given to it in Roman law. The commentators and digest-writers have, in effect, a task analogous to that of the jurisconsults. They are not expected to state law, properly so called, but to propose solutions to disputes, solutions which they approve and which they certify to be conformable to the texts. They prepare the way for the judge and they simplify his work, but they do not take it on. There were, in other respects, several notable points of resemblance between the role of the *prudentes* and that of our Hindu 'interpreters' (as I shall call them) which explain the high opinion which both groups had of the significance of their function. They both regarded it as a veritable priesthood.

sought itself, and has always aspired to its own rediscovery. The role of interpretation amounts to this: it offers society the means whereby it can rediscover itself in fact.

We have already noted the gigantic task to which the commentator was exposed by the equal value attributed to the different expressions of *smṛti,* chiefly because of the enormous mass of texts which he must assemble and classify before any kind of construction could be undertaken. If citations from the *dharma-sūtras* and *dharma-śāstras* occupy the largest place in the commentaries and digests, the other works contained within the concept of *smṛti,* especially the epics and *purāṇas,* are likewise laid under contribution, and Vedic texts too. There is one observation we must make. The commentators and the digest-writers were bound to make a choice between rules found in the works which they had before them or carried in their memories. Now every choice implies a rejection, and the rules which are *not* retained, whatever might have been the authority of the work which contained them, are in every sense of the word dead letters. As for the works which we know only from the commentators' citations—and we have seen how numerous these are—only the citations matter, for they alone have been taken into account in the working out of the law. It follows that, if one were so lucky as to discover the *dharma-śāstra* attributed to Hārīta, for example, one could not make anything of that part of the discovery which is at this moment hidden from us. It will be appreciated how such a hypothesis must inflict uncertainty upon the study of institutions belonging to a pre-commentary epoch! Interpretation has fixed the totality of authoritative texts; it has demarcated the scope of *smṛti.* Law owes nothing to what interpretation neglected or spontaneously rejected. An arbitrary element has thus entered into the constructions which the commentators made, for they selected their sources for themselves. It could be said in reply that the texts utilised are sufficiently numerous and varied, and that they afford sufficient diversity and variations for us to be able to trust the commentators and concede that their citations do correspond faithfully to the totality of *smṛti* rules. One might add that the interpretors are numerous and of divergent views, and that omission of an essential text by one of them could not have failed to be detected and reprehended by others. However, before the luxuriant flowering of works classified as *smṛti* which, according to everyone, must have continued during more than a millennium, the problem must still be considered an open one. And where an author of the sixteenth century produces passages from *dharma-sūtras* which cannot be traced in the published versions which we owe to their commentators, we are bound to retain some doubts.[2]

[2]I allude to the *Sarasvatī-vilāsa* and its citations of the *dharma-sūtras* of Viṣṇu and

If interpretation aims to play upon all *smṛti* (and *śruti*) literature, by contrast it leaves all texts not belonging to *smṛti* severely alone.[2a] Not only do we find no reference to any ordinances passed by any historical king in our commentaries or digests, nor any documents used in practice—which the system of interpretation itself suffices to explain—but it is only quite exceptionally that any account is taken of works which are indeed neighbours of the *dharma-śāstras* and are devoted to the *arthaśāstra*. This omission from the sources used by our writers should now be explained.

Just like *dharmaśāstra,* the compound word *arthaśāstra* has two senses, as the word *śāstra* is taken in the sense of "science" or in that of "treatise". *Artha* signifies wealth or means, economic profit, and the science of *artha (arthaśāstra)* tries to teach men generally the means of securing their material welfare; whilst the science of *dharma (dharmaśāstra)* is aimed at teaching them the means of acquiring merit and thus securing their salvation. Each of these sciences has its distinct domain, and the rules regulating human activity which they inspire meet upon an approximately equal footing in the elaboration of law-in-action. Manu himself observes that men are very frequently guided by interest, and he says that the ideal of the Sage is to know how to reconcile the practice of virtue *(dharma)* with interest *(artha)* and pleasure *(kāma)*. Thus the authors of the *dharma-śāstra* (the treatise) could not confine themselves to *dharmaśāstra* (the science), and they were bound to make some room for *artha* in their precepts. Yājñavalkya (II.21), Nārada (I.37), Kātyāyana (32) and others, in verses which we shall study later, name *arthaśāstra* (the discipline) expressly beside *dharmaśāstra* (in the same sense) as the foundation of a judicial decision. Aparārka (on *Yāj.*, I.3) ranges *arthaśāstra* amongst the auxiliary sciences; he sees in it a *dṛṣṭa-smṛti,* a discipline directed to matters having a "seen", that is to say worldly, end or object. As such it is doubtless inferior to *dharma-śāstra* which is primarily concerned with actions whose effect is "unseen", that is to say supernatural, but knowledge of it is no less indispensable for the government of men. As a science the *arthaśāstra* is an integral part of the knowledge required of the interpreter, even though research into and study of the rule of *dharma* must be his predominating concern.

In the sense of a treatise, *arthaśāstra* means a class of works whose domain is much less vast and more precise than their title suggests.

Gautama. Derrett, 'Kuttā', *B.S.O.A.S.*, 21 (1958), 69; 'A strange rule of *smṛti* and a suggested solution', *J.R.A.S.*, 1958, 24n. In his view the citations may well be authentic, since they could have been eliminated by commentators who had before them versions more complete than our surviving texts.

[2a]See L. Rocher at *Journal of the Oriental Institute*, III (1953–4), 1–7. [trs.]

Their real object is to give counsel in practical wisdom to kings, which is intended to secure the prosperity of the kingdom and the stability of the throne. They are treatises on royal policies, viewed as the interest of the king and of the state. Composition of such works went back very far, to the period of the *sūtras,* and it continued parallel to that of the *dharma-śāstras,* providing a literature which must once have been as large. From this old *arthaśāstra* literature only two works have actually survived, Kauṭilya's *Arthaśāstra,* the date (or dates) of which are in debate, and Kāmandaka's *Nītisāra.* Kāmandaka describes himself as a disciple of Viṣṇugupta, another name for Kauṭilya.[3] Apart from these, and apart again from citations (the most numerous of which are found in the Śāntiparvan of the *Mahābhārata*), we know only the names of authors to whom such works are attributed and who are sometimes the same as those to whom *dharma-śāstras* are assigned, namely Manu, Bṛhaspati, Nārada, Parāśara, etc., besides Uśanas (alias Śukra).

We might surely suppose that this literature must have had some influence on that of the *dharmaśāstra,* at least on the portions of the *śāstras* devoted to the function and duties of the king.[4] However no author of the *arthaśāstra* is so much as named in the *śāstras* themselves, so that any such influence must remain conjectural. By contrast the commentators and digest-writers certainly know of such treatises. They refer to them occasionally, or simply refer their readers thither.[5] Above

[3]Kauṭilya's *Arthaśāstra,* rediscovered in 1905, has given rise to an abundant literature (Kāṇe, I, 86). We need mention here only the translations of R. Shāmasāstry (Mysore, 1908–10), of J.J. Meyer (Leipzig, 1925) and of R.P. Kāngle (Bombay, 1963). Kauṭilya, alias Viṣṇugupta or Cāṇakya, is supposed to have been the preceptor and later the minister of Candragupta, the founder of the Maurya dynasty who owed his elevation to the throne to his political successes. Some scholars would place the composition of the *Arthaśāstra* in Candragupta's era (the first quarter of the fourth century B.C.). Others attribute it to the third or fourth century A.D. Renou, *L'Inde classique* II, s. 1598. The *Nītisāra* of Kāmandaka (often called simply the *Kāmandakīya*) is generally dated in the eighth century. We cannot mention Jain works here, and must pass with a bare mention the oft-cited *Śukranīti,* the apocryphal character of which is fully established (Lallanji Gopal, 'The Śukranīti, a nineteenth-century text', *B.S.O.A.S.,* 25 (1962), 524–56). On the relationship between Kauṭilya and related works on the one hand and *dharma-śāstra* texts on the other valuable information has been gathered by L. Sternbach in his 'Quotations from the Kauṭilīya-Arthaśāstra, I; II', *J.A.O.S.,* 88 (1968), 495–520, 717–27. That Kauṭilya was not Cāṇakya has been suggested by T. Burrow. [trs.]

[4]H. Jacobi, J.J. Meyer, P.V. Kāṇe, K.V. Raṅgaswāmī Aiyaṅgār, and U.N. Ghoshāl have pointed out undeniable correspondencies between the *Arthaśāstra* of Kauṭilya and the *smṛtis* of Manu, Yājñavalkya and Nārada. It is quite hypothetical to conclude from these affinities that one author borrowed from another or that there was a direct influence.

[5]For Bhāruci, see above, p. 94, n. 9. For Sternbach's investigation see above, n. 3. Aparārka cites prose passages from Uśanas. Viśvarūpa on *Yāj.,* I. 307 advises the king to appoint ministers according to the opinions expressed in the works of Bṛhaspati and Uśanas. Vijñāneśvara on *Yāj.,* II.21 also names Uśanas as a classical author in the field of *arthaśāstra.* Medhātithi on *M.,* VII.43 declares that the word *daṇḍa-nīti* in the text

all in the parts of digests devoted to the royal function we may expect to find citations borrowed from *arthaśāstra* works. Yet, even there citations are rare. The case of Bhāruci has already been mentioned, and Medhātithi followed him to that extent. However, Lakṣmīdhara in his *Rājadharma-kāṇḍa* and Ananta-deva in his *Rājadharma-kaustubha* stick strictly to *smṛti* texts. Nīlakaṇṭha in the *Nīti-mayūkha* and Mitra-miśra in his *Rājanīti-prakāśa* cite only the *Kāmandakīya*. Caṇḍeśvara is a notable exception. Though he takes Lakṣmīdhara for his model, his *Rājanīti-ratnākara* contains numerous extracts from works of *artha-śāstra*.

The interpreters' reticence with regard to *arthaśāstra* treatises does not depend upon a fundamental opposition between the characters of those works and that of the *dharma-śāstras*. Under the title of *rāja-dharma* the *dharma-śāstras* teach the king, as *arthaśāstra* works do, how he should govern if he is to perform his task properly. Manu (VII.99–100) and Yājñavalkya (I.317) recommend him a programme of action which does not differ from the quadruple object of the *arthaśāstra* according to the definition of Kauṭilya (I.4.3). Likewise the preoccupation with *artha,* profit or economic interests, especially when the context is the exercise of royal power, cannot be totally foreign to the outlook of *dharmaśāstra* writers, any more than could a concern for *dharma*, religious and moral duties, remain absolutely a matter of indifference to *artha-śāstra* authors. As Vijñāneśvara, the author of the *Mitākṣarā*, observes (on *Yāj*., II.21), there is no essential difference between the two sorts of works; it is only that *dharma* occupies the principal place in the first and a subordinate place in the others. In fact the distinction relates not to the object, which is similar, but to the way of seeing things. In the *dharma-śāstras* the function of the king is seen under its aspect of the duties incumbent on him in order that his mission should be accomplished. It is studied as an element in the social system of which it forms the keystone. In the *arthaśāstra* works it is studied in and for itself, in its aspect as an institution whose stability must be secured by the means appropriate to it.[6] It follows that if their precepts furnish a picture much more complete than the *dharma-śāstras* do of the machinery of a kingdom's administration and the various instruments of royal policy, these precepts, inspired by the interests of the state, could have only a weak response from the commentators and authors of digests. For them, royalty, which they believed to be as indispensable to the pros-

refers to the works of Cāṇakya (alias Kauṭilya) and others. The relationship between the *arthaśāstra* and the *dharmaśāstra* as two sciences and two literatures must remain something of a puzzle, in spite of the detailed studies of R.C. Hazra in *Our Heritage*.

[6]Cf the very relevant remarks of U.N. Ghoshāl, *A History of Indian Political Ideas* (Oxford, 1959), 82.

perity of the kingdom as did the *arthaśāstra* authors, could not be regarded as an end in itself. In their eyes it was essentially a source of duties which above all, it was important that kings should be taught to know.

2. *The Method of Interpretation*

The interpreter must first of all explain, if the need arises, the meaning of the words of his text. That is the simplest part of his task, but not the least useful, for at the period of the commentators certain terms were no longer in general use in the sense in which they were used in the *smṛtis*; and the text itself might be obscure by reason of its formulation or its conciseness. In this respect the value of interpretation is such that a *sūtra* or a verse unaccompanied by commentary is sometimes unintelligible. This does not mean that the commentators always agree as to the meaning of a word or a phrase. At the very least their opinions, however diverse they may turn out to be, have the merit of not being arbitrary.

But one of the essential tasks of interpretation distinguishes it completely from literary exegesis. It is the search from amongst the rules of *smṛti,* for that which ought to be held for an obligatory rule of conduct, viz. a rule the breach of which is a sin, a rule of *dharma.* As for our juridical texts, but with still more amplitude, there are multiple distinctions to be made between the rules of the *smṛti* so far as concerns their nature and their significance. The western jurist appeals to the intention of the legislator or to the end which he pursued. Such criteria cannot assist the interpreter, for the rule of *dharma* rests on a divine commandment whose profound reasons are beyond human intellects. Its formal aspect enables it to be grasped; its expression, and its expression alone, reveals what it means. This explains the importance of certain disciplines for the method of interpretation. Grammar, Logic, and above all the Mīmāṃsā have played a great role. Of the last one writer has no hesitation in saying that without a profound knowledge of that system it is out of the question to debate problems in Hindu law.[7]

Besides the sources *(mūla)* properly so called of *dharma,* Yājñavalkya (I.3) ranks the Mīmāṃsā amongst the bases *(sthānas)* of the knowledge of *dharma,* along with Nyāya (the system of formal logic) and the Vedāṅgas. Vasiṣṭha (III.20), Baudhāyana (I.1.1.8), and Manu (XII.111) call a *mīmāṃsaka* to sit in the *pariṣads* which are given the role of resolving controversial questions. It seems that very early the Mīmāṃsā was regarded as an indispensable science for the interpreter.

The Mīmāṃsā ("investigation")[8] is a method of exegesis which was

[7]Gaṅgānātha Jhā, Introduction to his translation of the *Vivāda-cintāmaṇi* (Baroda, 1942), vii.

[8]Also known as *pūrva-mīmāṃsā* to distinguish it from a 'subsequent' investigation *(uttara-mīmāṃsā),* namely the Vedānta.

originally confined to the Vedic texts. Its object was to secure the correct performance of sacrificial rites. Since the content of these rites is fixed by the "injunctions" *(codanā, vidhi)* of the Veda, the Mīmāṃsā propounds rules which enable the scholar to recognise a true injunction and to determine its sense and significance.[9]

The oldest treatise is the collection of *sūtras* attributed to Jaimini (whose date differs between the third century B.C. and the third century A.D. according to different scholars). The text is accompanied by a commentary *(bhāṣya)* of Śabarasvāmin (fifth cent.?), which was itself commented upon by Kumārila-bhaṭṭa (end of the seventh cent.) and by Prabhākara (called Guru), who was slightly later.[10] There are many more recent commentaries.

The *sūtras* of Jaimini were divided into 12 *adhyāyas*, each one of which is divided into many (generally four) *pādas* (quarters) and in each *pāda* one or more *sūtras* are grouped into *adhikaraṇas* (topics, subjects). Each topic is in principle subdivided into five parts : the subject of the investigation *(viṣaya)*, the doubt which it raises *(saṃśaya)*, the hypothesis or *prima facie* view *(pūrva-pakṣa)*, the reply *(uttara-pakṣa)*, and the conclusion *(siddhānta* or *nirṇaya)*.

As Colebrooke observes,[10a] this method of discussion is not without relevance to the method followed by the jurist in elucidating a point of law. This alone would suffice to explain why the Mīmāṃsā was the school where interpreters were trained for argument. But above all, since the real object of Mīmāṃsā was to study the injunctions and to develop a theory about them, interpretation found in it material ready to subserve its ends. It is true that the word *dharma* as understood in Mīmāṃsā is merely the ritual act, and that the Vedic injunction is only studied with a view to the correct execution of rituals; but the transposition of ideas was the easier for the fact that under the orthodox doctrine the rule of conduct which conforms to *dharma* takes its own source, directed or presumed, in the Veda. Likewise the Mīmāṃsā rules of interpretation found a domain of application ready-made in the *śāstras'* precepts concerning Good Custom and penances. But even in what concerns the rules of a specifically juridical character which go to make up the *vyavahāra* chapter(s), the extension of this method to the texts of *smṛti* was in no need of justification. The regulation of

[9]On the Mīmāṃsā in general see L. Renou, *L'Inde classique*, II, ss. 1370ff. There is a bibliography in Jhā's *Pūrva-mīmāṃsā in its Sources* (Benares, 1942) and Kāṇe, V, 1200–1201. The same volume of Kāṇe's work gives an excellent chapter on the subject.

[10]The *bhāṣya* of Śabarasvāmin was translated by G. Jhā (Gaekwad's Or. Ser., Baroda, 1933–36); the same writer has also translated the *Tantravārtika* and the *Ślokavārtika*, Kumārila's commentaries on the work of Śabara (Bibl. Ind. ser., Calcutta, 1903–24 and 1900–08).

[10a]*Miscellaneous Essays* (London, 1873), I, 342.

disputes is presented by the *dharmaśāstra* authors as a sacrificial act, or as if it were a sacrificial act, the rules of which must be scrupulously observed under pain of sin.

The Mīmāṃsā appeared to interpreters from the oldest to the most recent as a source for references on the same basis as the texts of *smṛti* themselves. Some seem more versed in them than others, but all of them use those principles without debate. It is true that the *sūtras* of Jaimini themselves sometimes give rise to discussion and that the opinions of his commentators differ. The interpreters of *dharmaśāstra* simply adopt the point of view of whichever of the commentators appears favourable to their outlook. By their time, however, the ritual acts with which the Mīmāṃsā is occupied had for the most part fallen into desuetude. The Vedic religion had been virtually dead for centuries, or had lived on in a more or less antiquarian atmosphere. Further, the arguments which the interpreters borrow from the Mīmāṃsā occasionally give rise to astonishment. It had become pure casuistry, speculation whose object had virtually ceased to have a reality. It found in the interpretation of *smṛti* a happy hunting ground, and thereby took on a new life. That life actually went on long after commentaries and digests had ceased to be written, and it is not the least curious aspect of legal practice in our own days that one can see the Anglo-Indian courts right up to the Privy Council discussing the bearing and meaning of a Mīmāṃsā principle in litigation.[11]

The way in which the commentators have utilised the Mīmāṃsā throws light on the resources of their dialectic and illuminates their mentality too. A systematic exposition of the way they proceeded would not be possible here. We can only refer to writers who have tackled this subject.[12] I shall confine myself to giving some examples of the most frequent uses of the technique. We shall meet others in the course of this chapter.

In the view of J.D. Mayne,[13] the Mīmāṃsā rules of interpretation were for the most part rules of good sense which any jurist might be

[11] *Sri Balusu Gurulingaswami* v. *Sri Balusu Ramalakshmamma* (1899) Law Reports, 26 Ind. App. 113. J.D. Mayne, *Hindu Law and Usage*, 11th edn. (Madras, 1953), s. 20, p. 37. Kāṇe, III, 676, n. 1277.

[12] The classic work is K.L. Sarkār, *The Mimānsā* (sic) *Rules of Interpretation as applied to Hindu Law* (Tagore Law lectures for 1905, Calcutta, 1909). See also J.N. Bhaṭṭāchārya, *Commentaries on Hindu Law* 3rd edn. (Calcutta, 1909), I, 97–152; the short but substantial treatment by A.B. Keith in the last chapter of his *Karmamīmāṃsā* (London, 1921); A.S. Naṭarāja Ayyar, *Mīmāṃsā Jurisprudence (The Sources of Hindu Law)* (Allahabad, 1952). Kāṇe's section in volume V (as noticed above) extending from p. 1152 to 1351 learnedly analyses the different forms of the Mīmāṃsā's contribution to the interpretation of *smṛti* precepts.

[13] *Op. cit.*, 8th edn. (Madras, 1914), s. 33. The passage has been retouched in the 11th edn, s. 20, pp. 35–6 and s. 21, p. 39.

brought naturally to use. The remark is only partly correct. There are maxims *(nyāyas)* taken from the Mīmāṃsā which are very like the Latin tags which western jurists are fond of citing to support or embellish their arguments and which express a generally accepted rule, a rule in many cases of simple good sense, such as *nemo dat quod non habet* (no one can transfer what he does not have). But such a citation strengthens the argument, and it is by no means useless to recall some primary truth in the course of juridical discussion. This is how it was with the use of certain axioms taken from the Mīmāṃsā which differ from ours only in point of their specifically Indian style. That is the case, for example, with the maxim of the black beans *(māṣa-mudga-nyāya)*. A Vedic text declares that black beans and some other cereals are unsuitable for sacrifices. Another text prescribes that on certain occasions offerings must be made with green beans *(mudga)*. If green beans are unobtainable can they be replaced by black ones? The question is examined according to the system indicated above (*Jai.,* VI.3.20). The conclusion *(siddhānta)* is that since the black kind have been expressly forbidden, one must avoid them even when they are mixed with the green variety and even when it would be difficult to distinguish the one from the other. When carried over into the usage of the *śāstric* interpreters, the rule means that every act contrary to the law is forbidden (cf. *contra legem facit qui id facit quod lex prohibet,* he breaks the law who does that which the law prohibits.). To some this may seem tautology, but none the less it elucidates numerous doubtful cases. For example, scholars are engaged in discussing whether a coheir who kept for himself property which was liable to partition, believing that it belonged exclusively to him, should be considered an offender. Jīmūtavāhana (*Dāy.,* XIII.8) believes that he can not be held to be a thief because that which he converted to his own use was at least partly his. He has not committed a sin, and all he must do is to bring into hotch-pot the goods in question. But Vijñāneśvara (*Mit.,* on *Yāj.,* II.127), referring to the maxim of the black beans, holds the selfish coheir to be an offender and deprives him of his quotient in the goods concealed or withdrawn. He relies on Manu (IX.213) according to whose terms "the eldest son who through cupidity has despoiled his younger brothers is no longer an elder brother; he should be deprived of his (preferential) share and be punished by the king". He concludes from this that since the prohibition of appropriating to oneself the goods of another is quite general it must be applied in a case even where the offender was a coproprietor.[14] From the very same maxim it has been concluded *e contrario* that everything which is not prohibited is permitted (cf. *quod non est lege prohibitum intelligitur concessum,* that which is not prohibited by law is understood to be

[14]Kāṇe, III, 636–7.

allowed). This is what Vācaspati Miśra does (*Vyav. cint.*, 298.1) à propos of Manu VIII.118, where the people are enumerated whose testimony is not to be accepted in court. When it is impossible to produce a witness possessing the required characteristics, it is permitted to substitute for him persons *not* fulfilling those conditions, *with the sole exception* of those explicitly disqualified by Manu's text. No one will doubt that in either case the reference to the maxim of the black beans is ineffectual: what has happened is simply that the authority of the Mīmāṃsā is used to reinforce the reasoning.

Further, when a precept taken from the Mīmāṃsā (III.2.1) lays down that the same word should not be taken in two senses in the same sentence *(barhir-nyāya)*, or even (VI.1.6–16) that the singular includes the plural and what is said of a male applies equally to a female *(grahaikatva-nyāya)*,[15] we are in the presence of rules (no doubt subject to their exceptions) which belong to the semantic stock in trade of the interpreter.

But we are in another sphere of application when the solution required by the Mīmāṃsā is regarded as an oracle in itself and justifies, or appears to justify, the interpretation. Thus Śaunaka, the author of a *dharma-śāstra* cited by Manu (III.16), declares that at the commencement of the ritual appropriate to an adoption the adopting parent shall honour the king and virtuous Brahmins with an offering of *madhuparka* (a mixture of honey, liquid butter and curds). Since the word is "Brahmins" in the plural, how many have the right to the offering? The author of the *Dattaka-candrikā*[16] resolves the difficulty by simply alluding to the maxim of the white partridges *(kapiñjala-nyāya)* (*Jai.*, II.1.38–45). A Vedic text prescribes that on the occasion of the horse-sacrifice one should sacrifice white partridges as an offering to Vasanta (the god of Spring). In this Mīmāṃsā passage the significance of the plural of the word partridge *(kapiñjalān)* is examined. At first sight the plural suggests any number exceeding two.[17] But the correct opinion is that here it means three only, for the Vedic injunction is entirely satisfied by the sacrifice of three partridges, and since one has done everything which the injunction prescribes by sacrificing three partridges one would be doing wrong if one went on and sacrificed more than the three. By analogy the author of the *Dattaka-candrikā* concludes that the plural *brāhmaṇāḥ* of the text ought to be understood as meaning three Brahmins and not more. In this case the solution which is adopted rests solely on the authority of the Mīmāṃsā.[18]

[15]Cf *genus masculinum complectitur et femininum* (words in the masculine include also the feminine). For the rule by statute in England see Maxwell, *Interpretation of Statutes*, 10th edn., 349, 412.

[16]In Sutherland's translation (Stokes's collection), p. 637.

[17]Sanskrit, like Greek, having the dual number and inflections accordingly.

[18]We may compare, from the *Sm. Cand.*, II, 297, an authoritative application of a

The few examples I have given so far of the application of Mīmāṃsā concepts to the interpretation of *śāstric* rules are intended to show the originality—some might say bizarreness—of such a use. But just as the Latin tags with which western jurists embellish their writings are far from representing what their professional education owes to the Roman or the common law, so the maxims *(nyāyas)* taken from the Mīmāṃsā of which the commentators make abundant use are only a feeble indication—a detritus—of the training which has made them what they are.[19] In reality the Mīmāṃsā has served the interpreters as a model even of exegetical methods. The deep discussion which they found there regarding questions of vocabulary, grammatical usage, syntax, and so on, has shown them the ways in which certain of their difficulties could be overcome and has given them help, almost philologically speaking, analogous to that afforded them from time to time by grammar. Only a transposition was needed to adapt to their own ends the reasoning of commentators on Jaimini and thus to find the key to a way of escape from their dilemmas.

The Mīmāṃsā has as its primary object the study of the injunction. It determined and examined the different forms under which it could present itself in the Vedic texts and undertook to define their respective scopes of application. Thus beside the primary injunction pure and simple *(utpatti-vidhi)*, it distinguished also the injunction of application *(viniyoga-vidhi)* which fixes the relation between the principal rite and a subsidiary action; the injunction of employment *(prayoga-vidhi)* which fixes the order in which the different parts of the rite should be performed; the injunction of qualification *(adhikāra-vidhi)* which fixes the conditions required if the doer of the action is to obtain the fruits of the ritual he has put into effect; the restrictive injunction *(niyama-vidhi)* which submits the doing of the act to determined conditions, excluding others which are equally possible; and the injunction of exclusive specification (*parisaṅkhyā-vidhi,* which operates as a prohibition), and so forth. These subtle distinctions furnish the *śāstric* interpreter with ready-formed means to analyse and classify the precepts of the *smṛti* and to define their nature and significance rigorously.[20]

But the prime task which the Mīmāṃsā undertook was to disengage the rules by which one could know from amongst the Vedic texts which were the propositions uttering a true injunction, distinguishing from

Mīmāṃsā rule of interpretation (*Jai.*, V.1, 14) to resolve a doubt about the dual *pitarau* in the text of *Yāj.*, II.135, in a manner diverging from that of Vijñāneśvara, who, for his part, relies upon Pāṇini and his commentators. Kāṇe, III, 720–3.

[19]Kāṇe, V, 1139–1351, gives a list of the maxims *(nyāyas)* which are most frequently cited by the commentators.

[20]On the different kinds of *vidhi* and the assistance which such distinctions can afford to the interpreters see Kāṇe, V, 1228–1232.

them those which were not imperative for the validity of the sacrificial act. First of all, an injunction emanating from the Veda, which is the very revelation of Truth, is peremptory, in the sense that one must conform to it for the sole reason that it is formulated. It requires no justification. It is self-validating. However, it often happens that the Vedic author adds to the utterance of the injunction some proposition which exalts the virtue of the act or has a bearing on some speciality of its performance. These subsidiary particulars, called *arthavādas,* have no bearing at all on the significance of the injunction and should not be understood to *explain* or justify the act. Thus it is prescribed in certain sacrifices that the *homa* libation[21] should be poured by means of the *śūrpa* (winnowing fan) and some texts add, "because it is by means of the *śūrpa* that that food is prepared". One wants to know whether these words supply the *reason* why one should use the *śūrpa*. Jaimini says not (I.2.26–30), for the injunction is self-sufficient. The phrase is an *arthavāda* which has no other object than to emphasise that the *śūrpa* should be used. If we understood it otherwise we might be led to think that the Veda prescribed the use of the *śūrpa* only because that utensil is used for the preparation of the *homa* and that therefore any utensil equally employed for that purpose could be used in the sacrificial act. Such a conclusion would be contrary to the contents of the injunction which mentions only the *śūrpa*.

There exist several varieties of *arthavāda*: descriptive passages, metaphorical passages, allusions to past events, allusions to current notions, etc. Vedic texts abound in them, and it is often difficult to know if what we have before us is an *arthavāda* or an injunction.[22]

The interpreters frequently avail themselves of the distinction between a *vidhi* and an *arthavāda,* either to resolve a conflict between the texts or to determine the meaning of a precept of *smṛti*. They use it with great virtuosity, as we shall see. Here we may confine ourselves to one particular case which is specially interesting because of the long controversy which the application of the Mīmāṃsā produced before the Anglo-Indian courts. Vasiṣṭha (XV.3) prescribed that one should neither receive nor give in adoption an only son. "For", says he, "[he should stay] to continue the line of his ancestors". It is clear that, by analogy with the rules of interpretation of the Mīmāṃsā, that last phrase should be taken as an *arthavāda,* intended merely to underline the importance of the only son. Vasiṣṭha wishes simply to prohibit the adoption of an only son. But if it is to be seen as the *reason* for the prohibition, the latter is weakened thereby, since a condition is imported into its application. The adoption of an only son would indeed be a sin on the father's part, but it would

[21] An oblation in fire, a ritual frequently prescribed for domestic ceremonies.
[22] Kāṇe, V, 1238–44.

not be invalid. Thus Vijñāneśvara (*Mit.*, on *Yāj.*, II.129–133), Nandapaṇḍita (*Dattaka-mimāṃsā* IV.1–6), the author of the *Dattaka-candrikā* (I.27) and Nīlakaṇṭha (*Vyav. may.*, IV.v.9, 16) pronounce in favour of absolute prohibition.[23]

On the other hand, if the authority of the injunction arises solely from the fact that it was formulated as such in the Veda, how can we recognise the same origin and consequently the same authority in prescriptions of the *smṛti* which do not happen to be referrable back to a Vedic text? Doubtless the rules set out in the *dharma-śāstras*, emanating from Sages versed in the Veda, are presumed to rest upon a Vedic injunction, even when their textual source cannot be verified. But this is only a presumption which the nature of the rule might rebut. Then there are in the *dharma-śāstras* precepts whose very form reveals that they could not derive their authority from a Vedic injunction. According to Śabara (on *Jai.*, I.3.3–4), the essential criterion is to be found in the motive which inspired them. The Vedic injunction really relies upon an invisible spiritual motive whose effect is not shown until the other world. If a precept of *smṛti* seems to be founded visibly on a worldly purpose, like the profit of him to whom it is addressed, that motive alone is the source from which its authority is drawn and that source cannot be located in the Veda, even in cases where it would not be in conflict with known Vedic texts. On the other hand, we may infer of a rule which appears to have no visible motive that it *is* founded on the Veda and that its authority stems solely from the Veda. Kumārila discusses this opinion at length and has a few reservations, observing that it is often impossible to dissociate in a Vedic injunction the invisible spiritual motive which inspired it from the visible motive—the two being inextricably blended.[24] To his mind one should find the criterion rather in the effect of the act. Every precept of *smṛti* whose effect cannot be experienced until the after-life and which remains as a result invisible in this world, should be presumed to have its basis in the Veda. Conversely a precept whose effect is shown in this life has no authority save that visible result.[25]

This criterion is of capital importance for the interpreters who refer sometimes to Śabara's commentary and sometimes to that of Kumārila.[26]

[23]However, the opposite conclusion was reached in Anglo-Hindu law after a debate which lasted the best part of the nineteenth century. Mayne, *op. cit.*, 11th edn., s. 174, p. 229.

[24]Thus, according to Kumārila, the rule that the *brahmacārin* must rise before the approach of his master as a sign of respect has a 'visible' motive, namely to please the master who will take a greater interest in teaching his pupil, and an 'invisible' motive, namely to secure that the Veda is taught him fully.

[25]The discussion is summarised by Kāṇe, III, 835–40 and V, 1260–3.

[26]Śabara's gloss is cited by Kullūka on *M.*, III.7. But Medhātithi, on *M.*, II.18, cites a passage of the *Tantravārtika* according to which 'a *smṛti* which is contrary to the Veda,

It allows them to distinguish between the precepts of the *smṛti* which have a religious value and consequently in their eyes a preeminently imperative character, and those precepts whose value is confined to their utility in the affairs of daily life. Surely this is evidence of their awareness of the difference between the profane (or secular) and the sacred. Thus Yājñavalkya lays down (I.52–53) amongst the conditions for marriage that the bride should not be affected by any incurable malady and that she should not be a *sapiṇḍa*[27] of her future husband nor of the same *gotra* (patrilineage) or *pravara* as he. Commenting on this text, Vijñāneśvara observes that the precept not to marry a girl with an incurable disease has a "visible" motive—the fear lest that disease should be transmitted to her offspring. This should be seen, consequently, as mere advice. On the other hand, the precept not to marry a girl who is a *sapiṇḍa* or of the same *gotra* is not founded on any visible motive and can have only a spiritual effect: it is therefore a rule of *dharma*. And Vijñāneśvara concludes from this that if a man marries a girl subject to an incurable disease he must risk the consequences (his children may inherit the disease) but the marriage is none the less valid. On the other hand, if he marries a girl who is a *sapiṇḍa* or of the same *gotra* the marriage ought to be treated as null and void.[28] Similarly, commenting on the verse of Kātyāyana (35) according to which "the king, having entered the court, shall look into the cases of the litigants, modestly clothed, with concentrated mind, seated facing the East", Vācaspati Miśra remarks that the precept that the king should be modestly dressed has a visible motive: the intention is to avoid intimidating the litigants. Conversely, that of being seated and facing the East, has no apparent motive. It must thus be founded on a motive of a spiritual kind, and to fail to observe it would be a sin on the king's part.[29]

We may note that the criterion founded on whether the object is visible or invisible *(dṛṣṭārtha,* or *adṛṣṭārtha)* comes from, or is connected with, the traditional classification established by the *trivarga* between the three ends or motive forces in human activity : *dharma* (righteousness, the Good), *artha* (the Useful) and *kāma* (the Pleasant). The rule of conduct which is inspired by a visible motive, that is to say a worldly one, is necessarily in the domain of *artha* or *kāma,* for this motive cannot be other than either the interest or the pleasure of the individual subject to it. By contrast a rule which is observed without reference to utility or pleasure in this world must belong to the domain of *dharma* from the

or disapproved by it, or which subserves a visible object and which proceeds from perceptible motives, can never depend upon the Veda'. It can never claim Vedic authority.

[27]On sapiṇḍaship according to Vijñāneśvara see Kāṇe, II, 452–8.

[28]Kāṇe, III, 837–8.

[29]*Vyav. cint.* 9.1–2 and n. 162.

moment when it is found prescribed in the *smṛti*. Its invisible effect, the *apūrva* ("non-previous") (the word could conceivably suggest also that the effect has no spontaneous motive), cannot be known until the after-life. The *dharmaśāstra* authors and their interpreters considered that conduct ruled by *dharma* was preferable to conduct inspired by interest or pleasure, because of the spiritual benefits which it secured. But this does not mean to say that a rule of *artha* or even of *kāma* must automatically be neglected, for, being the fruit of human experience, it might well formulate useful advice of current morality or provide a solution to difficulties of a practical nature. In other words, it could well have the status of a recommendation or even of a rule of law. This would not be the case where the rule of *dharma* is in contradiction with a rule of *artha* or *kāma* when, according to our authors, it must take priority. Thus Yājñavalkya declares (I.352) that the king must take pains to secure friends, for, he says, friends are worth more than gold or territory. This is valid advice in general, but given to the king in his own interest it appertains to the domain of *artha*. Likewise, when the same author enjoins the king to render justice according to the precepts of the *śāstras,* the king should decide the cases submitted to him without being concerned whether he makes friends thereby, for to follow the precepts of the *śāstra* is a religious duty for him, a rule of *dharma,* failure to observe which will react upon his future destiny through the operation of a cause otherwise unknown to us.

The principle is enunciated in the *smṛti* quite clearly: "A rule of *dharma* has more weight than a rule of *artha*" (*Yāj.*, II.21).[30] But one must note by the same token that where it is not repugnant to a rule of *dharma* a rule of *artha* is fully valid (as advice or as a rule of law).

It seems none the less curious on the part of the interpreters that they attribute superiority to dispositions of *smṛti* which are without any motive or visible object, i.e. without apparent utility. In reality nothing shows better than this criterion how very far their conception of their task was from that of a jurist in our sense of that word.

3. *Conflicts between texts*

THE PRINCIPAL task of the interpreters was to extract the rules of *dharma* from the mass of authoritative texts. Our first duty is to examine the means by which they managed to resolve the difficulties inevitably arising from the variety of legal propositions with which they were faced.

At the period of the commentators, *smṛti* had become the essential source for the knowledge of *dharma*. It had encompassed the precepts

[30]*arthaśāstrāt tu balavad dharmaśāstram iti sthitiḥ*. The same rule appears at *Nār.*, Intr. I.39 and *Kāt*. 32.

of *śruti*, and wherever the rule it contained could not be traced back to a known Vedic text, it was presumed to be founded on a passage which had escaped human knowledge. Manu himself (II.10) declares that *śruti* and *smṛti* "ought to be above all discussion *(amīmāṃsye)* on any point, for it is from those two that *dharma* proceeds". And Bṛhaspati (*Aiy.*, saṃskāra 228) compares to a one-eyed man any Brahmin who is versed only in *śruti*, since *śruti* and *smṛti* are like a pair of eyes. So the two written sources of *dharma* tend to be confused in a common interpretation.

When à propos of the same sacrificial act, the Vedic texts prescribe two different rules, it is possible, according to the Mīmāṃsā, to opt for either. This principle is found in Manu (II.14): "In a case of divergence between two precepts of *śruti* both are taken for [rules of] *dharma (dharmāv ubhau smṛtau)*, for both of them were declared *dharma* by the Sages". Medhātithi, like Vijñāneśvara (*Mit.*, on *Yāj.*, I.4–5) extends this principle to texts of *smṛti* itself. If there is a conflict between a precept of *śruti* and one of *smṛti*, the majority of the interpreters, following the opinion of Kumārila, believe that the rule formulated in *smṛti* will not lose any authority, and in consequence an option is permitted between them.[31]

But this option is not a solution which can be generalised. It may be that in a ritual context it is often possible to leave the choice between two methods of performing the act to the sacrificer himself. But, by their very nature, precepts of a juridical character generally demand that in any given context one must pronounce for one alternative and against the other. To admit an option is never better than a last resort. Therefore we are not allowed to admit that a conflict exists unless no other solution is conceivable.[32]

To resolve such difficulties we can take no account whatever of the relative age of works in which the conflicting texts are found. A verse attributed to Pitāmaha has as much force as one from the *Yājñavalkya-smṛti*. Bṛhaspati (*Aiy.*, saṃskāra 13) gives superiority to Manu above all the other *smṛtis* and declares that a *smṛti* which contradicts Manu has no authority *(manvartha-viparitā tu yā smṛtiḥ sā na śasyate)*. But this opinion has not prevailed, and Bṛhaspati himself often differs from Manu on important points.[33] Likewise no more than an echo has been heard of the verses of the *Parāśara-smṛti* (I.22–23) according to which the rules proclaimed by Parāśara alone would be valid for the

[31]Cf the passage of the *Ācārasāra* of Lakṣmaṇa-bhaṭṭa, cited by Maṇḍlik in the Introduction to the *Vyavahāra-mayūkha*, p. xxvii. Medhātithi admits the option (on *M.*, II.6) but thinks, as indeed does Kumārila, that it is preferable to follow the rule of *śruti*.

[32]That is the principle which is accepted by the Mīmāṃsā elsewhere, according to which option *(vikalpa)* is subject to eight faults. Kāṇe, V, 1250.

[33]Kāṇe, I², 487.

Kali Age. In any case, the fact that this *smṛti* deals only with Good Custom *(ācāra)* and penances and leaves *vyavahāra* alone withdraws a good deal of interest from its pretensions. For its part, the *Gobhila-smṛti* (alias the *Karma-pradīpa* of Kātyāyana) declares that in a case of conflict it is the rule accepted by the *majority* of authors which should be observed. This mechanical method of resolving conflicts (which recalls the curious "Law of Citations" of the late Roman empire)[34] seems never to have been employed by our interpreters.

Thus the interpreters were obliged to attempt to resolve by reasoning alone the apparent contradictions between texts of equal authority. Manu (II.11) inveighs against the critical spirit which would seek to undermine the authority of the sacred texts, and he even declares (IV.30) that a logician has no more right to the hospitality of a *dvija* than has a heretic. But he is only condemning the ill use which could be made of reasoning, and his commentators explain that the word for logician *(hetuka)* means here sceptics or adherents of false doctrines. Manu (XII.111) does grant a place in *pariṣads* to a logician *(hetuka)* beside the *mimāṃsaka*. And he fully recognises the value of reasoning when he says (XII.106), "He alone and no other knows *dharma* who ponders on [the teachings] of the *ṛṣis* and on the precepts of *dharma* relying on [a method of] reasoning not opposed to the Veda". This method of reasoning (here *tarka*),[35] is nothing other than Mīmāṃsā for interpreters such as Medhātithi and Kullūka. And all the resources of a dialectic which scrupulously respects the sacred texts are laid under contribution by the interpreters in general.

In order for a conflict to exist, both texts must state a genuine precept. If it is admitted that one of them does not have an imperative quality, the conflict disappears. The interpreters often have recourse to this point of view to remove texts which, otherwise, would have been embarrassing. Thus, a passage in the *Taittirīya-saṃhitā* (III.5.2.7) declares that the eldest son takes a larger share of his paternal estate than that of his brothers. Some authors do not accept this inequality at a partition. They say that it is inoperative, for the text contains no injunction, but a mere recital of events past *(anuvāda)* : it tells us what certain people do or have done.[36] Likewise a passage in the *Ṛgveda* (VII.4.7–8) seems to condemn adoption. But *smṛti* texts provide for adoption with a ritual under the form of a *homa* sacrifice, which allows us to presume that there was a Vedic injunction behind the *smṛti*. Consequently the Vedic

[34] I.3 C. Th. *de resp. prud.* (1.4). R. Sohm, *The Institutes, a textbook of the history and system of Roman Private Law*, 3rd edn. (Oxford, 1907), 118–9. [trs.]

[35] Gautama, XI.22–3 uses the same word *tarka* to indicate reasoning such as enables the king to unravel the truth in a dispute.

[36] Kāṇe, III, 622. The discussion is found at Āpastamba, II.6.14, 13.

text which disapproves of adoption is a simple *arthavāda* which cannot annual a *smṛti* precept recommending adoption and followed by an obligatory *homa*.[37] The same argument is employed, sometimes with an astonishing virtuosity, with regard to the precepts of the *dharma-śāstras* which appear to conflict.

Thus Nārada (I.81) says, "An object given as a pledge, boundaries *(sīmā)*, the property of a child, a deposit, a loan *(upanidhi)*, women, the property of the king or *śrotriyas* does not cease to belong [to their owners] by being in the possession of another". But the following verse decides, "Only excepting a woman or the property of the king, even pledges, etc. *(ādhyādiny api)* are lost to their owner when they have been openly in the possession of another during twice ten years". It seems that we are in the presence of two contradictory texts, the one not admitting that the owner of a pledge can lose his ownership, the other admitting on the contrary that, save for women and the property of the king, ownership is lost at the end of a certain lapse of time. Vācaspati Miśra (*Vyav. cint.,* 510–511) gets rid of this contradiction by seeing in the second text an *arthavāda* intended only to bring out the non-liability of a pledge to be acquired by prescription. He relies on the word *api* ("even") which signifies emphasis and he calls to mind, as an analogy, a phrase like this: "Even drinking poison would be better than to dine in that man's house". The words "even drinking poison" obviously do not mean that it is ever permissible to drink poison. Their only object is to emphasise the recommendation not to eat in that house. In the same way, the second verse of Nārada is simply directed to reenforce the rule laid down in the first. Medhātithi has recourse to the same special method of reasoning to deprive of all significance that verse of Manu (VIII.350) by which he allows that in self-defense one may kill even a Brahmin. For Medhātithi the killing of a Brahmin is always an inexpiable sin, for Manu elsewhere (IV.162) formally and unconditionally prohibits the doing of any harm to a Brahmin. Thus the first verse of Manu can only be taken to justify fully the right of self-defense in general: "If a natural reaction drives one who is attacked to kill even a Brahmin, who is a sacred person [whom no one has the right to touch] what need be said when the assailant is a non-Brahmin?"[38]

When this attempt at exclusion of conflicts cannot apply, and we are confronted with two precepts really dealing with the same matter, they should, in principle, be held to be mutually complementary. The interpreter must attempt to reconcile them, especially by trying to see whether one does not express the general rule and the other the exception,

[37] *Vīr., par.,* 27. *Nirṇaya-sindhu* cited by Kāṇe, III, 657 n. 1244.

[38] The same process of reasoning is found at Vijñāneśvara, *Mit.,* on *Yāj.,* II.21.

or whether each does not have its own proper scope of application.[39] We cannot fail to remark how the method of reasoning is always abstract. Our authors discuss only texts and existing opinions about texts. They never presuppose a standard other than pure logic, aiming—or at any rate *seeming* to aim—at nothing other than a rational solution.[40] They do not hesitate to have recourse to quibbles in order to support a solution which they believe to be well-founded, but the best of them deploy in their handling of the texts a technique which might well be the envy of our most subtle casuists or experts in distinguishing decided cases.

Let us take as an example the commentary of the *Mitākṣarā* on verse 24 of Book II of the *Yājñavalkya-smṛti*. The text goes as follows :

paśyato 'bruvato bhūmer hānir viṃśati-vārṣikī
pareṇa bhujyamānāya dhanasya daśa-vārṣikī.

"Of him who sees without objection his land occupied by another, a loss *(hāni)* is undergone with regard to that land at the end of twenty years; [if it is] a moveable asset *(dhana)*, ten years [are sufficient]".

According to certain commentators anterior to Vijñāneśvara, especially Asahāya (on *Nār.*, I.78), this verse would signify that after an uninterrupted possession of twenty or ten years under the eyes of the owner and without protest on his part, the possessor acquires property in the object. The word "loss" *(hāni)* would mean the loss of the thing itself, loss by the true owner of his right of property. Vijñāneśvara discards this opinion as conflicting with a verse of Nārada (I.87) which says "He who enjoys [the asset of another] without title, even for centuries, the lord of the land [i.e. the king] should inflict on that sinner the penalty

[39]Mīmāṃsā principles (II.1, 46) recalled especially by Vijñāneśvara, *Mit.*, on *Yāj.*, I.4–5 and by Medhātithi on *M.*, XI.216.

[40]Cf the verse from the (unpublished) *Bhaviṣya Purāṇa* cited in the *Vyav. cint.*, 10. *smṛtyarthayor virodhe tu arthaśāstrasya bādhanam, paraspara-virodhe tu nyāya-yuktaṃ pramāṇavat.* 'Where there is a conflict between *smṛti* and *artha*, the rule of *artha* is barred. Where there is a conflict between two rules of the same nature that which conforms to logic *(nyāya-yukta)* is authoritative.' The translation of *nyāya* by equity, preferred by L. Rocher, is debatable, for *nyāya* refers to a process of reasoning which facilitates a choice between the two rules, rather than a subjective notion which would make the choice depend upon the interpreter's assessment. Equity, as we know it, has no place here, but rather in the administration of justice where the king or his delegate, the deciding judge, is free to take into account the circumstances surrounding the matter before him. The interpreter, for his part, is confined to speculating on the texts. I do not think we need pay attention here to *Nār.*, I.40, which also is cited in the *Vyav. cint.* 11 : *dharmaśāstra-virodhe tu yukti-yukto vidhiḥ smṛtaḥ*, or, according to Bhavasvāmin's version (I.34) : *-yukto 'pi dharmataḥ.* 'Where there is a conflict between two precepts of the *śāstras*, it is the injunction which is obtained by reasoning *(yukti-yukto)* which should be respected.' For that verse refers to the administration of justice and the word *yukti* envisages reasoning based upon the circumstances of the case. Lingat, 'Les quatre pieds du procès', *J.A.*, 1962, 502 n. 18.

denounced against thieves". Whence it would appear to result that possession without title cannot lead to the acquisition of the property.

It is true that Vijñāneśvara recognises that the verse of Nārada applies only to the trespasser, to one who knows that neither he nor any of his predecessors have ever had any title to ownership of that asset. As for the possessor in good faith verse 27 of Yājñavalkya provides that possession without title cannot serve as proof of ownership unless it is prolonged through a line of ancestors *(pūrva-kramāgata)*, that is to say three generations, which Vijñāneśvara equates with a century.[41] After all, facts going back further escape human memory, and one can not expect a possessor to justify the origin of his possession. In other words, immemorial possession dispenses with title or enables it to be presumed. But wherever possession does not have this character it is entirely inoperative, because, since it cannot enable ownership to be presumed, it cannot *a fortiori* enable it to be acquired.[42] Now this is precisely the case with a period as short as ten or twenty years envisaged in *v*.24. Therefore this text cannot mean that property in the asset has passed to the possessor.

Vijñāneśvara then takes up another interpretation which connects *v*.24 with the preceding verse.[43] Verse 23 stands contrary to the general rule that when two contracts have been entered into successively the later in date prevails. It declares that if the same asset has been offered as a pledge, given, or sold successively to two people, it is the first contract which is binding. In other words the asset should belong to him to whom it was offered as a pledge, given, or sold in the first place. To this exception the following verse, namely our *v*.24, would in turn provide an exception: if he to whom the asset was pledged, given or sold in the second instance

[41]The same rule is expressed by *Kāt.*, 317 and by *Nār.*, I.91, both of which speak of possession extending through three generations *(tri-puruṣāgata)*. However, the verse of *Nār.* gives some little difficulty, because it provides that the possessor cannot be evicted even if his possession has been irregular *(anyāyenāpi)*, which is in contradiction with his verse 87 which is cited above. Vijñāneśvara *(Mit.*, on *Yāj.*, II.27) extricates himself from the difficulty by relying on the word *api* (as do Vācaspati Miśra and Medhātithi in the examples cited above, and as he has already done on *Yāj.*, II.21). This word *api* ('even') should, he says, indicate that if a possessor cannot be evicted when his possession is irregular, it follows *a fortiori* (and that would be the true sense of the line) that he cannot be evicted if his possession is not tainted by any irregularity. We could also understand *anyāyena* as simply meaning 'without title', *vināgamam*, which is what Asahāya actually does (on *Nār.*, I.91). On Bṛhaspati VII.73–74 see L. Rocher, *Adyar Library Bulletin*, XVIII, 3/4, 171–7. [trs.]

[42]Vijñāneśvara presents the argument as an application of the principles of Nyāya: that which is a means of proof *(pramāṇa)* cannot produce that which has to be proved *(prameya)*.

[43]This interpretation is to be found in the *Vyavahāra-mātṛkā* of Jīmūtavāhana (Kāṇe, III, 324 n. 464), but the author is not actually named in the *Mitākṣarā* (they seem to have been roughly contemporary).

had actually entered into possession and continued to possess it for ten or twenty years in full knowledge of the first without any protest on the latter's part, he would win the case. The loss *(hāni)* would fall upon the first lender who had required a pledge, or the first donee or vendee. Vijñāneśvara refutes this interpretation. He observes that it is not allowed for one who has already disposed of his asset to dispose of it again. The second transaction is thus void, and cannot affect the rights of the first transferee. Further, if the dispute is about a gift, it exposes both the donee and the donor to a heavy punishment (the *uttama-sāhasa*) (*Nār.*, IV.12).

Vijñāneśvara encounters another interpretation (proposed in fact by Viśvarūpa, on *Yāj.*, II.26, who is not actually named), founded on the following text of Nārada (*ed. Sāmb.*, II.71): "Of him who shows indifference *(upekṣā)* or who stays silent *(tūṣṇīm-bhūta)*, when the time prescribed [for suit] has elapsed, action is no longer allowed *(vyavahāro na sidhyati)*." The words *upekṣā* and *tūṣṇīm-bhūta* correspond (so it seems) to *paśyataḥ* and *abruvataḥ* in the *Yājñavalkya-smṛti*. Thus *v.*24 would signify that after having left a third party to enjoy his asset in his presence without protest for ten or twenty years, the true owner has lost his right of action. *Hāni* would be loss of judicial remedy. The owner could not go to court to recover his asset, but he would not necessarily have lost his right of property.

This loss of a judicial remedy does not necessarily produce the same result as if the right of property itself had been extinguished. Devaṇṇabhaṭṭa (*Sm. cand.*, II. pp. 68–69), who supports this theory, contends in effect that the only loss is that of proof in court by the human means of proof *(mānuṣa-pramāṇāt)*; but the owner would be permitted to take recourse to an ordeal. This opinion is supported by a passage of the *Saṃgraha-kāra*,[44] where it is said that written proof or witnesses are of no value when property is sought to be recovered from a possessor. Aparārka, whose theory is closely similar, speaks only of the owner's right to take recourse to an ordeal. But he considers that *v.*24 merely states the presumption of ownership in a possessor's favour, a presumption adequate to bar the action of the owner in a court of justice, but such as a scrupulous possessor should hesitate to rely upon or exploit. He who knows that the asset which he enjoys really belongs to another, even though he cannot be evicted from it by legal means, can nevertheless restore it to its rightful owner out of regard for sin which would otherwise be incurred.

Thus the expiry of a period of ten or twenty years could well have the effect of paralysing the proprietor's legal action, but it would not put

[44]Mys. edn. III/1 (1914), 157. On this *smṛti* which is often cited in the *Sm. cand.*, see Kāṇe, I, 239–42 (and I², 541).

an end to the ownership as such. The latter may still be recognised, whether by the true owner's taking recourse to an ordeal, or through the free consent of the third party who is in possession.

This theory is severely criticised by Vijñāneśvara. First of all he declares that inactivity *(upekṣā)* or silence *(tūṣṇīm-bhāva)* on the part of the true owner cannot be held by itself to be sufficient reason for his loss of the right of action, for it could have been due to causes over which he had no control. Thus texts of Manu (VIII.148) and Nārada (I.80) provide that the owner who allows a stranger to enjoy his asset is not deprived of his rights if he (the owner) is of unsound mind or a minor. Now Medhātithi observes that the cases of unsoundness of mind *(jaḍatva)* or of minority *(pogaṇḍatva)* are cited only as examples, and what is really envisaged in those texts is the complete series of cases in which a person is found incapable of undertaking litigation. So, according to Vijñāneśvara, Manu's and Nārada's intention is not to make the loss of a judicial remedy depend from the simple passivity of the true owner or a simple default on his part in exercising his right, but from the absence of causes which would explain or account for his passivity. When none of those causes seems to exist, as for example, when the true owner is neither a lunatic nor a minor, the possessor can defend an action for ejectment in the following way: "The plaintiff is neither of unsound mind nor a minor. I have enjoyed his asset to his knowledge for twenty years without interruption. If my possession commenced in an irregular way why has he remained inactive and silent for so long a period? To support what I say I can produce witnesses." In such a case it is likely that the plaintiff would be unable to reply to this, and he would lose his case. But after all the only problem there was one of fact, and if the true owner has arguments to pursue to establish his right, there is no reason to hinder his doing that. And Vijñāneśvara recalls that it is the duty of the king, when a case is before him, to decide according to the merits of the action, without allowing himself to be distracted from that task by chicanery *(chala)* (*Yāj.*, II.19).

One could equally contend, continues Vijñāneśvara, that *v*.24 intends merely to induce the true owner not to be inactive, for if he does not exert himself while his asset is in the hands of a stranger, he runs the risk of seeing the latter pleading prolonged possession as a means of keeping himself *in* that possession. This theory is taken up again later by Vācaspati Miśra (*Vyav., cint.*, 467–469) who cites a text of Vyāsa in support: "Just as a cow is lost to her owner when he does not take care of her and lets her wander unguarded, so, at the end of a particular period, land is lost when it is enjoyed by others under the eyes of its true owner". In other words, the loss of his asset would be a sort of punishment for the owner's negligence.

Vijñāneśvara refutes this theory too. He remarks that if the text of Yājñavalkya ought to be interpreted as containing an injunction to the owner not to remain inactive it would be impossible to find a plausible explanation for the sanction attached to the period of ten or twenty years. A possession for so short a period cannot raise any presumption in favour of the possessor's proprietary right. The text of Vyāsa can only be referred to on the hypothesis that it deals with *immemorial* possession.

After refuting in this way, one after another, the different interpretations suggested before his time, Vijñāneśvara concludes with his own. For him the word *hāni* in *v.*24 signifies the loss, not of the asset, nor of the right of action, but of the produce or profits (*phala,* fruit) of the asset. Thus if the true owner is to sue successfully he can expect nothing but the asset itself: he cannot obtain from the trespasser whom he has ejected the value of the profits obtained by the possessor during the period of his possession. This loss of profits is due to his wrongly remaining inactive throughout that period. Vijñāneśvara remarks that, in any case, it *could* happen that the asset itself would be lost to the owner: this could well be the case if enjoyment of it (e.g. of an article of clothing) actually implies using it up or wearing it out. It is only if the fruits or profits can be detached from the source of those profits, as is the case if the asset possessed is, for example, a jack-tree, that the true owner can recover his asset.

Reading this long commentary, of which I have given only a summary, a jurist is put in mind of the different solutions which an analogous problem has called forth in Roman law and in the older and modern common law. This deployment of arguments cannot be treated as a mere joke. What we know of the personal standing of Vijñāneśvara[45] and above all the authority which his work has enjoyed leave us no room for doubt that he wanted to give a solution of a rational character to difficulties which arose out of the diversity of the texts which he had before him. It is clear that he was profoundly hostile to acquisition by prescription against the true owner and that in his eyes possession, no matter how long, could not be a means of acquiring ownership. It is this preconceived opinion which guides his steps through the maze of texts, which induces him to align them one after another like landmarks leading whither he knew he would arrive, and brings him finally to reduce to a minimum the significance of the rule actually expressed by his author, Yājñavalkya.

It is clear that if the reasoning had been directed otherwise it could have arrived at a very different conclusion. Authors who, like Viśvarūpa

[45]Vijñāneśvara belonged to a celebrated Brahmin family. It is known that he wrote the *Mitākṣarā* at the request of Vikramāditya VI of the dynasty of the Cālukyas of Kalyāṇi.

or Aparārka, give possession for ten or twenty years the status of a means of defense, analogous to the *praescriptio longi temporis* of classical Roman law,[46] use arguments which render such a solution perfectly valid. As for those who, taking *v*.24 literally, attribute an acquisitive power to prolonged possession by the trespasser, their arguments do not fail to support their opinion and to dispose of the texts followed by Vijñāneśvara. They hold, for example, with Śrīkara[47] that *v*.24 only applies when the owner is present, while *v*.27 and analogous texts which provide for possession for three generations only come into effect if the possessor came into possession while the owner was absent or dwells in another region. As for the verse of Nārada (I.87) which says that he who enjoys without title even for centuries should be punished by the king, we could believe, with Raghunandana, that it applies only to possession of an asset belonging to a woman *(strī-dhana)* or to the king;[48] or even, with Śūlapāṇi, that this text is a rule of *arthaśāstra* which cannot prevail against *v*.27 of Yājñavalkya which expresses a rule of *dharma*;[49] or even, again, with Devaṇṇa-bhaṭṭa and others, that it applies only when there is no doubt that the possessor has no title to the asset.[50] Finally for others *v*.24 has only an even more limited application. It applies only between co-heirs where one of them has obtained at the partition a portion smaller than that to which he was entitled; or between two possessors in succession equally without title, in which case the first, no matter how long he had possession, was evicted by the second after twenty or ten years of peaceful possession; or even in favour of a possessor whose title was affected by some flaw. Possession for ten or twenty years without protest on the part of the true owner would thus serve to cover the irregularity in the title, etc.

There is no occasion to be surprised that interpretation should terminate in conclusions differing from writer to writer. Our own legal treatises evince divergencies striking enough in their way. Given the abundance and great diversity of the texts which constitute *smṛti*, the commentators and digest-writers had a good hand to play. But interpretation as such

[46]Sohm, *op. cit.*, 319. D. Nörr, *Die Entstehung der* longi temporis praescriptio (Cologne and Opladen, 1969). [trs.]

[47]Cited in the *Vyavahāra-mātṛkā* (Kāṇe, III, 324). Śrīkara, according to Kāṇe (I, 268) lived between 800 and 1060. His work is known to us only from quotations made by commentators.

[48]To support this interpretation Raghunandana invokes *Nār.*, I.83, which provides that the property of a woman or the king is never lost (to its owner) even if it has been in the possession of another for centuries. *Vyavahāra-tattva*, 53.

[49]Cited in the *Vyavahāra-tattva*, *ubi cit.*

[50]*Sm. cand.*, II, 74.

[51]Medhātithi (on *M.*, VIII.148) reviews most of these interpretations. A. Ṭhākur, *Hindu Law of Evidence* (Calcutta, 1933), 240–63. Kāṇe, III, 320–5.

played a larger part than did juridical theory as we know it. Whether we are considering the work of Vijñāneśvara or any other, there is no reason whatever to doubt the good faith of the interpreters. Each of them is convinced that the solution he proposes is the one which emerges from the totality of the *smṛti*, and which consequently expresses the rule of *dharma*. One may well say that the Indian mentality is not so sensitive to contradiction as we are, and conceives that there may be, in this domain if not in many others, ways of looking at things which are divergent but at the same time equally plausible. However that may be, it is certain that each of the proposed solutions was an authority (I do not say that it was necessarily received and adopted) at a particular period and in a particular place. Thus if we wish to envisage a general evolution of ideas—in default of an evolution of law, which remains beyond our power to achieve—it is upon such solutions as these that we must rely. So, to return to *v*.24 of Book II of the *Yājñavalkya-smṛti,* A. Ṭhākur[52] thinks it possible to conclude from the various interpretations to which the verse gave rise that originally the general opinion of the writers was favourable to the priority of possession over title, then placed title above possession, and then reverted, at a period which Ṭhākur places a little before Vācaspati Miśra, to the first solution which gives plain effect to *v*.24. The uncertainty which surrounds the periods at which some authors must have lived renders this kind of work far from easy. Then we must take account of the fact that opinions differed from place to place.[53] So this example is only given here to illustrate how idle it is, so far as the commentators are concerned during the period when the law was being constructed and probably so far as the previous epoch was concerned also, to keep close to the letter of the *śāstras* with the idea of forming a notion of what was the law actually in force. In reality multiple solutions were derived from the texts, all believed to be equally valid, proffered to different ages and different milieux of Indian society in order that *dharma* might be realised.

They were so preoccupied with the task of extracting the rule of *dharma* by the application of pure reasoning, and their taste for debate was so lively, that it would be perverse to think that the interpreters voluntarily forswore an attempt to write a book that would be useful. The solutions they commended must have been those which, in their eyes, had the greatest chance of passing into actual practice. If the texts were capable of several different interpretations, that one should be preferred (to their minds) which best fitted the needs of their times and was nearest to current usage.[54] A rule taken from *smṛti* which is confirmed

[52]*Op. cit.*, 234.

[53]Mitra-miśra (*Vīr.*, *vyav.*; *Dh. k.*, 392–96) and Nīlakaṇṭha (*Vyav. may.*, II, ii, pp. 5–6) follow the opinion of Vijñāneśvara and they wrote in the middle of the seventeenth century.

[54]Derrett, at *Adyar Library Bulletin* 31–2 (1967–8), 531–53; 33 (1969), 135–81.

by practice acquires a particular force, for the religious sanction is accompanied then by a social sanction: it becomes a juridical rule. Usage would thus be a sort of test for interpretation.

There is a text of Yājñavalkya (II.21) as taken by certain commentators, which would support our point of view :

smṛtyor virodhe nyāyas tu balavān vyavahārataḥ

Vijñāneśvara connects *vyavahārataḥ* with *nyāya* and construes, "determined according to the practices of the past". Thus the text can be translated, "In case of a conflict between two *smṛtis*, reasoning *(nyāya)* guided by the practices of the past has (more) force".[55]

It is presumed, therefore, that the usages practised by the men of the past, that is to say from time immemorial, are conformable to the teaching of the Sages. If those usages are corroborated by an interpretation of *smṛti* texts, then that is the interpretation which ought to be preferred.

Nīlakaṇṭha has recourse to this criterion to fix the sense to be attributed to Manu (IX.210) on the subject of a second partition of family property. This text says that "when brothers, who were first separated, have rejoined in a state of indivision and then proceed to a new partition, the shares must be equal : there is no special share for the eldest". Certain commentators (Aparārka, Mādhava, Kamalākara and others) rely upon the last phrase of the verse and contend that Manu only intends to prohibit any inequality arising from the right of the eldest son[56] but not any inequality which might result from differences between the values of the parts of the formerly joint family property which had been put together to form a reunited stock. Nīlakaṇṭha rejects this opinion, first because he considers the last phrase as an *arthavāda,* intended solely to emphasise the equality of partition ("even the eldest" must renounce his preferential share) and because equality of participation is a rule confirmed by custom : "Because it is possible to construe the text in a sense which conforms to usage, it would be incorrect to suppose that the text could enunciate a solution contrary to it".[57]

Likewise one finds in *smṛti* contradictory provisions regarding the *sapiṇḍī-karaṇa* to be done by a son for his dead mother. The son has a choice amongst three solutions: but the practice of his family should prevail if we follow Vijñāneśvara (*Mit.,* on *Yāj.,* I.253–254).[58]

[55]This hardly seems a natural translation; but it is accepted by Kāṇe, III, 866. Ghārpure and Maṇḍlik translate *nyāya* by 'equity', but see above, p.161, n. 40. Commentators agree in taking the word in the sense of rules of logic.

[56]Some *smṛtis*, especially Manu (IX.114–116) allow the eldest son a preferential share *(uddhāra)* when the paternal estate is being partitioned. Kāṇe, III, 624–6. The question was agitated as recently as the case of *Siromani* v. *Hemkumar* A.I.R. 1968 S.C. 1299. [trs.]

[57]*Vyav. may.* IV.ix.2–3.

[58]Kāṇe, IV, 524. *Sapiṇḍī-karaṇa* is a *śrāddha* which takes place in principle one year

Another example where usage confirms the text is particularly interesting. It is the interpretation presented by Mādhava of verses 172–173 of Book IX of Manu, which reprehend the marriage of a boy with his maternal uncle's daughter or his paternal aunt's daughter (an exceedingly common match amongst South Indians) and hold it to be a grave sin. "He who has relations with the daughter of the sister of his father [who is for him] a sister *(bhaginī)*, or with the daughter of the sister of his mother, or with (the daughter) of his mother's brother [who is] *āpta*, should observe the lunar penance *(cāndrāyaṇa)*."[59] "A wise man will not take as his wife [any of] these three women; because of sapiṇḍaship one must not marry them, for he who marries one of these falls into hell."

Other *dharma-śāstras* (Śātātapa, Paiṭhīnasi, Sumantu, Vyāsa) state the same prohibition without qualification, emphasising solely the closeness of *sapiṇḍa* relationship. What the rule really amounts to is that one should not marry a *sapiṇḍa* girl. Now the uncle's or aunt's daughter is a cousin through an ancestor found in the third degree. However narrowly one may construe the rule as to the minimum number of degrees required to be a *sapiṇḍa* no one can doubt that the marriage falls within the scope of the prohibition.

Moreover the majority of interpreters agree that the text of Manu has general application. Medhātithi (on *M.*, II.18) knows very well that marriage with the maternal uncle's daughter occurs in certain regions, but he pronounces such usage *adharma (non-dharmic*, or even *anti-dharmic)*.

But Mādhava, who is a man of the South where such marriages have not only been allowed for an immense period[60] but are actually viewed as desirable, evades the *smṛti* texts. He first places in opposition to them some Vedic passages which, in his view, refer to marriage with the maternal uncle's daughter or the paternal aunt's daughter. Then he shows, by applying Mīmāṃsā principles, that these passages must indeed be understood as formulating an injunction *(vidhi)* and that they are not simply descriptive *(arthavādas)*.[60a] Mādhava could have stopped there, given the rule that in case of conflict between *śruti* and *smṛti* the *śruti* rule must prevail. But he was evidently anxious to respect

after the death. The deceased thereafter ceases to be a *preta* (ghost) and is raised to the status of *pitṛ* (one of the *manes* or departed ancestors).

59 *paitṛṣvaseyīṃ bhaginīṃ svasrīyāṃ mātur eva ca*
mātuś ca bhrātur āptasya gantvā cāndrāyaṇaṃ caret.

60 *Gaut.*, XI.20, and *Baudh.*, I.1.2, 3 cite marriage with the maternal uncle's daughter as one of the special customs of the 'South'.

60a *Parāśara-Mādhavīya* I, 2, pp. 63–8. Mādhava's commentary is reproduced by Maṇḍlik in an appendix to his translation of the *Vyavahāra-mayūkha*, 417–21. In Setlur's collection it appears at pp. 550–3. Kāṇe, II, 460–3.

Manu's authority, and he tries hard to show that his precepts merely do not have so large an application as one might suspect.

For this purpose he relies on the words *bhaginī* and *āpta* in *v*.172 in order to contend that that verse applies only upon the hypothesis that the father's sister or mother's sister or the mother herself were married in an inferior form of marriage, say the *gāndharva, āsura,* etc. It is only in this case, he says, that the daughter of the paternal aunt *(paitṛ-ṣvaseyī)* or maternal aunt *(svasrīyā mātur)* could be called *bhaginī,* "sister", by her bridegroom! If the aunt is married in the Brahmā, Daiva or other approved form of marriage, she passes into the *gotra* of the family of her husband, the sapiṇḍaship relation is broken with her natal family, and the word *bhaginī,* "sister", cannot be employed. Similarly, the mother's brother can only be called an *āpta*[61] (i.e. a close relation of his sister) if she has retained her relationship with her natal family by marrying in one of the unapproved forms of marriage. Thus the prohibition which Manu utters is not general. It does not apply to the case where the daughter who has been married is the child of a marriage contracted in one of the higher forms, i.e. the Brāhma or other approved forms.

It is true, Mādhava adds, that this reasoning would permit us equally to recognise the validity of a marriage with the maternal *aunt's* daughter. But such a union has always and everywhere been reprehended by the *śiṣṭas*. This raises the presumption that there was a Vedic injunction condemning such unions. On the other hand, although marriage with the maternal uncle's daughter is rejected by the (majority of) the *śiṣṭas* of Northern India it is admitted by those of the South. This usage on the part of Southerners cannot be attributed to license, for it is practised by pious people who are learned in the sacred texts. Further, since it is corroborated by the interpretation given to texts, it must be recognised as valid in the regions where it is an immemorial custom.[62]

In order to provide *smṛti* rules applicable to a population with manners and customs as varied as those of the vast subcontinent of India, the interpreters were bound to use their ingenuity to justify varied solutions. We have just seen that marriage with the maternal uncle's daughter is *dharma* for Southerners but *adharma* for Northerners. No one can doubt that Mādhava was orientated here in his reasoning by custom, since in the end he expressly cites it as the criterion of his interpretation. But we can hardly doubt that even in the many cases where our authors make no allusion to custom at all and base themselves solely on logic

[61] An *āpta* is so close a relation that his evidence cannot be tendered in litigation on behalf of his kin. Medhātithi on *M.*, VIII.64 illustrates the word *āpta* in that context by paternal and maternal uncles.

[62] The same reasoning is followed by Devaṇṇa-bhaṭṭa, *Sm. cand.*, I, 70–4.

and a purely literal exegesis, they have been guided by a desire to validate a practice which struck them as blameless. In the same way, the western judge tries to use the texts—when they permit it—to arrive at a solution which, on the facts of the case, seems to him most equitable or most practical. Thus there were formed in India, according to the different writers, different currents of interpretation responding to different customs. A given group would find in a given author, in preference to certain others, a formulation suitable to its usages. Different juridical systems actually grew up, based on the same totality of texts and drawing their authority from nowhere else but the texts which they all held sacred.

To these juridical systems the British (Colebrooke was the first) gave the name of "schools", the schools of Benares, Mithilā, Bengal, and so on. The expression was justly criticised because it seemed to give a regional basis to divergencies of opinion which were essentially personal.[62a] Diversity of interpretation finds only a feeble echo in the West. The Cour de Cassation (in France), the House of Lords (in Great Britain) and the Supreme Court (in the United States and even more so in India) have jurisdiction to secure the unity of the case-law and so much of jurisprudence as is based squarely upon it. To understand what happened in India as a result of this recognition of "schools" we should take for comparison politically autonomous countries which have adopted the same laws. France, Belgium, and Holland for example, have what is virtually the same civil code. The very same article of the code can be, and sometimes is, differently interpreted in each of the three countries. In India where local populations have always had the benefit of measures of autonomy, and where a great variety of tribunals used to coexist, the real diversity of customs must have involved a diversity of laws.

But I do not mean to say that commentators and digest-writers had no object but to confirm or canonise customary rules. Such rules must be able to find a point of contact with *smṛti*, and there are some customs which no amount of text-torturing could legitimise. A scope of conflict thus makes its appearance which we shall make our special study in the next chapter. Further the customary rule must present characteristics which permit of a *dharmic* rule's being seen in it. In particular it must not rest upon a "visible" motive, a worldly purpose. We have seen how Mādhava does not fail to observe that the custom of marrying the maternal uncle's daughter had the sanction of the *śiṣṭas* and those who were learned in the sacred texts. The interpreters were thus brought to make a choice between customs, rejecting some, amending others, following, though perhaps in a different spirit, the slow work of "āryanisation" which the authors of the *dharma-śāstra* itself carried on. But

[62a] K.V. Raṅgaswāmī Aiyaṅgār, *Rājadharma* (Madras, 1941), 112.

above all, interpretation could only provide legal foundation for an institution which was originally customary by deducing the principle from the *śāstras*. The interpreters constructed the institution from that principle upwards, connecting by a logical thread the different precepts which they contained. In other words, as we have already observed à propos of the commentary on *v*.24 of Book II of the *Yājñavalkya-smṛti,* interpretation ends in a harmonisation of texts scattered in the *smṛti,* which is intended to gather them into a coherent system. It is rare for customary rules relative to an institution of law to be met with in a connected form, linked so rigorously. They are often imprecise and incomplete. Interpretation offers them a framework which demands adjustments and correctives in enunciation, at the same time as it allows their gaps to be filled. It is true that the interpreter does not work upon customary data, but he is inspired by them and makes for them, if not actually with them, a system to which they are invited to adapt themselves. We grasp thereby the influence which interpretation could exercise upon custom, even when custom has not directed its choice.

A good example of the systematisation thus offered to customary data is furnished by the celebrated divergence between doctrines of the *Dāyabhāga* and those of the *Mitākṣarā* on the subject of the rights of the son (and further male lineal descendants) in succession to ancestral property.[63]

For Vijñāneśvara the sons' right arises from their relationship as sons. It is acquired by birth alone. From the moment of birth (or rather conception in the case of a live birth) the sons have a right over the ancestral estate, they are coproprietors with their father. For Jīmūtavāhana, the author of the *Dāyabhāga,* on the other hand, the issue have no right in the said estate during the lifetime of their father. Their right arises only on his death (or on events assimilated to death, namely exclusion from caste, and the adoption of the status of ascetic), whereupon they become coheirs and coproprietors *inter se*.

We must pass over the long argumentation by which the two authors play with the *smṛti* texts and come to such violently opposed theses.[64] What especially interest us are the consequences of a juridical character which they have drawn from them. Each relied solely on the *smṛti* and refuted by reasoning the surface meaning of texts which seemed to be in opposition to him. Those consequences which naturally differ on each point can be summarised as follows :

1. In the *Dāyabhāga* system a son cannot in the lifetime of his father

[63]Called *paitāmaha,* i.e. assets received by the father from the grandfather (or other lineal ascendant). *G. Lakshminarasamma* v. *Rama Brahman* Indian Law Reports 1950 Madras, 1084. [trs.]

[64]*Dāy.*, I, 11–30; *Mit.,* on *Yāj.,* II.114. Kāṇe, III, 552–4.

obtain a partition of the ancestral property unless the father consents to this. In principle the partition will not take effect until the death (or civil death) of the father. Jīmūtavāhana is even of the opinion that it should not take place until the death of the mother, if she survives him.[65] In the *Mitākṣarā* system, by contrast, the son has a right to demand partition of the ancestral property, even against his father's will.[66]

2. In the *Dāyabhāga* system the father possesses in principle the same powers of alienation over the ancestral estate as he has over his personal assets.[67] In the *Mitākṣarā* system he can dispose at his pleasure of only his personal property. In respect of ancestral property his powers are limited. Beyond acts which the law allows him he requires the consent of his sons.[68]

3. On the death of the father, in the *Dāyabhāga* system, there is a real succession, a transfer of property, with the sons inheriting from the father. If they remain undivided their shares remain fixed at the proportion it was at the father's death. There is common possession, but not common property: they are tenants-in-common, not joint tenants. Each can dispose of his undivided share in the common estate. If one dies succession opens and his estate, including his share in his father's estate, passes to his heirs.[69] In the *Mitākṣarā* system there is no succession on the father's death. The sons enter into possession of the goods he leaves by right of "survivorship". Their portions have received an accretion from the portion which was their father's. If they remain undivided none of them can dispose of his share without the consent of the others: they have a common possession and a common property. They are mere joint tenants. If one of them dies there is no question whatsoever of a succession. His interest accrues to those of the others. The result is that each one's share, instead of being defined once for all as in the *Dāyabhāga* system, is capable of being enlarged (by deaths) just as it is capable of being diminished by the birth of, for example, a grandson.[70]

We must note that these provisions have not been presented in the

[65] *Dāy.*, I, 44 and II, 5.

[66] *Mit.*, on *Yāj.*, II.122.

[67] *Dāy.*, II, 22–4.

[68] *Mit.*, on *Yāj.* II.114. This position was once more complicated than at present. Originally the consent of adult male issue was required to validate even justified acts. But the position in British India is now universally adopted, namely that major as well as minor issue are bound by justified transfers entered into by their father. Derrett at (1965) 67 Bombay Law Reporter, Journ., 96–8 (a criticism of *Balmukand* v. *Kamla Wati* All India Rep. 1964 S.C. 1385). *Raghubanchmani* v. *Ambica* A.I.R. 1971 S.C. 776; *Rani* v. *Santa* A.I.R. 1971 S.C. 1028; also App. 2 to *Critique of Modern Hindu Law* (Bombay, Tripathi, 1970). [trs.]

[69] *Dāy.*, II, 28–31.

[70] *Mit.*, on *Yāj.* II.114. For a more detailed comparison see Kāṇe, III, 591–4. The Hindu Succession Act, 1956, ss. 6 and 8, provides that where a coparcener dies leaving a mother,

theoretical guise in which I have set them down here. They are accompanied by nuances imposed or justified by the texts. In the *Dāyabhāga* family, for example, the father is master of all the family property. If however, he wishes to proceed in his lifetime to make a partition, he can distribute at his will and pleasure only his personal wealth, whereas in respect of ancestral property the partition between himself and his sons must follow certain rules.[71] Conversely in the *Mitākṣarā* family where the father is merely a coproprietor in the family property, his powers of administration are much more extensive than those which are given to an ordinary co-owner appointed to the management of property in co-ownership.[72] But none the less the two systems are rigorously worked out, and each can claim the authority of the *smṛti* behind it.

These two systems correspond to two types of family : the one resembles a patriarchal family in which the father is the sole master of the estate; the other a joint family where the assets are the collective property of the members. Debate continues on the question which is the more ancient.[73] But anyone who places himself in the period when these two systems were worked out cannot doubt that both types of family involved were co-existing, and that Vijñāneśvara and Jīmūtavāhana, in succession to others, have simply tried to give a structure to them, offering thereby a valid intellectual organisation of their family customs to different social groups (which were, perhaps, very dispersed originally).

But it would be difficult to say to what degree the data and the construct were ultimately combined in each of the systems. No one could take them as simple expressions of customary rules (to which, in any case, they make no reference, except in the vaguest terms).[74] Yet they were models which could not fail to have a normalising effect in course of time. Further we note that the writers (and they are numerous) who followed the *Mitākṣarā* system in broad outline often introduced variations to Vijñāneśvara's propositions, variations doubtless justified by local peculiarities at least in part.

So despite their appearance as pure logicians, the interpreters have achieved a useful work. Some of them gave life, or have regiven life,

a widow, a daughter, a daughter's son and certain other very close relations the undivided interest shall not pass by survivorship (so as to enlarge the presumptive shares of other coparceners), but it shall pass by testamentary or intestate succession. But in somewhat rare cases (as where an unmarried and issueless male dies) survivorship may still operate. [trs.]

[71] *Dāy.*, II, 35–79.

[72] *Mit.*, on *Yāj.* II.114. Kāṇe, III, 592–3. Mayne, *op. cit.*, 11th edn., chh. viii and ix.

[73] On this see especially N.C. Sen-Gupta, *The Evolution of Law*, app. 'The Hindu Joint Family' (Calcutta, 1926), 158–67. Kāṇe, III, 557–60.

[74] This is well demonstrated by the opposition which the Anglo-Indian courts encountered in the course of their attempts to apply Mitākṣarā rules uniformly.

to precepts in the *śāstras* which were incapable of being employed without the aid of a commentary. Placed as they were between the immutable texts of *smṛti* and the mobile traditions of custom, they facilitated the passage from the one to the other, fixing the latter with the indispensable aid of the former. We could say that they were the real organisers of Hindu law. Their work, of course, remains theoretical in so far as it has not been sanctioned by practical application. It is still an expression of the human intellect: subject, as all such expressions are, to criticism and amendment. But the weakness of interpretation is far from being a defect. It calls forth a constant renewal of jurisprudence. It obviates the immobility to which a purely imperative exegesis of the texts would have led. It justifies in time and in space a variety of solutions to problems, a variety in which India, the one and the many, recognises her own face.[75]

[75]This could not be illustrated better than in the difference of opinion between Hegde, J., who took a progressive view, and the majority of his brother judges on the Supreme Court bench (who took a conservative view), as to the meaning (for the present age) of the ancient Mitākṣarā texts relating to acquisition of joint family property through the investment or disposition of family funds: *V.D. Dhanwatey* v. *Commr. of I.-T., Madhya Pradesh* All India Rep. 1968 S.C., 683. Hegde, J., had his way (leaving the texts to one side) in *Shri Raj Kumar Singh* v. *C.I.T., M.P.* (1970) 2 S.C.W.R. 674. [trs.]

CHAPTER II

DHARMA AND CUSTOM

1. *The Contrast between Law and Custom*

THE PROBLEM of the relationship between law and custom arises in Hindu law very differently from the manner in which it arises in western law. For the jurist who is trained after the Roman style, both law and custom rest finally on the *consensus omnium* (the consent of all), the agreement, expressed in the first case and tacit in the second, of the population which they both govern.[1] Both are sources of law of the same nature, distinguished only by the way in which they develop and in their technical method of expression and promulgation. But they apply at the same level of social activity.

But the law which is promulgated by the *śāstras* differs from custom both by object and by origin. As its intention is to teach *dharma,* it prescribes duties and obligations of a religious character. It shows men the conduct they should follow in order to acquire spiritual benefits. To act in conformity with it is to secure merits which, according to the law of *karma,* will produce fruits in the course of this life or after it. The transgressor is a sinner. He is exposed to calamities which can only be avoided by his performing certain penances.

By contrast, the rule of custom is in principle indifferent to the religious consequences of an act. It could be in accord with the precepts of the *śāstra*; it could equally be in conflict with them. Kātyāyana (37) defines custom (under the name *caritra*) as "all that a person practises, whether or not it conforms to *dharma (dharmyaṃ vādharmyam eva ca),* simply because that is the constant usage of the country".[2]

Again, the law which the *śāstras* communicate to us does not arise from the will of men. It rules the moral world just as a physical law rules the phenomena of nature. The rules of conduct and the duties which it enunciates are preconditions of the realisation of the social order as it was intended by the Creator. These rules preexisted the expression of them. They were not conceived by the authors of the *dharmaśāstra* themselves, but were discovered in the texts where divine will is expressed or in traditions in which it is manifested. The rules govern the activity of men : they are not influenced by man.

[1]Cf the celebrated text of Julian at Dig. I.3.32 : ... *nam quid interest, suffragio populus voluntatem suam declaret, an rebus ipsis et factis*? Facts may be as good an indication of the popular will as the votes of an assembly.

[2]An analogous verse is attributed to Pitāmaha (*Dh. k.,* I, p. 105).

Custom, on the other hand, is a purely human development in the sense that it develops at the level of the human groups involved. However, Hindus did not attribute it, as did the Roman jurisconsults of the classical period, to an origin by way of *convention*.[3] It is not born of a more or less conscious agreement of the wills of those called upon to obey it. Its origin eludes human memory, which confers upon it in Hindu eyes an almost sacred character and gives it a force which it neither had nor has in western civilisations. But the customary rule as such seems to be a simple fact, a rule produced by conditions contingent upon time and place without relation to the divine injunction which is at the root of the *śāstric* rule. As Kātyāyana puts it in the definition we have just seen, it is observed simply because it has always been observed. It owes its authority to its *inveterate* character.

Thus law and custom have in India entirely different natures. Custom is a social phenomenon, while law has a transcendant character.

Apart from this, law's independence relative to custom flows directly from the application of Mīmāṃsā principles to the interpretation of *smṛti* texts. *Śāstric* rules which rest upon a Vedic injunction cannot have their source in human activity. Their reason escapes our means of knowledge, and even their effects are hidden from us. The Veda is not the composition of any human author.[4]

But we may ask whether this conception is really what flows from the texts themselves. Would it not be possible to extract from them a different conception, which would make a place for custom at the genesis of *dharma*? We limit our enquiry, for the present, to this question: not whether the human authors of the *smṛtis* were effectively inspired by custom, but whether they really considered custom, as such, a source of *dharma*. A widely spread theory, which tends to confuse the two questions, pronouces an affirmative answer.

The value of such a discussion is far from being merely theoretical. If law and custom are of the same nature, the one may act directly upon the other. Consequently the legal rule is capable of being abrogated by a custom to the contrary effect.[5] If their natures are different, each acts in its own sphere, and there can be no direct mutual interaction. All that the *dharmaśāstra* authors could do was to put men who were

[3]But we must notice that conventional rules arrived at by members of professional bodies amongst others, which can give rise to a particular *vivāda-pada* (when they are broken), are often designated by the same name as custom itself, viz. *caritra*.

[4]G. Jhā, *Pūrvamīmāṃsā in its Sources* (Benares, 1942), 126–7.

[5]In the passage in the *Digest*, cited above at p. 176, n. 1, Julian concludes that a legal rule can be abrogated *per desuetudinem*, by a contrary custom. In Hindu law it is admitted that certain śāstric rules can become obsolete. Derrett, *Religion, Law and the State in India*, 313. And the obsolescence of a custom can be proved from ancient texts to the same effect! *Siromani* v. *Hemkumar* cited above at p.168, n. 56. [trs.]

concerned for their salvation on their guard against law-breaking. In other words the very solution to the conflict of *dharma* with custom depends on the answer to the questions we have just posed.

A.S. Altekar, who was one of the scholars most hostile to the orthodox interpretation, argues from the first *sūtras* of the *Āpastamba-dharma-sūtra* where it is said that the rules of *dharma* are *sāmayācārika,* an expression which Haradatta glosses by *pauruṣeyī vyavasthā,* or "human regulation", which Altekar renders "social conventions". He then concludes that at the period of the *dharma-sūtras* the rules of *dharma* were founded upon custom, tradition, or convention accepted by the public. His notion is that the rules of *dharma,* resulting from a meeting of wills, must originally have varied according to the circumstances which gave rise to their enunciation; they became fixed much later, with the literature of the *dharma-śāstras.*[6]

First of all we must note that the meaning attributed to *sāmayācārika* seems very quaint in the mouth of Āpastamba who, as his teaching shows, was a faithful *mīmāṃsaka.* True enough, the word does evoke a notion of usage or of practices sanctioned by conventions (*samaya,* gathering).[7] But the text of Āpastamba continues, *dharma-jña-samayaḥ pramāṇam vedas ca*: "The authority (or criterion) [of these rules of *dharma*] is the accord (or opinion) of those who know *dharma* and the Vedas". Thus it is not because it is customary that this or that practice is elevated into a rule of *dharma* but because it is held to be such by those who know *dharma,* or because it is prescribed by the Veda. The agreement or consensus of men only relates to the certification that it does conform to one or the other of those conditions.[8] The origin of the rule itself escapes human will altogether. In other words Āpastamba wants to say simply that the rules of *dharma* which he is about to explain are the practices which the Sages agree to recognise because they are connected either with a Vedic injunction or with Good Custom. By "those who know *dharma*" Āpastamba clearly means the *śiṣṭas,* people who are learned and virtuous. The text upon which so much unexpected weight is placed means no more than an allusion to the two sources of *dharma* recognised at the *dharma-sūtra* period: the Veda and Good Custom.

[6]Altekar, *Sources of Hindu Dharma,* 12–3.

[7]Monier-Williams, s.v. *sāmayācārika*: 'relating to conventional practice or usage'. Bühler translates, 'customs of the daily life as they have been settled by the agreement (of those who know law)'. Kāṇe, III, 825 translates simply by 'evolved from conventions and practices'.

[8]As it recognises the Sages' mission to show men which are the rules of *dharma,* the text of Āpastamba can be the origin of a subsequent theory which we shall refer to later, according to which it was the Sages' task at the commencement of each Age to determine the rules of *dharma* which it would no longer be possible to observe because of the (progressive) 'deterioriation of the Ages'.

But does this merely defer the problem? Could we not see two parallel sources, the Vedic texts on the one hand and Good Custom on the other, the first alone having a transcendant origin, but the second having, as its name suggests, a customary origin?

Manu sees (II.17–18) in Good Custom the primitive Āryan custom, that which is perpetuated by tradition amongst the *varṇas* and the mixtures between them *(antarāla)* in Brahmāvarta, "that land created by the gods which extends between the two divine rivers, the Sarasvatī and the Dṛṣadvatī". There no doubt a territorial custom is envisaged, but it is purely mythical, and the author of the Code of Manu invokes it only to glorify Good Custom itself of which he is about to give the outlines. Moreover the majority of the *dharma-śāstras* define *sadācāra* as the custom of the *śiṣṭas*, that is to say the rules of conduct observed by those who are instructed in the Veda and are virtuous and "free from all attachment" *(a-kāmātmā)* as Vasiṣṭha puts it (I.6). He is not referring to a localised custom, but to the usages of people whose lives can serve as a model. And if their usages form an accessory source of *dharma* it is because, being versed in the sacred texts and pure conduct, they presumably act in conformity with the teaching of the Sages to whom the divine law was revealed. In any case this is only a presumption, for such usages ought not to be followed, even when not opposed to the precepts of *smṛti*, if they hide an interested motive. This reservation is expressly formulated by Vasiṣṭha (I.7) who, soon after his definition of *śiṣṭa*, adds: "only an act in which one cannot perceive a worldly motive *(a-gṛhyamāṇa-kāraṇa)* is considered *dharma*", which brings us back to the Mīmāṃsā conception of an act of *dharma*.[9] So it is not in its quality as custom that *sadācāra* is a source of *dharma*, and it is not because it is practised by *śiṣṭas* that their act is *dharma*, but because of its intrinsic qualities. Even the practices observed on the sacred soil of Brahmāvarta, where only virtuous people are born, says Medhātithi (on *M.*, II.18), are not to be followed in their entirety: some of them are *adharma*.[10] *Dharma* can then be inferred from the practice of the *śiṣṭas*: its origin, or its cause, is not to be found there.

The real criterion is found in the disinterested character of the act, accompanied by a belief on the part of those who do it that they only do, in performing it, what obedience to the divine law requires. The *śiṣṭas* are held to be Sages not simply because of their conduct but also because they are learned in the Veda and scrupulously observe the rites prescribed by the Vedic texts. Further, since the reasons for their actions elude us, we may suppose that they obey some Vedic injunction which is unknown

[9]Mīmāṃsā influence is equally obvious in the analogous rules of Āpastamba, I.1.4, 8–9 and 4.12, 8–12.

[10]Aparārka on *Yāj.*, I.7 makes a similar observation à propos of *M.*, II.18 and *Vas.*, I.10.

to us but perpetuated through the memory of their family. The Veda is definitively the deeper source, it is the true source of Good Custom, and that which confers authority upon it.[11]

The *śiṣṭa,* of course, can only be a learned Brahmin, a *śrotriya,* and in fact the *varṇa* of Brahmins was created precisely to instruct men in their duties. That Good Custom is a source of *dharma* thus amounts to saying that the conduct of everyone should be ruled by that of Brahmins.[12]

Nevertheless the interpreters' way of putting this tends to suggest a somewhat wider meaning. Commenting upon Manu II.6, Medhātithi enumerates amongst the sources of *dharma* the practices of the *sādhus (ācāraḥ sādhūnām),* and the word *sādhu* is glossed by *śiṣṭa.*[13] But the examples which he gives of these practices—examples taken up again by the majority of later commentators—refer to usages of secondary importance which, he says, are extremely varied and differ according to circumstances, places and individual disposition, such as the custom of tying a bracelet after the ceremony of marriage, the worship paid by the bride on her wedding day to certain trees, *yakṣas* (demons), cross-roads and other places, the custom of keeping a number of tufts on the head, the precise manner of receiving guests, etc. We gather a propensity on the part of interpreters to rank under Good Custom, and thus to regard as acts of *dharma,* many sorts of practices whose connection with *śruti* becomes quite artificial. Certain late writers, like Mitra-miśra, see nothing in *sadācāra* but the practices of good people, even when they are *not* learned in the Veda; and they admit that even for Śūdras the customs of their ancestors are a source of knowledge of their *dharma* which are authoritatively binding upon the descendants.[14] However, even at that level of interpretation there is no confusion between ordinary custom and the rule of *dharma*. In order to be counted as a rule of *dharma* every custom must be not only immemorial but also free from all apparent worldly motive, interest, or utilitarian consideration.

2. *The Doctrine of Consensus*

Whether it proceeds from inveterate usage or from convention, custom is essentially variable and diverse. It varies not only according to milieu but also according to period. A practice which was honored at one

[11]As an echo of the Mīmāṃsā doctrine Āpastamba says (I.4.12, 10) that the authority of Good Custom rests upon the presumption that it originates in the *śruti.*

[12]Cf *Vas.,* I.39–40 and *M.,* II.20 : "(it is) from a Brahmin originating in this land (Brahmāvarta) that all men on earth should learn their usages and customs."

[13]*M.,* II.6 : *Vedo 'khilo dharma-mūlaṃ smṛti-śīle ca tad-vidām, ācāraś caiva sādhūnām ātmanas tuṣṭir eva ca.* Some commentators connect *sādhūnām* with *ātmanas tuṣṭi* : 'internal consent' of virtuous people.

[14]*Vīr., par.,* p. 9. Kāṇe, III.875–6, 881.

moment can, in the next period, fall into desuetude so that new practices may arise and develop. By contrast, the rule of *dharma,* whether its source is *smṛti* or *sadācāra,* takes its origin and draws its authority from that eternal Law which is the Veda and is, like it, immutable. Whatever its expression over the course of time, it is always the same rule which is being prescribed. Here we recognise the doctrine of consensus, according to which a complete unity of opinion must be presumed as between all authors of *smṛti*. According to Jaimini and Śabara all recensions of the Veda and of the *brāhmaṇas* form a single body, so that a rite like the *agnihotra* must be considered one and the same in all recensions, even though certain details figure in many of them and are omitted in others.[15] The commentators and digest-writers have extended that conception to *smṛti,*[16] so that it lies at the root of their system of interpretation.

Modern scholars have found themselves in conflict with the orthodox conception of *dharma*, above all, in finding fault with the doctrine of consensus. Indeed if it could be established that *dharma* does not have in the *śāstras* that immutability which the interpreters attribute to it, but that it represents a notion which has varied with the centuries, we should be led to admit that without necessarily being confused with ordinary custom, it must have some close relationship to it. The dogma of the unanimity of texts of *smṛti* would then seem like a fiction, perhaps useful for facilitating flexibility of interpretation but foreign to the *smṛti* itself and valueless for the period of the *dharma-śāstras*.[17]

Two kinds of argument have been presented against the doctrine of consensus, one founded on a comparative examination of the *dharma-śāstras'* contents, the other upon certain texts of the *dharma-śāstras* themselves.

Arguments founded on an examination of the texts are certainly the stronger.

The authors of the *dharma-śāstras* are undoubtedly inspired in the composition of their works largely by usages which they saw going on before their eyes. Those which they present to us as constituting Good Custom, whatever foundation might be attributed to them, must correspond in great part to the rules of conduct effectively laid down for

[15]This is the maxim of *sarva-śākhā-pratyaya* or *śākhāntarādhikaraṇa*. *Jai.*, II.4.8–33. Kāṇe, IV, 453–5; V, 1273.

[16]Notably Viśvarūpa and Vijñāneśvara on *Yāj.*, I.4–5; Medhātithi on *M.*, II.29 and XI.216; Aparārka on *Yāj.*, III.243; Vijñāneśvara on *Yāj.*, III.325. The interpreters also rely on the principle of syntactical unity of adjacent propositions, formulated by Jaimini II.1.46 and expressed in the maxim of *eka-vākyatā* (texts must speak with one voice). C. Saṅkararāma Śāstrī, *Fictions in the Development of the Hindu Law Texts* (Madras, 1926), 170–4; G. Jhā, *Pūrvamīmāṃsā* ..., 189–191; Kāṇe, III, 443 and V, 1297–8.

[17]Cf Saṅkararāma Śāstrī, *op. cit., ubi cit.*

the *dvijas*. As for precepts concerning the hearing of cases, the commentators themselves do not hesitate to admit their origin in custom. Nīlakaṇṭha (*Vyav. may.*, IV.ix.3) does not hesitate to compare them to rules of grammar in that they also are generally founded on usage. A propos of the regulation of succession, Vijñāneśvara (*Mit.*, on *Yāj.*, II.118–119) remarks that the *śāstras* hardly do more in this connection than reproduce rules prevailing in the world. Mitra-miśra (*Vīr.*, on *Yāj.*, II.135–136) makes the same remark, and adds that all the authors of digests agree in viewing the part of the *dharma-śāstras* devoted to *vyavahāra* as reproducing rules habitually followed by the public.

The influence of customary facts on the precepts of the *dharma-śāstras* appears plainly enough in the obvious contradictions in Manu. Manu (III.15–19), like Vasiṣṭha (I.27) and Yājñavalkya (I.56), condemns the marriage of a *dvija* with a Śūdra woman; however, he must recognise the existence of such unions, because he fixes the share of the paternal estate which will come to the son of a Brahmin, of a Kṣatriya, or a Vaiśya born of a female Śūdra (*M.*, IX.153; cf *Yāj.*, II.125). Similarly he holds it a grave sin to eat meat (V.55, XI.159) but he declares that the *snātaka* should not refuse meat which is offered to him (IV.250), and he places meat amongst the foods to be offered to Brahmins invited to *śrāddha* ceremonies (III.227). Likewise he considers *niyoga* a bestial practice *(paśu-dharma)* (IX.66), but he explains how it is done and fixes the rights of the *kṣetraja* (field-born) son in succession to his pater (IX.120–121). Similarly, according to him, a widow ought not to remarry (V.157, 162, IX.65), but he fixes the lengths of time she should wait in case her husband is missing (IX.76) and regulates the rights of succession of sons born of one mother by two different fathers (IX.191).

It emerges from these texts that the author of the Code of Manu was hostile to marriage between a *dvija* and a Śūdrā, to the act of meat-eating, to *niyoga*, and to second marriages of widows, but he was confronted by customs too deeply rooted for prohibition to be efficacious. All he could do was to try to discredit them and to limit their practice and their importance. Thus he gives the son of the Śūdra born to a *dvija* male a clearly inferior position from the point of view of succession (IX.153–155, Cf *Yāj.*, II.125) and he places him in a very low caste (X.8–10, Cf *Yāj.*, I.91–92). He limits the application of *niyoga* to the case (not necessarily rare) where the girl's betrothed bridegroom died before the marriage could be consummated (IX.69–70) and submits the actual implementation of *niyoga* to strict regulation (IX.59–63).

This way of proceeding on the part of the author of the *dharma-śāstra* reveals how he felt the force of custom. But it also shows that he did not accept it uncritically. As we have shown in trying to extract the image which one could obtain of Indian society from the *dharma-sūtras*, the *smṛti*-writers' borrowings from custom are always selective. They keep only what answers to their notion of morality. Even when they believe they are only confirming it they necessarily import aspects of precision which mere oral transmission could not have had. If it is possible to admit, for example, that precepts belonging to the control of litigation were for the most part taken from actual practice, it is beyond doubt that they are presented in the *dharma-śāstras* quite otherwise than in their original form. Custom knows only *brocards* (maxims, apothegms). It is true that some such are to be found in the *dharma-śāstras*. But the classifications, the distinctions, the subtle and complex solutions which we find in the *smṛtis* imply most clearly the intervention of the author himself or even of a school. In short, we are confronted by works which doubtless owe much to custom, but of which the least one can say is that they are *compositions*. It would be hazardous to imagine social reality through their precepts or to take their precepts for rules of law in force in their times. One can only draw from a comparative examination of the texts indications about some currents of opinion amongst the writers, currents which plausibly reflect changes of ideas or of manners in the population. In default of a history of the ancient law, i.e. of society properly so called, one might perhaps attempt a history of social ideas, using the different and sometimes contradictory views which we recognise when we compare the *dharma-śāstras* with each other. But the grave uncertainty of the chronology and the huge gaps in our knowledge about the *dharma-śāstra* literature leaves hardly any solid ground for such an enterprise.

Nevertheless, even if the state of our texts makes it impossible for the historian to profit from them, it is undeniable that the composers of the *dharma-śāstras* have been influenced by their times and their environments. To this extent, the criticisms directed against the doctrine of consensus are justified. Given the very long period during which the literature developed, it could not conceivably escape bearing traces of the evolution of ideas and changes of manners undergone in the heart of Indian society. But the question is whether the authors themselves intended only to legislate for their own times, if their aim was really to supply a new law. Now, at least at first sight, a negative reply seems certain. Each writer presents his work as the expression of the eternal Law which rules men's activities. Even the fact that he attributes the exposition to a mythical person, to the dawn of time, shows that he had, if not the conviction (who can tell?), at least the desire to produce it as such.

However, now we come to the second class of arguments aimed to demolish the theory of consensus: certain texts of *dharma-śāstra* origin seem themselves to contradict the idea that *dharma* is one immutable law, and to admit that, on the contrary, it changes from age to age.

The most important text in this respect is found in the first Book of the *Manu-smṛti*, where the celebrated theory of the *yugas* is set out. According to Hindu cosmogony the world is subject to alternate periods of creation and destruction called periods of Manu. Each of these periods is subdivided into four ages *(yugas)* of which the first, the *kṛta* age, is the age of Gold, and the last, the *kali* age, is our own. In the *kṛta* age men were pure, virtuous, and lived 400 years. In the following ages their virtues decreased like their lives, until the Kali Age is one of supreme decadence. This is what Manu says in the first Book :

> 84. The duration of human life, as announced in the Veda, the benedictions *(āśiḥ)* (resulting) from sacrificial acts and the (supernatural) powers of corporeal beings bear fruit amongst men according to the Age.
>
> 85. Distinct are the *dharmas* of the *kṛta* Age, distinct in the *tretā* and the *dvāpara* Age, distinct in the *kali* Age, because of the worsening of those Ages.
>
> 86. In the *kṛta* Age what is essential is austerity *(tapas)*, in the *tretā* knowledge *(jñāna)*, in the *dvāpara* sacrifice *(yajña)*, in the *kali* Age, simply gift *(dāna)*.[18]

After having reproduced verses 85–86 of Manu, the *Parāśara-smṛti* lays down that the rules of *dharma* have been proclaimed for the *kṛta* Age by Manu, for the *tretā* Age by Gautama, for the *dvāpara* Age by Śaṅkha-Likhita and for the *kali* Age by Parāśara himself (I.24).[19]

It has been thought possible to conclude from these texts that the authors of the *dharma-śāstras* were themselves well aware that the concept of morality changed with the ages, and that that which was held for good and meritorious in a given age could be adjudged in the next to be immoral and wicked.[20] Thus, in their eyes, *dharma* was not the intangible law that orthodox doctrine supposed.

Verse 85 of Manu cannot but be held embarrassing, for it clearly says (literally): "others are the *dharmas*" *(anye dharmāḥ)*, according to the Ages. However, the plural employed for *dharma* seems to suggest that he is not talking here about *dharma* in general, but of the *dharmas*, i.e. particular meritorious acts, which would change according to the Ages, some being practised in preference to others. This is what the next following verse confirms : "In the *kṛta* Age, the essential is austerity . . .". Thus : in the *kṛta* Age the act of *dharma par excellence* is the practice of austerities, while in the Ages that follow it is successively the study of sacred texts, sacrificial acts, and gift (i.e. commended generosity).

[18]These verses are to be found also in the *Mahābhārata*, Śāntip., 232, 26–8. A verse similar to *v.*86 is attributed to Bṛhaspati (*Aiy.*, p. 231, 4); for the Kali Age it adds to gift *(dāna)* compassion *(dayā)* and self-control *(dama)* or, according to a variant reading, long-suffering *(kṣama)*.

[19] *kṛte tu mānavā dharmās tretāyāṃ gautamāḥ smṛtāḥ*
dvāpare śankha-likhitāḥ kalau pārāśarāḥ smṛtāḥ.

[20]Cf especially Altekar, *op. cit.*, 40–1.

But that does not mean that the practice of austerities has lost its value in the *tretā* Age, or that in the next Age the study of sacred texts has become fruitless. If the *dharmas* vary, it is "because of the worsening of the Ages", i.e. because the progressive diminution of the length of human life no longer allows men to be sufficiently instructed in their duties, and because humanity has lost the innocence of the Golden Age in the course of its ever-deepening corruption. Men therefore grasp at the act of *dharma* which is the least troublesome or the easiest to perform. It is interesting that the "dharmas" listed in *v*.86, from austerity to gift, actually demand less and less effort on the part of those who perform them, so that their succession really corresponds to the progressive deterioration of the Ages. That deterioration also tends to decrease the efficacy of the act of *dharma,* because such an act is performed by inadequately instructed men who are corrupted by sins. Medhātithi says this neatly in his commentary on *v*.82: "Since those who officiate, who institute sacrifices, who make gifts, and who receive them are all subject to the faults which this verse alludes to, the meritorious act is not performed as it should be, and as a result the fruit which it ought to have procured is not attained".[21]

Medhātithi (no one knows why) denies all connection between verses 85 and 86 and interprets the first differently. He attributes to the word *dharma* not the sense of sacrificial act or act prescribed by the Veda, but that of "character" or quality *(guṇa)* of things in general. Philologically this is a possible translation. The verse would not mean that *dharma,* the moral law, changes with the Ages, but that the characters or qualities of things vary from Age to Age, like the duration of human life which goes on decreasing, or the aspects of nature which change with the seasons. The use of the plural for *dharmas* and the diversity of senses of the word do authorise this possible interpretation, which is taken up again by Mitra-miśra. The latter also thinks, à propos of Manu's *v*.85, that the difference between the *dharmas* in question envisages solely the modalities *(prakāras)* of the act and not its essential features.[22]

However, Medhātithi comes to an explanation close to ours in his commentary on Manu's *v*.81. There figures in that verse the celebrated picture of Dharma compared with a bull: he stands on four feet in the *kṛta* Age, but he loses one foot successively in each of the following Ages—a symbol of the diminution of the physical faculties and moral sense of men in course of time. For Medhātithi (as for other commentators on Manu, viz. Kullūka and Nārāyaṇa), the four feet of the bull Dharma correspond to the four principal means of acquiring merit:

[21] Verse 84 means the same.

[22] *Vīr., par.,* p. 47. The same interpretation is given again by Mādhava, on *Par.,* I.22, reproducing *M.,* I.85.

the practice of austerities, knowledge of sacred texts, sacrifices, and gifts, which Manu mentions in *v*.86 as being the virtues successively in esteem in the four Ages of the world. In other words, if Dharma totters, it is not because he has changed his nature but because, through men's neglect or weakness, he has ceased to be held up. And Medhātithi observes, on *v*.86 itself, that the practice of one or another of the four virtues spoken of is not special to a particular *yuga,* but that they are prescribed, all four of them, for all time. He means that the perfection of *dharma* is not attained unless they are all esteemed equally.

Thus the *yugas'* rolling onwards affects only human capabilities. It makes the accomplishment of the divine will more and more difficult, but this divine will is always expressed within the timeless law that is *dharma*. As that law has been proclaimed in *smṛti* and can be known by all, it behoves those who have the mission to instruct men in their duties to develop it and render it accessible, in order to keep open the way of virtue in spite of the corruption of the times. And it especially behoves the king to secure conditions for his subjects through well-advised policies, which will permit them to engage and to persevere in that law. When he explains the king's function, Manu himself declares that the king, by his conduct, is identified with the Ages of the world: "Asleep he is the *kali* Age; awake he is the *dvāpara,* ready for action the *tretā*; and acting he is the *kṛta* Age". (*M.,* IX.302). Thus, the passing of the *yugas* can be made illusory by the support which the king brings to *dharma* if he fulfills his duty.[23] The Sage can, by trying to conform to the precepts of the eternal law, escape from the *kali* Age. If he does this he is not turning backwards through Time, he is submitting himself simply to the order of things.

The text of Parāśara seem to be more difficult than Manu's to reconcile with the doctrine of consensus, at least at first sight. In fact he specifies at the beginning of his work that it contains exclusively precepts valid for our Age. The famous *v*.24 of the first Book, taken literally, seems to signify that each *yuga* has had its peculiar rules of *dharma,* enunciated by Manu for the *kṛta* Age, Gautama for the *tretā,* Śaṅkha-Likhita for the *dvāpara,* and lastly Parāśara for the *kali* Age. We need not notice the singularity of this list, which places Manu before Gautama and gives Śaṇkha-Likhita an importance which the work passing under that name appears not to have enjoyed.[24] On the other hand, we cannot

[23]Medhātithi on *M.,* IX.301, observes that the *yugas* should not be taken here as if they were historical periods. It is the king's methods which create conditions belonging to one or other of them. Lingat, 'Dharma et temps', *J.A.*, 259 (1961), 487–95, available in English as 'Time and the Dharma: on Manu I.85–6', *Contributions to Indian Sociology* 6 (1962), 7–16.

[24]U.C. Sarkār, *Epochs in Hindu Legal History* (Hoshiarpur, 1958), 122–3, observes that Manu here means the *Mānava-dharma-sūtra* rather than the *Manu-smṛti* which is

evade the difficulties which this text presents by merely observing that the author has declared his work made specially for our times in order to attribute more authority to his book. This may well be true. But the observation would imply nonetheless that the author, who knew the theory of the *yugas*, had understood it in the same sense as the present-day antagonist of the orthodox doctrine. He would have seen in verses 84–85 of Manu (which have become verses 22–23 of the first chapter of the *Parāśara-smṛti*) the expression of the changeableness of *dharma*.

Now if his intention really was to write especially for our Iron Age, he apparently did not think it followed that the prescriptions offered by the new *smṛti* must supersede those which were designed for anterior Ages. In fact he evinces a veritable veneration for Manu who is "the sole (amongst the Sages) to know all the *śāstras*" (IX.51).[25] In many places, he puts his own precepts under the authority of Manu (VI.1, VII.31–32, IX.26, XI.19, XII.38), where he does not actually reproduce Manu's verses literally or almost literally. "The Veda is without an author", says he (I.21), "it is (simply) recalled (for the world of men) by (the god) with four faces (Brahmā); in the same way, at the commencement of each *kalpa*, Manu puts (men) in mind of their duties *(dharmas)*".[26] The preeminent place accorded to Manu shows that the author of the *Parāśara-smṛti* had no intention to substitute for the *dharmas* hallowed by Manu other *dharmas* valid for our Age. His intention seems clear from the verses which follow *v*.24, in which he explains how men's conduct differs from Age to Age. The differences arise because little by little men lose their primitive purity, and they become more and more incapable of correctly performing the sacrificial acts. Thus while during the *kṛta* Age no one would wish to live in a country where a sinner was found, in the succeeding Ages, men were content to avoid successively the village where he lived, then his family, and finally, in the *kali* Age the sinner himself (I.25). In the *kṛta* Age, it was a sin to speak with a sinner, while in the *kali* Age a man is degraded only by acts which he himself commits (I.26). Rites lose their efficacy little by little. While in the *kṛta* Age their effect was instantaneous, in the following Ages it was only produced within ten days, then within a month, and at last within the year of their being performed (I.27). Even charity, which remains the essential virtue of the *kali* Age, is no longer

certainly later than the *dharma-sūtra* of Gautama (*M*., III.16 in effect cites Gautama). This hypothesis can hardly be accepted (apart from the absence of proof that such a *sūtra* ever existed) because of numerous references to the *Manu-smṛti* which figure in the *Parāśara-smṛti*.

25 *manunā caivam ekena sarva-śāstrāṇi jānatā.*

26 *na kaścid veda-kartā ca vedaṃ smṛtvā catur-mukhaḥ*
tathaiva dharmān smarati manuḥ kalpāntare 'ntare.

practised as it should be, for men do not make gifts except to remunerate services, which deprives the act of all merit (I.28–29).

Thus the author of the *Parāśara-smṛti* shares the idea which illuminates verses 84–85 of Manu, namely that it is the degeneration of humanity which no longer permits men to perform their duties perfectly. His scheme is thus to teach them the rules of conduct which it remains possible for them to follow, and also the penances which are appropriate. Basically, here is nothing new. Already we have found Gautama (I.3) and Āpastamba (II.6.13.7–8) recognising that what was permitted to the ancient Sages because of their sanctity could not be permitted in our Age of sin. The Good Custom proclaimed by the *dharma-śāstras* is an ideal of life which is available only to saints. It is in this sense only that we can call it the morality of an age other than our own. It is impossible to demand that the generality of people observe it with rigour. Certain practices, ill understood, ill applied, should actually be discouraged. The *Parāśara-smṛti* recommends him who is ill to try by all possible means to recover health and, when he is physically capable of it, to observe the precepts of *dharma* just once (VII.37). It places the need for self-preservation before all religious duties (VII.36), and declares that there is no need to care for rules of purity in a period of distress (VII.38). Even if they are not put quite so crudely, such propositions have their echo in other *dharma-śāstras*.[27]

Parāśara's affirmation that his rules are valid for the *kali* Age can be regarded as the germ of the theory of the *kali-varjyas*, which we shall discuss later. But one must own that it had hardly any influence upon the composition of his work, because in the rather restricted domain which its author has chosen the *Parāśara-smṛti* has nothing to distinguish it specifically from other *smṛtis*.

Thus neither the verses of the *Parāśara-smṛti* nor those of the Code of Manu permit us to conclude that the authors of the *dharma-śāstras* intended to legislate for their own days. Doubtless they felt the influence of their milieux and the aspirations of their age, and this influence is unquestionably to be seen in their works. But for them the Law which they proclaimed, taking its ultimate source in the Veda, could only be, like it, one and eternal.[28] Likewise, the idea that Good and Evil are relative terms, that the moral value of an act is susceptible to be appreciated differently from epoch to epoch, is an idea of the modern world which could not have come into our authors' heads. For them Dharma

[27]The *Mīmāṃsā* itself (*Jai.*, VI.3, 1 cited by Mādhava on *Par.*, I.22), à propos of the *agnihotra* and other obligatory rituals, concludes that the sacrificer is bound to perform only those rites which it is within his power to perform. That self-preservation takes precedence over all religious imperatives explains the immunity which the majority of the *dharma-śāstras* allow to the slayer of a Brahmin aggressor *(ātatāyin)*.

[28]This is Mādhava's principal argument on *Par.*, I.22 (otherwise *M.*, I.85).

is synonymous with Truth. Since however, they were conscious of the occurrence of changes in ideas and morals, they had recourse to the theory of the *yugas*. It is not the moral imperatives which vary according to the Ages, but men's progressively weakening capacity to obey the moral law. As for divergencies between the precepts of the *smṛtis,* not even they can be attributed to the influence of time. They only appear divergent by reason of the weakness of human intelligence, which is incapable of grasping truth under all her guises. It is up to the interpreter to rediscover the underlying unanimity.

If the doctrine of consensus was only a fiction at the time of the commentators—which is hardly likely—we must concede that it has rendered a priceless service to interpretation. To consider all the *dharma-śāstras* and in a general sense all the works ranked within *smṛti* as a single law was to open the way to multiple solutions to problems. Interpretation acquired a flexibility it could not have had if it were applied to only one text, designated the most recent or the most complete. In a country like India where customs are so diverse, diversity of interpretation is the very condition of the birth of law.

3. *Prohibitions proper to the Kali Age*

The theory of the *yugas* (Ages) has led us little by little to the idea that, although the rules of conduct prescribed by the *śāstras* retain eternally their redemptive quality, they are not always good to follow. Laid down by Sages for the perfect man of the Golden Age, they cannot be enjoined upon men of our days without discretion. The latter find, as Manu says (IX.2–4), that the pursuit of interest or pleasure tends to take precedence over the acquisition of spiritual merit. Human nature is such that one cannot force it without destroying the effect desired. Hence it would be better to dissuade men from, or even to prohibit certain precepts of the *śāstras* than to try to impose them without regard for whether they will work.

A verse of Manu, which does not refer, at least explicitly, to the theory of the *yugas,* brings some confirmation of this point of view. The verse is placed in the part of Book IV devoted to the duties of the *snātaka,* or the Brahminical student during the last phase of his training when he prepares himself to marry and found a family. But it unquestionably applies also to a householder. After having enjoined him above all to avoid wealth and pleasures which are repugnant to *dharma,* Manu adds that he should refrain "also (from observing) *dharma* that has inauspicious consequences *(a-sukhodarkam)* or which is reproved by the world *(loka-vikruṣṭam)*" (IV.176).[29] Thus, according to Manu, there can be

29 *parityajed artha-kāmau yau syātāṃ dharma-varjitau*
dharmaṃ cāpy asukhodarkaṃ loka-vikruṣṭam eva ca.

two cases in which the *dvija* is not only allowed but even required not to follow the precepts of the law. As an example of the first case, Medhātithi cites the possibility that a head of the family might give away all his property. Even though the gift might well be in itself a meritorious act, such a donation should not be made because of the painful effects it would have upon the donor and his family. The rule can be explained further by the idea, expressed elsewhere by Manu (II.224), that the ideal of the Sage, or rather of the respectable man, is to reconcile in the course of his conduct virtue with profit and pleasure, so that it might be better to abstain from a meritorious act if the act would threaten that equilibrium. Here we have a note with a modern sound to it, a realistic one, to which Manu is not always a stranger.[30] He does not prevent considerations of profit or welfare being in some way measured in the same scales with the authority which attaches to precepts of *dharma,* and being thought capable of counterbalancing them.

The assault on *dharma's* authority is much more grave in the second case proposed by Manu, in which the rule of conduct hallowed by texts must still be avoided because it is "reproved by the world" (*vikruṣṭa,* literally "decried, despised"). Here we do not have an exception justified by individual reasons to prevent the performance of an act which is generally valid. We have an entire and definitive condemnation of certain practices, a prohibition based on a reason related to public order, namely the reaction of society which regards as blameworthy such practices, though they are hallowed by the texts.

There is a verse of Yājñavalkya (I.156) which corresponds to that verse of Manu. He too declares à propos of the duties of the *snātaka,* "In act, thought, and speech he should practise *dharma* assiduously; however he should not observe *dharma* [or 'that which is consistent with *dharma*'] if it does not lead to heaven and/or is odious to the world *(loka-vidviṣṭam)*".[31]

Although the expression "if it does not lead to heaven" *(a-svargya)* may not have precisely the same sense as "having inauspicious consequences",[32] it seems that Yājñavalkya, like Manu, understood by it

This principle has been evoked in the last thirty years in support of the movement to reform by legislation the Hindu law of India. [trs.]

[30]We may compare with this verse that by which Manu recommends sons to proceed to a partition of the paternal estate, for this is more meritorious (*dharma-vṛddhi* results), but still leaves them free to remain undivided if they think it more useful (*M.*, IX.111, identical with *Gaut.*, XXVIII.4).

[31] *karmaṇā manasā vācā yatnād dharmaṃ samācaret*
asvargyaṃ loka-vidviṣṭaṃ dharmam apy ācaren na tu.

There are significant variations in the reading of the last quarter as transmitted by the different commentators, but it is not necessary to dilate upon them here.

[32]*asukhodarka.* Mitra-miśra, glossing *asvargyam,* applies it to ritual practices and gives as an example recourse to *abhicāras,* magic spells done with evil intent. Viśvarūpa evidences

an obedience to the rule which would be an abuse, which would involve more harm than good. But *loka-vidviṣṭa* ("odious to the world")[32a] agrees plainly with the *loka-vikruṣṭa* ("reproved by the world") of Manu.

There are commentators who rely expressly on these verses of Manu and Yājñavalkya to condemn practices hallowed by *smṛti*. Thus Medhātithi (on *M.*, IV.176) reports that, following the opinion of older commentators, it is no longer permitted to sacrifice a bull or to eat beef, since such usages are "reproved by the world". Vijñāneśvara (*Mit.*, on *Yāj.*, II.117) prohibits the eldest son's being given a larger share at a partition of ancestral property than any of his younger brothers, even though such a preferential share is permitted by Manu and Yājñavalkya. "It is true", he says, "that unequal partitions are authorised by the texts, but they should not be made, because they are rejected by the world". And he adds that it would be the same as to sacrifice a barren cow to Mitra and Varuṇa (enjoined in a Vedic text) and to offer a bull or a goat to a learned Brahmin when he comes to the house as a guest (an offering recommended by Yājñavalkya at I.109).[33]

How are we to explain that popular aversion could justify in the eyes of the *smṛti* the prohibition of practices which it has itself laid down? Doubtless we shall agree that certain rites, however obligatory, will cease to be observed in the course of time. But, as Medhātithi remarks (on *M.*, IX.112) à propos of *sattras* (sacrifices of long duration), if they are no longer performed that could be explained by the fact that no one in our days has the means to perform them, or desires the results which performance of them procures, or even that faith in their efficacy has vanished. But they do not any the less retain their validity, and they are always capable of being performed. A rule of *dharma* cannot be abrogated by dissuetude. By contrast what we have here are not rules which have simply been abandoned or have fallen into dissuetude, but practices which have been formally forbidden and treated as bad.

The old commentators to whom Medhātithi alludes (on *M.*, IV.176) present a really curious explanation for the prohibition of any sacrifice of a bull. In their view, the great majority of men of our days, failing to be sufficiently instructed in such matters, are unaware that such a sacrifice is permitted in particular cases, and they therefore regard the sacrificer in all cases as a reprobate who should be shunned. Rather than scandalise the masses and provoke their indignation (even if unjustified), it is better that people should abstain from that sacrifice

a reading *asvantam* (which ends ill), which recalls Manu's *asukhodarkam*. Many commentators, notably Vijñāneśvara, simply relate *asvargyam* to *loka-vidviṣṭam*.

[32a] The same expression is found in *Viṣ.*, LXXI.85 : *loka-vidviṣṭaṃ dharmam api (nācaret)*.

[33] Derrett, 'Showing a big bull : a piece of hypocrisy in the Mitākṣarā?', *Annals of the Bhandarkar Or. Res. Inst.* 48–9 (1968), 45–53.

altogether. Such an explanation protects the validity of the sacrifice itself, and of the texts which prescribe it! Abstention is recommended to the intending sacrificer in order to spare him from the hostile reactions of his environment. Here is a counsel of practical wisdom, analogous to that which foresees that some acts will be "having inauspicious consequences".

However, the prohibition of practices "odious to the world" is not generally understood in this way. In putting on the same level the sacrifice of a bull and unequal partition, Vijñāneśvara certainly envisages those practices, which were once permitted, as now completely reprehensible.

Devaṇṇa-bhaṭṭa (*Sm. cand.,* II, p. 266) rightly remarks that the parallelism between the sacrifice of a bull and unequal partition is unsure, for the prohibition of sacrificing a bull has only a negative aspect. It does not substitute another act contrary to the act prohibited, whereas the prohibition of unequal partition implies a new form of partition different from that which is taught in the *smṛti*. In other words, Devaṇṇa-bhaṭṭa seems disposed to accept that popular aversion suffices to justify the condemnation of a practice; while on the other hand he will not admit that a contrary custom can abrogate a rule laid down in the *śāstras*. This is a perfectly orthodox position. However it is only certain in a case where the precepts of the *śāstras* make no difficulty and do not open the way to alternative interpretations. We have seen that, on this hypothesis, usage should guide the interpreter towards the solution which should be adopted, in the sense that conformity with usage guarantees in some sense the correctness of that interpretation. We could see in the rejection of acts "odious to the world" the counterpart to this proposition. Amongst possible solutions, that which conflicts with usage ought to be eliminated, not because of popular opposition to it but because that hostility is the sign that it is incorrect. Such a way of looking at the matter is by no means wanting amongst the commentators.[34]

It seems very difficult to agree that the *smṛti*-writers referred to popular reaction to determine which of their precepts should not be obeyed. In any case such a criterion is far from secure. Observe the divergence of opinion on the subject of unequal partition. Vijñāneśvara holds that the public is hostile to it, while Devaṇṇa-bhaṭṭa and other commentators believe that it is still held to be right to give a special share to the eldest

[34]When condemning unequal partitions, Vijñāneśvara (*Mit.,* on *Yāj.,* II.117) does not stop at saying that they are 'odious to the world'. He regards it as desirable to show that there is some disagreement between the precepts of Manu and Yājñavalkya and those of Āpastamba (II.6.14, 1–14) and even of the Veda : hence the meaning of the first two could be open to debate. Mādhava, for his part, relies on *Yāj.,* I.156 to limit the bearing of his interpretation of *M.,* XI.172, and to support the prohibition of marriage with the daughter of the paternal aunt (see above). Yājñavalkya's precept is thus, for him, a criterion of interpretation.

son when he particularly merits it.[35] But above all how can the verdict of people of low status, or the mere populace, who have no acquaintance with the sacred texts, render a practice disreputable and so justify its being condemned? Moreover, Mitra-miśra holds that the word *loka* in the phrase *loka-vidviṣṭa* really means *yuga*. It is not acts which are "odious to the world" which Yājñavalkya intends to proscribe, but those which have become odious in the *yuga* in which we are.

The theory of the *yugas* in effect offers the commentators a means, no doubt more orthodox than recourse to popular aversion, to bring the *śāstric* precepts into touch with their times, ranging practices which had become "odious" amongst those which are condemned in the Kali Age. Condemnation of them rests, then, not only on the sentiments of the population in regard to them, but also on the progressive worsening of the Ages, since in the Kali Age men are no longer capable of accomplishing as they should all the acts hallowed by Good Custom. Consequently, certain of these acts have lost their meritorious quality and vitiated by evil inclinations, have even become acts of perdition. This explains why the Sages have prohibited them.

The Sages then, and not human beings themselves, must tell which practices have ceased to be salutary. The author of the *Parāśara-smṛti* already purports to legislate only for the Kali Age, but he omits to lay down those prohibitions. Other *smṛtis,* beginning from Bṛhaspati,[36] specify the prohibited actions and begin to formulate, little by little, a long list of *kali-varjyas* (acts prohibited in the Kali Age).[37]

During the period of the commentators, recourse to the theory of the *yugas* to explain how certain practices hallowed by the texts were put on the Index (and so banned) was in full vigour. Al Bīrūnī, whose stay in India occurred at the beginning of the eleventh century, testifies to this effect. The Arab traveller reports that the Hindus had told him there was once a time when it was permitted to eat cow's meat. There were sacrifices in which cows were put to death, but later this was prohibited "because of the weakness of men who had become too weak to perform their duties".[38] From the twelfth to the thirteenth century this theory came into frequent use. The digests or commentaries cite a long passage from a *purāṇa* which mentions fifty *kali-varjyas*.[39] The end of this passage says that, for the protection of the world, at the beginning of the Kali Age, the said practices were censured by mutual consent of the Sages, and the joint opinion of the good *(samayaḥ sādhūnām)*

[35] Kāṇe. III. 627–30. See above. p. 168, n. 56.

[36] Prohibition of killing a Brahmin agressor (*Aiy.*, XXIII.4), disallowance of *niyoga* (XXV.12. *Aiy.*, XXVI.58) and of secondary sons (XXV.14, *Aiy.*, XXVI.18).

[37] Kāṇe. III, 926–7.

[38] *Al Biruni's India,* trans. Sachau, II, 152.

[39] Kāṇe. III. gives the passage as an appendix, p. 1013, n. 1783.

has the same authority as the Veda.[40] We need only notice in this fable how it conforms to orthodoxy : these practices have really been condemned in the interest of humanity, and the condemnations are believed to have been pronounced once for all at the beginning of the Kali Age in order to signify that they fall beyond the judgement of the men of the Kali Age.

Kāṇe, who gives a whole series of forbidden acts (III., pp. 930–968), concludes by saying that the theory of the *kali-varjyas* furnishes a "peremptory" argument against the still widespread prejudice of the "Unchanging East". In India, as elsewhere, society has evolved. The fiction of an agreement between the Sages to establish rules, which should not be followed during the Kali Age is the means the writers have used to register changes in religious practices and moral notions. Kāṇe says also that the *Kali-varjya* theory is a peremptory argument against the idea that *dharma* is immutable and unchanging. Thanks to it, the most solemn prescriptions of the Veda and the ancient Sages can be put to one side and considered as having no authority, because they run counter to the prevailing notions of society.

The *kali-varjya* theory undoubtedly served to hallow changes that took place in opinion and manners, and to justify that popular reaction which Manu and Yājñavalkya refer to without explaining. One must admit that the theory often looks a bit artificial, and that the argument it provided for our writers is seldom more than a formality. It is quite probable that revulsion from certain practices, such as bloody sacrifices, secondary sons, and *niyoga,* is due to a refinement of the moral sense and a softening of manners, rather than to a "progressive worsening of the Ages". But does this mean to say that in the eyes of the Hindus themselves the *kali-varjya* theory was only a fiction intended to mask the effect which time had been having upon the very concept of *dharma*? We cannot affirm this without throwing overboard the beliefs upon which rest both the teaching of *smṛti* and the system of its interpretation. Perhaps though it seems very specious to us, the explanation really satisfied minds different from our own, penetrated as they were by the notion that perfect wisdom existed only at the dawn of days. All that we can say is that, in attaching a natural, cosmic cause, independent of human will, to changes in ideas and manners, it turned into a general rule prohibitions which, for want of such a foundation, would have had a very limited significance. Consequently groups that continued to

[40]Cf the text of Āpastamba, I.1.1. 2–3, discussed above. The Sages have the authority to fix the acts of *dharma*, to determine those which should be observed and those which should be no longer because of the deterioration of the Ages, not to lay down new rules. It would be going much too far to conclude from the passage referred to here that the Sages' opinion could make law.

observe the prohibited acts affirmed thereby their incapacity to break away from sin and their moral inferiority relative to those who condemned them. The prohibition amounted to a *degradation*.[41] Thus what happened, after the *smṛti* period, was a movement to purify or refine custom, without compromising (indeed perhaps rather reinforcing) the previously established social hierarchy.

Yet we should note that, whatever the basis we give it, the *kali-varjya* theory has only a negative aspect. It merely explains and legitimises the disappearance of certain customs. Now it is one thing to hallow the abrogation or desuetude of an institution, but another thing to install a new law. If the disappearance of certain practices indicates a change of manners or opinion, it does not imply, conversely, anything fundamentally new. Transformation of society is marked rather by the appearance of new rules which not only abrogate the previous ones but substitute something in their stead. This creative function has undeniably been played in India by custom. If in certain limited domains the *kali-varjya* theory has allowed a triumph of the resistance which custom offers to sacred tradition, it would be going too far to attribute to it the birth of new institutions.

Finally, that theory could only function in the face of practices which were susceptible to a general application. It has no role when the question is one of a strictly local usage or one restricted to a definite social group, a family, a caste, a corporation, or the like. Yet it is precisely with regard to these sorts of custom that conflict presents itself most frequently.

4. *Conflicts between Dharma and Custom*

From a very early period, the rules and customs observed in the various social groups; castes, corporations or guilds, families, etc., or in different regions of India formed a sort of special law within the bosom of the common law which the *smṛtis* expounded. Manu (VIII.41), following Vasiṣṭha (XIX.7) recommends the king to inform himself about the usages[42] of castes, countries, guilds, and families, and thus to fix everyone's duty. Many of these customs are immaterial from the religious point of view, and are sanctioned ultimately by human justice alone.[43] Others are thought to conform to the precepts of the *śāstra* and see their authority

[41] Viśvarūpa (on *Yāj.*, I.69) already suggests that the texts relating to *niyoga* concerned the Śūdras only. Kāṇe, II, 604. However, when the prohibition of meat-eating was extended even to those cases in which the *śāstras* permitted it, meat-eaters became declassified. degraded, relative to those who abstained. Kāṇe, II, 772–82; III. 945; IV, 422–5.

[42] Here (as in corresponding passages) the term employed is *dharma*, taken in the sense of a customary rule.

[43] That seems to be the case with the majority of the examples furnished by the commentators expounding this text.

confirmed accordingly. But what are we to think of those which, traditionally followed in a given milieu, are in contradiction with the precepts of the sacred texts?

The question arose very early. Baudhāyana (I.2.1–4) enumerates aberrant practices peculiar to the Brahmins of the North and those of the South. "There is", says he, "a difference between the South and the North on five points. We shall describe the practices of the South: to eat with a person not having received Brahminical initiation; to eat with one's wife; to eat food prepared the previous day; to marry the daughter of the maternal uncle or the paternal aunt. And for the North: to sell wool; to drink spirits; to traffic in animals with two rows of teeth; to take up the profession of arms; to make sea-voyages."

The orthodox point of view is known: a practice contrary to the precepts of *śruti* or *smṛti* cannot be good and he who observes it commits a sin. Likewise Baudhāyana (I.1.2.5–8) reports that Gautama condemns the particular practices with which he deals because they are contrary to the traditions of the *śiṣṭas*. But he does not share this opinion. He believes that the Brahmin of the North or the South who follows the customs of his district cannot be blamed, for, he says, local usage merits respect *(tatra tatra deśa-prāmāṇyam eva syāt)*; he admits, conversely, that in any other locality than that in which they prevail, it would be a sin to follow them.

We have already seen the special force enjoyed in India by custom because of its immemorial origin. But usage cannot be erected into a rule of conduct unless it is practised by *śiṣṭas,* the learned and the virtuous, whose conduct may be presumed to rest upon the divine will. Baudhāyana (I.1.5–6), who is faithful to the teaching of the Mīmāṃsā, is very strict on what should be understood about a *śiṣṭa*. Not only should the *śiṣṭa* have a profound knowledge of the Veda, but he should know how to draw all the consequences which flow from the Vedic injunctions for conduct to be followed. It is precisely because of his knowledge of the sacred texts and his scrupulous observance of the precepts that it is permitted to presume that he always acts in conformity with a Vedic injunction, even if the latter cannot be verified in the texts now at our disposal. Thus it can hardly be doubted that, for Baudhāyana as for Gautama, usages contrary to the traditions of the *śiṣṭas* and *a fortiori* those which are contrary to precepts of *śruti* or *smṛti* are *adharma*.[44] That is why he adds that it is not allowed to follow them anywhere else than in the districts where they prevail. However he admits that the force of usage is such that even *adharma* practices, such as these which

[44]Moreover, Baudh., I.1.1–4 demonstrates the hierarchy between the three sources of *dharma*: first the Veda, then *smṛti*, and then only in the third rank (hence in default of the first two) Good Custom *(śiṣṭācāra)*.

he mentions, deserve respect,[45] and consequently cannot be reprobated after the time when they passed into custom. Does this mean that he believes that the sin is wiped out? Let us confine ourselves for the present to acknowledging that from the *dharma-sūtra* period onwards the question gave rise to controversy between the schools.

Other passages of *smṛti* seem to allow certain customs an authority large enough to counterbalance that of the *śāstras*. Thus Āpastamba (I.7.2.6–7), agreeing that it is difficult to distinguish that which is *dharma* from that which is not, advises that one should hold fast to the usages of good people.[46] Strictly speaking, one could see in this no more than the application of the criterion of custom where the texts contradict each other. Manu (IV.178) in the same vein, recommends the *snātaka* to "walk in the way of virtuous people which his father and ancestors have trodden; in following that he will do no wrong". Family customs here have for Manu the validity of rules of conduct.

The same Manu (VIII.46) counsels the king to cause to be observed as law "all the practices of virtuous *dvijas,* attached to *dharma,* if they are not contrary to the customs of countries, families, and castes",[47] which seems indeed to imply that particular customs have more weight than the custom of the Sages. What is intended there, however, is only advice in the nature of political wisdom addressed to the king which does not touch the bottom of the problem, for a *dvija* who is concerned for his own salvation tries to conform his conduct to the precepts of the *śāstras* and consequently avoids following usages which are opposed to them (*Vas.,* I.17, XIX.7; *Gaut.,* XI.20). Yet if the text of the verse seems clear to us, the commentators are divided in the interpretation which they place upon it. Medhātithi (followed by Govindarāja) and Devaṇṇa-bhaṭṭa (*Sm. cand.,* I, p. 10) understand, on the contrary, that he recommends the king not to allow to be observed as law in countries, families, and castes any practices other than those conforming to the sacred texts.[48]

The most important text of Manu on the subject which now concerns us is verse 108 of the first Book, because it has served as the basis of

[45] We note that Baudhāyana does not say that custom is *dharmya* (conformable to *dharma*) but that it is *prāmāṇya* (from *māna,* opinion), worthy of respect, authoritative, without any religious connotation.

[46] 'Dharma and Adharma do not show themselves to us in bodily form and say "here we are". Nor do the gods, or the Gandharvas, or the *manes* say, "this is *dharma,* that is *adharma*". Consequently what good people approve of is *dharma,* and that which they condemn is *adharma.*'

[47] *sadbhir ācaritaṃ yat syād dharmikaiś ca dvijātibhiḥ*
tad deśa-kula-jātīnām aviruddhaṃ prakalpayet.

A similar text attributed by the *Sm. cand.* to an anonymous *smṛti* is reproduced by Jolly in his edition of *Bṛhaspati* (XXVII.24) and by Aiyaṅgār (Additional Texts, p. 495).

[48] Cf Bühler's note to his translation, and the translation which G. Jhā gives of it.

the Anglo-Indian case-law which has confirmed the primacy of custom over the written law.[49] This is the text :

ācāraḥ paramo dharmaḥ śrutyuktaḥ smārta eva ca
tasmād asmin sadā yukto nityaṃ syād ātmavān dvijaḥ.

The British judges, following Sir William Jones, translated the first line of this couplet (the second provides no difficulty) giving a disjunctive value to the words *eva ca*. Then it would mean, "Custom is supreme Law, as is that which is said in *śruti* and *smṛti*. The twice-born concerned for the good of his soul must always be attentive to it." Thus Manu would acknowledge in custom the same value in affording a rule of *dharma* as have the precepts of the Veda and the *śāstras*. Now this construction of the verse is far from settled.[50] The majority of the commentators, relating the words *śrutyuktaḥ* and *smārta* to the word *ācāra,* understand the verse of Manu to signify that the *ācāra,* rules of conduct, as they are propounded in *śruti* and *smṛti,* are supreme *dharma*.[51] In other words Manu insisted upon practice of the rules of life prescribed by the sacred texts, for it is not by simply knowing texts that the *dvija* acquires spiritual merit *(dharma),* but by his application to their observation in action. Thus *ācāra,* the way of life, is the supreme source of merit when it conforms to precepts. This second interpretation would reflect the thought of Manu better than the first.[52] This does not mean to say that the first has not some support in texts throughout *smṛti* (notably some passages of the *Mahābhārata*) and that it has been received as correct by some commentators on Manu, viz. Govindarāja and Nandana.[53]

Even with that view of Manu's verse, and with whatever extension acquired in course of time by the notion of Good Custom, a customary rule cannot replace a precept of the sacred texts except on condition of presenting the characteristics of a rule of *dharma,* defined long ago by the Mīmāṃsā. Custom could not prevail against a contrary precept

[49]The principal decision was that given in 1868 by the Privy Council in the Ramnad Case, *Collector of Madura* v. *Moottoo Ramalinga Sathupathy* 12 Moore's Ind. Appeals. 397.

[50]Mayne, *op. cit.,* 11th edn., s. 33, p. 59 n. *(d)*. Whatever the original meaning of the verse, it is relevant only to topics within the concept of Good Custom. It is at best very doubtful whether it applies to judicial questions, for the powers of the judge were in no way limited by texts of this type.

[51]The translations of Bühler, Strehly and G. Jhā reveal that this was (in their view) the sense.

[52]Cf *M.*, IV.155–8. At *v.*155 the words *śruti-smṛtyudita*, corresponding to *śrutyuktaḥ smārta* in our verse, are connected with *ācāra*. The importance of practical application is neatly underlined in the precepts of *Vas.,* VI.1–7, of which the verses of Manu are an echo (*M.*, IV.156 in any case reproduces *Vas.*, VI.7).

[53]Kāṇe, III, 875.

unless it does not appear to be visibly inspired by utilitarian or hedonistic considerations. And we must add that interpreters faithful to orthodoxy do not even approve that point of view. They hold that it is always a sin to follow a particular usage, even if it is clear of all mundane motives, should it be opposed to the written rule.

But here another consideration intervenes to which an allusion was made earlier. The totality of rules posited in *śruti* and *smṛti* can only be observed entire by those whose sole concern is to deserve heaven. Even some of them must be rejected today because of the worsening of manners in the Age in which we live (the *kali-varjya* theory). *A fortiori* we cannot ask an oridinary man to submit to all the obligations laid down in the course of the four stages of life. This is an ideal to which only saints may aspire. From the generality of men absorbed in their daily task, such an effort cannot be demanded, for "virtue is not taught", wisdom is an innate gift. It is not realistic to reproach him who does not have that gift and who confines himself to following the rules of the social group to which he belongs.

A group of precepts incontestably belonging to *smṛti* tends to favour recognition of a juridical value in custom whether or not it agrees with the sacred texts. First of all we have the well-known verse of Yājñavalkya (I.342) which recommends that when the king has conquered a country, he maintain intact the customs *(ācāra)*, the rules of procedure (or the rules followed in transactions: *vyavahāra)* and the usages of families *(kula-sthiti)*, just as they are observed there.[54] A propos of this text, Vijñāneśvara insists that the king ought not to try to impose the usages of his own country upon the population of a country which he has conquered. Dealing with his own subjects, Yājñavalkya (II.192) counsels the king to cause the observance of conventions entered into by members of groups such as the *naigamas, pākhaṇḍis* and so on. Nārada (XIII.2) declares also that the king should cause usages and conventions *(samaya)* to be observed which prevail in the *pākhaṇḍi, naigama* and other fraternities, whether in fortresses or in the provinces. According to Vijñāneśvara (*Mit.*, on *Yāj.*, I.192) and Nīlakaṇṭha (*Vyav. may.*, XII.1) *pākhaṇḍi* means merchants and other groups of people who reject the authority of the Veda, whilst *naigama* signifies merchants and other people who, conversely, do accept the authority of the Veda. Similarly the king is bound to respect, and to cause to be respected by others, the customs of populations living on the frontiers or in the mountains (whose manners could be very different—as they still are—from those of the Hindus) and even those which are established by heretics. Medhātithi (on *M.*, VIII.41) remarks on this subject that there is no anomaly on the king's part if, installed to safeguard *dharma*, he applies to barbarians the

[54]The same rule appears at *Viṣ.*, III.42 and *M.*, VII.203.

customs of their society even if they are repugnant to the sacred texts, for to such people the concept of *purity* is meaningless.

But there can be no precise demarcation between the Āryan and the non-Āryan worlds. Even in the heart of the Hindu community there exist peoples too ignorant or too weak to observe completely the precepts of the *śāstras*. They do not conceive that they commit any sin in following the customs of their ancestors. How could one impose rules of the *śāstras* to the letter on them, when heretics and barbarians are legally authorised to practice customs repugnant to the Veda?

This is the context in which it is fitting to read the verse of Bṛhaspati (II.28): "Customs *(dharmas)* of countries, castes, families and other (groups) must be maintained intact; otherwise the public would revolt, the subjects would take an aversion to (their king), and the army and the treasury would be destroyed."[55]

It would hardly be possible to show more neatly how the interests of the state must prevail over the rule of *dharma* when one encounters a custom firmly entrenched. But this is a principle of royal policy. The king's mission is, above all, to make peace reign within the realm and to protect his subjects against perils from abroad. Where strict observance of the rules of *dharma* would lead to disorder he must abstain from intervention and must allow his subjects to continue to observe their customs.

Does this mean that a contrary custom abrogates the rule of *dharma*? It goes without saying that a person who observes the former cannot be considered at fault by the members of group to which he belongs, who are the sole judges of his conduct in practice. In other words, he cannot be held socially culpable. But is it the same from the religious point of view? He has violated *dharma,* unconsciously no doubt, but unawareness is not a means of absolution from sin. Had custom, by itself, a power of that kind?

The question is debated. We have seen that Baudhāyana seems to admit that customs which he reports to us as belonging to Brahmins of the North and the South were only *adharma* when practised in a region where they were not traditionally followed. We have also seen that according to Manu (IV.178) he who follows the custom of his ancestors does no wrong. But what should be understood by "he does no wrong [to himself or to another] *(na riṣyate)*"? Commenting on this verse, Medhātithi says that it is not applicable except to ignorant

[55]Aiyaṅgār, I.126b–127, following the citation in the *Kṛtyakalpataru* is a reduplication of this verse and adds to the customs of countries, etc., those proper to people born of irregular unions *(pratiloma-prasūta)* and those proper to inhabitants of strongholds *(durga-nivāsin)*, which echoes Nārada XIII.2.

people who are incapable of consulting texts, for whom the best way of knowing their duties is to act as their ancestors have done. Or even, he adds, the verse's only object is to show, where there is an option between several rules of conduct, that the rule to follow is that which has been adopted in the past in the same environment. Still unresolved is the question whether one is protected from all *sin* if one observes family customs, *whatever they might be.*

But Bṛhaspati (II.31; *Aiy.*, I.130 cd), after listing a series of practices which are aberrant but observed in certain regions of India,[56] ends with the line:

anena karmaṇā naite prāyaścitta-damārhakāḥ.

Literally translated this seems to mean, "for such practices these (people) incur neither penance nor secular punishment". According to this text a contrary custom would have the effect of paralysing the rule of *dharma*, not to make an aberrant usage into an act of *dharma* carrying spiritual benefits, but to abolish the religious sanction which accompanies the violation of the rule, as much as to say that it is no longer sinful to act in that way. Here, we must emphasise, is a set back of a much graver character to the obligatory quality of the rule of *dharma* than was constituted by the prohibitions of the Kali Age. After all, those prohibitions allowed the *dharmic* rule to stand for regenerate humanity. They were founded on a general theme: the weakness of men of our present Age. The abrogation effectuated by a contrary custom however, has no other foundation than the particular traditions of a particular social group.

Even so a section of the interpreters refused to admit that the line of Bṛhaspati had the sense and significance which we have just given to it. "According to some authors", writes Nīlakaṇṭha (*Vyav. may.*, I.1.13),[56a] "the reference to penances and secular punishments for the acts concerned applies to countries not comprised in the text mentioned before. Others who explain *prāyaścitta-dama* by *prāyaścitta-rūpo yo damaḥ* [secular punishment taking the form of a penance] only allow exemption from secular punishment in those cases, but hold that there is occasion for punishment and penance at the same time in other cases". In other words, according to these last writers, the immunity extends only to those penalties which can be inflicted by way of penance; certain penances

[56] 'Some *dvijas*, in the South, marry the daughter of their maternal uncle. In the central regions artisans and manual workers eat cow's flesh. In the East fish is eaten and wives practise adultery. In the North women drink alcohol and it is permitted to have intercourse with them during their periods. The people of the Khasa country take to wife the widows of their brothers.'

[56a] Cf P.V. Kāṇe and S.G. Patwardhan, *The Vyavahāramayukha of Nilakaṇṭha* ... (Bombay, 1933), 7–8.

indeed constitute veritable punishments. And no punishment can be inflicted on those who have only followed the customs of their country. The sin thus remains without immediate sanction, but it subsists none the less. Mitra-miśra,[57] who shares this second opinion, observes for his part that only judicial action is paralysed as against such customs, because to reform them would risk upheavals amongst the subjects (as is said in the passage of Bṛhaspati which we saw above). No penalty can be inflicted by the king on those who practice them. But penance eludes the judicial sphere. Its object is not to punish but to purify the sinner in the interests of his afterlife. It may as a consequence be imposed even where judicial action is not contemplated. Thus Mitra-miśra considers that there is always a sin in infringing the religious law, even when the infringement, being protected by custom, cannot be redressed by penal action.[58] In sum this suggests that the rule of *dharma* and the rule of custom has each its own level of application. If the rule of *dharma* cannot abrogate the customary rule, the latter certainly cannot abrogate the rule of *dharma* as such, that is to say as instrument of the law of *karma*.

Moreover, in a hierarchical society such as is the Indian, it would be very difficult to understand how people who practised usages contrary to Good Custom could be immunised against the degrading consequences of their sin, and be considered as "pure" as the *dvijas* who were faithful to the *śāstras'* precepts. Like others in their group, they would remain degraded in the eyes of the "pure" or the less "impure" unless they expiated their sins. They would occupy an inferior place in the social hierarchy. But they could none the less continue to live under their customs, and the *śāstras* even advised the king, for reasons of wise policy, to take care that they are observed. These customs were not on that account legitimated; they were only tolerated.

From the developments above-mentioned it is apparent that the rule of *dharma* did not become a juridical rule until it entered into behaviour and was accepted by the population as a customary rule. But how could such a process take place if it was assumed that customary rules should prevail over the rule of the *śāstras*? Are not the two principles mutually contradictory? Or should one conclude simply that only custom counts in Hindu law, and that the *śāstras* are only useful when they are in agreement with custom? To these questions the following answers may be attempted.

[57]*Vīr. vyav.*, p. 22, quoted at *Dh. k.*, p. 101. Kāṇe, III, 861.

[58]Devaṇṇa-bhaṭṭa (*Sm. cand.* I, 10) citing the verses of Bṛhaspati discussed above, omits the last verse *anena karmaṇā* . . ., which makes one wonder whether it figured in certain versions of the text of the *Bṛhaspati-smṛti*.

Because of the admitted predominance of the customary rule over the rules of the *śāstras,* custom certainly occupies an important place in Hindu law, so important that some observers, including very well informed men, have been able to believe and to write that India was without written law. This is the opinion of the Jesuit Father Bouchet who lived at Madura at the beginning of the eighteenth century, and of Abbé Dubois at the beginning of the nineteenth so far as concerns Mysore and the southern parts of the Madras Presidency. L. Sorg writes that in the eighteenth century in the provinces governed by the East India Company, justice as dispensed by the heads of the castes or the village or by the panchayats had no other rule but immemorial custom. That member of the French judiciary even writes that the authority of the texts is the result of European influence, espousing thereby the theses of Nelson.[59] He is right—partially. But what we know of the way in which justice was administered by the panchayats or the village courts leaves us with a subtler impression. In delicate questions appeals were indeed made to a Brahmin for advice, and recourse was made, if not to the *śāstras* themselves, at least to treatises which provided a local interpretation of them.

Even where the *śāstras* agreed with custom (and we have seen that the interpreters frequently tried to establish that they did) the role of the written law was far from negligible. It is thanks to the digest-writers and the commentators that custom could be organised in a juridical framework following a pre-established plan, which opened the way to refinements and to a certain influence of technique upon the data themselves. In what concerns topics within *vyavahāra* our authors managed to extract a veritable common law, without which no juridical science would have been possible.

But it would be wrong to confine the influence exercised by the *dharmaśāstras* and the commentaries to the areas in which they agreed, on broad lines, with custom. Their influence has really been very much wider than that. We must take account of the attraction which the *dharmic* rule has exercised upon custom by virtue of its religious significance and the veneration always attaching to the sacred books which supply it.

Even when not followed, the rule of *dharma* always appears to the Hindu as a model towards which one should tend, for it is a principle of classification. A caste rises in the social hierarchy only as it approaches the usages practised by the higher castes, i.e. those who most respect the traditions set out in the *smṛti.* Thus there will be a tendency, at least amongst the élite, to remove from custom usages frankly contrary to orthodoxy and to incline the group, or a part of the group, towards a

[59]Léon Sorg, *Introduction à l'étude du droit hindou* (Pondicherry, 1895).

mode of life regarded as more pure, or less impure. Now custom is generally oral and is transmitted by being observed. It is essentially unfixed. It is modified to keep pace with progress in manners and culture, with the evolution of opinions. On the other hand the rule of *dharma* is a written rule and presents all the advantages of a written law: it is certain (except, naturally, for the divergencies due to interpretation, which are nothing compared with the difficulties experienced when establishing the existence, the bearing, or the meaning of a customary rule). Further, it is immutable, fixed once for ever in the sacred books. It alone is the object of a study, or rather of a science, since *law* is studied only as a bonus, so to speak, where, and only where, it maintains and upholds *dharma*. Thus there are many reasons why the original mobility of custom should be retained with all its imprecision, and why it should be kept ready to model itself on the rules of the *śāstras*.

Yet we should observe that if the interpreters of the Middle Ages allow custom to prevail over the written law, they believe conversely that a usage in contradiction with the law is not capable of extension, i.e. it can be allowed only in the group where its existence is proved.[60] Thus an unorthodox rule of custom has no chance of extending its domain.[61] It remains a particularity, a peculiarity. By contrast, the rule of *dharma* has an unlimited power of radiation. It offers itself as a model to every group. It fills the gaps in custom and tends to insinuate itself into the customary structure. And once it is established there it is fixed thereafter; it is and remains *dharma*, the group's law.

I cannot refrain from comparing this influence of *dharma* with that which Roman law exercised in the Middle Ages upon the customs of western Europe in the regions called the "lands of custom" (as opposed to regions of book-law). In those regions germanic invasions had established the supremacy of customs. With the renaissance of studies of Roman law, the latter appeared to the jurists as a veritable revelation of law, the *ratio scripta*, or "written reason". The authority which Roman law then enjoyed as an expression of juridical science is of the same nature as that of our *dharma-śāstras* in India. It too was regarded as an ideal legislation to which one should conform, not, surely, for any reason of a religious character but because of the intrinsic merits which were recognised to reside in it. As in India, that authority seemed fragile enough, for the adage went: "custom exceeds law". But there too,

[60]Cf Kāṇe, III, 876–7.

[61]It cannot be adopted by those to whom the book-law applies, and those whom it binds may at any time abandon it for the book-law. These rules are accepted in Anglo-Indian jurisprudence. Derrett, *Introduction to Modern Hindu Law*, s. 15; see also *per* Devadoss, J., at *Mokka* v. *Ammakutti* Indian Law Reports (1927) 51 Madras, 1 at p. 28 (a full bench decision), a point of view confirmed by Krishnaswami Ayyangar, J., in *Durgaprasada* v. *Sudarsanaswami* Indian Law Reports 1940 Madras, 653 at p. 665. [trs.]

as in India, recourse was had to written law to fill the numerous gaps in the customary wardrobe, to organise the customary mass into rational frameworks, and to give it order and logic, so that the written law tended to attract customary rules to itself, forming an ideal common law which was preferable to the diversity of customs. And, as in India still, the customary rule which was repugnant to written law found itself confined to its actual territory. In the fourteenth century, two sorts of customs were distinguished, those which were conformable to the written law and on that account were considered to be common law, and the others, "malignant law", which were held to be narrow and could not be extended either by analogy or from one custom to another.[62] Thus Roman law could penetrate into customary French law, without dispelling it entirely (far from that!), but making it a beneficiary of its technique.

The admission of Roman law in this guise into so many parts of western Europe did not have an exact counterpart in England. But from what we have seen no one will be surprised to learn that the ascendancy of the true Common Law of England over the multitudes of local customs was achieved more notably and more intimately by the systematised reasoning of the Common Lawyers than by the operation of statute.[63] It is not irrelevant to speak of the strict, even harsh tests to which the Judges submitted customs before they were allowed to displace the common law; nor of the phenomenon whereby mercantile customs were admitted into English equity and became part of the law of the land. Though nominally following the experience of the Common Law, India, in her strict, if not harsh ascertainment and application of customs in derogation from the Hindu and Islamic law, and in her willingness to allow oft-proved customs to pass into judicial knowledge, has actually worked out to its logical conclusion the very procedure which I have been describing.[64] Custom may be used to throw light upon book law, but it is much more common for the book law to illuminate and define custom. The book law is the goal towards which those formerly governed by customs are presumed to tend.[65]

In the vast subcontinent of India, where all levels of culture are represented and where the most diverse human types coexist, customs are of an infinite variety. And yet the moment that these peoples, the

[62]J. Declareuil, *Histoire générale du droit français* (Paris, 1925), 833.

[63]W. Blackstone, *Commentaries on the Laws of England* (1765), I, 74–9. [trs.]

[64]To the instances given in Derrett, s. 15 add the cases of *Fateh Ali Shah* v. *Muhammad Bakhsh* Indian Law Reports (1927) 9 Lahore, 428 (prostitutes do not forfeit their property by marrying); *P. Latchamma* v. *M. Appalaswamy* All India Reporter 1961 An. Prad. 55 (a woman does not forfeit wedding presents by remarrying); *Sheikriyammada N. Koya* v. *Adm., Laccadives* 1967 Kerala Law Times 395 (a custom of inalienability is repugnant to the right of property). [trs.]

[65]See Derrett cited above, p. 204, n. 61.

most disparate *inter se* in the world, proclaim themselves to be Hindus, they have all some point in common with Brahminical orthodoxy. However low they may be in the social scale they are not barbarians, *mlecchas*. They participate at least to a humble degree in the maintenance of the eternal order, of *dharma*. They have their functions and duties to perform. In performing them they expiate the faults of the past and prepare themselves for higher births.[66] Under the influence of Hindu civilisation their customs tend to lose the aspects which are most shocking in the eyes of more Hinduised groups and tend to assimilate the usages of the latter. Though venerated everywhere, the rules of the *dharma-śāstras* are not obeyed as a whole except in the higher classes of society. In the lower classes, their field of action diminishes as one descends, and custom becomes more and more supreme. At the bottom, amongst peoples who are hardly Hinduised at all, the domain of *dharma* is reduced to practically nothing. Yet even in a population firmly rebellious against all progress and totally void of ambition, once *dharma* is accepted on one point, it begins little by little to be accepted on others also by a kind of invisible radiation. That is where the authority of the written law lies. Masson-Oursel put it very well. "That authority exists in the substrata . . . , and not, as in the West, so to say on the surface, following the territorial extension of the political power."[67]

However, such a formula leaves in the shadow or presupposes already resolved the problem which is posed in India by the very existence of that political power. If *dharma* is indeed a personal law which attaches to a man to the degree that he can call himself a Hindu, the Hindu as an individual is also the subject of a ruler to whom he owes obedience and who possesses the means to compel obedience. The authority of the written law is thus historically counterbalanced by that of the prince. The law actually in force, at least for a specific period and in a limited territory, is really the offspring of the solution to this new conflict between the two sources of authority.

[66]According to *M.*, IX.335 the Śūdra who fulfils his duties loyally obtains rebirth in a higher caste.

[67]*L'Inde antique et la civilisation indienne* (Paris, 1933), 99.

CHAPTER III

DHARMA AND ROYAL ORDINANCE

1. *The Function of the King*

(a) *Kṣatra* and *Dharma*

THE THEORY of the function of the king is absent from the *dharma-sūtras* which mention only some elements of it. It takes an important place in the *dharma-śāstras*, starting with the Code of Manu, who moreover furnishes the most complete expression of it.[1]

Kingship[2] is regarded as an institution necessary to the maintenance of the social order established by the Creator for the good of creatures. Only in the Golden Age could men dispense with a king, because all of them had full knowledge of their duties and conformed to them naturally. "There were no law-suits then, nor did hatred exist, nor greed" (*Nār.*, Intr., I.1). Consequent on the degeneration of humanity through the Ages, men lost the inborn sense of their duties. Society was handed over to disorder. The strong oppressed the weak. There was no longer a barrier to contain appetites. There was no property and no family.

Here we meet one of the dogmas of Indian thought: A society without a king *(a-rājaka)* is not viable. It is the "logic of the fish" (i.e. the law of the jungle) which is law.[3]

Therefore the gods instituted the royal function, giving him who is invested with power of command *(kṣatra)* the mission to protect the creatures[4] and to give them, as Yājñavalkya says I.323), the guarantee

[1]In this context, my interest does not extend beyond those aspects which illuminate the nature and extent of the royal authority, in order to determine the basis of the royal activity in the juridical domain. For a more complete account of the theory see Ghoshāl. *History of Indian Political Ideas* (Oxford, 1959), to which I owe no little inspiration.

[2]The *dharma-śāstras* envisage no other form of government than monarchy.

[3]*Mātsya-nyāya*. The expression is found only in the epic (notably at *Mahābhārata*, Śāntip., 15.30, 67.16) and in the works of *arthaśāstra* (*Kaut.*, I.4. 13). But the metaphor is ancient, for one finds it in the Flood passage in the *Śatapatha-brāhmaṇa* (I.8.1. 1–10) and it underlies several passages in the *dharma-śāstras* (esp. *M.*, VII.20; *Nār.*, XVIII.15). It is odd that it turns up again in the mouth of the bishops of the province of Rheims, assembled at Trosly in 909; 'Everywhere the powerful oppresses the weak, and men are like fish in the sea which are devoured pell-mell by each other' (quoted by M. Bloch. *La Société féodale, La formation des liens de dépendance*, Paris, 1939, 9). On the other hand it is in frequent use in European political literature of the seventeenth century. C. Drekmeier, *Kingship and Community in Early India* (Stanford, 1962), 249 n.*d.*

[4]'The first duty of the Kṣatriya is the protection of his people' (*kṣatriyasya pradhānaṃ karma prajānāṃ paripālanam*: *Yāj.*, I.119).

of security *(abhaya-dāna)*. That mission and function is a *dharma*, a religious duty, and since each man's performance of his own duty *(sva-dharma)* depends on the protection secured by the king, it is perfectly correct for the *Mahābhārata* to declare (Śāntip.63.25) that all *dharmas* are comprised in the *rāja-dharma* and that all have *rāja-dharma* at their head.

Certain verses in the *dharma-śāstras* attribute a divine origin to the king himself (*M.*, VII.3-8; *Nār. Sāmb.*, XVIII.13,20). This conception is foreign to the *dharma-sūtras*. It doubtless originated in certain Vedic texts which attribute a divine nature to the king because of his participation in rites which identify him with a god. But it is taken up again primarily to give the king a halo of glory and to justify the respect due to his person (cf.*M.*, VII.8; *Nār.*, XVIII.54-55), rather than being presented as the essential reason why his orders should be obeyed. The same *dharma-śāstras* (*M.*, IX.303-311; *Nār.*, XVIII.26-31) tell another tale about the divine creation of royalty, which boils down to some analogies between the royal function and the essential functions of certain deities. The king rises to the status of a god and maintains this by applying himself to the duties of his office.[5] He is more than an ordinary mortal, but he occupies the throne of Indra, as Vasiṣṭha says (XIX.48) and Manu repeats (V.93). Thus it is only by exercising the royal function as it was created by the gods that the king is assimilated to a deity.[6] The dominant idea of the *dharmaśāstra* writers seems to have been that it was not the king who had a divine nature, but the royal function itself.[7] That an abstraction should be presented as a divinity cannot surprise us, since punishment *(daṇḍa)* is also presented as a deity, a particularly powerful deity which is issue of Brahmā himself (*M.*, VII.14; *Yāj.*, I.354).

The *dharma-śāstras* take the arrival of the king for granted and do not concern themselves with the manner in which he came to his throne. The king is he who has been anointed *(abhiṣikta)*, i.e. for whom the

[5]Cf *Kāt.*, 7–9. *Nār. Sāmb.*, XVIII.13.

[6]Cf the verse of Śaṅkha cited in the *Rājadharmakāṇḍa*, p. 85; 'the king gains heaven not by vows, fasts, or various kinds of sacrifices, but by securing the protection of his subjects' *(na vratair nopavāsena na ca yajñaiḥ pṛthag-vidhaiḥ, rājā svargam avāpnoti paripālanāt)*, which puts the exercise of the royal function above the practice of austerities and the performance of sacrificial rituals.

[7]The question has been hotly debated (cf. U.N. Ghoshāl, *op. cit.*, 546–7 and n. 20), but common opinion seems today to favour the doctrine given above. Altekar, *State and Government in Ancient India* (Benares, 1955), 86–7; B.K. Sarkār, *Political Institutions and Theories of the Hindus* (Leipzig, 1922), 179–80; A.K. Sen, *Studies in Hindu Political Thought* (Calcutta, 1926), 57; K.V. Aiyaṅgār, *Aspects of the Social and Political System of Manusmṛti* (Lucknow, 1949), 175, and lastly L. and R. Rocher, 'La sacralité du Pouvoir dans l'Inde ancienne d'après les textes de Dharma', *Annales du Centre d'étudés des Religions* (Brussels, 1962), 123–37, and Drekmeier, *op. cit.*, 250–2. According to Hopkins ('The divinity of Kings', *J.A.O.S.*, 51, 1931, 309–316) the same conclusion is to be drawn from the epic texts.

coronation rites have been celebrated. All interpreters, save Caṇḍeśvara,[8] believe that the ceremony is necessary to invest the king with supreme authority, but no rule lays down why or how a particular individual is fit to qualify.[9] Doubtless the *dharma-śāstras* list the qualities which the king should possess to be worthy of that title (cf.especially *Gaut.*, XI.2.4-6; *M.*, VII.38-52; *Yāj.*, I.309-311). But these qualities are only put forward to serve as a model for the king. He is praised for having them. He is presumed to have them, in order that he may actually have them, following the current procedure of the authors of *praśastis,* the official eulogies paid to a ruling king.[10] We cannot see in them conditions for accession to royalty, suggesting an election or even popular approbation.

Basically, for the authors of the *dharmaśāstra* as for Voltaire, "The first to be king was a jolly soldier". A soldier: it fits well enough that the king should be a warrior, in order to secure the protection of his subjects and the defense of his realm. And it is usual that he should be a Kṣatriya, for it was to the Kṣatriya *varṇa* that Brahmā reserved in principle the right to bear arms and the duty to protect the lives and properties of the creatures. Manu (VII.2) does not allow him to be otherwise.[11] If he envisages that a non-Kṣatriya could be king it is only to stigmatise him crudely (IV.85) and to forbid a *brahmacārin* to receive any gift from him (IV.84). He is particularly hostile to the idea that a Śūdra could be king (IV.61). Yājñavalkya is less clear. He does not fail to recall that the first duty of a Kṣatriya is to protect the people (I.119). But, when he enumerates the qualities which a *narādhipa,* a "protector

[8]After having cited the orthodox opinion on the necessity of a coronation, Caṇḍeśvara (*Rāj. rat.*, 2–3) rejects it, arguing that it does not take account of the authority of a conqueror over territory won for him by his prowess.

[9]The interpreters are agreed, however, that his eldest son should succeed to the deceased ruler. Rules regarding succession to the throne are very rare in the *dharma-śāstras*. Manu (IX.323) only alludes to the transmission of the throne to a son *(putra)*, though during the king's own lifetime. Caṇḍeśvara (*Rāj. rat.*, p. 70) quotes a verse of Bṛhaspati (*Aiy.*, saṃskāra, 516) according to which 'In the matter of royalty, the order in which marriages take place, and the performing of the *sapiṇḍīkaraṇa* (see above p. 168, n. 58) of the father, the eldest is the one to whom the rights are given, even if his younger brothers are endowed with good qualities', and a verse of Nārada (not in the published text), 'The eldest is the liberator from hell, the most honourable (amongst sons) in the world; thus he is called a jewel-treasury *(ratnākara)*; only he is worthy of the throne *(rājyārho jyeṣṭhaḥ)*', which shows that the rule of primogeniture was based on the religious quality of the first-born son.

[10]Cf G. Dumézil, *Servius et la Fortune* (Paris, 1943).

[11]*brāhmaṃ prāptena saṃskāraṃ kṣatriyena yathāvidhi, sarvasyāsya yathānyāyaṃ kartavyam parirakṣaṇam*: 'It is by a Kṣatriya who has received the *saṃskāra* prescribed by the Veda that the protection of all shall be done according to rule.' It is remarkable that the majority of the commentators upon Manu, including Medhātithi, understood the word *saṃskāra* as the ceremony of initiation *(upanayana)*, or the series of sacraments prescribed for a *dvija*; and that only Nandana saw it as meaning the coronation.

of the people", i.e. a king, should possess, he confines himself to requiring that he should be a *kulīna,* of good family, of high birth, as Vijñāneśvara understands the word *(Mit.,* on *Yāj.,* I.309). And it is to be noted that, in the verse which corresponds to Manu (IV.84), it is not from a non-Kṣatriya king that gifts are to be refused, but from a king who is greedy *(lubdha)* or who transgresses the precepts of the *śāstras (ucchāstrā-vartin)* (I.140).

Certainly some commentators, notably Viśvarūpa, Mādhava, and Nanda-paṇḍita, influenced either by the Mīmāṃsā doctrine[12] or simply by the fact that their patrons were or pretended to be Kṣatriyas, insist that the king should be a Kṣatriya. But the majority neglect this requirement. Medhātithi does indeed say that the word Kṣatriya in Manu VII.2 indicates that only a Kṣatriya has the right to kingship. But he adds that in default of a Kṣatriya a man of another *varṇa* can be substituted for otherwise the realm, wanting a protector, will go to ruin. On verse 84 of Book IV he explains that the word *rāja* in the text means whoever exercises power in a territory, even if he is not a Kṣatriya. He employs very recherché arguments to deprive Manu IV.61 of all significance. That verse forbids a *dvija* to live in a country of which a Śūdra is king. For him everyone who assumes the duties of a Kṣatriya has a right to the title of king (on *M.,* VIII.1).[13] In the same way Kullūka (on *M.,* VII.1) declares that the word *rāja* at VII.1 includes anyone who has been crowned (literally, anointed) and who secures the country's protection, irrespective of his *varṇa.* Caṇḍeśvara (*Rāj. rat.,* p.2) approves of this opinion. Mitra-miśra (*Vīr., Rājanīti-prakāśa,* pp.10–15), citing the same verse, has a long discussion on the sense of the same word and concludes, like Kullūka, that *rāja* applies to another who assumes the task of protecting the subjects.[14] Yājñavalkya's commentators, Vijñāneśvara (*Mit.,* on *Yāj.,* I.368, II.1). Aparārka (on *Yāj.,* I.366), and Nīlakaṇṭha (*Vyav. may.,* I.1.5, citing *Yāj.,* II.1) share the same opinion. We can say that, in spite of Manu, the great majority of interpreters do *not* require that the king should be a Kṣatriya. Early on, no doubt under the pressure of events, kingship ceased to be the prerogative of the second *varṇa.* This must have indirectly affected the divinity of the king himself, because it was by divine predestination that a Kṣatriya would be called to mount the throne. The kingship, then, belonged to him who possessed *kṣatra* de facto, the *imperium,* "empire" in the broad sense, i.e. the power to command, whatever might have been his birth and whatever might have been the circumstances which brought him to the throne.[15]

[12]The maxim of the *aveṣṭi, Jai.* II.3, 3. Cf Kāṇe. III, 38; Ghoshāl, *op. cit.,* 324.

[13]There is a similar comment on *M.,* III.109; V.81, 92. etc.

[14]Kāṇe, III, 39.

[15]The concept of sovereignty, *imperium,* seems to be better expressed by the word *kṣatra*

Kṣatra, the foundation of all royalty, is associated in Indian doctrine with *rāja-dharma,* the totality of duties which constitute the king's mission, that which we have called the royal function, which is a divine institution. There are two distinct entities here and we should distinguish them.

Kṣatra confers on the king independence, the right to act to suit himself without depending upon anyone else. The king is independent of his subjects, as is the spiritual preceptor of his pupils and the head of the family of the members of his household (*Nār.,* I.32-33 and Asahāya thereon).[16] Yājñavalkya actually declares (I.334) that the king ought to be a father to his subjects, but Mitra-miśra glosses this text by adding that he must be qualified (like a father with regard to the members of his family) to secure their protection and control their actions and behaviour. It is true that the *dharma-śāstras* and their interpreters recommend the king not to take any decision without being supplied with counsels. But he is never bound to follow the opinions of his counsellors. He alone bears the responsibility for his actions (*M.,* VII.57; *Yāj.,* I.312).

By contrast, *Dharma* is essentially a rule of *interdependence,* founded on a hierarchy corresponding to the nature of things and necessary for the maintenance of the social order. To break away from it is to violate one's destiny and to expose oneself to the loss of one's salvation. The peculiar *dharma* of the king is the protection of his subjects. If he is free to act as he pleases without having to account to anyone for his acts, he acquires merit only when acting in conformity with his *dharma.* "Kings who remain faithful to their duties", says Kātyāyana (*śloka* 9) attain the status of Indra; but those whose actions depart (from the path of duty) will remain (after their deaths) in the hell called Avīci". So finally the destiny of the king depends on the way in which he has been able to protect his subjects. His merits and sins, the balance between which will determine his future, are measured by those of his subjects; it is because of the protection that he has afforded to them that *they* have been able to perform their duties, just as it is a fault on his part to have been *able* to keep them to their duties when they have actually sinned. The *smṛtis* go so far as to calculate the portion of merits and sins passing to the king. "A king who protects (his subjects) acquires the sixth of

than by any word derived from *rājan,* such as *rājyam* ('kingdom'). *Rājā* and *rājyam* evoke in Hindu eyes, if we follow the etymology current at the time of the commentators (*Bṛh. Aiy.,* I.66 and Renou's remark thereon) and recalled by Mitra-miśra in the passage cited above, the idea of splendor, magnificence, prestige attaching to the person of the king, rather than his power of command and the idea of power or force. Thus there is no reason for surprise that it was the word *kṣatriya* which passed with the sense of 'king' into the languages of certain South East Asian countries where the caste system was not in vogue.

[16]Cf *Nār.,* I.33: *asvatantrāḥ prajāḥ svatantraḥ pṛthivīpatiḥ.* On the subject see Derrett at *Recueils de la Société Jean Bodin* XXII, *Gouvernés et Gouvernants* (Brussels, 1969), 417–45.

the spiritual merit of each of them; conversely, he who fails to protect them gains the sixth of their demerits" (*M.*, VIII.304. Cf.*Gaut.*, XI.11; *Viṣ.*, III.98).[17] A sort of solidarity is thus established between the king and his subjects. The king's happiness depends on his subjects, for he suffers the consequences of their sins and profits from the merits they acquire. Conversely, the happiness of his subjects depends on the king, for if he protects them as he should he will prevent the rogues from roguery and will permit the good to devote themselves to their duties.[18] But "happiness" must be taken here, according to the point of view of the *dharmaśāstra* writers, not in the sense of material happiness, but in the sense of spiritual bliss. The real Indian formula to express that solidarity between king and subjects can best be stated thus: the salvation of the king depends on his subjects, just as the salvation of the subjects depends on their king.[19] That is how we show the relationship of interdependence which the rule of *dharma* sets up, in opposition to pure power which is *kṣatra*.

Kṣatra and *dharma* are equally opposed in another point of view. *Dharma* is a universal rule in this sense, that every king is subject to it and suffers its sanctions, whatever be the extent or situation of his kingdom. Moreover it is a duty and an obligation of a personal character which is incumbent on the king's conscience and obtains stability only through his will.

Kṣatra, however, is power of a territorial character, exercised within a given territory and stopping at the frontiers of the realm. In addition, it is conceived not as a sovereignty in the modern sense of that word, but as a real right over territory. Of the same nature as property, it implies a direct power over the soil. That is why the king is also called *svāmin,* a word which can be applied equally to a proprietor as to a husband or a chief, and which denotes an immediate power over a thing or over a person. Manu (IX.44) alludes to a version of the legend of Pṛthu, according to which Pṛthu married the earth. This image of a marriage between the king and his realm, which became a cliché in the epigraphical literature, translates the tight relation between the king and the territory

[17]As the commentators remark, these rules serve simply to indicate the weight of merit and sin accruing to the king without in any way diminishing the merits or sins of his subjects. Yājñavalkya (I.335, 337) retains the 'sixth' for merits, but enlarges the king's responsibility for sins, raising the proportion to a half.

[18]Cf *Viṣ.* III.98: *prajā-sukhe sukhī rājā tad-duḥkhe yaś ca duḥkhitaḥ.*

[19]However the balance leans undoubtedly to the king's side, for his subjects cannot fulfil meritorious acts unless the king secures their protection. He is the master of the time, following the Mahābhārata formula which Manu develops (IX.302). In other words, the policies which he means to pursue determine the spiritual happiness of his subjects: if he is just he participates in the merits they gain. But conversely his subjects do not participate in merit gained by the king, for he, in protecting them does no more than his *dharma,* and it is to that end that he enjoys the prerogatives appertaining to the function of royalty.

of his realm. The king regards his kingdom as his property, although it is agreed that other powers than his own could be exercised along with his over actual parcels of soil. Thus to fill the almost total silence of the *śāstras* on the rules relating to succession to the throne, the interpreters have not hesitated to apply to this subject, saving a few indispensable corrections, precepts relating to the devolution of property at death.[20]

Two prerogatives are attached to the royal function: the right to tax and the right to punish.

Numerous texts *(Baudh.,* I.10.1; *M.,* VII.144,VIII.307,308; *Yāj.,* I.337; *Nār.,* XVIII.48) establish a strict correlation between the duty of protection incumbent upon the king and his subjects' payment of taxes to which they are assessed. Nārada (XVIII.48) speaks of a tax *(bali)* of a sixth on the produce of the land as if it were a salary *(vetana)* awarded the king in return for his performing his duty. Certain authors conclude that the king is paid by his subjects for fulfilling his task. The duty of protection would be the consideration for the receipt of revenue, so that there would exist between the king and his subjects relations of a contractual nature or a quasi-contractual nature founded on the principle of equity which we express by the maxim, *ubi emolumentum ibi onus,* "the liability follows the consideration". But such a way of looking at the matter would go counter to the notion which we have already formulated of the absolute independence of the king vis-à-vis his subjects. To refute it, we need only note that if the duty of protection rested on the obligation of the subjects to pay their taxes, the king would not be held strictly to protect any subjects who did not pay tax. Now all interpreters are agreed in recognising that the duty of the king to protect extends to all his subjects, not only those who are exempt because of their status, but also those who are dispensed from payment because of their age, their infirmities or their want of resources.[21] In fact the right to take revenue is only an adjunct to the royal function, intended to give the king the means to secure his proper subsistence and to govern his realm.[22] True, the king who fails in his duty exposes himself to the danger

[20]This 'real' (i.e. proprietorial) character attributed to *kṣatra,* parallel to the similar concept of eminent domain developed by western feudal jurists, explains the controversy which still goes on as to who has the ultimate ownership of the soil in India. Kāṇe, III, 865–9, Ghoshāl, *The Agrarian System in Ancient India* (Calcutta, 1930), 81–103, *History of Indian Political Ideas,* passim; R. Shama Sastry, *Evolution of Indian Polity* (Calcutta, 1930), 172–6; Y. Bongert, 'La notion de propriété dans l'Inde', *Études de droit contemporain* 23 (1962), 149–62; A.S. Naṭarāja Ayyar, 'The king's right in the soil', *Vyavahāra Nirṇaya* (Delhi), 4 (1955), 25–45; D.N. Jhā, *Revenue System in Post-Maurya and Gupta Times* (Calcutta, 1967), ch. ii.

[21]Medhātithi, on *M.,* VII.2, 35, 40, 80; Kullūka on *M.,* VIII.304; Viśvarūpa on *Yāj.,* II.38.

[22]Cf Medhātithi on *M.,* VIII.1; Vijñāneśvara, *Mit.,* on *Yāj.,* I.119.

of losing his subjects' affection, and *dharmaśāstra* writers do not omit to paint, in emphatic terms, the risks which he runs (*M.*, VII.111–112; *Yāj.,* I.341). But it is their way of reminding the king that it is in his own interest to subserve his people's welfare. The real sanction against failure to protect does not lie in the threats which apply to the king's present life and which, in any case, might never be realised. It is in the inescapable sanction which the king's violation of his *dharma* puts in motion in the other world. The king is not bound to protect his subjects because he takes taxes from them, but because that is where his own peculiar duty lies.[23]

The right to punish is another prerogative attached to the royal function. Only the king may use punishment to secure the execution of his orders. It is remarkable that punishment is not presented as an accessory of the royal function, as is the right to demand revenue, but as a divine institution itself. Its origin is even more marvellous than that of royalty. Since the royal function is only a source of obligations for the king, no power of coercion could be produced from it; on the other hand, *kṣatra, de facto* power or unilateral will, could not find in itself any justification for the use of punishment. Consequently, punishment was personified under the name of *daṇḍa* (literally, "mace, sceptre") by the supreme god in the king's interest and for the good of creatures (*M.*, VII.14; *Yāj.*, I.354). But, above all, the exceptional importance of punishment in the government of men raised it to the point of being thought a deity. In celebrated verses (VII.20-25), Manu like Nārada (XVIII.14-16) shows forcefully the necessity of punishment, the only means of keeping men on the path of duty (*M.*, VII.22).[24] In effect, *Daṇḍa* is only pure force. Its sole object is to enable the king to perform his function. Thus it is identified with Dharma (*M.*, VII.17; *Yāj.*, I.354), and, while protecting the king when properly applied, it turns against him and brings his ruin if inflicted unjustly (*M.*, VII.27-29; *Yaj.*, I.356-357).

None the less punishment places a redoubtable weapon in the king's hands. Since the sanction is temporal, it immediately accompanies even an unjust order, whereas the king cannot suffer for any such misdeeds until the after-life. Several verses emphasise this absolute power of the king founded upon punishment (*M.*, VII.9,12,13; *Nār.*, XVIII.20,32) and admit all the dangers of investing the king with such a power (*M.*, VII.28,30; *Yāj.*, I.355). But this is to admit that, because of punishment, the king possesses an unlimited power on the temporal plane, and that he can do whatever he wishes. "Whatever the king does," says Nārada

[23]For a fuller discussion see Ghoshāl, *History*, 536–9, 564 n. 2.

[24]An evidently pessimistic view of human nature. But in reality Manu means this: the fear of punishment will restrain the wicked, and thus permit the good to fulfil their duties in peace.

(XVIII.21), "is justified: such is the rule".[25] In other words the king is the sole judge of the means to be employed to accomplish his mission. Complete liberty is allowed him. Only the result matters.

The king's activity is the more free for the fact that, in order that he shall fulfill his mission, the *śāstras* proclaim that while he is inflicting punishment he can incur no impurity. "Kings, like those who are bound by a vow or who perform a long sacrifice, commit no impurity, for they are seated upon the throne of Indra", declare Vasiṣṭha (XIX.48) and Manu (V.93) (cf. also *Gaut.*, XIV.45; *Viṣ.*, XXII.48 and *M.*, V.94,97, VIII.311). There are many texts in which the position of the king is closely compared to that of one who institutes a sacrifice. The exercise of the royal function is equivalent to the celebration of a sacrifice of a long duration *(sattra)*, and that is why the king remains pure, whatever acts he is led to commit, including condemnation to death or recourse to treacherous means to bring a culprit to justice.

In sum, from the doctrine deduced by the interpreters from the totality of *smṛti*, the king appears to owe his authority neither to the divine will, nor to his birth, nor to any social compact, but solely to the force at his disposal.[26] Certainly, kingship confers a great prestige upon him, but if he is called *rāja*, it is because "he pleases his subjects *(rañjayate)* because of his military might furnished with the Four Arms" *(Bṛh.Aiy.*, I.66), that is to say because of the deployment of his force. His authority is entirely temporal or secular. Punishment is the sole instrument of his policies. But, like every mortal, he has his own *dharma* which the *dharma-śāstra* writers continually rehearse. This must always be present to his mind, for the fulfilment of his *dharma* is the precondition of that of all other men. Though he is an absolute sovereign, he is subject to the law of *karma* which will play inescapably for him, or against him. That is why it is said in the *Bṛhad-āraṇyaka-upaniṣad* (I.14), "Dharma is the sovereignty of sovereignty *(kṣatrasya kṣatram yad dharmaḥ)*".

(b) *Kṣatra* and *Brahman*

If the king is called to undergo, like any sinner, the consequences of his acts in the after-life, he is entirely free in his lifetime to act as he wishes and as his conscience directs. The only bridle which the *dharma-śāstras* provide for his authority resides in the position given to the Brahmins

[25] *yad eva kurute rājā tat pramāṇam iti sthitiḥ*. [Perhaps *pramāṇam* implies 'valid', 'authoritative'. (trs.)]

[26] But if we follow Nārada XVIII.25 it is to the merits which he acquired in previous births that the king owes the power he now enjoys: *tapaḥ-krītāḥ prajā rājñā prabhur āsit tato nṛpaḥ, tasmāt tad vacasi stheyaṃ vārtā cāsāṃ tad āśrayā*. 'It is by austerities that the king has purchased his subjects, and that is why he is their master. Thus what he says must be observed, for their existence depends on him.' The proposition is isolated, and has a Buddhistic sound, but none the less, within the bounds of orthodox opinion, it simply restates the law of *karma*.

and in the role which has devolved upon them. Here the *smṛti*-writers have only taken up the Vedic doctrine on the relations between spiritual power *(brahman)* and temporal power *(kṣatra)*, matching up with them certain consequences of a juridical nature. This doctrine itself flows from the division of functions between the first two *varṇas*. The spiritual power was attributed to the Brahmin so that he might instruct the others in their duties. The temporal power was attributed to the Kṣatriya because he possessed the force necessary to obtain obedience. The one is thus complementary to the other. As is said in a passage in the *Śatapatha-brāhmaṇa* (IV.1.4.1), *brahma* is "he who conceives" *(abhigantṛ)* and *kṣatra* "he who does" *(kartṛ)*, or again, *brahma* is intelligence and *kṣatra* will.[27] Both of them aim to secure the reign of *dharma*. The Brahmin only performs his role successfully if he personifies *dharma* in his teaching and in his conduct. The Kṣatriya invested with the royal function is not successful in his role unless he too personifies *dharma* in his activity. At bottom there is identity of function between them; but *dharma* cannot be realised without their cooperation. This principle of the essential cooperation of the two powers is one of the fundamental elements in *smṛti's* theory of kingship. For Gautama (VIII.1-3,XI.27,31,32) the Brahmins and the king sustain the divine order of the world *(dhṛta-vrata)*, the Brahmins by their counsel, the king by punishment. Likewise Nārada (*Sāmb.*, XVIII.32) declares that temporal power, when associated with the spiritual, is the foundation (*mūla*, "root") of the protection of the people.[28] So the Brahmins are born counsellors for the king. The *śāstras* insist that, expressly because of the power with which the king is invested and which allows him to achieve anything, he cannot take a decision without asking the advice of competent and enlightened people, amongst the first of whom naturally are the Brahmins (*M.*, VII.55-59; *Yāj.*, I.312; *Kāt.*, 4-5). These have almost a vested right to participate in the court of justice. Not only are they clearly assigned the judicial function, but any learned Brahmin who is present when a case is heard is allowed to make his opinion known on the matter at issue *(Nār.*, III.2, with Asahāya). It is even a duty to do so. As a result, Vijñāneśvara and Mitra-miśra (on *Yāj.*, II.1-2) distinguish, amongst the members of the court, the *sabhyas* who are specially chosen and appointed *(yukta)* to this function by the king and the Brahmins who come voluntarily to the hearing without any appointment *(a-yukta)*. On the other hand, when the king cannot preside in person (which must be often), he must in principle see that his place is taken by a Brahmin (*M.*, VIII.9; *Yāj.*, II.3). Only in default of a Brahmin ready, willing,

[27]Cited by U.N. Ghoshāl, *op. cit.*, 33.

[28]*saṃyuktaṃ brāhmaṇaiḥ kṣatraṃ mūlaṃ lokābhirakṣaṇe.*

and fit to be appointed may he designate a Kṣatriya or a Vaiśya (*Kāt.*, 67) as his delegate or *prāḍvivāka* (presiding judge).

It is not only in the administration of justice that the advice of Brahmins is required, but in all affairs in which the interests of the state are at large. "As for the most important questions concerning the six means (of policy)[29]", says Manu (VIII.58-59), "he (the king) must discuss them with a learned Brahmin, the most eminent of all these (counsellors). Full of confidence (in him) he should always charge him with all his affairs; after having deliberated with him, he should do what it is appropriate to do." Thus the king is bound to choose amongst the Brahmins a *purohita* who will be his chief counsellor. Agreement between king and *purohita* is regarded by Gautama (XI.12-14) to be the very symbol of harmony between the two powers. And Vasiṣṭha (XIX.4) recalls that it is written in the Veda, "A realm where a Brahmin is appointed *purohita* flourishes". The role of the *purohita* is multiple, and the translation "chaplain" poorly indicates what his different functions are. He is far from being simply a priest with the duty to see that the king fulfils his religious obligations. Elsewhere Manu (VII.78) and Yājñavalkya (I.314) distinguish him from officiating priests whose duty it was to celebrate ritual ceremonies. Yājñavalkya (I.312) demands of him knowledge of astrology in order to know the influence of the planets and to be able to neutralise their effects if they are sinister; he should also be versed in the *atharva* and know the required spells to be cast, and magic prayers.[30] The same verse requires him to be knowledgeable in the art of politics *(daṇḍa-nīti)*. In reality the *purohita* is the brain of the king. As servant of *dharma* he is a servant of the state. For the rest, he occupies a singular position by reason of his functions. Vijñāneśvara (*Mit.*, on *Yāj.*, I.353) ranks him amongst the ministers *(mantrin)* and Manu (XII.46) classes him, with kings and Kṣatriyas, amongst those whose future destiny is dominated by *rajas* ("energy", "passion").[31]

It would be vain to look in Indian tradition on the relations between the two powers for an analogy with the Christian theory of the Two Swords. True, the Brahmin is master when the question is one of ritual and, as we shall see, of penance. But his scope extends in reality over all the field of royal activity, as much on its political side as on its religious. There are no two powers here each functioning in its proper sphere, the sacred to one side, and the profane to the other. Secular power alone

[29]*Ṣāḍguṇya* defined by Manu VII.160 as by Kauṭilya: *sandhi* (alliance), *vigraha* (war), *yāna* (movement of troops), *āsana* (encampment), *dvaidhībhāva* (division of forces), and *saṃśraya* (taking cover).

[30]Cf K.W. Kārambelkar, 'Brahman and Purohita in Atharvanic texts', *I.H.Q.* 26 (1950), 293–300.

[31]On the three *guṇas*, see above, p. 86.

has the capacity to act, but it is a blind force which needs to be directed before its application can be effectual. If the king were to disdain the advice of his Brahmins he would not only fail in his duty, but even incur the risk of governing badly.[32]

Furthermore, the authority of the king is balanced by the privileged situation of the Brahmins. It is true that they have no other source of revenue but the gifts of the faithful. But the donations made to them procure for the donor a recompense in the after-life much greater than that derived from gifts made to non-Brahmins (*M.*, VII.85). And there are many texts which make it a duty on the king's part to show himself generous towards Brahmins. He obtains for himself thereby, as Manu (VII.82) and Yājñavalkya (I.135) say, an "imperishable treasure" *(akṣayo nidhi)* of merits which will compensate for the sins which he might be led to commit in the course of his government.[33] *A fortiori* he must see to it that no Brahmin suffers privation in his kingdom, and he must even aid from his personal purse any who are found to be in need (*M.*, XI.22).

Through his birth in the first of the *varṇas,* the Brahmin occupies the first rank in the social hierarchy. Alluding to the famous hymn to Puruṣa in the *Ṛgveda,* Manu (I.93,95,99) declares him to be by right the lord of creation *(dharmataḥ prabhu).* (See also *M.*, IX.345, and the same style at *Yāj.*, I.199). Prajāpati has confided to him as to the king all the created beings (*M.*, IX.327). Manu recognises that he, like the king, has a residual right to property in everything, for it is "thanks to his benevolence that other men subsist" (IX.100-101). Just as even a child-king must never be despised, for he is a great divinity who resides within a human form (*M.*, VII.8), even an ignorant Brahmin, even a Brahmin addicted to low occupations, must always be honored, for he is the highest divinity *(daivataṃ paramam)* (*M.*, IX.317-319). The parallelism established by these verses between the attributes of the king and those of the Brahmin marks the independence of the two powers; it is explained by the identity of their functions. But the superiority of the spiritual power over the temporal is affirmed afresh by Manu, who, taking up a Vedic conception again, derives the temporal power from the spiritual: "Fire comes from water [when sticks, dried, kindle], the Kṣatriya from the Brahmin, iron from stone; their power which penetrates everywhere is powerless against (the element) from which they have issued" (IX.321). Manu (IX.32) accords even to the Brahmin a might in fact greater than that of the king, because of the power which his knowledge of the formulas of curses gives him.

[32]Manu IX.67 reminds the king that Vena, the king created by the gods, perished because he did not respect the *varṇa* hierarchy.

[33]According to the *Parāśarasmṛti* (VI.60) the sins or stains of sinners are washed away by the water of sacramental formulas.

Nothing shows better than the domain of penance how superior the Brahmin is to the members of other *varṇas* in the scale of social values, superior particularly to the king, for the gravity of a sin is bound to depend on considerations which are entirely spiritual. The person of the Brahmin is sacred, and to lay a hand on him is sacrilege. The slaying of a Brahmin *(brahmahatyā)* figures in the list of four *mahā-pātakas* and is even the most grave of the four according to Manu, for "there is not in the world a graver crime than the slaying of a Brahmin; even the thought of such a crime should not graze the mind of the king" (VIII. 381). It is an inexpiable sin if done intentionally (*Gaut.*, XXI.7; *Baudh.*, II.1.6; *M.*, XI.90) or expiable only by hard penance (cf Kāṇe, IV,pp. 88-94). One who threatens a Brahmin with death falls to hell for a hundred years; he who strikes him, for a thousand years (*M.*, XI.207). "As many grains of dust as a Brahmin's blood coagulates, for so many years does he who made (the blood flow) remain in hell" (*M.*, XI.208). The king, however, is not viewed especially as king, but simply as a Kṣatriya. The murder of a Kṣatriya is placed only amongst the *upa-pātakas* (*M.*, XI.67; *Yāj.*, III.236) and gives rise to a penance equal to a quarter fixed for the slaying of a Brahmin according to Manu (XI.127) and Yājñavalkya (III.267).[34]

This recognised superiority of the spiritual power gives the *varṇa* of Brahmins a privileged position which confers on its members an almost total independence with regard to the king's authority. "The king is master of all," says Gautama (XI.1), "with the exception of the Brahmins".[35] A number of exceptional provisions attest this independence.

The Brahmin does not escape as completely from royal justice as Gautama suggests (VIII.13), but the sacred character of his person prevents any corporal punishment being inflicted upon him. Banishment, tonsure, a mark on the forehead and a shameful parade are the gravest penalties with which he can be punished (*Vis.*, V.2-3; *M.*, VIII.379-380; *Bṛh.*, XXVII.11; *Nār.*, XIV.10). By contrast Manu (XI.31) allows him to dispense with the secular arm in order to obtain damages for offenses committed against him: "his own power suffices for him to chastise those who have done him wrong." The Brahmin is actually authorised to have recourse to magic prayers, to charms and incantations to annihilate his enemies, although such proceedings on the part of others are reprehended and are punished by a fine (*M.*, IX.290) or even by banishment (*Bṛh.*, XXII.16).

[34]The slaying of a Kṣatriya or even of a Vaiśya is assimilated to the slaying of a Brahmin and involves the same penance if the victim was in the course of a sacrifice, according to *Vas.*, XX.34; *M.*, XI.88, and *Yāj.*, III.251. But, as Medhātithi remarks on *M.*, XI.88, the sacrificer *at that time* becomes a Brahmin.

[35]*rājā sarvasyeṣṭe brāhmaṇavarjam.*

The Brahmin is exempt from all tax. This fiscal immunity is provided by numerous texts. Viṣṇu (III.27) justifies it with the notion that the Brahmins "pay tax under the form of religious merit" in which the king has his share. Expressing the same idea, Vasiṣṭha (I.44-46) adds, "the Brahmin cannot be a source of subsistence (for the king), for Soma is his king", recalling the famous formula pronounced twice by the officiating priest during the coronation ceremony *(rājasūya)*, by which the independence of the Brahmin vis-à-vis the king is affirmed. Bṛhaspati (*Aiy.*, āpad., 19-20) for his part, appeals to the residual right which the Brahmin, along with the king, has in the property in the soil: "The Brahmin who cultivates his ground holds it freely, at his pleasure, for he is the lord of all. He need give nothing to anyone.[35a] Therefore it is right that the Brahmin who cultivates his soil should pay no tax *(bali)* either to the headman or to the king." The same idea is put forward by Manu (VIII.37) to justify the right of the Brahmin to the whole of any treasure he finds, while the king is bound to give the half of any such to Brahmins (*M.*, VIII.38).

Like his person, the goods of the Brahmin are sacred. More terrible than poison which destroys only one man, they kill not only him who takes them but also his sons and grandsons (*Vas.*, XVII.85-86; *Baudh.*, I.5.16; *Bṛh.Aiy.*, āpad.43-46). Thus the king should never take the goods of Brahmins, even when, as Bṛhaspati makes clear (*Aiy.*, āpad., 42), he finds himself at the end of his resources. By this we can explain that law of succession peculiar to Brahmins, whereunder the goods left by a Brahmin who dies without an heir should be given to other Brahmins, instead of passing to the king as in a normal case of escheat (*Gaut.*, XXVIII.41; *Vas.*, 84; *Viṣ.*, XVII.13-14; *Baudh.*, I.5.15-16; *M.*, IX. 188-189). Finally, like those of the king, the goods of Brahmins cannot be acquired by prescription (*M.*, VIII.149; *Yāj.*, II.25; *Bṛh.*, IX.21,etc.).

The whole of these provisions and the traditions by which they are inspired give to Brahmins a prestige and an authority in the kingdom' which suggest to the king not only that these men should be respected but also that they should be humoured and induced to collaborate with him. Any discontent on their part, says Manu (IX.313) involves the annihilation of the king and his army. Recalling that the Kṣatriyas are born from Brahmins, he allows the latter the right to resist the king who arouses their anger and to oblige him to submit (IX.320). It is clear that for Manu the opinion of the Brahmins is the only counterbalance to the king's authority.[36] Certainly, their might would have been much greater had they organised themselves into a body, capable of showing a solid front to royal power. We know that nothing of the sort happened

[35] Reading *dadyāt* for Aiyaṅgār's erroneous *vidyāt*. [36]Cf U.N. Ghoshāl, *op. cit.*, 175, n. 1, 551. For a modern comment see R.S. Betai at *Umesha Mishra Comm. Vol.* (Allahabad, 1970), 279–98.

and that the *varṇa* of Brahmins was divided into multiple castes and sub-castes of very different status. If legend contains some memory of conflicts between Kṣatriyas and Brahmins, the quarrel was quite extinct by the time of the *dharma-śāstras* and their interpreters. We can not even say that there must have been a victor, for both were destined to complete each other mutually and not to oppose each other. Because of the Brahmin's position in charge of sacrifices and religious teaching, his superiority consisted, on a social plane, of his being bound more strictly than members of the other *varṇas* to the observance of rules of purity. The task of the king is essentially political. It demands diplomacy, compromises hardly compatible with the sacred character, and sometimes acts frankly reprehensible in the generality of men. This is what explains why, contrary to our system in which *cedant arma togae* (military command must give place to civil rule), the right to act and the responsibility for action are given in the Hindu system to warriors. A king cannot be a saint. But because of the great might he possesses, he needs disinterested counsellors, responsible to no one, who will guide him and represent to him the consequences and possible outcomes of the actions he proposes. Thus in glorifying the persons of Brahmins, the authors of the *dharmaśāstra* tended to persuade the king that it is not simply his duty but also in his best interests to have Brahmins by his side. The superiority of the spiritual power is put forward specially in order to underline the necessity of collaboration between the two powers.

In passing we may notice that the interpreters show a tendency in general to reduce the practical significance of the exceptional provisions about Brahmins. Manu's exaltation leaves them cold. For Medhātithi, if Manu (I.100) declares that the Brahmin is the lord of all creation, that simply means that one should approach him with humility and follow his instructions in spiritual matters. When Manu (VIII.37) justifies the Brahmin's right to the totality of buried treasure with the notion that he is master of all, what appears there is an *arthavāda* without juridical significance, and Medhātithi almost submits the Brahmin to the general law. That a Brahmin, learned or not, is a great deity (*M.*, IX.317) signifies that one should not despise one who is a Brahmin only in name and that the gifts which are made to him are none the less valid. In the eyes of Viśvarūpa (on *Yāj.*, I.199) and Aparārka (on *Yāj.*, I.198) the superiority of the Brahmins does not attach to their *varṇa*, i.e. to their birth, but to the fact that they are devoted to the study of the Veda and therefore qualified to instruct other people. They fill a need which they alone can satisfy. The accent is placed here on the degree of learning of which the Brahmin is capable. Thus the immunities from punishment are not possessed uniformly by all Brahmins. Vijñāneśvara (*Mit.*, on *Yāj.*, II.4) believes that total immunity belongs only to a Brahmin of exceptional learning *(bahu-śruta)*. Haradatta (on *Gaut.*, VIII.12-13) observes that even a learned Brahmin should not enjoy immunity unless he committed the offense without premeditation, in ignorance, or inadvertently. And Aparārka remarks on the verse of Manu (VIII.380) which prohibits inflicting the death penalty on Brahmins that the Brahmin *is* exposed to equivalent penalties.[37] However, an evolution, the reverse of what happened with penal immunity, led to the respect due to the Brahmin's person being pushed to the extreme. Contrary to the letter of the majority of the *smṛtis* (*Vas.*, III.15-18; *Viṣ.*, V.189-190; *M.*, VIII.350-351; *Kāt.*, 801), the interpreters have attached the sin of *brahma-hatyā* to all slayings of Brahmins, even if done in self-defense.[38] While they translate the *śāstric* provisions relative to the legal status of Brahmins very prosaically, the interpreters become lyrical when the subject is the sacred character of their persons. Their privileges reduced to a more normal scale, the Brahmins added others, because of their association with the celebration of rituals, and because their membership in the first of the *varṇas* subjected them to special restrictions. There cannot be any doubt, and it answers well in other respects to what the *śāstras* teach, that many Brahmins at the courts of rulers were devoted to the interests of the state and put their intelligence at the service of the king's policies. But it is also beyond doubt that a king concerned to rule in peace had to take careful notice of the only form of public opinion which could reveal itself before him; he was under every inducement in the exercise of his authority not to draw down upon himself the Brahmins' discontent.[39]

(c) Analysis of the functions of the king

The function of the king is fully expressed in the words *prajānāṃ paripālanam*, "protection of his subjects". This protection aims to remove two sorts of danger, those which come from outside and those which emerge inside his kingdom.

First of all, the king should protect his subjects against the aggressive inclinations of neighbouring states, whether by maintaining peace with

[37]Viśvarūpa on *Yāj.*, II.281 cites a verse of Kātyāyana (ś. 806) which recommends even the death penalty for a Brahmin guilty of certain crimes. Yama (Kāṇe. I. 234–5) provides that a Brahmin may be sentenced to imprisonment and hard labour.

[38]On the problem of the Brahmin aggressor *(ātatāyin)* cf Kāṇe, II, 148–51.

[39]One of the means possessed by Brahmins to express their dissatisfaction and put pressure on the king who refuses to be corrected or to follow their counsel is to fast. According to Āpastamba (II.10.25, 11) the king should not allow a Brahmin to suffer hunger even intentionally *(buddhi-pūrvam)*. The *Rājataraṅgiṇī* (VI.14) relates that in Kashmir there was an official whose duty it was to search out anyone who was on hunger-strike and to discover his purpose. The same chronicle relates several examples of *prāyopaveśa* or ceremonial fasting to which groups of Brahmins had recourse in order to force the king to remove a bad counsellor or to undertake a particular political act. J. Naudou. L'autorité royale au Kaśmīr médiéval et ses limitations', *J.A.*, 1963, 217–227.

them by adroit policies or by forestalling their attack by war and thus subjecting them to his authority. This first object of the royal function passes beyond the scope of this book. But we should not forget it. The *dharma-śāstras* devote to it a considerable number of verses, even though their precepts relate to the interests of the state, to the *arthaśāstra*.[40] What is dealt with there is the original task of the king. He is above all a warrior whose most splendid end is to die in battle (*Viṣ.*, III.44; *Gaut.*, X.16; *M.*, VII.87-89; *Yāj.*, I.322-323).

In the second place—and it is the only object of the royal function which need retain our attention at present—the king should protect his subjects against the perils that threaten them within the kingdom. This "protection" has a fourfold aspect.

1. The most grave peril is disorder caused by forgetfulness or neglect of the duties incumbent on men under the divine law. To what extent can the king intervene to make his subjects respect the rules of conduct prescribed in the *śāstras*? Here we find posed the question of the king's legislative power.

2. The king must see to it that penances enjoined upon sinners to expiate their sins are actually carried out, for this protects them against the fatal consequences which their unexpiated sins would involve. He must also warn his subjects against committing sins. This is the role of the king in regard to penances.

3. The king is the subjects' surety for peace and order within the realm. In order that they may be allowed to pursue peacefully the fulfilment of their duties, he should try to eliminate those who are a cause of disturbance by their reprehensible activities. This is the basis of the criminal law properly so called.

4. Lastly the king is equally surety for peace between his subjects. The *śāstras* act as supreme arbitrator in their disputes. This is a particularly important task, for, if there were no judge with authority to put an end to their quarrels, passions would break out afresh. It is the king's duty, then to secure a good administration of justice.

We shall find that this quadruple aspect of the duty of protection covers the whole scope of *dharma*, as the *smṛtis* conceived it to be: *ācāra*, *prāyaścitta*, and *vyavahāra*. It is true enough that *rāja-dharma* presides over all *dharmas*.

We must examine these various aspects of the royal function in succession, for the role of the king is not necessarily the same in each case. The mode in which he exercises his powers, and their extents, can even differ considerably.

[40]Cf especially the advice given to the king by Manu (VII.169ff.) on the attitude to be maintained towards neighbouring kings: war is solely justified by the advantage which may be drawn from it, and not by considerations of law or equity.

2. *The King's Legislative Power*

Lively debate continues on the subject whether, and if at all to what extent, the system of the *śāstras* permits the king to pass laws, to legislate.[41] In this connection we should remind ourselves that what is implied by "legislative power" is a right attributed to a constitutionally competent authority to pronounce rules having a general application and possessing, in principle, a permanent character. Particular orders, for example, would not be legislation within this definition.

Law must be distinguished from an order which is a command addressed occasionally to an individual or a group of individuals.[42] Even in modern western states which are familiar with what are known as "private statutes", it is evident that the *effect* of such commands is regarded, jurisprudentially, as quite different from that of general statutes—indeed the copies of legislation printed for the use of the public and their advisers frequently omit private statutes. In the sense of legislative power, the enacting body is equally the author of the private and the general statute; but it is only in a technical and narrow sense that private statutes can be called "legislation". In the sense in which I use the word only statutes of general application would be "legislation".[42a]

It is evident that every order of the king, whatever its nature, should be obeyed by the person or persons to whom it is addressed. The texts recommend the king not to allow himself to be carried away by anger or cupidity, nor by affection or partiality, nor to pass orders until he has maturely reflected and sought the advice of his counsellors. But, once an order has been given, it must be executed. Kātyāyana (670, the same rule in Nārada XVIII.13) punishes by fine and corporal punishment him who transgresses the royal order *(lopayan rāja-śāsanam)*.[43] No one could debate the king's order without putting the authority of the king in question. That authority is necessary for the protection of the subjects; To disturb it is to provoke disorder.[44] If an order is unjust, the king may well commit a sin, but that sin could be compensated for with the aid of merits which he has acquired from elsewhere. The interests of the

[41]U.N. Ghoshāl, 'The authority of the king in Kauṭilya's political thought', *I.H.Q.*, 28 (1952), 307–11 and the subsequent controversy with K.A. Nīlakanta Śāstrī in *I.H.Q.*, 29 (1953), 175–9 and 286–92. See also B.P. Sinha, 'The king in the Kauṭilīyan state', *J.B.R.S.*, 1954, 277–308, and Ghoshāl, *History of Indian Political Ideas*, 530–2. Derrett, 'Bhāruci on the royal regulative power in India', *J.A.O.S.*, 84 (1964), 392–5.

[42]Confusion can arise from the fact that *rāja-śāsana* can mean an order or an ordinance.

[42a][trs.]

[43]A verse of the *Bṛhat-parāśara-smṛti*, cited in the *Rājanīti-prakāśa* (of Mitra-miśra's *Vīramitrodaya*) (p. 23) goes so far as to prescribe the death penalty for disobedience to the royal order. Ghoshāl, *History*, 313.

[44]This is actually the basis of obedience to the royal order according to Nārada, XVIII.21 : 'Because the protection of the world is confided to him . . ., all that the king does is justified, that is the rule.'

state can demand recourse to acts which would be reprehensible in other contexts.

Conversely, it is clear that the king cannot, in a definitive and general way, substitute his will for the divine commandments touching rules of conduct to be observed by the *varṇas* at different stages of life, i.e. he should not and cannot legislate in the domain of Good Custom, not to speak of *dharma* in general. He should not, for it would be contrary to his very mission, which is to facilitate his subjects' performance of their duties; and he cannot because he lacks the necessary authority. His "law" cannot be imposed except by force and would disappear as soon as force ceased to uphold it.[45] So, when Manu provides (VII.13) that "none should transgress the *dharma* which the king decrees in favour of those he loves and (the orders) by which he inflicts penalties on those he does not love", Medhātithi and other commentators understand the word *dharma* as envisaging only occasional ordinances, and they add that this verse by no means allows the king the power of modifying precepts of a religious character.

If the king is allowed to interfere in this domain at all it is only to reestablish a rule of *dharma* which a custom, or even an ill-advised or perverse king has infringed. Nārada (XVIII.9) made it a duty of the king to reform the transactions of his predecessor which were unreasonable *(nyāyāpeta)*.[46] And, still more generally, Kātyāyana (42) recommends the king to abolish customs which turn out to be repugnant to reason *(viruddhaṃ nyāyataḥ)*.[47] It is to be noted that both of these texts speak of transactions or customs which are contrary to reason or to logic *(nyāya)*, which does not necessarily mean contrary to the precepts of the *śāstras*. Other texts which we have analysed above (especially *Bṛh.* II.28) recommend the king, on the contrary, not to touch customary rules, even when they are obviously opposed to the precepts of *smṛti*, for fear of causing his people's disaffection and thus threatening the stability of the throne.

As between these two recommended solutions the choice would be indicated to the king by his political wisdom. If the king is the support of *dharma* he is also the surety of the public peace, and *dharma* cannot prosper in disorder. If then he believes that the abrogation of a custom which is contrary to *smṛti* would be likely to provoke disorder, he will

[45]It is significant that when Kauṭilya himself lists (III.1, 43) the sources of positive law, he omits *rāja-śāsana* (unless we are to translate *nyāya* as edict, which is improbable). Ghoshāl, *I.H.Q.*, 29 (1953), 290.

[46]*nyāyāpetaṃ yad anyena rājñā'jñāna-kṛtaṃ ca yat, tad apy anyāya-vihitaṃ punarnyāye niveśayet. Dh. k.*, 90, 104, 549, 586.

[47]*viruddhaṃ nyāyato yas tu caritraṃ kalpyate nṛpaiḥ, evaṃ tatra nirasyeta caritraṃ tu nṛpājñayā.* An altogether different sense is extracted from this verse by Vācaspati Miśra (*Vyav. cint.* 718).

prefer to leave his subjects alone, rather than seek to impose on them a morality too high for them. That is doubtless why, at the beginning of his chapter on *rāja-dharma,* Yājñavalkya (I.311) asks that the king as well as his *purohita* (I.313) should be versed in the art of politics *(daṇḍa-nīti)*. The resources of politics are indispensable for him to preserve his kingdom from the excitements and catastrophes which an exclusive preoccupation with religious precepts could not fail to produce. Only when the rule introduced by usage or adopted by certain communities appears, from its immoral or unjust character, to be likely to excite stress and discontent amongst his subjects can the king usefully employ his authority and abrogate it.

In fact such interventions by the king in *dharma's* domain seem to have been very rare. The few historical examples which are cited emanate from kings who were heterodox or whose orthodoxy is doubtful.[48] The Hindu king is before all a warrior charged to protect his subjects and to secure the prosperity of the realm. Doubtless his protection extends particularly to those who fulfill their duties.[49] But it would *not* be his duty to make proselytes, and the conception which would see in him a reformer of public morals is certainly foreign to the *smṛti*.[50]

The manner in which the king is called to intervene on the occasion of agreements between members of certain local groups, such as villages,

[48]I have met only one historical example of the intervention of the king which has the effect of reviving a rule of *dharma*. It is the abolition by Kumārapāla (second half of the twelfth century) of the custom whereby the estate of a man who died without sons passed to the crown. The Jain chronicles attribute this measure to the humanitarian influence of Jainism. We may suspect, with other chroniclers, that the usage in question was abolished because it was repugnant to the *smṛtis* which called the king to the succession only in default of all other heirs. But the edict or edicts attributed to the same king prohibited killing all animals, eating meat, drinking spirits; and ordered that gaming-houses should be closed. And these were certainly inspired by Jainism (A.K. Majumdār, *Chaulukyas of Gujarat*, Bombay, 1956, 247, 315–6). The famous edicts of Aśoka prohibit animal sacrifices (in some places) (1st Rock Edict) or prohibit the killing of certain animals (5th Pillar Edict), and these proceed from a mind influenced by Buddhism. This outlook is revealed in reference to the conquest of Kaliṅga. It is difficult to believe that a king under the sole influence of his duties as a Kṣatriya could feel pity for the sufferings caused in a victorious war. It was a ruler favourable to Buddhism, Harṣavardhana, who, according to Hiuan-Tsang, ordered his subjects to abstain from meat-eating.

[49]According to Medhātithi and Kullūka (on *M.*, VII.35) the king incurs sin if he neglects to protect those who are attached to their duties, but, conversely, it is not a fault on his part if those who have abandoned their duties are oppressed by others. This implies that only those whose conduct is beyond reproach are entitled to the king's protection.

[50]We recall that, according to *M.*, VII.203, the king should not change the laws in force in countries he has conquered : *pramāṇāni ca kurvīta teṣāṃ dharmān yathoditān*. The same rule appears at *Yāj.*, I.343, who, instead of *dharmān,* uses the words *ācāra-kula-sthiti-vyavahāra* : customs, usages of families, and rules observed in transactions (or procedure?). Commenting upon *M.*, VII.203, Medhātithi observes that in so acting the king will bind the people to himself, which proves that the rule appertains to politics.

guilds, corporations, artisans, or religious fraternities, constituting in some sense their statutes or by-laws, reveals the essentially pragmatic character of the royal policies. We know that the *dharma-śāstras* attribute a very large autonomy to those groups, and that the disputes which can arise in that context are the object of a special title in the portion devoted to private litigation, under the name of "violation of regulations (or compacts)" *(saṃvid-vyatikrama)*.

The king is bound to insist upon these conventions or regulations being respected, even if, dealing with communities of heretics, for example, the rules would be in contradiction with the precepts of the *śāstra* (*Yāj.*, II.192; *Nār.*, XIII.2). According to Bṛhaspati (XVIII.7), the members' agreement appears simply as a solemn form, or a written stipulation, or the declaration of witnesses who are themselves strangers to the group. But Kātyāyana is more demanding. He declares that the statutes *(sthiti)* of the corporations of merchants, artisans, Brahmins, etc., cannot be proved (in court) except by written documents, not by ordeals or by witnesses. And the same writer (*śloka* 48) even prescribes that regulations *(vyavasthās)* established by the consent of the inhabitants of the same region or of a country *(deśasyānumatena)* should be consigned to writing and sealed with the royal seal *(mudritā rāja-mudrayā)*.

In the South of India in particular, a number of these *vyavasthās* sanctioned by the king survive to this day. They are not confined to conventions between the inhabitants of a locality or region, but also include accords concerning colonies of Brahmins, guilds, or corporations of tradesmen, which show that the custom of having these compacts confirmed by the king was very widespread. The majority are concerned with the maintenance of a temple, the celebration of a cult, the division of taxation amongst members, the making of a dam or a reservoir. But we also find provisions dealing with the law of succession, the forms of marriage, the legal status of children born out of regular marriage, the penalties applicable in those guilty of certain crimes, which are certainly within the domain of the *śāstras*. Some of them only recall or reinforce the *śāstric* rules, but at times they establish what are clear infractions of those rules.

J.D.M. Derrett sees in the king's intervention at least an indirect form of legislative activity within the very domain of *dharma*. Since the royal sanction applies even to rules which are contrary to *smṛti*, according to his view the king must be understood to be *de facto* qualified to legislate without being bound by the precepts of the *śāstras*.[51]

We can hardly speak of "legislation" à propos of the sanction which

[51]Derrett, *Hindu Law, Past and Present* (Calcutta, 1957), 43; 'The criteria for distinguishing between legal and religious commands in the Dharmaśāstra', *All India Reporter, Journ.*, 1953, 61; the whole article is to be seen, rewritten, at his *Religion* . . . , ch. 3.

the king gave to the compacts or conventions referred to above. Such regulations concerned only restricted circles in the population and had not the general application which is required by our definition of "legislation". Moreover they were not due ultimately to the king's own initiative. They were simply submitted to him in order that their application should be secured. The exercise of legislative power by the king, which would authorise him to make ordinances *proprio motu,* on his own initiative and at his pleasure, would be a very different matter.

In reality when the king accords his sanction, his attitude is determined by considerations of opportunity. Similarly in the tenth title of the *smṛti* bearing his name, a title devoted to collective regulations, Nārada describes clearly what points the king should supervise. After having said that he should authorise the existence of various bodies, even if they are composed of heretics, and cause their customs to be observed (X. 2.3), he adds that the king should prohibit those which are contrary to his wishes *(pratikūla),* naturally perverse *(prakṛtyavamata)*[52] or opposed to his interests *(bādhakam arthānām)* (X.4). He should not tolerate any which are formed amongst factious groups, nor the taking up of arms with an object prejudicial to the state, nor such as would provoke violence between them (X.5). Plainly the royal supervision bears especially on any clauses of the said regulations which would be likely to breed disorder or to be injurious to the interests of the state. When he confirms any such regulations he apparently acts not as a legislator but as an administrator concerned to keep the peace between his subjects.

That, even when sanctioned by the king, such regulations do not have a true legislative quality, results from the fact that the king himself is not bound to respect them, if the needs of government so require. According to Nārada (XVIII.24), "it is (only) for good order [or in the interests of the institution] that the scope of application of customs has been fixed by kings. (Thus) a royal order is held to have more weight than his customs."[53] Furthermore, Yājñavalkya explains (II.186) that "On condition of not being contrary to his own *dharma (nija-dharma)* [i.e. the duties peculiar to his caste, family, etc.], the *dharma* [i.e. the regulation] established by common consent *(sāmayika)* should be rigorously

[52]On perhaps rather 'blamed by the generality of the public', as Kāṇe, III, 158, prefers.

[53]*sthityartham pṛthivī-pālaiś caritra-viṣayāḥ kṛtāḥ, caritrebhyo 'sya tat prāhur garīyo rāja-śāsanam.* Jolly's translation of *caritra* by 'law' gives the verse a different sense. The example given by Aparārka in his commentary shows clearly enough that we should understand by that word the 'statutes' of bodies whose scope of application (viz. the provisions) have been sanctioned by the king. Let us suppose, says he, that an article of the statutes of a colony of Brahmins forbids royal officials to enter into the Brahmins' houses or certain other places. Those officials could still, at the king's order, make an entry into those houses to arrest thieves, for example. Ghoshāl, *op. cit.,* 414.

observed by (everyone), the same as the *dharma* made [i.e. sanctioned] by the king *(rāja-kṛta).*" Which leads us to believe that even a member of such a body is not bound to observe a regulation, even if it was sanctioned by the king, if it is in contradiction with religious duties.[54] Official approbation of a regulation was apparently no more than a formality especially useful to facilitate proof of its regularity, analogous to modern registration of authentic deeds and other documents. The king only supervised those clauses which could prejudice public order, and this supervision did not extend to fundamental questions of validity. What we have, therefore, was a system of making the regulations official: they were turned into public muniments.[55]

Far from legislating in the sphere reserved for *śrotriyas,* the kings of history tried to enlighten their subjects and themselves upon their duties, giving their patronage to commentators and digest-writers. This was only one way in which they acquired renown as pious princes, devoted to *dharma.* We have already seen how many interpreters whose life is vaguely known to us filled important posts at court. Their labours plainly had as their object to facilitate the king's task and that of his ministers, offering them a reasoned interpretation of the rules of the *śāstras.* Lakṣmīdhara, the author of the *Kalpataru,* does not hesitate to declare in the preliminary poem of the *Rāja-dharma-kāṇḍa* that it is thanks to his counsels and his *mantras* that the king Govindacandra (whose prime minister he was) managed to subjugate numerous kings and to progress on the road of justice and generosity towards his subjects. There is every reason to think that his monumental work is not a mere display of his knowledge, but a work through which he intended to carry out his task as counsellor. Certain kings themselves have lent their names to the compositions of digests or commentaries, either by officially patronising their authors, like Madanapāla, king of Kāṣṭhā (1360–1390) and Vīrasiṃha, king of Orccha (1605–1627), whose names figure in the actual titles of works composed at their requests by Viśveśvara and Mitra-miśra, or by presiding over the compilation or editing of the work and publishing it in their own names, as did Pratāpa-rudra, king of Orissa (beginning of the sixteenth century) for the *Sarasvatī-vilāsa.*

[54]Kātyāyana (ś. 669) formulates a similar rule: 'If a royal edict (or order, *rāja-śāsana*) is passed, not contrary to (precepts of) the *dharmaśāstra,* it should be observed before everything, because of the authority of the king *(nṛpājñayā)'.* This does not refer to an order addressed to an individual, for this would be in conflict with texts which forbid resistance to an order from the king. *Rāja-śāsana* must mean, then, the act by which the king sanctions a collective regulation. Therefore Kāṇe was quite right to place this verse in the section on 'breach of regulations' in his edition of the *Kātyāyana-smṛti.*

[55]*Kauṭ.* (II.7, 2) seems to provide that the 'superintendent of accounts' should register local statutes, professional regulations, and customs special to castes and families. Ghoshāl, *op. cit.,* 114.

It is difficult to doubt that royal patronage assured the works a measure of official status and consequently a certain authority. Mitra-miśra proclaims that his digest contains the sum of all *dharma* and makes it superfluous to consult other works. Pratāpa-rudra declares that he has composed the *Sarasvatī-vilāsa* to spare judges, ministers, and the *purohita* the trouble of harmonising the divergent opinions of earlier exegetes, and that his work renders all preceding writings useless. It really seems as if the king wished to confer an imperative character on the interpretation of the rules of the *smṛti* which he presented. It seems as if we have within the very framework of the *śāstras* an act having the character of positive law in the modern sense of the word, as Kāṇe has observed (I,p.412). Justinian, too, thought that the compilation of the Corpus Juris Civilis sufficed the needs of jurists and he forbade all further commentatorial activity. But the king of Cuttack did not manage to fix interpretation any more than did the Byzantine emperor. Interpretation is a human achievement, thus subject to error, and only the texts of *smṛti* make up the law. The path must remain open for new interpretations. The *Sarasvatī-vilāsa* is certainly an authority in certain contexts in Orissa, but it has been supplanted in others by the *Mitākṣarā* which is senior to it by five centuries.[56] This shows plainly enough that the king did not have the power to impose a general interpretation of texts of *smṛti.* He could favour certain enterprises in order to elucidate their meaning so that his subjects and he himself could know their duties better. But for all their bulk and elaboration the digests and commentaries have no more value than an *opinion,* and no one, starting with the king himself, could be held bound to follow the proposed solutions from the moment when other solutions seemed better or more appropriate to his circumstances.[57]

Because of the large sphere reserved for *dharma* the legislative activity of the king was limited very seriously, but there did remain a vast field in which it might operate. The majority of the topics which come within what we would call administrative law fell under royal authority. The *dharma-śāstras* confine themselves to indicating, for example, the qualities which ministers should have. But it fell to the king to divide amongst them the tasks of administration, to define the scope and the powers of each ministry. In Book 11, Kauṭilya presents a long list of rules for the conduct to be followed by the different heads of the public services

[56]Mayne, *Hindu Law and Usage,* 11th edn., 90, n. *(a).*

[57]According to T.V. Mahāliṅgam, *Administration and Social Life under Vijayanagara* (Madras, 1940), 107, the rules figuring in the *Vyavahāra-mādhava* do not correspond to practice during the reign of Bukka, especially so far as concerns judicial organisation. Nevertheless it was probably at the request of that king, whose *kula-guru* and minister he was, that Mādhava introduced that long digression into his commentary upon the *Parāśara-smṛti.*

(adhyakṣas), and such rules were clearly intended to be formulated in the shape of edicts.[58] For the organisation of local administration we can hardly find in the *dharma-śāstras* more than the most summary and theoretical indications.[59] Even though local groups enjoyed a substantial autonomy, it was certainly needful to settle how the king's officers should exercise control over the transactions of local bodies. Public finance likewise presupposed a whole body of rules relative to the collection of rates, taxes and customs duties to which the *śāstras* allude, necessitating a large body of officials whose duties had to be defined and their functions supervised. It seems impossible that every section of the administrative machine could have functioned under the direct orders of the king. The continuity of institutions must have demanded royal instructions having the effect of laws. Even in judicial contexts, the king's intervention must have given rise to actual legislation. First of all criminal justice would have to be organised from top to bottom. It was his own special department of justice. Although the *dharma-śāstras* provide lists of crimes the suppression of which must be effectuated by the king, they are silent on how criminal proceedings are to be organised. And once again we find those elements in the *arthaśāstra* treatises. The application of those rules lay wholly within the royal discretion.

Even in the sphere of private litigation, the *dharma-śāstras* give their attention indeed to formulating rules for the solution of disputes, but rules dealing with judicial organisation and even legal procedure are in need of completion. For example, appeal properly so called, i.e. the right of the litigant who has lost his case to take the decision before a court superior to that in which he was unsuccessful, is barely outlined in the *śāstras*, which do not specify the conditions, the periods, and the effect of an appeal. Once again, the reason is that here we have to do with a matter solely within the royal authority, pertaining to the means employed to give true justice, of which the king is the sole judge. Finally in the sphere of economics, if the *dharma-śāstras* enable us to catch a glimpse of the king's intervention in supervision of markets, prices, and wages, it is only if we read *arthaśāstra* works that we can form an idea of that encroaching quality which could regulate so many branches of human activity. We could say that the royal edicts penetrated substantially into the daily lives of individuals and communities.[60]

This royal legislation, which is foreign to *dharma*, remains largely unknown to us. The commentators and digest-writers know by the name *rāja-śāsana* only individual measures or occasional orders.[61] These

[58]Ghoshāl, *op. cit.*, 114–5.

[59]Cf *M.*, VII.115–22.

[60]B.P. Sinha, *J.B.R.S.*, 1954, 277–308.

[61]See the examples given by Medhātithi and other commentators on *M.*, VII.13. Kauṭilya too gives, as examples of *rāja-śāsana*, hardly any which are not occasional or individual measures (II.10, 38–46).

precepts had no other foundation or sanction than the will of the king, nor other object than to secure the government of the realm. But, by contrast, they belong to positive law, law-in-action, immediately applicable to the subjects, sanctioned by the king's agents. Alongside the rules of the *śāstras,* though in an entirely different sphere, they fashioned and controlled the social activity of the kingdoms of history.

Edicts, being only the expression of the royal will, could be supplemented, modified, or abrogated at the will of their author. They probably became void at the end of the reign, unless they were continued in effect by the new ruler. Only one text leads us to doubt this: Nārada (XVIII.9) prescribes that the king shall reform or amend the transactions of his predecessor which might seem to be contrary to equity; from which it might seem to follow that the unabrogated acts of a king continue to have effect during the reign of his successor. But this would be to attribute more meaning to the text than it deserves: it quite possibly envisages only royal acts injurious to individuals, and not legislative acts at all.

3. *The King's Role relative to Penance*

When his subjects have committed sins, the king is bound to see to it that they observe the penances which are prescribed by the *śāstras.* In so doing he protects them from the consequences of their unexpiated sins, which would inescapably affect their future destinies. As Medhātithi remarks (on *M.,* VIII.1) the king should guarantee his subjects not only against visible torments, such as those which the victim of robbery would suffer, but also against invisible torments, that is to say those which will await the robber himself because of the sin he committed in robbing the victim. When the breach of religious duties is only a sin and does not involve a penal sanction, the spiritual and temporal powers each have its distinct role. The Brahmins must decide the penance, and the king must secure that it is performed.

The procedure is clearly indicated by Āpastamba (II.5.10.12-16): "The *ācārya* shall prescribe to those who, participating according to the *śāstras* (in the rights and duties of their caste), have left the right path because of the weakness of their senses, to perform penances corresponding to their acts following the sacred precepts. If they transgress the order of their *ācārya* he will conduct them before the king. The king shall send them to his *purohita* versed in the *dharma-sūtra* and the art of government. He (the *purohita)* shall order them to perform their penances if they are Brahmins. He shall reduce them to obedience by the means of constraint, with the exception of corporal punishment or reduction to slavery."

The king only intervenes for the sake of the performance of the penance fixed by the *ācārya*. Nārada (XVIII.3), Kātyāyana (*śl.*949) and Bṛhaspati (*Aiy.*, XXIX.13) expressly mention the non-performance of penance amongst the matters which the king may take up *suo motu,* of his own motion. Certain texts, notably Parāśara (VIII.28), require the permission of the king before penance is performed, or at least prescribe that he should be informed of the performance of the gravest penances. But the king is strictly forbidden to decide upon the penance himself, and if he exceeds the opinion of the Brahmins, the sin which is committed is enlarged a hundredfold (*Par.,* VIII.29). The question escapes the king's jurisdiction and belongs exclusively to the spiritual power.[62]

When the penance to be observed is in doubt, the question should be taken before a *pariṣad.* "If one asks what should be done when the rule has not been specified (the reply is:) what the Brahmins (who are) *śiṣṭas* shall decide will incontestably be *dharma.*" Thus Manu (XII.108), and Yājñavalkya likewise (III.301): "He whose fault is known *(vikhyāta-doṣa)* shall perform the penance which has been approved by the *pariṣad*".[63]

The composition of a *pariṣad* has been explained above.[64] This gathering consists in principle of at least three persons, but it can be reduced to one: "Four (Brahmins) versed in the Vedas and the *dharmaśāstra,* or knowing only three Vedas, form a *pariṣad.* What they declare is *dharma,* or even what is declared by one alone, the best versed in knowledge of the *ātman (adhyātma-vittama)*" (*Yāj.,* I.9).

The *pariṣad* to determine penance takes account of the country, the time, the age and capacity of the offender, also the nature of the sin (*Yāj.,* III.294).

According to Vijñāneśvara (*Mit.,* on *Yāj.,* III.301), in case of doubt about the penance, recourse to a *pariṣad* is necessary, even if the sinner is learned in the *śāstras.* He should confer with its members and do only what they have approved. Vijñāneśvara cites on this subject a text of Aṅgiras which obliges the *pariṣad* to indicate the penance on pain of incurring the same sin as had been committed by the man who came to consult it. The same commentator also produces a *sūtra* of Vasiṣṭha (III.6) according to which "the sin of him whom fools, misled by darkness

[62]The same principle seems to flow from *M.*, VIII.390 also. Until the merger of the States of Travancore and Cochin with other territories to form the present State of Kerala in the Indian Union, the Mahārājas kept ministers specifically to attend to questions of breach of Hindu caste discipline, whose powers were legally recognised without prejudice to the rights of individual castes to excommunicate their members. [trs.]

[63]A text of Aṅgiras, quoted by Vijñāneśvara (*Mit.,* on *Yāj.,* III.301) prescribes the manner in which the sinner should approach the *pariṣad*: fasting, straight from his bath, with his garments still wet. He may complete his confession only after having paid the Brahmins their honoraria *(dakṣinā).* Kāṇe, IV, 84–5.

[64]Pt. I, ch. 1, pp. 15ff.

(tamonūḍha) and ignorant of the sacred law, have (ill) instructed (in his duty) rebounds multiplied a hundredfold on those who have explained (his duty) to him" (the same text is in *Baudh.,* I.1.11, and a closely similar text in *M.,* XII.115 and *Par.,* VIII.5). In other words, the sinner is purified even when the penance which he has performed has been settled for him by an ignorant *pariṣad.* This last text underlines the exclusive competence of Brahmins in the matter of penance.

It often happens that the sin also constitutes a crime and that the sinner is liable to a penalty that the king, as sole master of punishment, is charged to have inflicted upon him. Given that certain penances are already equivalent to veritable punishments, the question remains whether the two sanctions are cumulative and, if not, which ought to supplant the other.

The principle of the reply seems to be found in Vasiṣṭha (XIX.45), which Manu (VIII.318) and Nārada (pariś.,48) reproduce. "Men who have committed crimes and who have been punished by the king are purified and go to heaven like those who have performed good deeds".[65]

Taken literally, this text excludes a cumulative situation and gives priority to the penal sanction. But the commentators refuse to give it so general a significance. For Vijñāneśvara (*Mit.,* on *Yāj.,* III.359) it applies only in the case where the sinner undergoes a *capital* punishment; only sentence of death can have an expiatory effect. Medhātithi presented a wider interpretation. The verse of Manu is always applicable when the punishment inflicted is a corporal one. There is no occasion then for penance. But both must be undergone when the culprit is only liable to a fine. Medhātithi justifies this distinction in the following manner: the fine is useful to the king, for it is a source of revenue for him; but a corporal punishment, if it has any utility, is useful only to the criminal himself. We should be inclined to say that it is useful as a measure of "protection" (in the senses we have discussed above), whether for the victim's sake, or because of its exemplary quality. But Medhātithi believes that that would not suffice to justify recourse to corporal punishment. In what concerns the convict himself, the utility of the punishment can only be found in the purification of a culprit. Corporal punishment produces an effect of an invisible nature in the person who undergoes it, at the same time as it, in another way, serves the king's purposes (namely the protection of his subjects); or, to put it in other words, Medhātithi believed that punishment, when corporal, is a real chastisement which is not a simple punishment: it wipes out the sin and purifies the culprit.

It is difficult not to see in this text, so understood, a trespass on the

[65]*rājabhir dhṛta-daṇḍās tu kṛtvā pāpāni mānavāḥ, nirmalāḥ svargam āyānti santaḥ sukṛtino yathā.*

part of the temporal power over the spiritual, for when the two sanctions are called in to play, the king has either had the case brought before him or he has taken the case up of his own motion. The king substitutes himself for the Brahmin; by fixing the punishment he chastises the sinner and so absolves him.

But why does punishment operate as a penance? Medhātithi speaks of an invisible effect produced in the person of the convict by the application of the punishment, and this is an effect analogous in its results to the act of *dharma*. But this effect results from the execution of the sentence pronounced by the king, and not from actions performed voluntarily by the convict himself, as the case with penances usually is. Should we attribute a purifying effect to chastisement *(daṇḍa)* when it personifies *dharma*, i.e. when it is employed conformably to the precepts of *smṛti*? Or should we simply admit that the king here has a religious power which permits him to wash away sins?

A text which we have already met in the *dharma-sūtras* (*Baudh.*, II. 1.16-17; *Gaut.*, XII.43-45; *Āp.*, I.9.25.4-5),[66] would incline towards the latter hypothesis. It concerns the crime committed by him who has stolen a Brahmin's gold, and turns up again, with some variations, in the majority of the *dharma-śāstras*. Thus, Manu says (VIII.314-316): "The thief should present himself before the king in all haste, his locks untied, and confess the theft, saying, 'I have done this, punish me'. He should carry on his shoulders a stake or a club of *khadira* wood or a spear pointed at both ends, or a rod of iron. Punished or released the thief is purged [of the sin] of the theft, but the king, in not punishing him, takes the sin of theft upon himself." Likewise Yājñavalkya (III. 257): "He who has stolen a Brahmin's gold shall present a stake to the king, proclaiming his crime; killed or released, he shall be purified *(hato mukto 'pi vā śuciḥ)*".[67]

It is clear that these rules had no practical interest for the commentators. But the importance which the authors of the *dharma-śāstras* attached to them, marked by the care they have taken to reproduce them makes one think that they attributed a symbolic value to them. To steal a Brahmin's gold was indeed a *mahāpātaka,* one of the four (later five) "great sins" for which, if the weight of gold exceeded a certain quantity, the penance prescribed was equivalent to a death-sentence (Kāṇe, IV,p. 101). Now, on this hypothesis, it appears that the king has the power to purify the sinner, letting him go and taking the sin of the theft upon himself. It is true that, if we follow a variant of the text provided by Nārada

[66]See above, Pt. I, ch. 3, p. 68.

[67]Similar provisions appear in other *smṛtis*. Kāṇe, IV.73–4, Vasiṣṭha (XX.41) introduces a variation : it is the king who presents the thief with a wooden club with which he should kill himself. 'It is said in the Veda that he is purified by that death'.

(*pariś.*,46-47), this would be because of his spontaneous admission of his guilt that the thief is purified.[68] But admission is expected of *any* sinner who wishes to expiate his offence and who offers to undergo penance. The special circumstances revealed by our texts are these: the sinner's presenting himself directly before the king in the attitude of a penitent; and the gesture of the king in touching him with the club or letting him go. And these have the purifying effect. Medhātithi (on *M.*, VIII.316) does indeed say that the thief who is released must pay the prescribed fine for the theft, but the penance is remitted. The explanation which he had given for the expiatory quality of chastisment by invisible effects of corporal punishment can hardly be applied here, because the culprit undergoes no punishment at all. Even when the king uses the club (he need strike only one blow according to the commentators), the culprit is purified, whether he is killed by the blow or only hurt. How could an incomplete chastisement, incomplete through quite fortuitous circumstances, have the same value as a penance?

It seems that we cannot avoid admitting that the king appears here endowed with a religious power, the penance no less than the punishment emerging from his own unaided will. And one might think that the verse of Manu (VIII.318), stating the principle that the punishment inflicted by the king is equivalent to penance, was to be explained originally by the same idea of a power proper to the king, and not, as Medhātithi imagined, by the effect of the corporal chastisement.[69]

The rules relating to theft of a Brahmin's gold were perhaps vestiges of a time when the royal power had not yet been fully "desacralised", when the king still shared the nature of the magician. At the period of the commentators they had only one reason for remaining consigned to the *smṛti*. They confirmed by an exceptional text, having undisputed authority, the idea that at that point where the king dispensed chastisement the spiritual power gave way to the temporal. It really mattered that the king should be master of the sanction when the question was of an infringement of Good Custom, an infringement which was not

[68]Following the text in Jolly's edn.: 'The thief shall approach the king with his hair untied, running and proclaiming his crime: I have done such a deed, punish me! Acting in this way he is purified by the fact that he has confessed his act. The king shall touch him (with the sceptre), but he shall let him go, for he is freed from his crime' *(rājā tataḥ spṛśed enam utsṛjet tu hy akilbiṣam)*. Or, in Sāmbaśiva's edition (*prakīrṇ*. 105, p. 190): '. . . the thief is purified by the fact that he has confessed his act; (it is) the king who is touched by the sin, because he has allowed a culprit to go free' *(rājānaṃ tat spṛśed ena utsṛjantaṃ sakilbiṣam)*.

[69]Further we may note that *M.*, VIII.318 is only one verse away from the provisions relative to the thief of gold, and that Nārada (*pariś.* 48, *prakīrṇ*. 106), reproducing *M.*, VIII.318, both in the Nepalese ms. used by Jolly and in the text commented upon by Bhavasvāmin, appears immediately after them.

not only failure in respect of religious duty but also a breach of public order. The interests of the state were at stake, and one could not leave to Brahmins the care of fixing the penance, since their decision would prejudge the punishment of the culprit without appeal. The king should remain free to determine the entire chastisement which might be suitable. He should be entitled to go so far as to release the culprit (taking his sin upon himself) if the necessities of his policies demanded that he should show clemency.

4. *Criminal Justice*

After having dealt successively with the eighteen types of litigation in which private persons engage, Manu (IX.252ff.) ends his exposition of duties of the king by enjoining him to "root out the thorns" *(kaṇṭaka-śodhana)* of his realm. He means by this that the king should take care to render harmless those of his subjects who are liable to compromise public order by their action, or to prejudice his authority. Manu enumerates, in no special order, a certain number of reprehensible acts, more or less grave, for which he provides varied punishments, and recommends recourse to some unusual means of keeping himself informed. Yājñavalkya does the same in the last thirteen verses of Book II.

What is involved, as indeed the commentators on Yājñavalkya observe, is the part of *rāja-dharma* which is distinguished in other *dharma-śāstras* from cases in private law by the name *prakīrṇaka*. That word, which means "scattered, diverse, thus *miscellaneous* (rules)", is misleading, for the rules contained under that title are often regarded as a simple supplement intended to complete those which relate to lawsuits between individual litigants.[70]

In reality the scope of *prakīrṇaka* embraces topics quite distinct from private litigation. It denotes a different aspect of the royal activity, in which the king appears, not as a judge charged with the task of ending a dispute between two litigants, but as a magistrate who seeks out wrong-doers and applies chastisement to them in the name of the state. This is what we call criminal law, even if, in certain aspects, *prakīrṇaka* resembles rather the police activity of government than criminal justice as we know it, in which the adversary aspect is usually maintained.

Matters falling within *prakīrṇaka* are characterised by the fact that the king can take them up *ex officio*. By contrast, the king must abstain from taking up a case appertaining to private disputes when no one has addressed a plaint to him. "Neither the king nor any of his officers," says Manu (VIII.43) should ever take up a case by themselves, still less

[70]Both individual litigation and *prakīrṇaka* come within *vyavahāra* as understood in the sense of administration of justice in general. Moreover certain *dharma-śāstras* present *prakīrṇaka* as the last *vyavahāra-pada*. See the table given by Kāṇe at III, 249.

should they stifle *(nigiret)* a case brought by another", and Kātyāyana (*śl.* 27): "The king should not, whether due to pressure (brought to bear upon him), or through desire to obtain wealth [by way of fees and fines], take upon himself to regulate differences between his subjects when these do not wish to carry their disputes before him." This essential difference is put clearly in relief by Bṛihaspati (XXVII.1) who defines *prakīrṇaka,* the procedure which depends from the king *(nṛpāśraya),* in opposition to that which is commenced by the litigants *(vādi-kṛta)* and the object of which is the private dispute.[71] In other words the king is master of the case in a matter within *prakīrṇaka*: he acts when, and only when, he thinks it appropriate.

The *smṛti* texts provide different lists of matters suitable to fall within *prakīrṇaka.* Nārada (XVIII.1-4) mentions the following offences: transgressing the king's orders; causing misunderstandings between the heads of cities (with their subordinates) or between elements constituting the state;[72] violating the regulations of corporate bodies and others; differences between father and son; failure to perform penance; cheating (Brahmins) of gifts due to them; annoying ascetics; creating a mixture of *varṇas*; infringement of the rules concerning their (permitted) means of subsistence.

Kātyāyana provides a longer list (947-952). The crimes are divided into three groups according to the king's role therein, those in the first group constituting the ten *aparādhas* (offences).[73] The same list, but without division into three groups is found in Bṛhaspati (*Aiy.,* XXIX. 12-14).[74] It contains most of the offences mentioned by Nārada, but presents still more variety. Specially mentioned are: divulging secrets concerning a war; abuses regarding the revenue or excise; misappropriating property which has escheated: crimes which could be considered as prejudicing the interests of the state but also acts which are held to be contrary to public morality or which are crimes against common law, such as the fact of becoming rich suddenly, conspiring with thieves, committing an attack on another man's wife, destroying crops, and so on.

Even longer lists are attributed by commentators to Pitāmaha. A

[71]*eṣa vādi-kṛtaḥ prokto vyavahāraḥ samāsataḥ, nṛpāśrayaṃ pravakṣyāmi vyavahāraṃ prakīrṇakaṃ.* The word *nṛpāśraya* to qualify *prakīrṇaka* is found in Nārada XVIII.1: *prakīrṇake punar jñeyo vyavahāro nṛpāśrayaḥ.*

[72]Here I follow the reading of Sāmbaśiva (*prakirṇ.* 2): *pura-pradhāna-saṃbhedaḥ prakṛtīnām tathaiva ca,* instead of that of Jolly's edn.: *purapradāna* ... which seems unsatisfactory.

[73]Two more lists of the ten *aparādhas* are attributed to Saṃvarta (*Sm. cand.,* II, 28) and Nārada (*Quot.,* I, 11–12) respectively. Neither agrees fully with Kātyāyana's. The 'ten *aparādhas',* however, appear frequently in epigraphy as (collectively) crimes for which fines may be collected. Kāṇe, IV, 264–5.

[74]On the correspondence between the two lists see Renou, *Études védiques et paninéennes,* 11 (Paris, 1963), 140–2.

first list by this author gives 22 crimes, cognizance of which appertains to the king *(padāni nṛpa-jñeyāni)*, crimes as varied as those appearing in the verses of Kātyāyana, passing from high treason and the destruction of a constituent element of the state to the disembowelling of an animal and causing beasts to give birth on another's field. A second list of 50 crimes called *chalas* (abuses) includes especially breaches of etiquette in the king's presence, like blowing the nose before him or untying the hair, but also acts injurious to the nation like destroying a cistern or obstructing the public way.[75]

The extreme diversity of these crimes, the artificial nature of their classification, which varies moreover with the authors, contrasts strongly with the way in which litigation between individuals is handled. After Manu's time rules governing such litigation were reduced to eighteen titles *(vyavahāra-padas)* following a classification, ordered and systematical in its nature,[76] to which not only the authors of later *smṛtis* but also the interpreters themselves generally adhere, so that matters which do not correspond to one of these types are regulated only by way of analogy. Here we are faced by an unorganised law, whose development appears to have been quite late in *smṛti* literature. The very name *prakīrṇaka* gives us reason to suspect that the subject matter is one which the *dharmaśāstra* writers only touched upon because the "uprooting of thorns" is one of the king's duties, but which they have deliberately neglected. Similarly none of the lists which have given us the crimes appertaining to *prakīrṇaka* is exhaustive. Nārada (XVIII.4) and Kātyāna (946) say that *prakīrṇaka* includes all that has been omitted in the preceding chapters![77] Even if this were to be taken literally, it is not true, since certain crimes actually listed under *prakīrṇaka* are to be traced in the part devoted to private litigation.[77a] What is meant is that no complete list can be furnished, for it is up to the king himself to decide whether a particular act is or is not a misdeed punishable in the name of the state. Guardian of the peace in his kingdom, he decides as he thinks fit what shall be the means to safeguard it and to secure respect for his persons and his powers. In other words the whole subject belongs not to the science of *dharma* but to the science of *artha*, and it is to the authors

[75]For details of such classifications see Kāṇe, III, 263–6.

[76]See above, Pt. I, ch. 4, p.

[77]*Viṣṇu* XLII.1 confines himself to defining *prakīrṇaka* as *yad anuktam*, 'what has not already been said'.

[77a]This duality of actions should surprise no one. In criminal matters we distinguish between a civil action to which the victim is entitled (the action in tort) from the public prosecution launched in the name of the state. All that we need say here is that the *śāstras* say nothing about the relationship between the two kinds of action, which a western jurist would no doubt consider a serious omission.

of *artha-śāstras* that they left the responsibility for explaining the subject to the king.[78]

Given that miscreants who have done acts within *prakīrṇaka* are prosecuted under the order of the king, it is important that he should be promptly informed of improper activities committed by his subjects and that he should keep as strict a watch as possible on individuals who are suspected of criminal inclinations. Therefore he has at his disposal means of enquiry and investigation of which we can only say that its justification must be its efficiency.

Since the question is of maintaining his authority, which is the foundation of social peace, the king is free to take recourse to all useful expedients. As for the "thorns", the duty of protection no longer exists. They can be suppressed like external enemies, if necessary by tricks and bribery. Every means is good to discover and to arrest them, even those means which would only be used in completely exceptional cases between private litigants.

Manu (VII.16) alludes to two procedures for the application of chastisement, differing according as the acts were prejudicial to the state or delicts committed against individuals. The details of measures which it is possible to employ in order to eradicate "thorns" belong to *artha-śāstra* works and elude *dharmaśāstra* authors. However, Manu devotes to them several verses of Book IX (256-293) where he advises the king to employ spies and even *agents provocateurs*.[79] Yājñavalkya (I.338-339) and Nārada (pariś.,61) give the same advice, though more concisely.

Kātyāyana (947-952) distributes crimes within *prakīrṇaka* in three groups, according to the king's role. For those of the first group (the ten *aparādhas*), he urges the king to conduct the enquiry himself; those in the second are divulged to him by spies and he should take preventive

[78]Kauṭilya devotes an entire book (IV) to *kaṇṭaka-śodhana* and gives a long enumeration of the crimes to be counted in this class in the course of several chapters. Kāṇe, III, 252–7.

[79]Cf amongst others IX.256: 'Let the king who has spies for his eyes *(cara-cakṣus)* discover the two sorts of thieves who take the property of others, both those who are manifest and those who are hidden.' 261: 'Having detected them (the malefactors) by means of trustworthy persons who are disguised and follow the same occupations and by spies passing under various disguises, he must cause them to be instigated (to commit offences) and bring them under his power.' 267: 'By means of clever reformed thieves who associate with such (rogues), follow them and know their devices, he should discover them and incite them (to commit offences).' 268: 'Under the pretext of (offering them) various dainties, of introducing them to Brahmins, and on account of feats of strength, they (the spies) must lead them into the presence (of the king's officials).' 269: 'Those among them who do not come (to the rendezvous) and those who suspect the old (thieves in the king's pay) should be attacked by the king by force and slain along with their friends, relations, and close connexions.' See also *M.*, VII.122–4, recommending the use of spies to watch officials and inform against them if they are corrupt. The similarity of this with Kauṭilya (I.12, IV.4–5) is evident.

measures; and as for the third group he should try to repress them by means of the four expedients *(upāyas)* of royal policy.[80] The distribution of the crimes seems arbitrary enough. We can only deduce from it that the procedure employed differed with the circumstances and envisaged, according to the case in question, either repression or prevention.

The same author does not confine himself to alluding to the use of spies within the scope of *prakīrṇaka*. He distinguishes two kinds of them: the *stobhaka*, who is a part-time informer, and who is paid for his services, and the *sūcaka*, who is a functionary entrusted with police duties (*Kāt.*, 33-34).

It is clear that the preparation of these kinds of cases should be in different hands from those in which the settlement of private disputes lay. For such an expeditious procedure, for such manoeuvres of a police character, reliance must have been placed on people who placed the security of the king's person and the interests of the state before everything. For the decision that should be taken or the advice that should be tendered to the king, it would be appropriate to rely on different advisers than the ordinary judiciary, men more free in their way of judging things. In other words there must have been a special service, quite independent of the judicial administration properly so called.

No *dharma-śāstra* takes the matter up, probably because it belongs particularly to the science of *artha*. The *dharma-śāstras* confine themselves to insisting on the duty of the king to extirpate "thorns" but they leave it to him to orgānise this kind of justice, *his* justice, or rather they leave the *arthaśāstra* writers with the business of advising on this subject.

It is known that Kauṭilya (IV.1.1) distinguishes between two kinds of tribunal. The *dharma-sthīya* is held to look into contentious matters, cases between two litigants or where the question is how their dispute shall be settled; the *kaṇṭaka-śodhana* is charged with the task of extripating "thorns", a jurisdiction which is virtually criminal or in which the king acts of his own motion. In the *dharma-sthīya*, the inquiry is conducted by the *dharma-sthas*, magistrates or officials of the judiciary versed in the *dharmaśāstra*; while the *kaṇṭaka-śodhana* is entrusted to three functionaries called *pradeṣṭṛ*, agents of the executive. The distinction is thus very neatly set out.

It scarcely appears at all in epigraphy, doubtless because what is covered there is essentially administrative machinery and thus merged with other organs of the state. Moreover the decision, whether in a *kaṇṭaka-śodhana* matter or in private litigation, was actually or nominally taken by the king, an important factor which would mask the difference in the powers which he exercised in each of those capacities.[81]

[80]The four expedients : conciliation, corruption, division and force are the classic methods to be used towards external enemies. Kāṇe, III, 172–5, and above, Pt. I, ch. 4, p. 82.

[81]According to *Bṛh.*, XXVII.25, the two sorts of matters were adjudged by the king in

In the matter of fixing penalties, it is hardly to be doubted that the king enjoyed a great latitude in criminal matters. The *dharma-śāstras* prescribe fixed penalties for certain crimes, varying from one to another. But often enough they give a choice for the same crime between penalties of very different gravity, or even neglect to specify the amount of the penalty.[82] It is here that the *śāstras'* recommendations on the correct employment of *daṇḍa* come into their own. From that the *arthaśāstra* writers take a morsel of political wisdom: the king should not abuse punishment lest he pass for a tyrant, nor should he show himself too lax lest he lose all his authority (*Kauṭ.*, I.4.8–10). Manu (VII.16, VIII.126) and Yājñavalkya (I.387), for their part, recommend the king generally to observe the motive, the period and location of the offense, also the capacity of the culprit to endure the penalty, in particular his age and gender. In other words the sentence is determined by the circumstances of each case. It is extremely variable and depends in a large measure upon the will of the king who must remain master of his own justice.

Manu (VIII.129), Yājñavalkya (I.367) and Bṛhaspati (XVII.5) distinguish four sorts of penalties: simple reprimand, severe admonition, fine, and corporal punishment. The two last can be awarded only by the king (*Bṛh.*, XXVII.8). The *dharma-śāstras* furnish a rich arsenal of corporal punishments.[83] It is worthy of note that the penalty of imprisonment *(nirodha)* is rarely provided for, though it was far from unknown (cf. *M.*, VIII.310,375). Manu prescribes (IX.288) that the prisons *(bandhana)* should be located at the side of a main road in order that the convicts may be seen undergoing torture and disfigurement. It is not impossible that what are spoken of were places where criminals were exposed.[84]

the course of the same audience. However C. Mīnākshī, in *Administration and Social Life under the Pallavas* (Madras, 1938), 59, thought she had found the distinction between the two jurisdictions in inscriptions belonging to the later Pallavas or the earlier Coḷas (end of the ninth and beginning of the tenth century): the *dharmāsana* referred to in the inscriptions would correspond to the *dharmasthīya* of Kauṭilya, since the matters belonging to that tribunal were matters of private law, while the *adhikaraṇa*, which seems to have exercised criminal jurisdiction, would correspond to the *kaṇṭaka-śodhana*. We may hazard a guess that a closer examination of epigraphy in other states and periods might reveal this distinction between the two types of jurisdiction, a distinction which in any case emerges from the very nature of the matters in question.

[82]Cf, amongst others, *M.*, IX.275: 'On those who rob the king's treasury and those who persist in opposing (his orders), he shall inflict various kinds of capital punishment (or 'shall strike with various penalties', *vividhair daṇḍaiḥ*), likewise on those who conspire with his enemies'. Kātyāyana (ś. 956): 'Those who imitate the king in his appearance, those who amuse themselves (when they should be working), those who extort excessive revenue, and those who steal the king's wealth should be punished with various corporal punishments *(prāpnuyur vividhaṃ vadham)*'.

[83]Kāṇe, III, 399–406.

[84]Moreover we should note that Viṣṇu, V.71 lays down that the king should never release from fetters one who has put out a person's eyes: *yāvajjīvaṃ bandhanān na muñcet*, which

This liberty to fix the penalty marks the last difference between the *prakīrṇaka* and private litigation. This difference is easily explained. In a case between litigants, following the analysis which our writers make, the plaintiff addresses himself to the king either to obtain restitution of what belongs to him or the payment of what is due to him, or to obtain compensation for a wrong done to him (often in the guise of a fine). There we have objective elements which, if the claim is properly proved. leave little room for the judge's discretion. On the other hand when it is a question of chastising a culprit, the fixing of the penalty, depending on the circumstances and the gravity of the offence, must naturally be much more flexible. It is even more flexible for the fact that there is no precept of general application, analogous to our maxim *nulla poena sine lege* (no penalty may be inflicted without authority of law), and therefore, as contrasted with the laws of today, the powers of the judge are much less restricted.

5. *Private Litigation*

By "private litigation" I mean the disputes capable of being brought by individuals before a court. These are classified by Manu under eighteen heads or titles generally called *vyavahāra-pada* or *vivāda-pada*. The names given to these titles, such as recovery of debts, restitution of deposit, sale by a non-proprietor, rules between associates (or partners), withholding of things donated, sound very much like *jurisdictions*. It would be a mistake, however, to see in the enumeration a closed list of actions viewed procedurally, within which the plaintiff must file his suit in order to have access to a court. In reality Manu's enumeration, taken up by the majority of writers with a few variations, aims at an analysis of the subject-matter of litigation viewed objectively. These are different fundamental topics which can present themselves before a judge, not different forms which an action can assume. There was nothing in common here with the formulae of actions in the classical Roman law. In addition, even though in modern times the law has lost a great deal of its ancient formalism, there was nothing comparable even with the procedural differences which we still recognise, for example, between a real action and a personal action in continental jurisprudence, or between a panchayat case and a case in a civil court or between a civil cause and a revenue matter in Indian law.[84a] Of course the *dharma-śāstras* provide rules of procedure (grouped usually under the name *vyavahāra-mātṛkā*), but with rare exceptions they are rules of general application. Even in the exceptional

is equivalent to imprisonment for life. The next *sūtra* allows the king the alternative of imposing a retaliatory punishment. By contrast *Kauṭ*. (IV.9.22–7) has many rules on the management of prisons.

[84a] [trs.]

cases we find no definition or limitation of the action. The plaintiff is free to move the court as soon as his action fulfils the basic conditions required to found a *vyavahāra*.

Yājñavalkya (II.5) defines a *vyavahāra-pada*: "when a person, having been injured *(ādharṣita)* by others in a manner contrary to *smṛti* or *ācāra*, submits a complaint to the king".[85] This definition highlights three elements: the violation of a rule prescribed by the *śāstras* or by a customary rule; the existence of injury or damage resulting from that violation; and finally the victim's plaint.

Violation of a rule of *dharma* does not suffice by itself to constitute a case. For this particular (or "special") damage must have ensued from it. Likewise infractions of rules of conduct making up what we have called Good Custom do not as a general rule damage anyone. The culprit is bound to expiate his sin, which is another matter. He can be compelled to do this by social pressures. The king, for his part, can intervene to secure the performance of penance, and even add to a penal sanction if he thinks it appropriate. On the other hand, every case presupposes an injury unjustly suffered by the plaintiff. It may well be that the wrong of which he complains is equally a sin on the culprit's part, and that the latter is liable to penance. But this has nothing to do with the litigation, which is brought before the court by the plaintiff with the sole motive of being compensated for the damage he claims he has suffered. In other words the plaintiff acts in his own interest to obtain satisfaction and not in the interests of the social or moral order. To use the style of the interpreters, the cause of the action started by the plaintiff is not the invisible effect of the *adharmic* act complained of, but its visible effect.

The predominantly interest-orientated character of private litigation equally distinguishes it from the matters which make up *prakīrṇaka*. In the latter it is public order or the authority of the king which are thought to be threatened or infringed, and not simply the interests of an individual. That is why the king, invested as he is with the general duty of protection, can take them up on his own initiative. It can happen that an infringement of private rights can also be held to be an infringement of public order, and that the king has already decided to punish it. There we shall find the case instituted by the plaintiff joined by a proceeding carried on in the name of the state and tending towards the application of a penalty. But these two cases, though simultaneous, will remain governed by their own rules. It is known that the general evolution of criminal law tends to substitute crimes for torts, to take away the satisfaction of vengeance from the victim in order to transfer that concern to the state. Hindu law never followed out that evolution completely,

[85] *smṛtyācāra-vyapetena mārgenādharṣitaḥ paraiḥ, āvedayati ced rājñe vyavahāra-padaṃ hi tat.*

and the victim of a tort is often allowed to claim, personally, that penalties should be imposed on the alleged tortfeasor. But the penalties are inflicted by the state; when a fine is in question that passes, as a general rule, to the king. On the other hand it is not rare for the tort, irrespective of the sanctions relative to it in private law, to figure equally amongst the matters which the king may take cognizance of on his own initiative. Instead of the substitution of a crime for a tort—which would mark the end of the evolution of the law—we are confronted by two parallel solutions, not conceived of as cumulative. Here there are difficulties in matters of detail into which we cannot enter. Probably they emerge from the existence of rules belonging to very different periods within our *śāstras*.

The injury for which the plaintiff demands reparation and which is the real cause of the suit, can be of two kinds, depending upon whether it affects the goods or the person of the plaintiff. Bṛhaspati (II.5) and Kātyāyana (*śl*.30) develop this distinction to divide private litigation into two big categories: those whose object is to render to the plaintiff what it his due, and those which aim to have a penalty inflicted. Some have thought they could see in this the germ of the distinction which modern law makes between civil and criminal cases.[86] But, apart from the fact that civil matters include other disputes as well, which do not involve goods, one should not confuse the matters ranged in the second class with our criminal causes, because the punishment of the culprit is demanded by the victim himself by way of reparation for the evil, physical or moral, which he has undergone. It is really a question of torts,[87] a class which has tended to be drastically reduced in modern laws, which invest the state with large powers to suppress wrongs against the citizen. However it must be agreed that the transitional law which the law of the *śāstras* really is does not always make a clear distinction, as between private wrongs and public wrongs, and the elements of both tend to be confused.[88]

[86]Kāṇe, III, 258–9.

[87]*Délits privés*. It will be recollected that in common-law jurisdictions exemplary and even punitive damages may be obtained in the case of certain torts. See, for an example, *Loudon* v. *Ryder* All England Reports 1953, Vol. 1, 741 (Court of Appeal), and for the principles *Rookes* v. *Barnard* All England Reports 1964, Vol. 1, 367 (House of Lords); *McCarey* v. *Associated Newspapers* All England Reports 1964, Vol. 3, 947 (Court of Appeal), followed in India in *R.K. Karanjia* v. *Krishnaraj* (1969) 72 Bombay Law Reporter, 94; and for the broader Australian view *Australian Consolidated Press* v. *Uren* All England Reports 1967, Vol. 3, 523 (Privy Council). *Cassell & Co*. v. *Broome* All England Reports 1972, Vol. 1, 801 (House of Lords). [trs.]

[88]Taking in account texts which place in a special class certain types of cases because of the gravity of the offenses in question, L. Rocher, 'Ancient Hindu Criminal Law', *J.O.R.* 24 (1955), 15–34, concludes that that distinction amounts to the one which we make between criminal and civil cases. It seems natural that the gravity of the offense should have served as a criterion for some *dharmaśāstra* writers to classify different types of cases. However, we may note that such a criterion does not lead to a demarcation between the penal and

It is the king's responsibility to secure to his subjects an equitable solution of the disputes that arise between them. According to Nārada (Int.,I.1-2) the royal function was created in order that an end should be made to quarrels caused by the liberation of passions, the king alone having the power to punish (he is the *daṇḍa-dhara*). He is responsible for the organisation of justice, and he should supervise its efficiency throughout his kingdom.

Jurisdiction seems to have been largely decentralised and even disseminated amongst many elements in the population. Every body of persons exercising a particular activity seems to have been invested with the legal right to hear disputes between its members. "Cultivators, artisans, artists, money-lenders, guilds of merchants, dancers, those who wear the signs of a religious order, and thieves", says Bṛhaspati (I.26), "should arrange their affairs following the rules of their profession".[89] This clearly refers to a competence limited to matters which call conventional usages into play. But a more general competence is attributed to bodies called *kula, śreṇi, gaṇa,* or *pūga,* on the composition of which the interpreters differ (Kāṇe, III,pp.280-281). We are not better informed on their powers, even if it appears that, as Bṛhaspati says (I.28), they cannot decide cases involving serious crime *(sāhasa)*. These jurisdictions are probably of customary origin, and the *dharma-śāstras* only confirm their existence, submitting them to the king's control. They do not administer justice by virtue of delegation from the king (though in some historical instances he may have confirmed or defined their powers), but by virtue of their own power which is organically attached to the very existence of the body itself.[90] On the other hand there is a hierarchy

the civil, for all litigation in Hindu law was then considered as resting upon damage suffered by the plaintiff, indeed what we call a tort: to repudiate a debt or to refuse to return a deposit (*Kāty*. 28, 35) are torts, just as are misappropriating the goods of another or offering violence to his person. By misusing our juridical categories we could liken the first two examples to civil cases—wrongly, for they are in reality penal matters like the last two examples. Proof of this lies in the penalty which falls upon the debtor or depositary against whom the debt or the deposit's reality is established (*M*., VIII. 139, 191–2). Yet certain of these offences can only be tried at the suit of the victim, while others can be taken up by the king *ex officio*. Vardhamāna (end of the fifteenth cent.) relies on this technical criterion to delimit the scope of his treatise on 'criminal' law, the *Daṇḍaviveka*. This author's outlook, reported at the end of the article cited above, only reflects (in my view) an opinion which was traditional during the period of the commentators.

[89]A similar rule appears at Gautama XI.21 : 'Cultivators, merchants, shepherds, money-lenders, and artisans (are authorised to lay down rules) for their respective bodies.'

[90]The question has been discussed à propos of *Yājn*., II.30a : *nṛpenādhikṛtāḥ pugāḥ śrenayo 'tha kulāni ca*. Some commentators relate *nṛpenādhikṛtāḥ*, 'appointed by the king', to the following words and conclude that the *pūgas, śreṇis*, etc., derive their judicial powers from the king. But Vijñāneśvara sees in the *nṛpenā-* royal judicial officers, distinct from the *pūgas, śreṇis*, etc. This interpretation is corroborated by analogous texts of *Nār*., I.7 (cited below) and *Bṛh*. I.93.

amongst them, the *śreṇis* having an authority superior to the *kulas*, and the *pūgas* (or *gaṇas*) to the *śreṇis* (*Yāj.*, II.30; *Nār.*, Int.,I.7; *Kāt.*, 82).[91] Further, Vijñāneśvara (*Mit.*, on *Yāj.*, II.30) shows that there could be an appeal from one to another, and this right seems expressly confirmed by Bṛhaspati (I.29-30).

However, what Medhātithi says in his commentary on Manu VIII.2 (in the course of which he cites *Nār.*, Int.,I.7) on the relations between the three jurisdictions hardly corresponds to what we understand by the word "appeal". For him *kula* means a family group. When the members of the family have given judgment on a dispute submitted to them, their decision (he says) must be observed precisely. But if there is reason to fear that they might be partial towards one of the parties, perhaps because they are more closely related to him than to the other, the case should be submitted to the *śreṇi* (guild of persons exercising the same profession). This group, says Medhātithi, has more authority than the body of relations, for the latter, for fear of hurting family sentiments, might hesitate to be severe with one who has left the right path. The members of a *śreṇi*, however, have nothing to fear beyond being summoned before the king, which would give royal officials an excuse to interfere in their group's affairs. Thus they always take precautions to secure the performance of their sentence before proceeding to look into the dispute, precautions consisting in exacting surety from the parties to pay a fine, should the decision which will be passed not be observed, or to have it executed. This commentary by no means suggests a revision by the *śreṇi* of a decision passed by a meeting of relations. What follows seems to be no more than an estimate of the authority of a decision rendered by a *gaṇa* (which Medhātithi visualises as a body of builders or temple-Brahmins), the superiority of that decision over that of a *śreṇi* amounting to this, that the members of a *gaṇa* would always act collectively.

So it seems, at least in Medhātithi's opinion, that the *kulas, śreṇis* and *ganas* form independent jurisdictions, each subject directly to the sole control of the king.[92] Apart from that, it is difficult to see what jurisdictional relation there could be between gatherings of such different compositions. It is probable, as Colebrooke thought,[93] that their essential task was to arbitrate between their members and that a body called

[91] *Nār.*, I.7 (=*Kāt.*, 82): *kulāni śreṇayaś caiva gaṇāś cādhikṛto nṛpaḥ, pratiṣṭhā vyavahārāṇāṃ gurv ebhyas tūttarotaram.* 'The *kulas, śreṇis, gaṇas,* a person appointed (by the king), and the king are invested with the power to hear cases; each following one is more important than those that precede.'

[92] It is incumbent on the king, according to *Yāj.*, I.361, to watch and see that the *kulas, jātis, śreṇis,* and *gaṇas* do not swerve from duties, and to punish them if they do swerve from them. *A fortiori* this supervision must extend to their bodies' judicial functions.

[93] *Miscellaneous Essays*, I. 492.

"superior" could take cognizance only when the parties agreed to commit their dispute to its final award.

These jurisdictions of customary origin were linked with jurisdictions created by the king himself by means of a method of review which we can generally liken to an appeal. Following Kātyāyana (*śl.*496), "when (a plaintiff) is not satisfied *(saṃtoṣaṃ na gataḥ)* with the decision, even though it be passed by a *kula* or another (jurisdiction), the king should reexamine the case and reform any error in the judgment". An analogous text is attributed to Pitāmaha (*Dh. k.,* p. 62). The path was apparently wide open, since it was sufficient that the appellant was not satisfied with the decision that had been passed (whether for or against him).

Bṛhaspati (I.2–3), however, distinguishes four sorts of courts (*sabhās*) : those that are stationary *(pratiṣṭhā)* i.e. permanently established in a town or village: those that are itinerant *(a-pratiṣṭhā)* : those which are presided over by a judge entitled to use the royal seal *(mudritā)*; lastly those which are presided over by the king in person. The first seem to correspond to the *kulas, śreṇis,* etc., which we have just considered. The second seem to be special jurisdictions for populations living in forests, for soldiers, and the complements of caravans (*Bṛh.,* I.25). The last two refer to royal courts. *Kulas* and other analogous bodies are not institutions specialising in the administration of justice. Their function as judicial organs eludes us completely. We can only presume that they played the role of an arbitrator and tried above all to bring the parties to an arrangement. Failing to arrive at an agreement, the parties could in any case move to the court of the king.

The king's court is the only court whose jurisdiction is dealt with by the *dharma-śāstras,* the only one for which their rules relative to the composition of the tribunal, the procedure, or even the deciding of cases, really apply. The king is indeed the supreme judge in his realm, and is held as a matter of duty to protect his subjects and to warrant that their disputes shall be settled justly. It is reasonable that he should be guided and counselled by the *smṛti*-writers in the exercise of that important part of the royal function for which, however, he alone must shoulder the responsibility.

The king's court must have had a single jurisdiction throughout the kingdom, but we are not prevented from supposing that the important towns had officials to whom the king delegated his powers of judicature by commission.[94]

[94]Perhaps this is what the *mudritas* of *Bṛh.,* I.2–3 are. And perhaps some allusion is made to these provincial judges in Pitāmaha (*Dh. k.,* 62): *grāme dṛṣṭaḥ puraṃ yāyāt pure dṛṣṭas tu rājani,* 'what has been decided in the village goes to the city, and what has been decided in the city goes before the king', unless, of course, one sees in the city a court composed of citizens (which remains quite hypothetical).

The king's court is normally composed of the president *(prāḍvivāka, adhyakṣa)* and three judges or assessors *(sabhyas)*, all four appointed by the king, the first being chosen preferably from amongst Brahmins, and none from amongst Śūdras (*M.*, VIII.9; *Yāj.*, II.3; *Kāt.*, 67). In principle, the king should be present at the hearings daily, for he alone has the right to punish. When he takes his seat he should be accompanied by the *purohita*, ministers and Brahmins (*M.*, VIII.1-2; *Yāj.*, II.1). And the Brahmins, even when they are not appointed by the king, have the right to be present at the hearing and to express their opinions.

The king should never decide a case alone; he should always take the opinions of his counsellors (*Gaut.*, XII.48): i.e. he can only decide a matter falling within the scope of private litigation when he is in open court. According to Bṛhaspati (I.6), "the president pronounces [the sentence], the king chastises, the judges look into the merits of the case". And Nārada (I.35) seems to say that the king must follow the opinion of the president *(prāḍvivāka-mate sthitaḥ)*.[95] If the decision is unjust, the fault, i.e. the sin, falls equally on the culprit who has been acquitted, the witnesses, the judges, and the king (*M.*, VIII.18). Moreover the duty of the judges is to make the king resile from an opinion which they believe to be wrong. When they have advised him in this sense, they are no longer responsible for the decision he will take (*Kāt.*, 77).

Such rules show that if the king is really master in the judgment he is morally bound in a very strict sense by the precepts of the *smṛti*. Giving justice is equivalent, say Manu (VIII.306) and Yājñavalkya (I.359), to performing a sacrifice capable of procuring the highest spiritual benefits. Bṛhaspati repeats this formula on several occasions (I.5,11;II.42, and *Aiy.*, I.55) and does not hesitate to identify a law-case *(vyavahāra)* as a sacrificial act *(yajña)*. "In the sacrifice Viṣṇu is the object of worship, in the case, it is the king. The plaintiff who wins his suit is (equal) to the sacrificer *(yajamāna)* and he who loses is like the victim *(paśu,* sacrificial animal). The plaint and the defense are (like) clarified butter, and the grounds of the plaint *(pratijñā)* like a vegetable offering *(havis)*. The Vedas are here the *śāstras,* the judges the priests who officiate *(ṛtvij)*, and the fine resembles the ritual fees *(dakṣinā)*" (*Aiy.*, I.118-119). Just as if he were performing a sacrifice, the king ought, then, scrupulously to observe the rules laid down by the texts. He is bound by the terms of the *śāstras* like a sacrificer by the ritual-manual. "It excludes from heaven; it ruins the country; it brings on danger from enemy armies; it destroys the germ of life—so does the decision which kings take on their own when a text exists [having a bearing on the case]" (*Kāt.*, 44).

When the king is hearing a case between two litigants the essential

95Gautama XI.25 also says that in a difficult case the king should consult the Brahmins who are learned in the Vedas and follow their counsel.

quality required of him is impartiality. "When the king is seated on the justice-seat *(dharmāsana)*, let him be devoid of passion, equal towards all, performing the vow of Vivasvat (Yama, the god of the underworlds, who fixes the destinies of the dead according to their past actions, good and bad)", prescribes Nārada (Int., I.34). For his part, Yājñavalkya declares (II.1), "The king, free from anger and greed, should give justice assisted by learned Brahmins, in conformity with the (precepts of) treatises of *dharma*". And Vijñāneśvara, commenting on the words "free from anger and greed" remarks that this is a special injunction *(ādarārtham)* and not a mere formality. Having the role of an arbiter between his subjects, the king no longer has the liberty of decision which he has in other affairs of his kingdom where the interests of the state are involved. This is in Medhātithi's mind when, commenting on the word *dharmāsana* in Manu VIII.23, he writes "When he sits on the throne [i.e. when he takes up affairs of state], the king considers *artha*, contributing as it does to the prosperity of the realm, as the most important element in preference even to *dharma*; but if his function is to settle litigation it is *dharma* which he regards as the most important thing".

However the king must always seek out the truth and make sure that he does not come to a hasty judgment. Moreover no legal rule may be applied until he has obtained complete familiarity with the matter. "Having rejected all chicanery *(chala)*, the king shall decide according to the real state of the facts; for even a well-founded claim, if not properly presented, can miscarry in the course of the hearing", says Yājñavalkya (II.19). Bṛhaspati (II.12) says more neatly: "A judgment should not be passed in reliance upon the text of the *śāstras* alone, for a trial [of the case] without taking account of the circumstances of the case leads to a loss of *dharma* [an injustice or a sin]".[96] And Bṛhaspati, in the following verse, alludes to the classic story of the hermit Māṇḍavya (*Mahābh.*, Ādip., ch.116)—to which Nārada also refers (Int.,I.42)—,who was unjustly condemned for theft on the sole basis of a legal rule presuming to be the thief him in whose possession stolen objects are found.

On the other hand, the plaintiff in private suits undertakes the action only with the object of obtaining satisfaction from the other party. He acts in his personal interests. Thus, in reality, the trial presents a complex character, since the rules of the *śāstras* are invoked to someone's profit. If it puts in issue superior interests as well, such as those of the state or of the throne, the conflict is no longer merely between a rule of *dharma* and a rule of *artha*, but between two opposed orders of interest. One can only imagine that the rule of *dharma* would remain in suspense.

[96] *kevalaṃ śāstram āśritya na kartavyo vinirṇayaḥ, yukti-hīne vicāre tu dharma-hāniḥ prajāyate*. On the sense of *yukti* in this verse, see my 'Les quatre pieds du procès', *J.A.*, 1962, 502 n. 18.

The texts on procedure dealing with the validity of the plaint have the effect of limiting the exercise of judicial action in response to motives of an entirely political character. According to Bṛhaspati (*Aiy.*, II.13, 32,43; the last two verses are attributed to Hārīta also), the action cannot be started *(anādeya)* in three cases; firstly, when it is opposed (to the interests) of a city, a village, or high personalities *(pura-grāma-mahājana-virodhin)*; secondly, when it is directed against the interests of the inhabitants of a town, of all the realm, or of one of the constituent elements of the state *(paura-virodha-kṛd rāṣṭrasya vā samastasya prakṛtīnāṃ tathaiva ca)*; finally, when it is barred by the king *(rājñā apavarjita)*. Kātyāyana (*sl.*136) likewise prescribes that a plaint should be rejected if it is opposed (to the interests of) the state *(rāṣṭra-viruddha)*,[97] or barred by the king *(rājñā vivarjita)*. Explaining this last case, Aparārka says that there might be a royal order to the effect that "in my realm there should be no dealings in rupees" (and a plaint assessed the damages in rupees). Mitra-miśra cites instances when the plaint refers to taxes or other revenue which are the monopoly of the king. In other words this cause of a plaint's being rejected would operate when it is contrary to an order previously given by the king. This no doubt minimises the significance of the expression.[98] It really seems that the king is generally able to bar from the courts any plaints which he thinks could interfere with the peace or injure the interests of the state or even the mere prestige of the administration.

Texts which are more or less ambiguous are found to introduce the consideration of *artha,* here understood in the sense of utility, what is opportune, into the discussion of matters coming before the king's court. First of all there is the enigmatic verse of Manu (VIII.24) where it is said that the king *"arthānarthāv ubhau buddhvā dharmādharmau ca kevalau* shall examine all the cases of the litigants according to the order of *varṇas"*. The meaning of the first line, which I have left here untranslated, is difficult. Three interpretations are offered by the commentators according to the importance which they attach to the word *kevalau* ("alone", in the dual number).[99]

[97]There is a similar rule at *Nār.*, Int., II.12.

[98]The interpretation adopted by the commentators at least eliminates the notion that *rājñā vivarjita* could have meant a plea which the king had already considered and rejected, i.e. *res judicata.*

[99]This difficulty is reflected in the diversity of the translations: 'Considering that which is advantageous or noxious, and adhering principally to recognition of what is legal or illegal ...' (Loiseleur-Deslongchamps's version rendered into English: Sir William Jones had 'Understanding what is expedient or inexpedient, but considering only what is law or not law ...'); 'Considering what is useful or not useful, and what is in itself right or wrong ...' (Burnell and Hopkins); 'Knowing what is expedient or inexpedient, what is pure justice or injustice ...' (Bühler); 'Considérant ce qui est utile et ce qui ne l'est pas, et surtout ce qui est juste et injuste ...' (Strehly); and 'Understanding both 'desirable' and 'undesirable' to be only 'justice' or 'injustice' ...' (Jhā).

According to Rāghavānanda it would be suitable to translate: "Knowing that *dharma* and *a-dharma* alone are *artha* or *anartha*", i.e. knowing that *dharma* alone is desirable and *adharma* alone undesirable, the king, etc....

Kullūka thinks that the sense should be: knowing what is *artha* and *anartha* and also what is *dharma* and *adharma*. i.e. understanding the importance of *dharma* and the less importance of *artha*, or realising what is advantageous and what is not, but giving attention to *dharma* alone, since it alone can enable one to acquire spiritual merit, the king, etc...

These first two interpretations assume the priority of *dharma* over *artha*. The king should know which solution would be advantageous for the litigants, but he should always render his decision in conformity with the precepts of the *śāstra*.

But we are free to ask why Manu wishes the king to weigh up the interests involved if at the end he is bound to conform himself to the legal rules. Thus Medhātithi suggests a third interpretation which has some subtlety. When a solution is highly desirable and opportune, but contrary to the legal rules, if the element of *a-dharma*, i.e. failure to observe the rules of *smṛti*, could be regarded as of little importance, then the king should hesitate to pass a decision which would be inopportune, for it is possible to make good the breach of the precepts of the *śāstras* by means of charitable acts or expiatory rites. In other terms a light sin, deliberately committed and which could easily be expiated, can be useful in the administration of justice. The strict observance of the texts could lead to an undesirable condemnation. This interpretation goes further than the verse of Bṛhaspati (II.12), analysed above, which criticises a judgment founded on the literal sense of a text merely because it has been given without a complete acquaintance with the facts of the case. Here the case has been properly prepared and the text has been deliberately set aside for reasons of mere convenience. This makes us think of similarities with the texts of Manu himself (IV.176) and of Yājñavalkya (I.156) who recommend setting aside precepts of the *śāstras* when these would be "odious to the world". Here, as there, failure to observe the rules is due to the intervention of the notion of *artha*. But, given the litigation, it is for the king to raise this question, fluid if there ever was one and fit to justify the worst injustice, but also fit to make equity triumph.

Nārada (Int., I.37) (a verse also attributed to *Bṛh., Aiy.*, I.111) seems to be even more categorical than Manu (if we follow Medhātithi's interpretation) when he enjoins the king carefully to avoid transgressing either the precepts of *dharma* or those of *artha*.[100] But, two verses further

[100] *dharmaśāstrārthaśāstrābhyām avirodhena yatnataḥ, saṃpaśyamāno nipuṇaṃ vyavahāragatiṃ nayet.*

(Int., I.39) he requires the king, in case of conflict between the two kinds of precepts, always to follow those of *dharma,* thus returning to the orthodox doctrine (*Yāj.,* II.21). Meanwhile Kātyāyana (32) also attributes an equal role to *dharma* and *ārtha* in judging cases, when he declares that "the science of *dharma* and that of *artha* are the two principal branches *(skandha)* of the trial, of which victory or defeat (of the parties) are the fruit."[101]

Of the Brahmins who assist the king in the administration of justice the same author (*Kāt.,* 57) requires not merely that they shall know the meaning of the precepts of the *śāstras* well *(dharma-śāstrārtha-kuśala)* but also that they should be versed in the science of *artha (artha-śāstra-viśārada).* They must join a sense of utility to juridical rigor. It is true that Vācaspati Miśra (*Vyav. cint.,* 9.4) citing the verse of Kātyāyana, observes that the precepts of *artha* should not be taken into consideration unless they do not conflict with those of *dharma.* And Aparārka, commenting on the word *mantra-jña* ("expert in giving counsel") by which Manu (VIII.1) qualifies the Brahmin counsellors of the king, admits that the word means *artha-śāstra-jña* ("versed in the science of artha"). He adds, however, that the Brahmin who is charged with the trial of cases should not put into practice the resources of the science of *artha* beyond the point where they cease to be compatible with the precepts of the science of *dharma.*

To sum up: the ideal aimed at by these writers, as by judges of all times, was to manage to reconcile the demands of justice with the concern for equity (or expediency). Medhātithi, commenting on the same word *mantra-jña,* gives an example of the kind of advice which the king could expect from his Brahmins. Let us suppose, says he, that someone has commenced a suit against a client of the prime minister and that it appears to the trial court that he might well win his case. If the minister's protégé were not held to lose the case or were not compelled to comply with the judgment the administration of justice would be faulty and the king's subjects would not fail to accuse the king of either partiality or weakness. On the other hand if the minister's dependant were cast, that would grieve his patron and could provoke unrest in its turn. Under such conditions, if those who are in charge of the hearing are really *mantra-jña,* they would adjourn the decision on some pretext and would inform the king of the situation, with the suggestion that he should urge the parties to come to some compromise. Thereupon the king would tell the prime minister that his man was on the point of losing his case, that a respite had been arranged simply to save his (the minister's) prestige, and that it was up to him to arrange matters so that his protégé would escape

[101] *dharmaśāstrārthaśāstre tu skandha-dvayam udāhṛtam, jayaś caivāsāyaś ca dve phale samudāhṛte.*

judgment being given against him. The prime minister would of course follow the king's advice, and thus both *artha* and *dharma* would be satisfied.

That Medhātithi finds it quite natural and even recommends such an intervention on the king's part in the course of a trial gives food for thought. One has no difficulty in imagining what abuses could flow from the advice to try to reconcile *dharma* and *artha*, valid as that might seem to be in principle.

Once the case has been heard the decision which puts an end to the case should follow as a matter of course. According to Bṛhaspati (II.24) there are two cases in which the king should decide himself, i.e. in which the judges are bound to refer to him. The first is where adequate proof is wanting *(pramāṇa-rahita)*. The same case is foreseen by Pitāmaha (*Dh.k.*, p.105): "In default of a document, possession and witnesses and when recourse to an ordeal is not to be thought of, the king is the authority, for all the doubtful points in a case are elucidated by him" and by Vyāsa *(Dh.k.*, p.106) who, having enumerated the different sorts of proof declares, "When they are wanting, the order of the king is the mode of decision".[102]

The king is equally to be appealed to to cut the knot, according to Bṛhaspati (II.24) when "the [precepts of] *śāstra* and the members of the tribunal are in disagreement *(śāstra-sabhya-virodhe)*". This formula begs some discussion. Some commentators understand that the king should pass the sentence when the court is of an opinion contrary to the texts. As Mitra-miśra observes (*Vīr.vyav.*, cited at *Dh.k.*, p.100), the judges are then exposed to being punished by the king. Perhaps we should translate the phrase by "in a case of a disagreement between the members of the court *or* between the precepts of the *śāstras*". The first hypothesis, in which the members of the court are divided on the sentence which should be passed, seems a suitable case for the king's intervention. As for the second, it is accepted by Vācaspati Miśra (*Vyav.cint.*, 719,2-3), who takes it, perhaps in a somewhat far-fetched manner, from a verse of

[102]A verse of Bṛhaspati (XIII.6), placed under the heading of sale by a non-owner, repeats the same rule, and provides that in the absence of proof the king should look into the characters of the parties and give judgment himself on the basis of the degree of confidence which might be reposed in their words *(pramāṇa-hīne vāde tu puruṣāpekṣayā nṛpaḥ, samanyunādhikatvena svayaṃ kuryād vinirṇayam)*. In his gloss on this verse Caṇḍeśvara (*Ratnākara* quoted by Jagannātha Tarkapañcānana, *Colebrooke's Digest*, London, 1801, I, 507) advises the king to have recourse to spies to find out the characters of the litigants. This contamination of 'civil' procedure with forms appropriate to criminal procedure could be explained by the hybrid character of this type of case : he who sells a thing which does not belong to him risks the penalty for theft (*M.*, VIII, 197–8). Manu himself (VIII.182) recommends the judges, in the absence of witnesses, to take the aid of spies to track down a dishonest depositary of gold who refuses to restore a deposit. Cf p. 240, n. 79 sup.

Kātyāyana (*śl.*52) upon which he comments as follows: "In a case where there is a contradiction between two principles or between two texts, the matter should be settled by an order from the king".[103] Thus the king has the power to determine in the last resort, not only on questions of fact, but also on questions of law.[104]

A judgment is definitive as soon as the parties accept it. It is binding on the king too who can not modify it on his authority alone. According to Manu (IX.233), "when a case has been heard or a penalty inflicted [the king] should consider that it has proceeded regularly and he should never rehear [whatever has already been decided]".[105] But it is possible for a plaintiff or a defendant who has lost a case to obtain a fresh trial if he thinks it has been decided unjustly *(vidharmataḥ* or *vidharmaṇā)*, on condition that, should he fail in his review, he will pay double the fine (*Nār.*, Int., I.65; *Yāj.*, II.306).[106] The case should then be brought before the king, who, if the appeal succeeds, will make the judges who are guilty of having judged incorrectly pay the fine (*Nār.*, Int., I.66; *Yāj.*, II.305) or who will, according to Manu (IX.234), inflict a fine of 1,000 *paṇas* on them.

On the other hand, the king could probably order a fresh trial of his own motion if he has reason to suspect the judges of having given a decision vitiated by partiality, cupidity, or fear, in which case the matter would naturally be submitted to him (*Yāj.*, II.305).

Once the king has passed judgment, whether in the first resort or the last, the judgment is not susceptible of any review. "That which [kings] decide, false or true," says Nārada (XVIII.19), "is *dharma* for the litigants"[107] and Pitāmaha: "That which has been considered by the king, good or bad, cannot be put in question afterwards".[108] The sentence he has given establishes in an incontrovertible fashion the truth about the litigation which came before him. The litigant who won has thereafter an irrefutable proof of his right to the thing he claimed or of the reality of the damage which he claimed to have undergone. He has only

[103]*nyāyayoḥ śāstrayor vā yatra virodhas tatrāpi rājājñayā vyavahāra ity arthaḥ.*

[104]But we must recollect that, before coming to a decision, the king ought always to take advice, and that certain texts, mentioned above (*Gaut.*, XI.25; *Nār.*, I.35) make it obligatory upon him to follow the opinion of the judge or of learned Brahmins.

[105]*tīritaṃ cānuśiṣṭaṃ ca yatra kvacana yad bhavet, kṛtam tad dharmato vidyān na tad bhūyo nivartayet* (Kāṇe, III, 383). I have taken up the most generally accepted interpretation of this. However, the majority of the commentators take the verse as applying to a judgment passed by the king's court.

[106]There are other instances of revision *(punarnyāya)*, especially where the action has been brought by a person under a disability, or by an unauthorised person, or when the sentence has been passed by a person incompetent to pass it, etc. (*Nār.*, I.45 and *Quot.*, I.14), but it does not appear that the case must necessarily be brought before the king.

[107]*te yad brūyur asat sad vā dharmo vyavahāriṇām.*

[108]*rājñā dṛṣṭaḥ kudṛṣṭo vā nāsti tasya punarbhavaḥ* (*Dh. k.*, 62).

to produce the king's order which has put an end to his case, that is to say the judgment, to set aside all other possible means of proof by which one might attempt to contest his right.[109] This is in any case a normal aspect of the recognised power of the king. All his orders must be obeyed, not only, as says Bṛhaspati (I.32), because the intelligence of kings far surpasses that of other mortals, but because to admit the possibility of debating such an order would be contrary to the very principle of the royal function. The force of the judgment rests upon a motive much more imperious than that which we attribute to *res judicata*, which has not, of course, any other foundation than the quite practical need to put an end to litigation.

Conversely, the judgment is only an order. It could not fix the law! It could not even serve as an illustration. The interpeters have understood this well—they whose functions must often have called them actually to administer justice—since they never cite any judgment given by any historical king in support of their arguments.[110] Following the interpretation allowed by some commentators[111] of the verse cited above (p. 225), Nārada even foresees the possibility of the king's revising a judgment given by his predecessor if he believes it to be contrary to reason.

Although the intervention of the king in judicial matters may be decisive, it brings no new element to interpretation. In settling disputes between his subjects, the king merely does his duty, which is to secure order and peace in his realm. This is the office of an administrator and not a legislator.

Whether *rāja-śāsana* means edict or judgment, it is always merely an expression of the royal policies, which could be inspired by considerations of convenience, opportunism, or equity, of which the king is and must remain the sole judge. Consequently, we may say that the king's sentence cannot make any lines of authority.[112] It is *dharma* only for the two parties to the case (*Nār.,* XVIII.19). It cannot leave any trace in the sphere of the law itself.

[109]In my view that is the sense and scope of Nārada, Int., I.10: *dharmaś ca vyavahāraś ca caritraṃ rāja-śāsanam, catuṣpād vyavahāro 'yam uttaraḥ pūrva-bādhakaḥ.* Cf 'Les quatre pieds ...', *J.A.*, 1962, 489–503. For a contrary view, viz. that these four are sources of law see Derrett, *Religion* ..., 148–58.

[110]Cf however the case reported by Asahāya on *Nār.*, IV.4 (*S.B.E.* XXXIII, pp. 43–4), but, in any case, without any historical data and not as a precedent.

[111]Particularly Vijñāneśvara, *Mit.*, on *Yāj.*, II.306, and Vācaspati Miśra, *Vyav. cint.*, 17.

[112]Although we have no surviving examples of this it is not absolutely beyond the bounds of possibility that decisions of kings known for their sense of justice or their ingenuity in resolving difficult cases might have been collected and copied into handbooks to serve as models for judges, if not as precedents in the true sense of that word. Such a possibility is raised by what will be seen below (p. 271–2).

CONCLUSION

WESTERN JURIDICAL systems are based on the concept of legality. Whether strictly speaking a written law or the common law, the law is understood to express the will of all. Even in cases where it has done no more than declare the customary law or case law in the form of codes, its imperative force resides entirely in the popular will or constitutionally established authority which has sanctioned it, and not in the power of the usage or custom which lies behind, and has in a sense given birth to, that law. What is just, within the meaning of those systems, is that which is *legal*, i.e. that which conforms to law. What is unjust, and thus irregular and reprehensible, is that which is illegal, i.e. contrary to law, i.e. to an actual provision of a law. Law-in-action, which effectively governs relations between people, is deduced directly from the law. Courts cannot pass sentences or hand down judgments which are just unless they are also, in that sense, legal. True enough, the statute or positive law is not the only source of court-law. Case-law, legal doctrine, even jurisprudence, which fix or attempt to fix the meaning and importance of statutory provisions, all play creative roles to various degrees, and there are numerous contexts, particularly in India, in which law is discovered from custom. But primacy belongs always to the positive law and in particular to statute. The other sources, even when by no means inconsiderable, are only subsidiary to it.

This system is the product of a long evolution in the western world, of which many parts of the "Third World" have inherited much, in both form and substance, alongside their indigenous systems. It is a system which fits an egalitarian and individualistic society. The rule of law is established at the very level of the relations which it purports to govern. It starts with individuals, and it is a manifestation of their own picture of the social order.[1] If we wanted to find a near counterpart to this conception in the traditional system of India we should probably find it in the regulations and "statutes" of corporate bodies and others such as we have mentioned which, established by the interested parties

[1]On the circumstances which led in Europe to the appearance in the fourteenth century of this individualistic conception of law see M. Villey, *Cours d'histoire de la philosophie du droit*, fasc. 2, 'La formation de la pensée juridique moderne' (Paris, 1963). It is impossible to fail to observe how close to Indian tradition was the doctrine, until then the classical doctrine, to which that conception is opposed.

themselves or declaring their customs, fixed everyone's rights and obligations. No doubt there was positive law there, but it was not legislation in the proper sense of that word.

The classical legal system of India substitutes the notion of *authority* for that of legality.[2] The precepts of *smṛti* are an authority because in them was seen the expression of a law in the sense in which that word is used in the natural sciences, a law which rules human activity. Everyone knows that no one can escape from that law. As a result, one must try his utmost to conform to it. But it has no constraining power by itself. It puts itself forward, it shows the way which one should follow, but it does not impose that way.[3] Society is thus organised on the model of itself, with which it is presented, as if it had actually achieved it.

This conception would have ended in a complete divorce between reality and law, had not the law revealed by the Sages been profoundly based in the traditions and aspirations of the Hindu world. It is careful to explain that wherever it cannot conquer custom remains queen. But custom's triumph by no means diminishes the authority of the law. It can only fetter the application of the latter, perhaps only for a time. No rule is really legitimate and finally sanctified until it conforms to that law.

Further, this conception would have involved or justified a strict conservatism, incompatible even with the survival of legal realities. But that law contained within itself a variety of solutions permitting interpretation to diversify its effects according to plans and periods, even going so far as to limit and actually paralyse its application. But this is also the reason why we can hardly get a grip upon the law-in-action, for interpretation could not, any more than the law itself, go beyond proposing itself: it could not be imposed.

The king might well have the right to impose his own decision, and if it conforms to the law, as he is in duty bound to make it do, it could be worthy of amounting in some sense to case-law. But to the extent that it is interpretative—and its interest would have begun and ended there—it cannot have more value (it indeed has less value) than the

[2]*Autorité, auctoritas*. The latter was the power which, added to the act made it perfect. Cf *auctoritas patrum* (the 'authority' of fathers) and, in ancient times, *auctoritas tutoris* (the 'authority' of the guardian, as fictitious parent). A. Ernout and A. Meillet, *Dictionnaire étymologique*, s.v. *augeo* and its derivatives, especially *augur*, 'he who gives omens, assuring the development of an enterprise'.

[3]'Dharma is a code of conduct supported by the general conscience of the people. It is not subjective in the sense that the conscience of the individual imposes it, nor external in the sense that the law enforces it. Dharma does not force men into virtue, but trains them for it. It is not a fixed code of mechanical rules, but a living spirit which grows and moves in response to the development of society.' (S. Radhakrishnan, *The Heart of Hinduism*, Madras, 1936, 17–18).

opinion of a qualified interpreter. In reality the office of king is more complex than the office of judge, because of the duties peculiar to the ruler. Even though his judgments are really law-in-action, they remain singular and unrelated, staccato, without any future.

The text of the law floats alone, incessantly worked upon, discussed, orientated in diverse ways: all we can say of it is that it preserves all its authority. It would be presumptuous and vain to attempt to draw from it any picture of the law actually in force at any given period. This would only be to add one more interpretation to those which have reached us from the hands of men better placed than we are to evaluate the juridical solutions which suited each in his own day.

Such a system may well be imperfect in the eyes of a western jurist. But it presented unquestionable advantages over our system for India, a country with a population of such diversity. A system founded upon legality, even assuming it could have found a climate fit to hatch it, would have involved a veritable legislative chaos. Even if not, it could only have been maintained by a tyranny which ignored popular reactions completely. Profiting from maximum flexibility, the Hindu system sustained the unity of the Indian world, thanks to the undisputed authority of the law. That unity was unrealisable at a lower level, but was realised on the higher level in an ideal participation amongst all Hindus. That ideal received the dynamic imparted to it by faith, by Hinduism itself, with the result that custom and the written law were inextricably woven together to give rise to law.

Some scholars feel that it was the need to affirm and to maintain that faith, when menaced by Islam, which explains how the work of interpretation went on without a break under the rule of the Sultans of Delhi and the Mogul Emperors. Indeed it is a remarkable fact that, far from stopping or even bridling the composition of digests or treatises, the Muslim conquests seem on the contrary to have produced a renewal of interest in this class of literature. However, it would be going too far to attribute this renewal simply to the reactions of the orthodox faithful. Even at the height of Muslim power independent Hindu states always existed with an almost complete internal autonomy, as vassals of the Emperor. Looking at works which originated in these states, one can only wonder at their extraordinary diffusion throughout the whole country, especially when we think of works like the *Vīramitrodaya* of Mitra-miśra or the *Bhagavanta-bhāskara* of Nīlakaṇṭha, written in each case under the patronage of quite subordinate princelings. On the other hand many digests, and not the least important of them, were written in regions directly subject to Muslim rule! It is possible that the curiosity or spirit of tolerance of a ruler like Akbar will explain how he could prompt Ṭoḍar Mal to compose a digest. But it is difficult to imagine that he saw nothing in it beyond a literature inspired by the religious zeal of his minister. In reality the flowering of treatises and digests during the Muslim period seems to have been due to the need for a renewal of that literature, or rather for a new effort on the part of interpretation to adapt the law to the changes that must have come about in Hindu opinion and manners as a result of the Muslim conquest.

According to K.L. Sarkār,[4] if the author of the *Mitākṣarā* adopted a fully secular concept of proprietary right,[5] a possible motive was to facilitate the application of Hindu succession law by Muslim officials. Apart from the fact that Vijñāneśvara lived in a region and at a period when Muslim rule was a very dimly apprehended possibility, this suggestion is very debatable in itself. But the idea, taken abstractly, may not be entirely lacking in relevance. The political ideas expressed by Caṇḍeśvara in the *Rājanīti-ratnākara* could consist with impressions produced in the author by the extension of the power of the Sultanate of Delhi. Nīlakaṇṭha's ideas on the ruler's property in the soil are thought to reflect the new situation created by the appearance of a non-Hindu ruler.[5a] When Muslim rule was consolidated the prolonged coexistence on the soil of India of two communities each having its way of life must obviously have led to movements of ideas in the bosom of each, actions and reactions which must have affected their respective customs, if only marginally. If it was the mission of Muslim rulers to maintain the presence of Islam, those Hindus who were versed in the *śāstras* must for their part have been under obligation to propagate their teaching, not in a spirit of rivalry or opposition which doubtless would not have been tolerated, but in order to inform the Hindu population of what, in their view, were strict duties incumbent upon it, with which no compromise could be permitted.

Though the Muslim conquests aroused and maintained this renewal of interpretation, marked by many works of different tendencies, the very concept of law remained unchanged. The system which the invaders imported was fundamentally similar to that of the Hindus, so that the Hindu would find it quite natural that it should be applied to Muslims, while the latter could raise no theoretical objection to the application of India's classical law to the Hindus. In either case the authority of the law rested not on the will of those who were governed by it, but on divine revelation, on the one hand *The Koran* and the *Sunna,* and on the other hand the Vedas and *smṛti.* The Islamic law was applied only to the believ-

[4]*The Mīmānsā Rules of Interpretation,* 13.

[5]This view, endorsed by A.S. Naṭarāja Ayyar, is an exaggeration, for Vijñāneśvara had no such intention in general, and in the passages under consideration he was anticipated by Medhātithi. See Derrett, *Religion* . . ., 141 n. 1 and see also Medhātithi on Manu IV.226.

[5a][trs.]

ers, while the law of the *śāstras* was not applicable in its plenitude except to Hindus. In either system interpretation has the same importance, and custom holds a significant (if not the same) role, even though in principle it could not contradict a revealed text. Finally, in either system the decisions of the courts are not a source of law, and juridical rules are established by what we would call juridical doctrine.[6]

The general principles are the same and the two systems look as if they were made in order to coexist. But still the Hindu system lacked, over a greater and greater area of territory, an essential element required in order that it might function properly—the king. In the Muslim system as in the Hindu the king has no power of legislation. But this restriction applied only in the sphere reserved for Koranic law. Apart from the fact that this left him a wide margin, it did not concern the institutions of conquered countries, which, in his eyes, had only the status of customs. If Muslim rulers, for reasons of policy analogous to those that inspired some rules of the *śāstras,* generally respected the customs of their Hindu subjects, they were certainly not bound to protect them in the same way as a Hindu king, and they were indifferent to the religious significance of their practices. The only means which the Indian population retained whereby it might be reminded of its duties was the Brahmin who, despoiled of his privileges, had lost the preeminent place he had occupied in the state.

But the void left by the removal of the Hindu king had consequences of the gravest nature in the administration of justice. In both systems, the mission to keep peace between subjects is the primary function of the sovereign, and the Sultans, like the Emperors, usually tried zealously to fulfil this duty. In fact, at least under the reigns of the great Emperors, the administration seems to have attained a high degree of perfection for the period. The judicial authority, represented by the Kādi, always enjoyed in Isalm a great independence vis-à-vis the administration and the sovereign himself. But, and here we come to the Hindu system's first failing, criminal justice which belonged to the sovereign's temporal authority according to the *śāstras* themselves, passed under the control of Islam. The Hindus were submitted in criminal matters to the same régime as the Muslims, like all subjects of the state; and if exception was made in their favour in respect of crimes which only Muslims could commit, the breaches made by Hindus, conversely, against Good Custom ceased to be enquired into and punished in the highest quarter. On the other hand the Sultans, like the Emperors, generally admitted that the

[6]On the life of Hindus under Muslim rule see M.B. Ahmad, *The Administration of Justice in Medieval India* (Aligarh, 1941); Jadunāth Sarkār, *Mughal Administration* (4th edn., Calcutta, 1952); Ishtiaq Husain Qureshi, *The Administration of the Sultanate of Delhi* (4th edn., Karachi, 1958).

Hindus should remain subject to their laws and customs in matters of private law, such as family law, inheritance, partition, adoption, and the like.

But the court of the Kādi, instituted to give justice as between believers, could only judge according to the Islamic law. Following a practice employed in Iran by the Abassids, Sultan Iltutmish decided in the thirteenth century that, for matters between Hindus (unable to settle their differences amicably by arbitration), the Kādi should be assisted by a paṇḍit, to whom he should refer himself in questions of Hindu law, just as he was assisted by a mufti for questions of Islamic law. But although the Kādi, who was a professional judge, was versed in Islamic law like the mufti, by whose advice (by the way) he was not absolutely bound, he had no knowledge whatever of Hindu law and had no choice but to rely on the opinion of the paṇḍit. The system thus entailed serious inconvenience. However it was not universal, and some regions, like Bengal, seem never to have employed it. Especially in the Mogul period, there were occasions when, if the dispute was between Hindu notables, it was determined by the Emperor's own arbitration. But more often the differences were submitted by the parties themselves to a Brahmin's decision, or were referred to local jurisdictions. Early on, as internal politics suggested, the Muslim authorities left local bodies a large measure of autonomy, not different from that which they enjoyed under the Hindu rulers. In judicial matters, the control of the central authorities was only exercised gently, especially because litigants felt some embarrassment in appealing before a Kādi's court. As a result the bodies which the *śāstras* call *kula, śreṇi,* etc. took on a great importance, even though their jurisdiction was reduced to what we may call civil matters and to penal questions of minor importance. Village assemblies or caste tribunals, under the name *panchayat,* became the ordinary courts for Hindus, gradually usurping the attributes of the state courts and passing judgments from which there was no appeal. Whether it was arbitration by a Brahmin, the decision of a caste tribunal, or that of a *panchayat,* the law applied was that of the local community, a law based above all on tradition and precedent, attached more or less laxly to one or other of the schools of interpretation. What occurred was a sort of localisation, if not sclerosis, of law, an arrested development which was henceforth embedded in custom. The Hindu law was no longer that ocean of texts, incessantly conned over and brewed over by the interpreters. It was fragmented into a series of islands placed under the government, direct or indirect, of a particular classical treatise or association of

[7]Cf U.C. Sarkār, *Epochs in Hindu Legal History* (Hoshiarpur, 1958), ch. 11 : 'The history of village panchayats with special reference to the administration of Hindu law during the Muslim period', 238–67.

treatises. Against this legalisation, i.e. conversion into law, of the juridical doctrine of the interpreter-jurists, which was so contrary to the whole spirit of the Hindu law, the last of the interpreters protested with commendable vigour.

Muslim rule injured the functioning of the classical system, but it did not directly attack or subvert it. Thus the system emerged again, or tended to emerge, as soon as historical circumstances permitted.[8]

By contrast, the British conquest (for, *de facto,* conquest it was), entailed direct attacks upon the Hindu system. In 1772, however, Warren Hastings had not the remotest intention of touching such fundamental questions; he thought only of securing a better administration of justice. At that time in his famous *Plan,* he laid the foundations for the civil courts of the Dīwānī of Bengal, Bihar, and Orissa, which had been granted to the East India company by the Emperor of Delhi. Hindus and Muslims remained as in the past under their respective laws. Only the judicial mechanism was changed, for thenceforward the judgment would be passed by an English judge instead of by a Kādi. But although this change was inoffensive to all appearances, it contained in itself, so far as Hindu law was concerned, a threat to traditional concepts which later developments and improvements introduced into this system could only aggravate. Whether the English judge followed the opinion of the paṇḍit in default of detailed knowledge of his own, or whether he had better information about the juridical literature (e.g. from translations) and had access to the texts, he could only make his judgment conform to what he thought was the law. He was a foreigner in India. He was an organ superimposed upon the living sources of law and exterior to them. His principal concern was to search out the legal solution. In other words in his court *legality* became substituted for *authority,* a concept which did not and could not have any meaning for him; and in any case he had no means of making it work, of giving it voice. His only possible course was to determine the law as he found it. No doubt this conception, with which we have become quite familiar, had its advantages. After the successive reforms to which judicial administration was subjected, viz. the creation of the High Courts and the institution of a system of appeals leading up to the Privy Council in London, the public subject to it received a surety of certainty and objectivity which at present they could not better. But these advantages could only be obtained at the price of the ruin of the traditional system.

Whilst, in the classical system, the judgment had no other object or effect but to put an end to a dispute brought before the judge, it now began to constitute a precedent upon which the rule of *stare decisis*

[8]Cf the renaissance of Hindu institutions in the Maratha country under Shivaji. V.T. Guṇe, *The judicial system of the Marathas* (Poona, 1953).

conferred the status of a source of law. Thus law-in-action, which had not existed except potentially in the *śāstras* and treatises, henceforward became extracted and fixed in the case-law of these new courts. It is beyond our present scope to evaluate that judge-made law in itself. Very different estimates of its value have appeared.[9] The English judge, grappling with multiple difficulties, could only confer authority on the diversity of customs which he found before him and refer, where possible, to rules given in a treatise which passed as an authority in the region where he functioned. He could complete the gaps—or his own ignorance—of the Hindu law with notions borrowed from the only law with which he was (in a measure) conversant, namely English law, as he was in any case authorised to do.[10] What interest us here are the effects which the introduction of the English judicial system was bound to have upon the classical system, whatever might be correctness or appropriateness of the decisions which emerged from the courts.

The judgment of a Hindu judge left the authority of the law intact, always available thereafter for new interpretations. However, the English judge called upon to define law, fixed interpretation once and for all. The judgment (even if that of a Full Bench), which was basically only one of the ways in which the law could be understood, became at length its sole valid expression. The commentaries and the digests were treated as if they were the customals of the continent of Europe, each of which used to apply, before codification began, to a particular territory; at times they were allowed to exclude each other, and at other times it was as if they complemented each other, although all of them were originally nothing more than diverse forms of interpretation. The latter skill at once dried up. Further development of law could take place only through the cases. In the classical system the rule of the sacred law became the rule of law-in-action only when it was hallowed by custom, but custom as such had no power to legitimate the rule. Opposed to that law, custom was external to the court-law and likewise to the judicial decision, which, as a result, could maintain its susceptibility to change. The British courts also agreed that custom prevailed over the written law, but, once proved —and admittedly proof was much more difficult than had been the case previously—it remained a *legal* rule. It was imposed (in suitable

[9]Derrett, *Religion* . . ., ch. 9.

[10]In 1781, Impey, completing the formula approved by Warren Hastings, decided that in the absence of a legal rule the judge should decide according to justice, equity and good conscience, which would be equivalent to leaving the judgment to the discretion of the judge, but the latter naturally was led to refer to the principles of the system nearest to him, namely the common law. For the formula, 'justice equity, and good conscience' see Derrett in J.N.D. Anderson, ed., *Changing Law in Developing Countries* (London, 1963), ch. 7. For the important role of Impey see B.N. Pāṇḍey, *The Introduction of English Law into India* (London, 1967). [trs.]

cases) upon the future, so that the written law ceased to exert any influence upon it. Thus the reform instituted solely to ameliorate judicial administration ended in subverting the traditional system. Intending to reduce the judge to the status of an interpreter of scriptural law. Warren Hastings and his successors turned him into a creator of court-law.

Legislation next appeared on the scene, introducing a new element even more fatal to Hindu concepts. The British took this path only very gradually. The first legislative measures were passed in the interests of morality and seem as a whole like police measures: the abolition of *suttee* in 1829, the abolition of slavery in 1843; the abolition in 1850 of loss of rights due to exclusion from caste and change of religion; the validation of the remarriage of widows in 1856. However the British were not slow to discover that the judicial system which they had imported could not function well unless an end was put to the uncertainty in which the judge was often placed as to the law to be applied. The recourse to codification was suggested early on. Already Warren Hastings himself had recognised the need for "a well-digested code of laws compiled agreeably to the laws and tenets of the Mahomedans and Gentoos".[11] Sir William Jones and Colebrooke placed great faith in the digests which they had caused to be produced and which, they imagined, would fix the Hindu law. But this was to misconceive the power of the interpreter, and they soon discovered that they had only added several more works to that imposing literature without having in any way diminished its authority. It was necessary to wait until the Charter Act of 1833 which, having set up a single legislature for all India, enabled one to envisage the utilisation of a parliamentary legislative power. However the British hesitated for a long time to intervene in the sphere of the personal laws, thinking that "the Hindoo law and the Mahomedan law derive their authority respectively from the Hindoo and Mahomedan religion. It follows that as a British legislature cannot make Mahomedan or Hindoo religion so neither can it make Mahomedan or Hindoo law."[12] It was only after the government of India was taken over by the Crown in 1858 that, impelled by the Legislative Council, the movement for codification came into play. The first codes to be issued—and long since revised—were the Code of Civil Procedure (1859), the Penal Code (1860), and the Code of Criminal Procedure (1861), dealing with matters relating to the sovereign authority and involving, from our present point of view, no innovation.

The first texts touching the private law were called forth by the need to regularise legal relations which the indigenous practice had not pro-

[11]Sir G.C. Rankin, *Background to Indian Law* (Cambridge, 1946), 137.

[12]*Report of the Second Law Commission,* 13 December 1855, quoted by Rankin, *op. cit.,* 158.

vided for, such as the Succession Act of 1865, applicable to foreign communities settled in India whose personal law was uncertain because of the want of a *lex loci,* a territorial law. Statutes of 1866 and 1869 belonged to the same class: the first was the Native Converts Marriage Dissolution Act, the scope of which is sufficiently indicated by its title, and the second was the Indian Divorce Act, which was intended specifically for Christians. The Hindu Wills Act of 1870 only settled and arranged matters collateral to the practice of making testaments which antedated the British. The Contract Act of 1872 was inspired above all by the needs of commerce. The personal law of the Hindus was, as yet, scarcely touched. But the notion that a statute law, positive law, could be substituted for the authority of the *śāstras* had made its way into men's minds. Especially after the First World War, more and more statutes interfered with a sphere previously exempted, and undertook important reforms especially in the fields of marriage and succession. Sometimes ahead of public sentiment, this new legislation could not have managed to become effectual unless it had had the support of the Hindu public. In that reservation we find something of an echo of the traditional system.

With the inauguration of a purely Indian legislature, the Union Parliament which held itself qualified to express the will of the Hindu people, a definitive change in the nature of statute law ensued. From being a personal law, with the variability and flexibility which that purported to ensure, it has become since 1955/6 a territorial law, applying with few and relatively unimportant exceptions to all Hindus, whatever their castes and places of origin. It thus responds to that need for uniformity which all new nations feel if they are to become states in the full sense of that word. It remains to be seen if this new set of laws, emanating from an élite, will gain the fullest response from a society which still lives within traditional frameworks, or whether it will live on outside society, in the same way as the law of the *śāstras* did but on a different level, where the unity resolves itself into aspirations which are no longer religious but political.[13]

We must turn, now, to Further India, and particularly towards the Hinduised states of the former Indo-China, if we wish to watch a continuous development of the classical Hindu system which relied for its renewal upon no resources but its own. True, the ambience was new. It was that of Hīnayāna Buddhism, the *theravāda,* of which the Mons or people of Pegu were the zealous propagandists in South East Asia. In the lands of Sanskrit culture, Cambodia and Champā, it seems that the Hindu system was followed in its originial purity, even though it had to undergo some modifications as a result of the difference of environment. But,

[13]Derrett, *Critique of Modern Hindu Law* (Bombay, Tripathi, 1970).

so far as we can discover from epigraphy, the official doctrine conformed to Hindu orthodoxy.[14]

The appearance at the Pagan epoch in Burma of a literature composed locally in Pāli by Mon monks on the model of the *dharma-śāstras* in Sanskrit marks, on the other hand, the first stage of an evolution which went on until it was exhausted.[15] The *dhammasattha,* of which the Code of Wāgarū gives us an idea, in spite of the late date of the version which has come down to us, has managed to hazard the introduction or perhaps rather the conservation of the Hindu system in environments practically cut off from India and entirely won for the Buddhist faith. That their authors were inspired by Indian *śāstras* is beyond doubt, for it is evidenced by their classification of contentious matters into 18 types, corresponding to the 18 titles of litigation in the *smṛtis*. But, if they were content to "de-Brahminise" their model and to adapt its rules to the manners and customs of the public for whom they wrote, manners and customs very different from those of Indian society which appears through the *dharma-śāstras,* they only ended by making customals or handbooks of law. To give to them the authority which the *dharma-śāstras* enjoyed, they would have had to attach the rules to a supernatural source like the Veda. The difficulty arose from the fact that the Buddhist religion, the religion of "renouncers", did not contain any revelation on the social order. The canonical legend of Mahāsammata, the world's first king, chosen by his people to put an end to discord,[16] alone offered elements of a solution. It must have been tempting to attribute the precepts of the *dhammasatthas* to Mahāsammata, who turned out to be a Bodhisattva. But Mahāsammata had to remain above all the model of the just king and could only be the interpreter of the law. Thus our authors, seizing upon the legend, completed it conveniently. They gave Mahāsammata a counsellor, the hermit Manu, who plays in his court the role which the *prāḍvivāka* does in the *dharma-śāstras*. They imagined that that Sage was raised into the celestial regions and reached the *cakkavāla,* the wall which surrounds the world and which bears, carved in letters high as a bull, the law which rules it. It is this very text of the law which, rehearsed from memory by the hermit Manu, is set down in the *dhamma-satthas*.

The fable seems to us naive enough. Yet, after all, it is not more so

[14]Lingat, 'L'influence juridique de l'Inde au Champâ et au Cambodge d'apres l'épigraphie', *J.A.*, 1949, 273–290.

[15]What follows is a brief résumé of my article, 'La conception du droit dans l'Indochine hinayâniste', *B.E.F.E.O.*, 1951, 165–87. See also S.P. Khetarpal, 'Debt of Burmese jurists to Hindu law', *Jaipur Law J.*, 8 (1968), 6–25. [trs.]

[16]*Dīgha Nikāya*, XXVII, Agañña Suttanta (Rhys Davids, *Dialogues of the Buddha* III, 77–94). On this legend and its relations with Indian traditions see L. Dumont, 'Kingship in ancient India', *Contributions to Indian Sociology*, 6 (The Hague) (1962), 61–4. J.W. Spellman, *Political Theory of Ancient India* (Oxford, 1964), 22.

than that which places the precepts of the *dharma-śāstras* in the mouths of mythical personages. It evidences at least as great an ingenuity as theirs, for it achieves an exact transposition of the Hindu system to Buddhist environments. It is clear that the hermit Manu has no more than the name in common with the Manu of the *smṛti*, even though some *dhammasatthas* make out of him a son of Brahmā, reincarnated in the person of a hermit. But it is also evident that the name was not chosen at random. For the Buddhists, the law of Manu is really the law of the phenomenal world, that which governs laymen. It is thenceforward cut from its religious roots, independent of the law which the Buddha came to teach to the world. It reveals to men the conditions of social welfare, while the law of the Buddha reveals to them the conditions of salvation. Despite this dichotomy, which has remained one of the characteristic traits of Hīnayānist society, the law of the *dhammasatthas*, like the law of the *śāstras*, transcends the world which it rules. It also is bound to the cosmic order and is therefore free from the will of men, who will live in peace only so long as they obey its precepts. A king like Mahāsammata himself could introduce no changes into it, and his role is confined to insuring that it is respected.

Of course the authors of the *dhammasatthas*, like those of the *dharma-śāstras*, took a substantial number of the rules which they attributed to Manu from the facts of contemporary custom. But thereby they certified its authority. Likewise thereby they condemned or deprived of all power of expansion those usages which they did not retain, thus pursuing, though in a different spirit, the work of moral reform which the *dharmaśāstra* writers undertook in Indian society. In environments which were still corroded and bound down by their customs, they also introduced a kind of ideal image of their society in which, through frameworks borrowed from Indian learning, their legal life could be defined and organised.

The Burmans were for a long time tributary to the Mons in the domain of law as in the remainder of the cultural sphere. Thus the *dhammasatthas* appeared to them as the *dharma-śāstras* did to the Hindus, as the expression of a law which was universal so far as concerned the Buddhist universe, and from which it was natural that they should profit. But little by little the Mon or Pāli *dhammasatthas* were melted, absorbed in a prolix production, written most frequently in the vernacular, in which local traditions held a greater and greater place, and where borrowings from the Buddhist scriptures became more and more numerous. In this new guise the *dhammasatthas* lost their original nature. All repeat and embellish the story of the marvellous discovery of the text of the law, and base their precepts on the revelation of the hermit Manu. This literature is abundant. As in India, the genre has proliferated. There is a list enumerating a hundred *dhammasatthas* composed in Burma, and forty of them still exist. Like the *dharma-śāstras,* their chronological succession is uncertain : they copy each other, and also complete and differ from each other. It is from the totality of them that the rule of law must be extracted. However, in contrast to the Indian position, the commentaries are mixed with the texts and do not appear as independent works until the modern period, when the form of doctrinal treatises emerges. A "digest" has however been compiled at the request of the British. But up to our own time the *dhammasatthas* have remained the only written law on all questions relating to the personal law of Burmese Buddhists, even though a project of codification has recently been mooted. The Burman kings, like the British authorities, took care not to legislate in the sphere of the law of Manu and confined themselves to their role as judges. As in the Hindu system, the precepts of the *dhammasatthas,* while certainly being authoritative, are not imperative in the manner of the rules of our codes. They give way before a regularly proved custom. After the British conquest, the rule of *stare decisis* has undermined traditional concepts in attributing to the judicial decision the status of a legal rule, but this injury has not had the significance which it had in India.

The Indian conception was adapted by the Mon and Buddhist peoples and lived on thereafter only upon its own resources. But in Siam it found its limits. The collection of ancient laws of the Ayuthia period has come down to us framed in a *dhammasattha* which provides it at once with a preface and a table of contents. This *dhammasattha,* originally written in Pāli, purports to be of Mon origin. It seems to have been known to the Thai peoples settled in the Ménam basin before the foundation of the Ayuthia kingdom (1350), and it is possible that within its surviving version many works of the same type have been fused. However that may be, it is in many respects very close to the Code of Wāgarū. We find there king Mahāsammata and his minister Manu (called Manosāra), and the text is given by rehearsal on Manu's part from what he read on the wall which surrounds the world. But it marks an important piece of progress in juridical technique by means of the new divisions and distinctions which it introduces. For example, contentious matters, instead of being reduced to the classical 18 titles of law, are classified under 39 rubrics, 10 being rules of procedure and 29 rules of substantive law.[17] But the most important novelty is the appearance, beside these fundamental rules *(mūla-attha),* of a new source of law, constituted by the "ramifications of litigation" *(sākha-attha),* i.e. rules derived from the first. The fundamental rules are those which the hermit Manu

[17]This subdivision of litigation corresponds to the distinction made in certain Sanskrit treatises between the *mātṛkā* and the *vivāda-padas.*

(or Manosāra) read on the *cakkavāla* and are found set out in the *dhammasattha*. They are the expression of the eternal law which should inspire Mahāsammata and future kings when giving justice to their subjects. As for the derivative rules, these resulted, in course of time, from the application by Mahāsammata and his successors of the principles laid down in the *dhammasattha*. They could not be actually enumerated, although the fundamental rules are necessarily limited in number.

Thus the Siamese *dhammasattha* recognised in advance that there may be a legal value in decisions passed by kings in conformity with its precepts. A procedure is expressly provided for the transformation of a royal decision into a rule of law. They must be stripped of the features which gave rise to them, and reduced in abstract terms to the concise form of the precepts of the law. They could then be added to the text of the *dhammasattha* itself under the relevant rubric. It seems that such a procedure was actually followed during the Ayuthia period at every change in the reign, when it was entrusted to members of the High Court of Justice, composed principally of Brahmins versed in the science of law. The last corpus of the old Siamese laws that has come down to us presents, therefore, a partially finished codification, in which the derivative rules of law, forming as many articles, are classified under the various rubrics of the *dhammasattha*, after a brief account of the fundamental rules.

The passage from *dharma* to court-law is found to have been perfectly realised. The Siamese code, in its *dharmmasattha* frame, expressed a positive law which was applicable immediately. The royal will, in its capacity as interpreter of the law, developed from the simple order which it was into a true legislation, even though, at least in theory, the king had no legislative power properly speaking. The law he laid down had authority only when it conformed to the *dhammasattha* precepts, but that authority was now furnished with coercive power which belonged to none but the king. The fusion between the two constituent elements of court-law was completed.

Truly speaking, this evolution of the Hindu system towards a system having a legislative aspect was already suggested by the *dharma-śāstras* themselves, insistently warning the king that a judgment is not just unless it is given in conformity with the precepts of the *śāstras*. Certainly in the course of the Muslim period, judicial precedents, in so far as they expressed custom, played an important role in the local courts (which does not mean to say that they were always recorded).[18] As for the ancient period, only the Buddhist literature alludes to collections of judgments intended to facilitate the work of the judiciary. In the *Tuṇḍila-jātaka* (VI.2.3) and the *Tesakuṇa-jātaka* (XVIII.1) the Bodhi-

[18]Guṇe, *op. cit.*, 68; U.C. Sarkār, *op. cit.*, 251.

sattva compiles a collection of his judgments after the death of the king of Benares and exhorts the subjects of the kingdom to consult it in the disposal of their disputes. But one must note that these judgments were not given by the king as an application of a preexisting law, but by the Bodhisattva himself, guided by his innate sense of justice. The society depicted is a society without written law, living solely under its customs, in fact far removed in this respect from the picture of Indian society which the *smṛtis* give us. The stories which appear in the *Mahā-Ummaga-jātaka* (XXII.9) of sentences passed by the future Buddha throw light on the usefulness which one might expect of such compilations in a real society, assuming that the *jātakas* (the ages of which are not known) alluded to historical facts.

Mahosatha whilst still a child astonishes the world by his ability to solve difficult cases. The king of Mithilā, before inviting him to visit, submits to him a certain number of tests, from which he extricates himself adroitly. If we leave aside the edifying character which their authors attached above all to these stories, we find that their principal function is to highlight the ingenuity of the Bodhisattva when faced with complicated cases, in establishing the true facts, testing the veracity of the parties, and confounding the culprit by unexpected tricks. In other words, they aim to teach judges not how to apply the law, but the art, often difficult enough, of discerning the true from the false and of obtaining an exact knowledge of the facts of the case. In this way they assist and illustrate the teaching of the *smṛtis* which exhort the king not to judge lightly (*Yāj.*, II.19), and to pay careful attention to the presumptions of fact (*M.*, VIII.44), not to speak of indirect methods which may be utilised in criminal matters. But these are only the necessary qualities of perspecacity which they seek to develop in the judge, qualities needful if one is to try the case well. When at length the facts are established it remains to find out under which rule of the *śāstras* they will fall. Then another intelligence is needed, that of the interpreter.[19] There is every reason to think that, if the Hindus had ever effectively compiled collections of "judgments", it would have been the originality and subtlety of the means employed to justify the decision which would have guided their choice, and not the correctness of the juridical argumentation.

As a matter of fact the stories in the Jātaka have given rise to a literary genre which is extremely widespread throughout Southeast Asia and particularly in Burma, that of the law tale.[20] In Burma, collections of

[19]This division of judicial work between the magistrate-inquisitor and the magistrate who is the judge is clearly marked in the ancient Siamese procedure, of which it is one of the most original characteristics. Lingat, 'La preuve dans l'ancien droit siamois', *Recueils de la Société Jean Bodin*, XVIII, *La Preuve* (Brussels, 1964), 397–418.

[20]Maung Htin Aung, *Burmese Law Tales* (London, 1962).

judgments *(pyat-hton)* attributed to various Bodhisattvas (the names of Mahosatha, Vidhura, Mahātuṇḍila occur) or to legendary personages, have been published to a great number (one lists puts them at 35). They are evidently fictitious judgments in which the writers display their imagination and their ingenuity. But there are some serious works amongst these collections. They are inspired by the Buddhist faith and effort is made to use the Pāli scriptures to complete the law of Manu or to show its conformity with the law of Buddha. This literature developed parallel to that of the *dhammasatthas* and certainly exerted some influence on the later ones of that class. But these works were not a source of law and can by no means be considered as if they were collections of precedents. They are simply intended to teach the art of sound judgement to the king, whence the name of *rāja-sattha* is given to them. They express the science of kingship *par excellence,* that which teaches the king to pass equitable judgments. Further, the *rāja-satthas* not only complete the *dhammasatthas*; they also reinforce their authority by appealing to Buddhist sources. With the coming of Buddhism, the king is no longer the mere protector of his subjects. He is also and above all the protector of the religion and the defender of morality. Let him become, in turn, interpreter of the precepts of the *dhammasattha,* and his judgments will have the double sanctity of the secular law and the religious law, and will serve as a model to the kings of the future. The *Manu Kyé*, a compilation of Burmese *dhammasatthas* of the middle of the eighteenth century, enjoins upon judges, as from the mouth of Manu, to follow "the decisions of the ancient kings, embryos of Buddha, and those which have been passed in our days in conformity with the precepts of the *dhammasattha"*.[21] Thus, if the *rāja-sattha* continues to remain distinct from the *dhammasattha,* the Buddhist conception of the royal function has led writers to formulae which contain the germ of the legislative system of modern times whilst maintaining the essentials of the Hindu system.

[21] D. Richardson, *The Damathat or the Laws of Menoo* (Rangoon, 1874), 151.

APPENDIX BY THE TRANSLATOR

M. LINGAT rightly commented on the embarrassment we suffer because we have so little contemporary information upon how the *dharmaśāstra* was used. Very recently two extremely interesting inscriptions came to light, which go a long way to resolve some, though not all our doubts. Stone inscription No. 558 of 1904 of the South Indian epigraphical collection, an inscription at Tiruvārūr, Nāgapaṭṭanam Tāluk, Tanjore district, which can be dated epigraphically in the twelfth century, and No. 479 of 1908 at Uyyakoṇḍān Tirumalai in Trichinopoly district are concerned with the same subject, namely the status and caste functions of the Kammālas, who were admitted to correspond to the Sanskrit designation Rathakāras. The problem, which stemmed from an ambiguity in the texts of Yājñavalkya and other Vedic and *smṛti* sources, was submitted to two committees of Brahmins for their decision. The first inscription has been published (No. 603 of South Indian Inscriptions, vol. XVII [1964]) and we find that the sources are quoted *in extenso*, in a few cases with a Tamil translation, and with a short commentary giving their effect. A copy of No. 479 of 1908 was kindly provided by the Chief Epigraphist, Archaeological Survey of India. It appears to belong to A.D. 1118, and cites Kauṭilya, while several of the *smṛti* sources used in No. 558 of 1904 are quoted, so that the two inscriptions are to that extent alike in style as well as subject-matter.

Amongst *smṛti* sources Gautama, Nārada and Yājñavalkya are referred to. Śaṅkha is quoted, and so is Yājñavalkya in a form differing from the well-known printed text. The commentator on Gautama called Maskari is quoted in No. 558 (but under the name Maskara [sic]). An unknown verse commentary on Gautama is quoted. The Brāhma-purāṇa is cited but not quoted. Amongst religious works there appear the Pañcarātra, at least one Vaikhānasa work, and the Bhīma-saṃhitā. Amongst Śaiva architectural works (quoted in No. 558 alongside Vaishṇava treatises) there appear the *āgamas* known as Kāraṇa, Yogaja and Suprabheda. The Āgastya-vāstu-śāstra is quoted, also a Vāstu-vidyā differing from the printed text, and a Sārasvatīya. The remaining works quoted have not yet been identified: Prapañcottara-vidyā-sūtra, Laksaṇa-pramāṇa, Prapañca-tantra, Pañcarātra-kāpiñjala, and Parama-puruṣa-saṃhitā. The Viśvakarmīya, which also is quoted, is evidently a leading text on architecture.

The wealth of authority, certified separately by two groups of experts, led comfortably to the satisfactory conclusion that of the *two* types of Rathakāras, the *anulomas,* born of a respectable (hypergamic) mixture of twice-born castes, were entitled to Vedic initiation, though without all the consequences which followed in the three twice-born *varṇas*; whereas the *pratiloma* Rathakāras were assigned exclusively to menial tasks.

The whole affair shows not merely that skilled artisans, obliged to learn esoteric lore in order to function in the various branches of domestic and public architecture, were wealthy and important enough to face a challenge to their status and perhaps to challenge, themselves, the status of Brahmins, but that at such a juncture they could count on learned Brahmins to solve the problem with the aid of a mixture of śāstric, religious, and architectural written sources, upon which they relied literally, but with a commentary of their own authentication. Such instances dispose at once of the extreme notion, once commonly heard, that śāstric texts never played a practical role, or that if they did, they did so only when it pleased some individuals to invoke them.[1]

[1]Derrett, 'Two inscriptions concerning the status of Kammālas and the application of the dharmaśāstra', *Prof. K.A. Nilakanta Sastri 80th Birthday Felicitation Volume* (Madras, 1971), 32–55. On Rathakāras see also U.N. Ghoshāl at *Indian Culture*, XIV (1947), 26–7.

BIBLIOGRAPHY[1]

TEXTS AND TRANSLATIONS

Dharmasūtras

Āpastamba : ed. G. Bühler, Bombay Skt. Ser., 3rd ed., Poona, 1932; with the comm. of Haradatta: ed. A. Mahādeva Śāstrī and R.K. Raṅgācārya, Bibl. Sansk., Mysore, 1898; ed. A.C. and A.R. Śāstrī, Chowkhambā Sansk. Ser., Benares, 1932; trans. G. Bühler, *S.B.E.*, II, Oxford, 1897.

Baudhāyana : ed. E. Hultzsch, 2nd ed., Leipzig, 1922; with the comm. of Govindasvāmin: ed. L. Śrīnivāsācārya, Bibl. Sansk., Mysore, 1907; ed. A.C. Śāstrī, Chowkhambā Sansk. Ser., Benares, 1934; trans. G. Bühler, *S.B.E.*, XIV, Oxford, 1882.

Gautama : ed. A.F. Stenzler, London, 1876; with the comm. of Maskarin: ed. L. Śrīnivāsācārya, Bibil. Sansk., Mysore, 1917; with the comm. of Haradatta: ed. G. Śāstrī, Ānandāśrama Skt. Ser., Poona, 1931; trans. G. Bühler, *S.B.E.*, II, 1897.

Śaṅkha-Likhita : fragments assembled by P.V. Kāṇe, *Annals Bhandarkar Or. Res. Inst.*, Poona, 1926.

Sumantu : frag. ed. T.R. Chintamani, *Journal of Oriental Research* (Madras) 8 (1934), 75–88.

Vaikānasa-dharma-praśna : ed. T. Gaṇapati Śāstrī, Trivandrum Sansk. Ser., 1913. See also Caland's text (1927) and trans. (1929) of the *Vaikhānasa-smārta-sutra* in the Bibl. Ind. series.

Vasiṣṭha : ed. A.A. Führer, Bombay Skt. Ser. 3rd edn., Poona, 1930; trans. G. Bühler, *S.B.E.*, XIV, Oxford, 1882.

Viṣṇu : ed. J. Jolly. Bibl. Ind., Calcutta, 1881; with the comm. of Nandapaṇḍita: ed. V. Kṛṣṇamācārya. Adyar Library Ser., Adyar, 1964; trans. J. Jolly, *S.B.E.*, VII, Oxford, 1880.

Dharmaśāstras

Aṅgiras : *Āṅgirasa-smṛti*, collected and reconstructed from citations in digests at *Adyar Library Bulletin*, supplements to vols. XV–XVII (1951–53).

Bṛhaspati : ed. K.V. Raṅgaswāmī Aiyaṅgār, Gaekwad's Or. Ser., Baroda, 1941; trans. J. Jolly, *S.B.E.*, XXXIII, Oxford, 1889.

[1]This bibliography has been revised by the translator.

Caturviṃśati-mata : with the comm. of Bhaṭṭoji Dīkṣita : ed. Devidatta Parājuli, Benares Skt. Ser., 1907–8.

Hārīta : ed. and trans. from citations in digests by J. Jolly at *Abhandlungen der Königl. Bayerischen Akademie der Wissenschaften,* philos.—philol. Classe, 18 (1890), pt. 2, 505–24.

Kātyāyana : ed. and trans. P.V. Kāṇe, Poona, 1933.

Manu : ed. V.N. Mandlik, Bombay, 1886; with the comm. of Kullūka : ed. Jīvānanda Vidyāsāgara, Calcutta, 1874; ed. Vāsudeva L. Panśīkar, Bombay, 1920 (6th edn.); ed. Gopāla Śāstrī Nene, Benares, 1935; with the comm. of Medhātithi : ed. J.R. Ghārpure, *Hindu Law Texts Ser.,* Bombay, 1920; ed. Gaṅgānātha Jhā, Bibl. Ind., Calcutta 1932–9; trans. A. Loiseleur-Deslongchamps, Paris, 1833; A.C. Burnell and E.W. Hopkins, London, 1884; G. Bühler, *S.B.E.,* XXV, Oxford, 1886; G. Strehly, Paris, 1893; G. Jhā (with the comm. of Medhātithi), Calcutta, 1920–9. Russian trans. : S.D. Elmanovich, St. Petersburg, 1913. Kullūka : ed. B. Goswami, *Manusamhita I, II,* Calcutta, 1915.

Nārada : ed. J. Jolly (with the comm. of Asahāya), Bibl. Ind., Calcutta, 1885; ed. K. Sāmbaśiva Śāstrī (with the comm. of Bhavasvāmin), Trivandrum Skt. Ser., 1929; ed. Nārāyaṇcandra Smṛtitīrtha (with a Bengali trans.), Sanskrit College Res. Ser. 38, Calcutta, 1966; trans. J. Jolly, *S.B.E.,* XXXIII, Oxford, 1889.

Parāśara : with the comm. of Mādhava : ed. C. Tarkālaṅkāra, Bibl. Ind., Calcutta, 1890–9; ed. V.S. Islāmpurkar, Bombay Skt. Ser., 1893–1919; trans. Kṛṣṇakamal Bhaṭṭācārya, Bibl. Ind., Calcutta, 1887.

Pitāmaha : fragments ed. Manzini, *Atti del Reale Istituto Veneto de Scienze, Lettere, ed Arti,* vol. 63, pt. 2; ed. K. Scriba, Leipzig, 1902.

Yājñavalkya : ed. and trans. A.F. Stenzler, Berlin/London, 1849; ed. and trans. V.N. Mandlik, Bombay, 1880; with the comm. of Aparārka : ed. Hari Nārāyaṇ Āpte, Ānandāśrama Skt. Ser., Poona, 1903–4; with the comm. of Vijñāneśvara : ed. W.L. Panśīkar, Nirṇayasāgara, Bombay, 4th edn., 1936; ed. J.R. Ghārpure, *Hindu Law Text Ser.,* Bombay, 1914; ed. N.S.K. Sāhityācārya, Chowkhambā Skt. Ser., Benares, 1930; with the comm. of Viśvarūpa : ed. T. Gaṇapati Śāstrī, Trivandrum Skt. Ser., 1922–4; with the comm. of Śūlapāṇi : ed. J.R. Ghārpure, *Hindu Law Texts Ser.,* Bombay, 1939; with the comm. of Mitra-miśra : ed. N.S. Khiste, Chowkhambā Skt. Ser., Benares, 1924–30; trans. J.R. Ghārpure (with the commentaries of Vijñāneśvara, Mitra-miśra and Śūlapāṇi), *Hindu Law Texts,* Bombay, 1936–44. Commentaries on the *Mitākṣarā* of Vijñāneśvara : *Bālaṃbhaṭṭi,* ed. (*Vyavahāra* section) Nityānand Paṇt Parvatīya, Chowkhambā Skt. Ser., Benares, 1914; ed. J.R. Ghārpure, *Hindu Law Texts,* Bombay, 1914–24; ed. S.S. Setlur, Madras, 1912. *Subodhini,* ed. and trans. J.R. Gharpure, *Hindu Law Texts,* Bombay, 1914 and 1930 [*Mitākṣarā* alone, Bombay, 1920]; ed. S.S. Setlur, Madras, 1912. G.C. Tarkālaṅkār, *The Mitakshara* (Calcutta, 1871) contains his trans. of the Loans section and W.H. Macnaghten's trans. of the Administration of Justice section of Vijñāneśvara's *Mitākṣarā*. The *Vyavahāra* section, ed., with Eng. and Bengali trans. and *Mitākṣarā*, S. Ray, Calcutta, 1964.

Vyāsa : ed. Batakṛishṇa Ghosh, *Indian Culture* (Calcutta) IX (1942–3), 65–98.

Collections of Various Smṛtis : *Dharmaśāstrasaṅgraha* : ed. Jīvānanda Vidyāsāgara, Sarasvatī Press, Calcutta, 1876. Contains : Atri (Vṛddha and Laghu), Viṣṇu, Hārīta (Vṛddha and Laghu), Yājñavalkya; Uśanas, Aṅgiras, Yama, Āpastamba *(smṛti)*, Saṃvarta, Kātyāyana (Karmapradīpa), Bṛhaspati *(smṛti)*, Parāśara (Bṛhat). Vyāsa, Śaṅkha *(smṛti)*, Likhita *(smṛti)*, Dakṣa, Gautama, Śātātapa (Karmavipāka), and Vasiṣṭha, *Smṛtināṃ samuccaya*, ed. V. Ganeśa Āpṭe. Ānandāśrama Skt. Ser., Poona, 2nd edn., 1929. Contains : Aṅgiras, Atri, Āpastamba, Uśanas, Gobhila (Karmapradīpa). Dakṣa, Devala, Prajāpati, Yama (also Bṛhat), Bṛhaspati *(smṛti)*, Viṣṇu (Laghu), Śaṅkha (also Laghu), Śātātapa (Vṛddha), Hārīta (Bṛhat and Laghu), Āśvalāyana (Laghu), Likhita *(smṛti)*, Vasiṣṭha, Vyāsa, Śaṅkha-Likhita, Saṃvarta, Baudhāyana. ed. M.N. Dutt, *The Dharma Śāstras*, Calcutta, 1906–8. Contains (text and translation) : Yājñavalkya, Hārīta, Uśanas, Aṅgiras, Yama, Atri, Saṃvarta, Kātyāyana, Bṛhaspati, Dakṣa, Śātātapa, Likhita, Śaṅkha, Gautama, Āpastamba, Vasiṣṭha, Vyāsa, Parāśara, Viṣṇu, Manu.

Digests

Ananta-deva : *Smṛti-kaustubha*, ed. V.L. Panśīkar, Nirṇayasāgara, Bombay, 1909. *Dattaka-dīdhiti*, ed. Bharatcandra Śiromaṇi, Calcutta, 1867. *Rājadharma-kaustubha*, ed. K. Kṛṣṇa Smṛtitīrtha, Gaekwad's Or. Ser., Baroda, 1935.

Caṇḍeśvara : *Vivāda-ratnākara*, ed. Dīnanātha Vidyākaṅkāra, Bibl. Ind., Calcutta, 2nd edn., 1931; trans. G.C. Sarkar and D. Chatterjee, Calcutta, 1899. *Rājanīti-ratnākara*, ed. K.P. Jayaswāl, Patna, 2nd edn., 1936.

Dalapati : *Nṛsiṃha-prasāda, Vyavahāra-sāra*, ed. V.S. Tillu, Sarasvatī Bhavan Texts Ser., Benares, 1934.

Devanna-bhaṭṭa[2] : *Smṛticandrikā*, ed. L. Śrīnivāsācārya, Bibl. Sansk., Mysore, 1914–21; ed. J.R. Ghārpure, *Hindu Law Texts*, Bombay, 1919; trans. J.R. Ghārpure, *Hindu Law Texts*, Bombay, 1946–50.

[2]The spelling 'Devanna' usual in MSS. would agree with Andhra provenance : M. Mayrhofer, 'Zum Namen Sāyaṇa', *Anzeiger der phil.-hist. Kl., Oesterreichische Akademie der Wissenschaften*, 108 (1971), 79ff., 81 n. 15.

Halāyudha : *see* L. Rocher, *Journal of the Oriental Institute* (Baroda) III, no. 4 (1954), 328–44; IV, no. 1 (1954), 13–32.

Hemādri : *Caturvarga-cintāmaṇi,* ed. Bharatcandra Śiromaṇi, P.N. Tarkabhūṣaṇa, etc., Bibl. Ind., Calcutta, 1873–1911.

Jīmūtavāhana : *Dāyabhāga,* ed. Bharatcandra Śiromaṇi (with the comm. of Raghunandana), Calcutta, 1863–4; ed. Jīvānanda Vidyāsāgara, Calcutta, 1893; trans. Colebrooke, Madras, 1864 (and earlier editions of the *Two Treatises*). *Vyavahāra-mātṛkā,*[3] ed. A. Mookerjee, Calcutta, 1912. *Kāla-viveka,* ed. Pramathanātha Tarkabhūṣaṇa, Bibl. Ind., Calcutta, 1905.

Kamalākara-bhaṭṭa : *Nirṇaya-sindhu,* ed. Kṛṣṇa-śāstrin Navate, Nirṇayasāgara, Bombay, 2nd edn., 1905; ed. Gopāla Śāstrin Nene, Chowkhambā Sansk. Ser., Benares, 1930–56. *Śūdra-kamalākara,* ed. Sāvajī Dādāji, Nirṇayasāgara, Bombay, 1880. *Vivāda-tāṇḍava,* ed. Maṇilāla Nabhubhāī Dvivedin, Lakṣmī Vilās Press, Baroda, 1901; ed. H.N. Chattopadhyaya in *Our Heritage,* 7–13 (1959–65).

Kāśīnātha Upādhyaya : *Dharma-sindhu,* ed. Bāpu-śāstrin Moghe, Nirṇayasāgara, Bombay, 6th edn., 1936; trans. in *Mélanges, Ann. Guimet* (1884), 1ff., 150ff., 225ff.

Kubera : *Dattaka-candrikā,* ed. Yajñeśvara Bhaṭṭācārya (with the comm. of Bharatacandra Śiromaṇi), Calcutta, 1885 (2nd edn.); trans. Sutherland, Calcutta, 1821; G. Orianne, Paris, 1844.

Lakṣmaṇa-śāstrī Joshī : *Dharma-kośa,* Wai, 1937–41.

Lakṣmīdhara : *Kṛtyakalpataru,* ed. K.V. Raṅgasvāmī Aiyaṅgār, Gaekwad's Or. Ser., Baroda, 1941–53.

Madana-siṃha : *Madana-ratna-pradīpa* : *Vyavahāra-viveka-uddyota* ed. P.V. Kāṇe, Gaṅgā Or. Ser., Bikaner (Anup Skt. Lib.), 1948.

Misaru-miśra : *Vivāda-candra,* ed. Priyanāth Mitra, Vidyāpati Press, Calcutta, 1931; also Vidyā Vīlās Press, Patna, 1931.

Mitra-miśra : *Vīramitrodaya,* ed. Jīvānanda Vidyāsāgara (*Vyavahāra-prakāśa* only), Calcutta, 1873; ed. V.P. Bhāndārī, Chowkhambā Skt. Ser., Benares, 1932–7; ed. and trans. (in part), G.C. Sarkar Śāstrī, Calcutta, 1879.

Nanda-paṇḍita : *Dattaka-mimāṃsā,* ed. Yajñeśvara Bhaṭṭācārya (with the comm. of Bharatachandra Śiromaṇi), Calcutta, 2nd edn., 1885; ed. Śaṅkara Śāstrī Mārulkar, Ānandāśrama Skt. Ser., Poona, 1954; trans. Sutherland, Calcutta, 1821.

Nīlakaṇṭha-bhaṭṭa : *Bhagavanta-bhāskara,* ed. J.R. Ghārpure, *Hindu Law Texts,* Bombay, 1921–7. *Vyavahāra-mayūkha,* ed. and trans. V.N. Mandlik, Bombay, 1880; ed. P.V. Kāṇe, Bombay Skt. Ser., Poona, 1926; trans. Borradaile, Surat, 1827; J.R. Ghārpure, *Hindu Law Texts,* Bombay, 1921; P.V. Kāṇe and S.G. Patawardhan, Bombay, 1933.

[3]See L. Rocher at *Journal of the Oriental Institute* (Baroda), III, no. 2 (1953), 134–46.

Pratāpa-rudra : *Sarasvatī-vilāsa,* ed. R. Shāma Shāstry (Śāstrī) (*Vyavahāra-kāṇḍa* only), Bibl. Sansk., Mysore, 1927; ed. and trans. (*Dāyavibhāga* portion), T. Foulkes, London, 1881.

Pṛthvīcandra : *Pṛthvīcandrodaya, Vyavahāra-prakāśa,* Pt. I, ed., J.H. Dave, Bhāratīya Vidyā Ser., Bombay, 1962.

Raghunandana : *Smṛti-tattva,* ed., Jīvānanda Vidyāsāgara, Calcutta, 1895. *Dāya-tattva,* ed. and trans. G.C. Sarkar, Calcutta, 1904. *Udvāha-tattva,* ed. H.N. Chatterjee, Skt. College Res. Ser., Calcutta, 1963.

Ratnākara : *Jayasiṃha-kalpadruma,* ed. Harinārāyaṇa Śarman, Bombay, 1903.

Śaṅkara-bhaṭṭa : *Dharma-dvaita-nirṇaya,* ed., J.R. Ghārpure, *Hindu Law Texts,* Bombay, 1943.

Śrī Kṛṣṇa Tarkālaṅkāra : *Dāyakrama-saṅgraha,* ed. Nīlakamala Vidyānidhi, Calcutta, 1930; trans., P.M. Wynch, Calcutta, 1818; G. Orianne, Pondicherry, 1843.

Śūlapāṇi : *Prāyaścitta-viveka,* ed., Jīvānanda Vidyāsāgara, 1893. *Saṃbandha-viveka,* ed. J.B. Chaudhuri, Calcutta, 1942. *Śrāddha-viveka,* ed., Śrī Cārukṛṣṇa Darśanācārya, Calcutta, 1939.

Toḍar Mal : *Toḍarānanda,* ed., P.L. Vaidya, Gaṅgā Or. Ser., Bikaner, 1948.

Vācaspati Miśra : *Vivāda-cintāmaṇi,* ed. R.C. Vidyāvāgīśa, Calcutta, 1837; ed. L. Jhā, Patna, 1937; trans. P.K. Tagore, Calcutta, 1863; G. Jhā, Gaekwad's Or. Ser., Baroda, 1942. *Vyavahāra-cintāmaṇi,* ed. and trans. L. Rocher, Ghent, 1956.

Vaidyanātha Dīkṣita : *Smṛti-muktāphala,* ed. J.R. Ghārpure, *Hindu Law Texts,* Bombay, 1937–40.

Varadarāja : *Vyavahāra-nirṇaya,* ed., K.V. Raṅgaswāmī Aiyaṅgār and A.N. Kṛishṇa Aiyaṅgār, Adyar, 1942; trans. (*Dāyabhāga* portion only) A.C. Burnell, Mangalore, 1872.

Viśveśvara-bhaṭṭa : *Madana-pārijāta,* ed. Madhusūdana Smṛtiratna, Bibl. Ind., Calcutta, 1893.

Collections of Hindu Law Books

I. For copious extracts in the original Sanskrit see J.C. Ghose, *Principles of Hindu Law* (3rd edn., below).

II. For entire texts translated see :

Stokes, W : *Hindu Law Books,* Madras, 1865. It contains: *Vyavahāra-mayūkha,* trans. Borradaile; *Dāyabhāga,* trans. Colebrooke; *Mitākṣarā,* Inheritance portion trans. Colebrooke; *Dāyakrama-saṅgraha,* trans. Wynch; *Dattaka-mimāṃsā* and *Dattaka-candrikā,* trans. Sutherland.

Dutt, Manmatha Nath : *The Dharma Sastra or the Hindu Law Codes . . .,* Calcutta, 1908 (3 vols. 1500 pp.).

Setlur, S : *Hindu Law Books on Inheritance*, Madras, 1911. It contains : Vol. 1 : *Mitākṣarā, Vyavahāra-mayūkha, Sarasvatī-vilāsa, Smṛti-candrikā, Vyavahāra-mayukha, Dattaka-mimāṃsā, Dattaka-candrikā.* Vol. 2 : *Dāyabhāga, Dāyakrama-saṅgraha, Vivāda-ratnākara, Vivāda-cintāmaṇi, Vīramitrodaya, Dāyatattva, Madana-pārijāta,* with an appendix containing extracts on sapiṇḍaship from the following works : *Mitākṣarā, Smṛti-muktāphala, Parāśara-mādhavīya, Dharma-sindhu, Saṃskāra-kaustubha, Saṃskāra-mayūkha, Saṃskāra-bhāskara, Madana-pārijāta.*

SECONDARY WORKS

General Works

Aiyangar, K.V. Rangaswami, *Some Aspects of Ancient Indian Polity* (Madras, 1935);

——— *Rājadharma* (Adyar, 1941);

——— *Aspects of the Social and Political System of Manusmṛti* (Lucknow, 1949);

——— *Indian Cameralism* (Adyar, 1949);

——— *Some Aspects of the Hindu View of Life according to Dharmaśāstra* (Baroda, 1952).

Altekar, A.S., *Sources of Hindu Dharma* (Sholapur, 1952);

——— *State and Government in Ancient India,* 3rd edn. (Benares, 1958).

Ayyar, A.S. Nataraja, *Mīmāṃsā Jurisprudence (The Sources of Hindu Law)* (Allahabad, 1952).

Bandyopadhyaya, N.C., *Development of Hindu Polity and Political Theories* (Calcutta, 1927–8).

Bandyopadhyaya, S.C., *Smṛti-śāstre Bāṅgālī* (Calcutta, 1962).

Banerjee, P.N., *Public Administration in Ancient India* (London, 1916).

Bhandarkar, D.R., *Some Aspects of Ancient Hindu Polity* (Madras, 1940).

Cunha Gonçalves, Luís da., *Direito hindú e mahometano* (Coimbra, 1924).

Das, Babu Bhagavan, *The Science of Social Organization, or the Laws of Manu,* 2nd edn. (Madras, 1935).

Derrett, J.D.M., *Hindu Law, Past and Present* (Calcutta, 1957);

——— *Religion, Law and the State in India* (London, 1968).

Dikshitar, V.R. Ramachandra, *Hindu Administrative Institutions* (Madras, 1929).

Drekmeier, Ch., *Kingship and Community in Early India* (Stanford, 1962).

Dutt, B.N., *Studies in Indian Social Polity* (Calcutta, 1944).

Ghosh, B.K., *Hindu Ideal of Life* (Calcutta, 1947).

Ghoshal, U.N., *A History of Hindu Political Theories* (Oxford, 1959).

Gupta, R.K., *Political Thought in the Smṛti Literature* (University of Allahabad, [? c. 1961]).

Jayaswal, K.P., *Manu and Yājñavalkya, a Basic History of Hindu Law* (Calcutta, 1930);

——— *Hindu Polity*, 3rd edn. (Bangalore, 1955).
Jolly, J., *Recht und Sitte* (Strasburg, 1896);
——— *Hindu Law and Custom* (a trans. of the above) (Calcutta, 1928).
Kāṇe, P.V., *History of Dharmaśāstra* (Poona, 1930–62 : 2nd ed., I/1, 1968).
Law, N.N., *Aspects of Ancient Indian Polity* (Oxford, 1921).
Majumdar, R.C., *Corporate Life in Ancient India*, 2nd. edn. (Calcutta, 1922).
Mazzarella, G., *Etnologia analitica dello antico diritto indiano* (Catania, 1913–38).
Mees, G.H., *Dharma and Society* (The Hague, 1935).
Mookerji, R.K., *Local Government in Ancient India*, 2nd edn. (Oxford, 1920).
Motwani, K., *Manu : a Study in Hindu Social Theory* (Madras, 1934).
Pargiter, F.E., *Ancient Indian Historical Tradition* (London, 1922).
Prabhu, P.N., *Hindu Social Organization*, 2nd edn. (Bombay, 1954).
Prasad, Beni, *Theory of Government in Ancient India (Post Vedic)* (Allahabad, 1927);
——— The State in Ancient India (Allahabad, 1928).
Rankin, Sir G.C., *Background to Indian Law* (Cambridge, 1946).
Raychaudhury, H.C., *Political History of Ancient India*, 5th edn. (Calcutta, 1950).
Ruben, W., *Die gesellschaftliche Entwicklung im alten Indien. II. Die Entwicklung von Staat und Recht* (Berlin, 1968).
Sankararama Sastri, C., *Fictions in the Development of the Hindu Law Texts* (Madras, 1926).
Sarkar, B.K., *Political Institutions and Theories of the Hindus* (Leipzig, 1922).
Sarkar, U.C., *Epochs in Hindu Legal History* (Hoshiarpur, 1958).
Sarkar, Kishori Lal, *Mīmānsā Rules of Interpretation* (Calcutta, 1909).
Scharfe, H., *Untersuchungen zur Staatsrechtslehre des Kauṭalya* (Wiesbaden, 1968).
Sen, A.K., *Studies in Hindu Political Thought* (Calcutta, 1926).
Sen, P.N., *The General Principles of Hindu Jurisprudence* (Calcutta, 1918).
Sen-Gupta, N.C., *Sources of Law and Society in Ancient India* (Calcutta, 1914);
——— *The Evolution of Law* (Calcutta, 1926);
——— *Evolution of Ancient Indian Law* (Calcutta/London, 1953).
Sharma, R.S., *Aspects of Political Ideas and Institutions in Ancient India* (Delhi, 1959);
——— *Śūdras in Ancient India* (Delhi, 1958).
Shastry, R.S., *Evolution of Indian Polity* (Calcutta, 1930).
Sinha, H.N., *Sovereignty in Ancient Indian Polity* (London, 1938).
Spellman, J.W., *Political Theory of Ancient India* (Oxford, 1964).

Trautmann, T.R., *Kauṭilya and the Arthaśāstra* (Leiden, Brill, 1971).
Varadachariar, Sir S., *The Hindu Judicial System* (Lucknow, 1946).

Treatises and Textbooks of Law

Bhattacharya, J., *Commentaries on the Hindu Law* (Calcutta, 1909).
Cowell, H., *The Hindu Law ... the Law Administered ... in India* (Calcutta, 1870–1).
Derrett, J.D.M., *Introduction to Modern Hindu Law* (Bombay, 1963); ——— *Critique of Modern Hindu Law* (Bombay, 1970).
Diagou, Gnanou, *Principes de droit hindou* (Pondicherry, 1929–32).
Ghārpure, J.R., *Hindu Law,* 4th edn. (Bombay, 1931).
Ghose, J.C., *The Principles of Hindu Law,* 3rd edn. (Calcutta, 1917–19).
Gupte, S.V., *Hindu Law in British India* (Bombay, 1947, with supplement, 1955).
Heramba, Chatterjee Sastri, *The Law of Debt in Ancient India* (Calcutta, 1971) (a work of exceptional interest).
Jha, Sir Ganganatha, *Hindu Law in its Sources* (Allahabad, 1930–1) (this work concentrates on the ancient source-material with an occasional glance at the current law then moving towards codification).
Macnaghten, F.W., *Considerations on the Hindoo Law as it is Current in Bengal* (Serampore, 1824) (this curious work is the first textbook on the subject).
Mayne, J.D., *Treatise on Hindu Law and Usage,* 11th edn., by N. Chandrasekhara Aiyar (Madras, 1953).
Mulla, D.F., *Principles of Hindu Law,* 13th edn., by S.T. Desai (Bombay, 1966).
Raghavachariar, N.R., *Hindu Law, Principles and Precedents,* 5th edn. (Madras, 1965).
Sarkar Sastri, G.C., *A Treatise on Hindu Law,* 7th edn. (Calcutta, 1933).
Sorg, L., *Introduction à l'ètude du droit hindou* (Pondicherry, 1895); ——— *Traité théorique et pratique de droit hindou* (Pondicherry, 1897).
Strange, Sir T., *Hindu Law,* 4th edn., by J.D. Mayne (Madras, 1864).
Trevelyan, Sir E.J., *Hindu Law,* 3rd edn. (Calcutta, 1929).
West, Sir R., and Bühler, G., *A Digest of the Hindu Law of Inheritance* ..., 3rd, and best, edn. (Bombay, 1884).

Note

Many more bibliographical details, especially with reference to the secondary literature on the ancient periods and the modern law and its problems, may be found in J. Gilissen, ed., *Bibliographical Introduction to Legal History and Ethnology* (Brussels), the following sections :

Rocher, Ludo, Section E/6, *Droit Hindou Ancien* (1965).
Derrett, J.D.M., Section E/8, *The Indian Subcontinent under European Influence* (1970).

GLOSSARY

ācāra : custom, especially religious usage, synonymous with *sadācāra*.
ācārya : Head of a Vedic school, spiritual preceptor.
adharma (when referred to an action) : opposed to the rule of *dharma*.
āraṇyaka : a work of religious instruction, of an esoteric character, belonging to Revelation.
arthavāda : phrases or sentences accessory to a Vedic injunctive formula.
āśrama : stage or phase of life.
bhāṣya : commentary, of a fully exegetical type.
brahmacārin : Brahminical student, belonging to the first stage of life.
brahman : spiritual power, an attribute of the Brahmin.
brāhmaṇa : a Vedic ceremonial treatise.
caraṇa : Vedic school.
caritra : customs or usage, particularly of a secular character.
daṇḍa : chastisement, the right to punish.
daṇḍanīti : the art of punishment, political science, synonymous with *arthaśāstra*.
dattaka : adoptive child (normally a son).
dvija : 'twice-born', a member of the three higher *varṇas* who has undergone Vedic initiation.
gaṇa : body of persons having the same profession in the same locality.
gṛhastha : householder, the second stage of life.
gṛhyasūtra : domestic ritual manual.
guru : spiritual teacher.
jāti : caste or sub-caste.
kalivarjya : practices forbidden in the Kali Age.
kalpasūtra : totality of ritual precepts in manual form.
kāṇḍa : section.
kaṇṭaka : 'thorn', fomenter of discord or disorder.
karma (the law of) : effects of actions upon the actor's destiny.
kṣatra : warlike force, the attribute of the Kṣatriya.
kṣatriya : a member of the second *varṇa*.
kṣetraja : a child born of the union called *niyoga*.
kula : family, family group or unit.
mahāpātaka : grave sin (four or five in all).
mantra : formula recited during a Vedic sacrifice.
mīmāṃsaka : scholar versed in the Mīmāṃsā.

mleccha : barbarian, non-Hindu.
nibandha : a literary work, especially a digest.
niyoga : procreation by one other than the husband when there is no son of the marriage.
nyāya : maxim taken from the Mīmāṃsā; reasoning, logic.
piṇḍa : rice-ball offered during the *śrāddha* ceremony.
prāḍvivāka : presiding judge in the royal court.
prakīrṇaka : (in effect) criminal justice.
pūga : assembly of members of a locality; cf. *gaṇa*.
purāṇa : texts inspired by religion, containing legends, attached to *smṛti*.
rāja, rājyam : king, kingdom.
rājadharma : duties of the king, the royal function.
rājaśāsana : royal order, ordinance.
ṛṣi : inspired bard, mythical sage.
sadācāra : Good Custom (the customs of the good), a source of *dharma*.
saṃhitā : collection of (liturgical) texts.
saṃnyāsin : ascetic, the fourth stage of life.
saṃskāra : purificatory ceremony, sacrament.
śāstra : science; an authoritative treatise in a science.
satī : suicide of a widow on the pyre of her husband or by fire alone (from *satī*, 'a good (wife)').
śiṣṭa : an instructed person, devoted to the application of the rules.
śiṣṭācāra : custom of the *śiṣṭa(s)*, synonymous with *sadācāra*.
śloka : a stanza formed of two lines, each having two groups of eight feet.
smṛti : tradition, a source of *dharma*; a work in which Tradition is communicated.
smṛtikāra : the author of a *smṛti*.
snātaka : a Brahminical student who has completed his studentship.
soma : the juice of a (hallucinating) plant used in certain Vedic sacrifices.
śrāddha : ceremony in commemoration of the dead, in ancestor-worship, figuring also in connection with funerals.
śrautasūtra : manual for Vedic sacrifices.
śreṇi : corporation or guild.
śrotriya : learned Brahmin performing the duties prescribed in *dharma*.
śruti : Revelation, the Vedic texts.
śūdra : a member of the fourth *varṇa*.
sūtra : an instructive phrase cast into an aphoristic style.
sūtrakāra : an author of works in the *sūtra* style.
ṭīkā : a commentary (of a more literal type), often upon a commentary.
upanayana : Brahminical initiation, the thread ceremony.
upaniṣad : a didactic work of a speculative character, belonging to Revelation.

vaiśya : a member of the third *varṇa*.
vidhi : a Vedic injunction.
vivāda : a dispute, in litigation, especially private litigation.
vivādapada : a little, or type, of legal dispute, a juridical division of the subject-matter of disputes in general.
vyavahāra : administration of justice, the judicial process, especially judicial procedure (viewed practically).
vyavahārapada : a class of litigation or trial, synonymous with *vivādapada*.
yuga : an Age of the world.

AN AID TO THE PRONUNCIATION OF SANSKRIT WORDS

All letters are sounded. The accent usually falls on the penultimate syllable unless this is short and is preceded by a long vowel: thus *para-mánanda, ārányaka,* but *ācárya.* Vowels marked long are pronounced as in Italian. *ā* is the a in *father*; *ū* is the oo in *pool. a* is the u in *butter*; *u* is the oo in *foot*; *i* is the i in *sit,* but *ī* is the ee in *feet.* ṛ is counted as a vowel, and sounds very like the re in *pretty. ai* is a diphthong and is the ie in *pie.*

c is the ch in *church*; *g* is always hard as in *gate*; *h* is always sounded as a full aspirate; when it follows a consonant that consonant is aspirated, so that *ph* is not an f sound but as in *drop him* spoken quickly with the aspirate sounded; *ḥ* is the sign for a light aspirant, but many pronounce it as if it repeated the previous vowel, e.g. *pādaḥ* is pronounced *pādahà. j* is the j in *joke. ṃ* nasalises the preceding vowel, but at the end of a word (not the final word of the phrase) it is equivalent to *m. ñ* is pronounced as in Spanish. *ś* is like the ssi in *passion*; *ṣ* is the sh in *push. t* and *d* are dental consonants, with the tongue close to the teeth; *ṭ* and *ḍ,* on the other hand are retroflex, with the tongue in the roof of the mouth, giving a nasal and tapping quality to the sound; both are rather a nuisance as English t and d are produced with the tongue in a position midway between the two.

The names of modern Indians are often hard to pronounce without help, and the deviations, both in North and in South India, from Sanskritic patterns can be disconcerting. In many cases the translator has added diacritical marks to assist in pronunciation, but consistency has not been sought; and where error in pronunciation would not be too embarrassing, modern names have been left as their owners spelt them.

ROBERT LINGAT

Life

Born at Charleville (Ardennes) in 1892.
Diplôme of the École des Langues Orientales Vivantes, Paris, 1919.
Doctorate in Law (with the Paul Deschanel Prize), Paris, 1932.
Legal Adviser, Bangkok, 1924–1940.
Lecturer in the History of Siamese Law at the University of Moral and Political Sciences, Bangkok, 1935–1939.
Professor in the Faculty of Law of Indo-China. 1941–1955.
'Conseiller légiste' (Law Member) to the Government of Cambodia, 1945.
'Directeur d'études' (Professor) at the École Pratique des Hautes Études (Section 6), Sorbonne, Paris, 1961—
Died at Paris, 7 May, 1972.

Works

1. *Buddhism*

La vie religieuse du roi Mongkut, *J.S.S.*, 20 (1926), 129–48.
History of Wat Saket, *J.S.S.*, 23 (1930), 125–34.
History of Wat Mahādhātu, *J.S.S.*, 24 (1930), 1–27.
History of Wat Pavaraniveça, *J.S.S.*, 26 (1933), 73–102.
Le culte du Bouddha d'éreraude, *J.S.S.*, 27 (1934), 9–38.
La double crise de l'Église bouddhique au Siam (1767–1851), *Cahiers d'histoire mondiale,* 4/2 (Neuchatel) (1958), 402–425.
Le Wat Rājapratiṣṭha, *Artibus Asiae, Felicitation Volume,* 24 (Ascona, 1961), 314–23.
Les suicides religieux au Siam, *Felicitation Volumes of Southeast-Asian Studies,* I (Bangkok, 1965), 71–5.
Encore *ayāya saṃbodhim,* à propos de l'inscription gréco-araméenne d'Aśoka, *J.A.,* 255 (1968), 195–8.

2. *History of Siam*

Chronique du Siam. Cent cinquantième anniversaire de Bangkok, *B.E.F.E.O.,* 333 (1933), 536–48.
Les trois Bangkok Recorders, *J.S.S.,* 28 (1935), 203–13.
Une lettre de Véret sur la Révolution siamoise de 1688, *T'oung Pao,* 31 (1935), 330–362.

3. *Siamese Law*

Note sur la revision des lois siamoises en 1805, *J.S.S.,* 23 (1929), 1–9.

L'esclavage privé dans le vieux droit siamois. xi, 395 pp. (Paris, 1931).

La succession des Bhikku (in Siamese), *Pramuon k'adi* (Bangkok) (1932), 633–52.

La responsabilité collective au Siam, *Rev. hist. de droit français et étranger,* 1936, 523–39.

Histoire du droit siamois (droit privé) (in Siamese), 3 vols., 102, 253, and 139 pp. (Bangkok, 1935–40).

Code du 1er *règne* [*de la dynastie de Bangkok*], C.S. 1166, 3 vols. (University of Moral and Political Sciences, Bangkok, 1938–39).

Effect de la pabbajjâ sur le mariage (in Siamese). 29 pp. (Bangkok, 1939).

Le régime des biens entre époux en Thaïlande, *Rev. Indochinoise juridique et économique* (Hanoi), 1943, 63 pp.

Les Ordalies au Siam, *L'Éducation* (Saigon), 1949, 19 pp.

Les origines du prêt à intérêt au Siam, *Rev. hist. de droit francais et étranger,* 1950, 213–35.

La condition des étrangers au Siam au XVIIe siécle, *Recueils de la Société Jean Bodin,* IX, *L'Étranger* (Brussels, 1958), 255–66.

Le statut de la femme au Siam, *Recueils de la Société Jean Bodin,* XI, *La Femme* (Brussels, 1959), 275–92.

Le délit de voisinage maléfique dans le vieux droit siamois, *J.A.,* 249 (1961), 63–84.

La preuve dans l'ancien droit siamois, *Recueils de la Société Jean Bodin,* XVIII, *La Preuve* (Brussels, 1964), 397–418.

Siam (Thailande). In J. Gilissen, ed., *Introduction Bibliographique à l'histoire du droit et à l'ethnologie juridique (Bibliographical Introduction to Legal History and Ethnology),* Sec. E/9 (Brussels, 1965), 17 pp.

4. *Indochinese Law*

Vinaya et droit laïque, *B.E.F.E.O.,* 37 (1937), 415–76.

Evolution of the conception of Law in Burma and Siam, *J.S.S.,* 38 (1950), 8–31.

La conception du droit dans l'Indochine hînayâniste, *B.E.F.E.O.,* 44 (1951), 163–87.

Les régimes matrimoniaux du Sud-Est de l'Asie. Essai de droit comparé indochinois. Tome I, Les régimes traditionnels 176 pp. (Paris, 1952); *Tome II, Les droits codifiés.* 195 pp. (Paris, 1965).

Pour un droit comparé indochinois. 14 pp. (Saigon, 1955).

5. *Hindu Law*

L'influence hindoue dans l'ancien droit siamois. In R. Lingat and Denise Paulme, *Conférences* 1936. *Études de sociologie et d'ethnologie juridiques, pub. sous la direction de René Maunier*...25 (Paris, 1937), 1–29.

L'influence juridique de l'Inde au Champa et au Cambodge d'après l'épigraphie, *J.A.*, 237 (1949), 273–90.

The Buddhist Manu or the Propagation of Hindu law in Hinayanist Indochina, *Annals of the Bhandarkar Oriental Research Institute* 30 (1949) (appeared in 1950), 284–97.

Dharma et temps, à propos de Manu, 1.85–86, *J.A.*, 249 (1961), 487–95; in English under the title 'Time and the Dharma', *Contributions to Indian Sociology*, 6 (The Hague) (1962), 7–16.

Les quatre pieds du procès, *J.A.*, 250 (1962), 489–503.

Les Sources du Droit dans le Système Traditionnel de l'Inde, 323 pp. (The Hague, 1967).

6. *Book Reviews*

Reviews appeared in *J.S.S.*, *B.E.F.E.O.*, *J.A.*, *Rev. hist. de droit*, *T'oung Pao*, *Recueil de jurisprudence Penant*, and *Artibus Asiae*.

INDEX*

ācāra : see Custom, Good.
accessories : 55.
adharma : 4, 55, 197 n.46, 244.
adoption : 24, 60–1, 84, 129; *mimāṃsā* rules applied : 152, 154–5, 159–60.
advice, the role of the jurist : 71–2, 248.
age, golden : 15.
ages of the world : 79, 184–7, 193.
agents provocateurs : 240.
agriculture : 31, 40, 71.
Ahmad, M.B. : 261 n.6.
Aiyangar, K.V. Rangaswami : 46 n.21, 104, 105, 123, 126 nn., 127 and n.12, 128 n.14, 129 n.16, 130, 132 n.18, 146 n.4, 171 n., 197 n. 47, 208 n.7.
Al Bīrunī : 48, 193.
Altekar, A.S. : 17 n.16, 106 n.16, 124, 178, 184 n.20, 208 n.7.
ambiguous smṛti, illustrated : 251–2.
Anantadeva, author of *Smṛtikaustubha* : 120; see *Rājadharma-kaustubha*.
ancestors, walking in their ways : 197.
Āndhras, 22.
Aṅgiras (smṛti) : 106, 233 and n.63.
Aparārka, commentator on Yājñavalkya : 113, 124 n.4, 129, 145, 146 n.5, 166, 168, 179 n.10, 181 n.16, 210, 221, 228 n.53, 251,·253, 276.
Āpastamba (dharma-sūtra) : 20–23, 41, 124 n.4, 129, 194 n.40, 178;
I.1.1.1–2 : 16, 178
I.1.1.4–5 : 30.
I.1.4.8 : 16.
I.1.14.25 : 31.
I.6.18.14 : 41.
I.7.2.6–7 : 197.
I.9.24.15 : 63.
I.10.29.6 : 31 n.5.
II.2.4.14 : 52.
II.5.10.11 : 65.
II.5.10.12–16 : 232.
II.5.12.4 : 59.
II.6.13.7 : 61.
II.9.21.10 : 47.
II.9.23.3–12 : 49–50.
II.10.27.4 : 61.
II.10.27.6–7 : 61.
II.10.27.15 : 40.
II.11.28.1 : 71.
II.11.28.13 : 66.
appeals : from one court to another : 247; before the king : 248; from judgment passed in the king's court : 255.
Arrian : 33 n.8, 51 n.33.

*[It is well known that French scholarly books are, on the whole, less well supplied with indexes than their counterparts in the English-speaking world. M. Lingat, by contrast, supplied an index which dealt faithfully with leading concepts and with proper names. It was still far from sufficient, and this present index attempts to rectify the chief deficiencies. But M. Lingat's decisions have been respected in two respects : a complete index to all references to the *sūtra* and *smṛti* writers would have been meaningless, or, if filled out with complete indications, impossible. Therefore these writers have been indexed, if their works survive in continuous published form, only if M. Lingat actually *quotes* them, even though the distinction between a quotation and a substantial summary or citation is an artificial one. Secondly, no systematic attempt has been made to index the Bibliography, which is, to a large extent, self-indexing.] [trs.]

artha, interest, profit, one of the motives of human conduct: 5; see also *artha-śāstra, trivarga.*
artha-śāstra, a science: definition of, 145; part of the knowledge required of an exegete: 145–7; value of a rule founded on *artha*: 156–7; inspired some *dharmaśāstra* rules: 145–6, 207 n.3, 223 and n., 241.
Asahāya. commentator on Nārada: 100 and n.7, 103, 114, 161, 162 n.41, 211, 216, 256 n.110.
ascetic, fourth stage of life: 46–7; leaves worldly morality: 5; the jurists' reservations about: 50–1; competing with Brahmins: 50.
Asian handling of 'precept': xiii n.2.
Aśoka: 226 n.48.
Atharvaveda: 7.
Atri (dharma-sūtra): 24.
authority of a rule of *dharma*: superior to that of a rule based on *artha*: 5, 157; based on its origin in a Vedic injunction: 7, 149; and its religious implications: 3–4, 135, 176, 203–4; and not on custom: 177–8; but it yields to custom: 196–7, 200; varies with the levels of society: 203–4; disappears in the domain of politics: 200, 225–6, 250; see also *dharma.*
authority, not legality, the key to the system: 258.
Ayyar, A.S.N.: 150 n.12, 213 n.20, 260 n.5.

Bālambhaṭṭa: 113.
Bandyopadhyaya, S.C., *see* Banerji.
Banerji, S.C.: 22 n.3, 24 n.4, 29 n.2, 89 n.7, 280.
Barth, A.: 51 n.32, 63 and n., 102, 125, 139–42.
bath, ritual: 46, 47.
battle, death in: 223.
Baudhāyana (dharma-sūtra): 18, 20–1, 22;
I.1.9–10: 15.
I.1.11: 233–4:
I.2.1–4: 196.
I.3.5: 45.
I.11.20.12: 60.
I.11.20.13–15: 59.
I.11.20.16: 59.
I.11.21.1: 59.
I.11.21.2–3: 59.
I.18.2–5: 30.
II.1.17: 68.
II.2.3.14: 61 n.
II.2.3.34–5: 61.
II.3.45: 57.
II.6.11.34: 50, 51.
II.17.16: 46.
III.3.13–14: 46.
IV.5.31: 56.
Beaman, G.B.: 81 n. 4a.
Betai, R.S.: 220 n.36.
Bhagavad-gītā: 4, 26, 77.
Bhagavanta-bhāskara: 117, 259.
Bhandarkar, R.G.: 99, 124.
Bhāruci, commentator on Manu: 94 and n., 111–12, 143, 146 n.5.
Bhattacharya, B.: 120 n.25, 124 n.3.
Bhattacharya, J.N.: 150 n.12.
Bhavasvāmin, commentator on Nārada: 100 and nn.6,7, 101 n.9, 103, 126 n.11.
Bhaviṣya-purāṇa: 92, 161 n.40.
Bhṛgu: 78–9, 87, 91, 93, 100, 105.
Blackstone, Sir W.: 205 n.63.
Bloch, M.: 207 n.3.
blood-money: 64.
Bongert, Y.: 213 n.20.
brāhmaṇa, meaning of: 7.

the principal: 77ff.; a critique of their chronology: 123ff.
dharma-sūtras: 12–13, 19ff.; their period: 20; general character of: 28; contents of: 52; juridical rules in, deriving from Good Custom: 57; authors' outlook: 57, 58–9, 71–2; the king's duties: 64; elements of administrative law in: 66—7; and of penal law: 67–8; and of procedure: 68, 69; and of civil law: 70–1; commentaries on: 114f.
Dīkṣita, Vaidyanātha, author of *Smṛti-muktāphala*: 120.
disapproval of practices: 60, 61.
distress (time of): in the *dharma-sūtras*: 39–40.
divine nature of kings: 208.
divine origin of laws: 74, 86.
Drekmeier, C.: 207 n.3, 208 n.7.
Dumézil, G.: 36–7, 209 n.10.
Dumont, L.: xv and n., 5 n.8, 15 n.14, 267 n.16.

enemies, foreign: the prime duty to keep peace: 66, 222–3; policies towards neighbouring lands: 82, 241 n.80; towards conquered countries: 82, 199–200, 226 n.50; *see* war (laws of).
epigraphy: xiii n.3, 101, 138 n.3, 267, 273–4.
escheat: 58, 62, 226 n.48, 238.
evaluation of rules: 59.
evolution and chronology of texts: 128–9.
excommunication: 53–4.
exegesis, *see* interpretation.
expediency: 253.

facultative rules: 49.
fasting: 46, 55.
females, and inheritance: 62.
Finot, L.: 101 n.8.
flexibility: 175, 259.
force: 214.
function, *see* Brahmin, king.
Fürer-Haimendorf, C.von: 43 n.20.

gambling: 84.
Gautama (dharma-sūtra): 19f., 273;
V.35–6: 52.
VIII.12–13: 67.
X.39–42: 71.
XI.1: 219.
XI.20: 38.
XI.21: 246 n.89.
XII.4–6: 40.
XII.7: 40.
XII.37–8: 71.
XII.44–5: 68.
gāyatrī: 45, 56.
Gerhardsson, B.: 75 n.2.
Ghārpure, J.R.: 113, 120, 168 n.55.
Ghose, B.K.: 22 n.3.
Ghose, J.C.: 98, 279.
Ghoshāl, U.N.: 146 n.4, 147 n., 207 n.1, 208 n.7, 213 n.20, 214 n.23, 216 n.27, 220 n.36, 224 nn., 228 n.53, 229 n.55, 231 n.58, 280.
Gobhila-smṛti: 159.
Gopal, L.: 146 n.3.
gotras: 31, 57.
Govindarāja, commentator on Manu: 112, 197, 198.

of his subjects in temporal matters: 211; sole judge of the means to do his duty: 214; in punishing incurs no impurity; 215; duty to *consult* his counsellors: 217; interest of in coping with Brahmins: 218, 220, 222 and n.39; techniques in dealing with a repugnant custom: 225; not to proselytise for any custom or law: 226 and n.50.
king's function: 207ff.; divine institution legitimises temporal power: 214–15; establishes a spiritual solidarity between the king and his subjects: 212 and nn.; imposes on him the duty of protection: 213; assimilated to the celebration of a sacrifice: 215; *see also* justice, administration of; justice, criminal; penance; power, temporal; protection; punishment.
Krishan, Y.: 51 n.34.
Kṣatriya: 4, 30, 33, 36, 39, 43 n.19, 65, 209ff.
Kullūka, commentator on Manu: 14, 17, 112, 155 n.26, 159, 185, 210, 213 n.21, 226 n.49, 252.
Kumaon: 120.
Kumārila, commentator on Śabara: 13, 149 n.10, 155 and n.24, 158.

Lakṣmaṇa-bhaṭṭa: 158 n.31.
Lakṣmīdhara: 115, 229, 278; see *Kalpataru*.
law, meaning of: xii, 256, 257.
lawsuits, private: in the *dharma-sūtras*: 67–8, 70–1; in Manu: 82–4; definition of: 243–4; necessity of injury against the plaintiff: 244; double action possible: 244; distinction between injury to the person and to property: 245; complex character of the action: 251; cases that will not lie because of public policy: 251; *artha* concepts may arise during the hearing: 251–4.
lawsuits, types of: 82, 101, 244.
Laszlo, F.: 92 n.
legal instruments, want of in Indian legal history: xiii.
legislation, royal: cannot modify the śāstra's rules: 225; abrogation of a custom repugnant to *dharma*: 225–6; the meaning of patronage awarded to jurists: 229–30; scope of the royal 'legislation': 230; its nature and significance: 231–2.
Lekhapaddhati: xiii n.3.
Lingat, R.: x–xi, 287–9; articles of referred to: 161 n.40, 186 n.23, 250 n., 256 n.109, 267 nn.14,15, 271 n.19.
liquor-drinking: 55, 84.
litigation, heads of: 82–3, 243.
Loiseleur-Deslongchamps, A.: 78, 94, 251 n.99.

Macnaghten, W.H.: 113, 277.
Mādhava, commentator on Parāśara: 103, 114, 168, 169–71, 185 n.22, 188 n.28, 192 n., 210, 230 n.57, 276.
Mahābhārata: its relation with Manu: 90, 91, 92, 95; miscellaneous references: 3 n.2, 10, 61 n., 91, 97, 103, 115, 146, 184 n.18, 198, 207 n.3, 208, 212 n.19, 250.
Mahāliṅgam, T.V.: 230 n.57.
Mahāsammata: 267.
Maity, S.K.: 124 n.2.
Majumdar, A.K.: 226 n.48.
Mānava-dharma-sūtra, hypothetical prototype of the Manu-smṛti: 88–91, 186 n.24.
Mandlik, V.N.: 112 n.4, 117, 158 n.31, 168 n.55, 169 n.60a.
mantras: 30, 44, 55.
Manu, mythical person: 9, 62, 78–9, 87, 100; hermit: 267–8.
Manu (smṛti): 77ff.; analysis: 78–87; origins: 87–92; successive versions: 91, 101; older than other smṛtis: 92–3; date: 95, 126–7, 130; contradictions: 182; commentaries on: 111–12; and the *Bhaviṣya-purāṇa*: 92 n.